Power, Money, and Trade

Power, Money,

and Trade

Decisions that Shape
Global Economic Relations

MARK R. BRAWLEY

broadview
press

Library and Archives Canada Cataloguing in Publication

Brawley, Mark R. (Mark Randal), 1960–
  Power, money and trade : decisions that shape global economic relations / by Mark R. Brawley.

Includes bibliographical references and index
ISBN 1-55111-683-9

1. International economic relations—History—Textbooks.   I. Title.

HF1359.B72 2005   337'.09   C2004-907348-6

Broadview Press, Ltd. is an independent, international publishing house, incorporated in 1985. Broadview believes in shared ownership, both with its employees and with the general public; since the year 2000 Broadview shares have traded publicly on the Toronto Venture Exchange under the symbol BDP.

We welcome any comments and suggestions regarding any aspect of our publications — please feel free to contact us at the addresses below, or at broadview@broadviewpress.com / www.broadviewpress.com

North America	*UK, Ireland, and*	*Australia and*
Post Office Box 1243,	*Continental Europe*	*New Zealand*
Peterborough, Ontario,	NBN International	UNIREPS
Canada K9J 7H5	Estover Road	University of
Tel: (705) 743-8990	Plymouth, Devon PL6 7PY	New South Wales
Fax: (705) 743-8353	United Kingdom	Sydney, NSW, 2052
customerservice	Tel: +44 (0) 1752 202300	Tel: + 61296 640 999
@broadviewpress.com	Fax: +44 (0) 1752 202330	Fax: + 61296 645 420
	Customer Service:	info.press@unsw.edu.au
3576 California Road,	cservs@nbninternational.com	
Orchard Park, NY	orders@nbninternational.com	
USA 14127		

Broadview Press Ltd. gratefully acknowledges the financial support of the Government of Canada through the Book Publishing Industry Development Program for our publishing activities.

Edited by Betsy Struthers. Cover design and typeset by Zack Taylor, www.zacktaylor.com.
Printed in Canada

For Adèle

Contents

Acknowledgements

In the first edition, I singled out Mike Lusztig and Charles Lipson for helping me get started with this project, and I still owe them thanks for their encouragement. I now owe thanks to Michael Harrison of Broadview Press, twice over, for giving me the opportunity to do this text and for seeing it through to successful completion again. Three anonymous reviewers gave me excellent criticisms, and if the themes and arguments in the text run tightly together, it is partly through their efforts as well as mine.

While I alone am responsible for the material herein, the book reflects the training I received from a great set of instructors: Jeff Frieden, David Lake, and Art Stein. I also wish to thank my colleagues at McGill and my partners in the McGill/Université de Montréal Joint Research Group in International Security, whom I have enjoyed working with over the years. I should also thank McGill University and the Political Science Department more directly, for the original version of the text was completed during my first sabbatical.

Special thanks also go to Donna Aronson, who assisted in the original research. I would also like to thank Betsy Struthers for her excellent editing. This book is much easier to read because of her efforts. Naturally, I want to thank Annette, Adèle, and Matt for being patient (as always), as I had to struggle with making work balance with the rest of life.

Mark R. Brawley
Montreal

Note to Instructors

This textbook was designed with certain goals in mind; thus, I find it important to remark on what is and is not included here. The contents reflect my own thinking about the different tasks that texts, lectures, and discussions serve. While some may argue that students need to be given only a small amount of information, and that the same information should be presented to them as many times as possible and in as many forms as possible, I disagree. In my view, a textbook should provide a guide. Combined with lectures, the textbook should provide the framework for piecing together a wider array of materials. Additional readings should provide the further information students require. Thus, this book has a limited set of aims.

First, the chapters laying out theories and paradigms in Part I introduce the fundamental concepts and arguments in international relations. These first chapters are not specific to international political economy (IPE). The examples presented are those used in the original classics we associate with particular paradigms or levels of analysis; thus, they are usually not examples from IPE at all. To illustrate how such approaches are employed in IPE, one must provide examples in lectures.

The cases in Part III are drawn from a variety of time periods and from all three issue-areas. They are presented in chronological order, but need not be presented that way. For instance, Chapters 10, 11, 12, 14, and 19 cover trade policy. Some consider turns to protectionism, some to liberalization, and a couple represent examples where policy did not change at all. Chapters 13, 15, 17, 20, and 21 examine decisions regarding international monetary policy. Within that group, two chapters (13 and 17) examine what happens when a national money is used as the key currency, and a currency overhang develops. As such, these chapters also reflect some of the consequences of international investment on the source country; the receivers' point of view can be found in Chapter 18 and, to a lesser extent, in Chapter 16. Chapters 16 and 18 look more closely at the causes and consequences of different development strategies. These cases can also be structured in ways that stress different theoretical purposes, depending on the instructor's goals.

Each case ends with comments about the consequences of the decisions taken. These include consequences for the evolution of IPE. This allows instructors to place cases in context with each other, but also helps lay out broader changes in the system. They do not provide evaluations of the theories applied in the cases. Instead, the results are usually left fairly open. Since there is room for interpretation and debate about the relative importance of each argument, such issues are best left for discussion in conferences, though lectures too could draw some conclusions. Moreover, each of the historical cases is constructed using a limited set of sources. The Additional References at the end of each chapter are normally (but not always) additional, in the sense that their points of view are not well-represented in the case. These lists can serve as an excellent source for extra reading assignments to complement this book. The contrasting points of view can then be explored in lectures and discussions.

INTRODUCTION

Themes and Goals

This book addresses the substance and analysis of international relations. It is designed for students who have no prior experience with theories of international relations, let alone international political economy. It illustrates how political scientists theorize about international relations, and the cases presented in Part III are drawn from international political economy. The book therefore introduces the core issues of international political economy to illustrate how *theories* from *international relations* handle the specific challenges of studying the politics of international economic relations. [Note: Words appearing in italics can be found in the Glossary.] In the initial chapters, we will learn how to categorize theories, as well as come to understand why theories falling in each category share common characteristics. In Part II, the central issues of international political economy are addressed. When we reach the cases in Part III, we should be able to combine the theories described in Part I with the substantive issues discussed in Part II in applications to historical events. As an introductory text, the book does not explore every aspect of *international political economy*, instead focusing on the chief issues attracting our attention. The goal is to provide students with a set of concepts and analytical tools they can build upon in later classes.

Why Should We Study International Relations?

Many different types of events, which we wish to understand, occur at the international level. Whether we are concerned with extremely hostile actions (such as the outbreak of wars or the issuance of military threats), or want to understand examples of cooperation or mutual benefit (such as an agreement to lower barriers to trade between two countries or the formation of an alliance), we try to understand these events in terms of patterns of activity. As a pair of theorists put it, "the facts do not speak for themselves ... what we know depends on how we go about organizing all the events and trends to which we attach significance."[1] More importantly, we want to understand the world in terms of causal patterns. We want answers to many different questions: why will one thing happen rather than another? when will it happen? how will other actors react? The list of possible questions is endless.

Our task as political scientists in the field of international relations is to make sense of these events. The first major point for students to understand is that we use theories or models to simplify things. The world is a complex place, and international relations is no different—it is very complicated. All sorts of factors shape the international political economy or the actions of particular states. As political scientists, our objective is to understand international relations by selecting and focusing on the most important forces influencing events. Why? Because we are concerned with the future. We want to take some control over future events. That means the theories or issues we will consider in this book are causal theories. We will be focusing on explaining why certain things happened in the past in order to establish causal patterns, which we hope will provide some guidelines as to how to act in the future. Without some understanding of how things happen, we have little guidance for action. With little understanding of what causes war, or what brings about a trade agreement, we lack a useful basis for intervening in the process to bring about more desirable results. Without an understanding of cause and effect, we would be basing decisions between various plans of action on nothing more than faith.

On the other hand, we can never have a perfectly accurate predictive model of the future because one can never anticipate how the future may differ from the past; this is especially true when one tries to predict human behaviour—and predicting human behaviour is very difficult! Since political science is not a pure science, but social in nature, political scientists will always have trouble making absolutely accurate predictions. The future may differ from the past in innumerable ways, so there is always the possibility—even the likelihood—that any predictions we make based on models of past behaviour will be somewhat inaccurate. But just because we cannot predict the future with total certainty does not mean we should forego any planning or any attempt to make educated or informed analyses of the possibilities (or probabilities) of something happening.

In fact, in the field of international relations, there are usually all sorts of people making recommendations about foreign policy. Many are ready and willing to give advice on policy, usually without giving us the causal model they are basing their arguments on. Journalists make recommendations in their editorials, suggesting that one particular policy will produce a set of particular outcomes, while a different policy would lead to an alternative result—they therefore have a causal theory implicit in their argument. The same can be said for politicians. Historians frequently describe past events in causal terms—they too often use theories, usually implicitly. Simply by emphasizing one aspect of a story over another, they are implicitly supporting one theory over another. The news media, by stressing particular bits of information and ignoring an infinite amount of other detail, are using implicit models of causality. They do so in an attempt to provide only the bits of information relevant to our lives. But in deciding what is relevant, they must rely on some sense of what shapes events—and that requires a sense of causality.

A Theoretical Approach to International Relations and International Political Economy

Political science differs from history or journalism precisely because it emphasizes the development of causal theories. Though we discuss the same events as historians or journalists, our efforts are much more self-consciously an effort in theory construction, and this requires us to lay out the logic of our arguments in an explicit form.[2] We seek to understand the linkage between cause and effect, and to clarify that linkage through comparisons of various past events.[3] We are searching for connections we can generalize; historians, on the other hand, are experts on the specific. While we use the same evidence as historians, we use that evidence in rather different ways. A good political scientist should also stress a sense of humility and awe in theory construction, recognizing the limits of his or her own knowledge and the limited range of our probabilistic statements.[4]

What is a Theory?

Since theories are the central theme throughout this book, we need to understand more specifically what we mean when we use this term. I follow the definition Kenneth Waltz uses in his book *Theory of International Politics*. He discusses both "laws" and "theories," defining a *law* as a way to establish relationships between variables, as facts of observation.[5] Of course, the most interesting associations are those relating a cause and an effect.

We use the term *variable* to refer to the forces or factors of both cause and effect, because when we take repeated observations of a relationship we are trying to locate changes in each side of the equation—that is, we want to see how both the cause and the effect *vary*. For example, we may think that good grades are the result of studying. We would want, therefore, to take observations of students who do varying amounts of studying. We would expect to see that as a student does more of the assigned reading for a course, the grade he or she receives will rise—the variation in grades depends on the variation in completing the readings. In more technical language, the effect is referred to as the *dependent variable*, because we are expecting changes in it to depend upon changes in the value of the causal variables. The causal variables will presumably also change in value, but since we are only concerned with explaining one thing at a time, we do not worry about why they vary; thus, we refer to them as *independent variables* (i.e., their values will change independently from other parts of our theory).[6] A theory can have more than one independent variable. For instance, grades are not merely a function of reading all the assigned texts—attending lectures, participating in discussion groups, prior experience in a similar course, and a host of other factors presumably affect grades as well. A more complex theory would elaborate the relationship between a variety of independent variables and the dependent variable.

In this text, in terms of the effects, we will be concerned with variations in the behaviour of states (foreign economic policy, to be specific) or the behaviour of other actors (such as corporations, political parties, bureaucracies, or individuals) as one side of the equation. The separate fields within social science reflect different interests in the subject we are trying to explain. International relations is primarily about describing and predicting the variation in state policies towards other states or towards international organizations or foreigners, though increasingly we try to describe and predict the behaviour of non-state actors. Comparative politics is primarily about describing and predicting the variation in state policies within states, and it, too, is now focusing on describing and predicting the behaviour of non-state actors.

Laws are connections between variables of which we have repeated observations of such strength and number that we can safely expect the relations to continue into the future. Laws are few and far between in the social sciences, however, precisely because so little fits this definition. A *theory*, on the other hand, Waltz defines as a speculative process for explaining observed relationships between variables.[7] Causality is thus an important aspect of any theory, since we are speculating that changes in the independent variables have some sort of impact on the dependent variables. Probability is another important facet of our understanding of a theory, since by Waltz's definition we are not certain about the relationship between the variables. (If we were certain, we would have a law.) Because we are not certain about the relationship between the variables, and because there are an infinite number of potential variables to consider, it is quite possible to have more than one causal theory consistent with the same facts. Since we lack definitive causal relationships (or laws), and several different causal relationships appear possible, political science is rife with debates about which theories are more persuasive. That is precisely where the main thrust of this text lies—in the debates between specialists in international relations over the persuasiveness of various theories as explanations for changes in foreign economic policies.

Some people point out that our ability to make predictions will never be very good. These pessimists go on to argue that any attempt to predict, or, even worse, to prescribe policies based on a prediction, would be unwise and risky. I would argue that simply because we cannot be certain in our predictions does not mean we should give up on building theories; rather, it means we must try, but be wary of the fact that perfect predictions are unattainable. The pessimists must do more than criticize the endeavours here, they must also offer an alternative. If we wish to take control over the future, how should we do so? If we don't develop prescriptions through the creation, criticism, and refinement of theories attempting to explain causal relationships, how then are we to develop policy prescriptions?[8] More importantly, how do we convince others to adopt one prescription rather than another?

Since theories are statements of probability, and since theories are used within political or policy debates, how can we pick one theory over another? There are several important characteristics of theories we can employ when comparing them. Obviously we can contrast theories in terms of the *accuracy* of their predictions or descriptions of past events, but accuracy is only one point of comparison among several. We can compare theories in terms of the range of tasks they are intended to perform.[9]

The Qualities of Theories

Our theories or models are simplifications of reality, so naturally many things are lost in the process of constructing them. As stated above, predictive theories are probability statements. That means that one of the qualities of a theory which we can always talk about is *accuracy*. No theory will be right 100 per cent of the time, but we can compare theories that are correct half of the time to theories that are right only a third of the time. Because theories are simplifications of reality, they focus on some independent variables at the expense of others. They do not work perfectly because some of these other variables could come into play, so there are always excuses for a theory's failure to provide an accurate prediction or description. Theorists expect a certain amount of inaccuracy and, therefore, often cover themselves by including the statement that their theoretical predictions will hold *ceteris paribus*, or "all other things being equal." Sometimes the theorist creates so many caveats that the theory is nearly impossible to test!

Besides accuracy, two other important aspects of theories are traditionally used as bases of comparison: *generalizability* and *parsimony*. Generalizability means "how broadly can I apply this theory?" or "for how many cases will this theory be useful?" Since we want to understand causality across several cases, and may want to use our theory in future situations, generalizability is important. As noted above, this emphasis on generalizable arguments is one of the characteristics differentiating political scientists from historians.

Parsimony refers to the degree of simplicity. Is the theory simpler than other theories attempting to explain the same phenomenon? Is it "cleaner" or "neater"?[10] Parsimony reflects the ability to explain much of the variation in the dependent variable with as little information or theory as possible. It serves as a proxy measure for efficiency—how much "mileage" in terms of explanation can we get out of a little bit of theory and a little bit of evidence. More recently, some scholars have begun to use the term *leverage* to refer to much the same idea: according to Gary King, Robert Keohane, and Sidney Verba, leverage is the ability to explain as much as possible with as little as possible.[11]

Yet another quality of theories we can identify for the purposes of comparison is *falsifiability*.[12] Essentially, philosophers of science have warned us to keep a perspective on what we consider as an explanation. In the natural sciences, different explanations for the transit of the sun across the earth's sky have been accepted as fact. But with new information, new scientific techniques, and new models or theories, these explanations have evolved. In hindsight, what was accepted as the explanation at one point in the past looks ridiculous to us today; our understanding today will perhaps look just as ridiculous to our grandchildren. Thomas Kuhn explored issues of knowledge creation in his work, *The Structure of Scientific Revolutions*, which drew examples from the evolution of physics. The conclusions of Kuhn, Imre Lakatos, and other scholars who study science and the pursuit of knowledge is that we can never know anything for sure—our explanations are never certain. Something else could be going on which we have yet to grasp or understand. We can ascertain, however, the incorrectness of our theories. Thus, our goal should not be to prove something completely correct, since that would be impossible, but rather to be putting our best explanations constantly to the test. By trying to disprove them, we can come to appreciate their strengths and weaknesses. That is where the notion of falsifiability comes in: we need to construct our theories in such a way that we can test them and disprove them. We should make explicit the grounds for rejecting our theories as being too often incorrect, at the same time recognizing that we can never know for certain that they are correct![13]

Kuhn's work on the development of physics is also appreciated for its illustration of how scientists often internalize the paradigm they are applying. His examples laid out how much a well-established paradigm or set of theories had to be questioned and criticized before the scientists were willing to abandon the theory and turn to an alternative. Kuhn discussed such shifts in thinking in surprising terms—he compared them to changes in faith, or psychological dramas, rather than the result of cool calculation. While we should certainly aim for rational decisions in our own search for theories in international relations, we should be aware of how difficult it is for these shifts in thinking to occur.

The trickiest aspect of comparing theories is balancing considerations of these various properties. An accurate theory or model, one that fits reality closely, is often quite complicated and takes many different factors into account. Some theories include so much, they are tailored to a single case. The gains in accuracy produce a loss in generalizability and/or parsimony. Making a generalizable theory often means dropping out details, losing accuracy. One thing to note once we examine specific theories is the manner in which different types of theories embody these trade-offs. We should also be sensitive to the fact that theories do different things, and that clearly affects how we should evaluate theories in terms of accuracy or generalizability.

We must also remember that more than one theory can fit the evidence. Philosophers and historians of science have pointed this fact out over and over again.[14] In the specific examples considered in later chapters, historical events may often be overdetermined. That is, several theories may provide explanations entirely consistent with each other, as well as with the historical record. One way to deal with overdetermination, however, is to explore the details of how events unfolded in such a way that one explanation appears to be more consistent with the facts than another.

Given what these last few paragraphs say about comparing theories, how does one ultimately resolve choices between them? Well, for starters, theories can be compared along one dimension: accuracy in prediction, perhaps. But is a very good description of the past more important than a good prediction? Is parsimony more important than generalizability? Those are questions of taste. Two rational people, interested in the scientific pursuit of knowledge, can disagree over which quality matters most.[15] Only when one theory can do just as well as another in all categories, but also performs better in at least one, can we clearly judge it to be preferable.

The Tasks of Theory

What do theories do? They serve us in several ways. We've been discussing how we use theories to *predict*, but that isn't all they can do for us. We may also use theories to *describe* the world of today or to help us understand the past. That means they tell us about the past and the present. They hopefully tell us something about the future also, so they may be used to predict as well. Theories can also be used to *prescribe* policies—that is, they should also tell us about how to take control over the future. Sometimes, theories also offer a *normative goal*—they provide us with a vision of the way things ought to be.

A good example of a theory performing all four of these tasks (description, prediction, prescription, and provision of a normative goal) fairly evenly is Marxism. Karl Marx developed a view of the world based on an analysis of historical development (description), arguing that capitalism would create all sorts of social and political problems because of its inherent contradictions (prediction), but that such problems could be solved through a world socialist revolution (prescription), which would deliver mankind to a socialist utopia (the normative goal). The *Communist Manifesto*, a rather short document, presents Marx's theory performing each of these tasks.

Since theories or models are simplifications or representations of reality, a theory begins with a set of things assumed to be true. These *assumptions* are useful for eliminating some of the confusion of the real world. As things assumed to be true, and as simplifications, assumptions are bound to be false some of the time (if not quite often). The value of an assumption is determined not by seeing if it passes a true-false test, but by examining how it shapes the theory. Is the assumption logically consistent with the theory? Does the assumption make the theory more accurate, or parsimonious, or generalizable? Those are the appropriate questions to ask about an assumption. Try to remember that, as political scientists, we are building models of reality, not reconstructing reality itself. A model airplane is rather different from the real thing; one is merely a representation of the other. Assumptions are elements of abstract thinking that help us create these representations by eliminating parts of reality.

Categorizing Theories

Theories that share assumptions can be gathered into groups; theories constructed in a similar fashion share similar qualities. Hence, people who construct theories in a similar fashion are usually referred to under a single title. The group may then be referred to as a "school of thought" or practitioners of a "paradigm" or "approach." Debates in international relations often come down to disagreements over the utility of different assumptions. Theories built on different assumptions usually reach very different predictions and, therefore, different policy prescriptions. It is through the comparison of theories' abilities to carry out the tasks discussed above, in terms of the qualities listed earlier, that we try to settle disputes between schools of thought.

One of the earliest schools of thought to form in modern times is known as *idealism*. Members of this approach constructed theories that shared the assumption that people were basically good—or at least that laws and institutions could bring out the goodness in people. They earned the name idealists because their assumption about human nature led them to build theories

INTRODUCTION | *Themes and Goals* [21]

prescribing paths to achieving an ideal world, a world of peace, love, and understanding. There were different theories within this group, but because of their underlying assumptions, the link to their normative goals was strong. Those more cynical about mankind emphasized a different set of assumptions and constructed theories by first assuming that people are selfish and desire domination over others. To highlight their distinction from the idealists, they were known as the *realists*. These two groups, plus the *radicals* who stand outside these two groups (and who are often from a *Marxist* tradition) are the three main groups of theorists in international relations,[16] although we will also be discussing groups such as *liberals, constructivists,* and *institutionalists* (and there are still others). We often refer to such groupings of assumptions as *paradigms*. A paradigm is an example, but in political science the term is used to refer to an example which others copy and employ as well. The set of core assumptions that define a set of theories is what separates one paradigm from another.[17] Because the assumptions can be grouped in several different ways, discussions of paradigms can be confusing. We will employ two different principles when organizing theories into groups. First, we will look at variants of idealism, realism, Marxism, liberalism, and other popular approaches in international political economy. Second, we will try to organize the same theories in a different fashion on the *levels of analysis*.

The original split between realists and idealists was over assumptions about human nature. But that is not the only assumption one might make; a Marxist or a constructivist might not worry about human nature at all when setting out to create a theory. So another way of grouping theories would be to look at some other defining assumption, such as the type of actor assumed to be most important. This approach was once one of the most popular methods for organizing theories into groups and is known as grouping theories by the levels of analysis.[18] As can be seen in the social sciences, scholars often understand human activity as the result of either the characteristics of individual units within the society (i.e., people, households, or business firms) or of characteristics of the social organization itself. In economics, for instance, we find this in the distinction made between macro- and micro-economics.

In the study of foreign policies, or foreign economic policies, things are a bit more complex. We have a number of different divisions to make, since we are talking about the behaviour or action of states and about how citizens from different countries interact to create international outcomes. So we find two levels of explanation or analysis right away. There are those explanations that focus on the characteristics of the state itself, which we will call *state-level* or *national-level* theories, and others that focus on the society of states or international *system level*.

Figure 1: The Levels of Analysis

System level
State level
National Characteristics
Domestic Politics
Bureaucratic Politics
Individual Idiosyncrasies

Just as an example of each type of explanation, consider Canada's membership in the North Atlantic Treaty Organization (NATO). How do we understand Canada's decision to join this organization? A system-level explanation would focus on the characteristics of the international system to understand this event: Canada belongs to NATO because in the 1950s there were two superpowers, and to be safe a country had to join an alliance led by a superpower. The existence of the two superpowers is critical for understanding Canada's decision in this theory. What about state-level explanations? Well, these would focus on Canada's domestic characteristics to explain the decision: the cultural, social, and political aspects of Canada would be used to understand Canada's entry into NATO.

We can come up with other levels of analysis by considering the composition of states. States are made up of government bodies, or social classes, or interest groups, etc., and each of those is, in turn, composed of individuals. It is possible to explain the policies of states as the result of the characteristics of groups or individuals within states, or of the ways these actors are configured relative to each other. This provides us with several other categories of theories, at these levels: *societal, bureaucratic,* and *individual.* When Canada signs a treaty with another country, is it the result of all Canada acting together? Or is it the result of some specific subset of Canadians determining the outcome? Or can it only be understood as the result of the actions or thoughts of a particular person, perhaps an influential leader or negotiator? Each of these levels will become clearer to us as we spend some time thinking about them and employing them. And, remember, each level of analysis represents a group of theories, not simply one theory.

We refer to them as the levels of analysis, because they can be stacked hierarchically (see Figure 1), with the narrowest form of social organization at the bottom (the individual) and the broadest at the top (the international system).

In Chapter 1, we will begin with a discussion of the evolution of the various paradigms, beginning with the debate between the realists and the idealists. In Chapter 2 we take a different tack and arrange theories by the levels of analysis. If we look closely at the definitions of the paradigms discussed in the next chapter, we will see that theories within each paradigm can usually be placed on a different level of analysis. Realists focus on states as the primary actor, and their arguments are about states interacting—thus, they fall into the system level. Idealists tend to focus on individuals, so their theories can often be grouped on that level. Marxists focus on classes as the primary actor, and classes interact within societies, so that is where they tend to be found. Some modifications of Marxism have come to focus on characteristics of capitalist states (i.e., on the state level) and on how states organize the international economy (i.e., on the system level). As we can see from this simple discussion, the various ways to organize theories overlap, although often these fits are imperfect.

In Part II, we examine three issue-areas in international political economy. These three issue-areas (trade, international investment, and international monetary relations) cover the most important aspects of the international economy, though they are not completely comprehensive. Each chapter in Part II will discuss some of the relevant economic theories on the subject, but will explore especially the political ramifications of economic activity in these areas. The goal is to establish a critical understanding of the interaction of political and economic issues concerning the international economy.

In Part III, particular examples of regime change or foreign economic policy behaviour are examined. Each case offers us an opportunity to test various theories. By viewing the theories as they are applied, and comparing their abilities to describe and explain events, the reader can learn to evaluate them. Moreover, each case is a pivotal change, a turning point in the evolution of the international political economy.

Finally, in Conclusion, questions concerning the refinement of theories are engaged, and the overall evolution of the international political economy is discussed in brief.

Notes

1. James R. Rosenau and Mary Durfee, *Thinking Theory Thoroughly* (Boulder, CO: Westview, 1995) 57.

2. Or at least we *should* make our theories explicit; see the recommendations made in Rosenau and Durfee 5.

3. It is possible to use "thought-experiments" (or counterfactuals) as well as the historical record, though one must take special care in how this is executed. For more on counterfactuals see Robert Keohane, Gary King, and Sidney Verba *Designing Social Inquiry* (Princeton, NJ: Princeton University Press, 1994).

4. Rosenau and Durfee 2.

5. Kenneth Waltz, *Theory of International Politics* (Reading, MA: Addison-Wesley, 1979) 1.

6. Sometimes we will be interested in understanding why the independent variable changes, of course, but that may require us to create a whole separate theory.

7. Waltz 6.

8. The one possible counter to this argument is that one can make such decisions based on faith rather than logic.

9. Waltz (69-70) talks about explanatory power, predictive power and elegance. The sorts of qualities I will discuss below appear in Thomas Kuhn's *The Structure of Scientific Revolutions* (Chicago, IL: University of Chicago Press, 1962). The same ideas also appear in Adam Pzerworski and Henry Teune, *The Logic of Comparative Social Inquiry* (New York, NY: Wiley, 1970).

10. See Kuhn's thoughts in *The Structure of Scientific Revolutions* 155. This is similar to the term *elegance* which Waltz uses.

11. Keohane, King, and Verba 29-31.

12. See Imre Lakatos, "Falsification and the Methodology of Scientific Research Programmes," *Criticism and the Growth of Knowledge*, ed. Imre Lakatos and Alan Musgrave (New York, NY: Cambridge University Press, 1970) 91-196. Lakatos is building on the ideas of Karl Popper, who discussed falsifiability in *The Logic of Scientific Discovery* (New York, NY: Basic Books, 1959).

13. For a discussion of how Kuhn's views of falsifiability differ from Popper's, see the interpretation offered by Lakatos in the article cited above. Lakatos develops the notion of "sophisticated methodological falsificationism," which stresses, among other things, that disproof is not the same thing as rejection of a theory and the need to test sets of theories rather than just a single theory. In other words, finding out that a theory doesn't work all the time doesn't disprove it, so much as show its level of accuracy. However, there are certain instances where a theory must be accurate if it is to viable at all; falsifiability is about establishing the grounds for rejecting a theory (or set of theories).

14. See Kuhn, *The Structure of Scientific Revolutions* 76.

15. For a broader discussion of such issues, see Kuhn, *The Structure of Scientific Revolutions* 199-201; also see Kuhn's comments on p. 262 in "Reflections on my Critics," *Criticism and the Growth of Knowledge*, ed. Imre Lakatos and Alan Musgrave (New York, NY: Cambridge University Press, 1970) 231-78.

16. See for instance, Robert Gilpin, *U.S. Power and the Multinational Corporation* (New York, NY: Basic Books, 1975) 26-33.

17. See the discussion in John A. Vasquez, *The Power of Power Politics: A Critique* (New Brunswick, NJ: Rutgers University Press, 1983) Chapter 1, esp. 2-5.

18. One of the first articles to discuss this technique was John David Singer, "The Level-of-Analysis Problem in International Relations," *The International System: Theoretical Essays*, ed. Klaus Knorr and Sidney Verba (Princeton, NJ: Princeton University Press, 1961) 77-92 (published in *World Politics* that year as well). A later exposition of this method for organizing theories can be found in S.J. Andriole, "The Levels of Analysis Problems and the Study of Foreign, International and Global Affairs: A Review Critique, and Another Final Solution," *International Interactions* 5 (2/3), 1978: 113-33.

PART I
Approaches to International Relations

CHAPTER I

Competing Theories and the Evolution of Paradigms

The Modern Study of International Relations

As a field within political science, international relations got its start thanks to the psychological, political, and emotional impact of World War I. While earlier scholars wrote about international relations, their work differed from current ways in which we study the subject; in fact, we would consider their way of study haphazard and unscientific. Academic inquiry in international relations was primarily the study of diplomatic history with some current events and international law mixed in. The emphasis was often on practical knowledge for diplomats. Students would have learned such things as who was who in current international political circles, which diplomats were posted where, or what the contents of recent treaties contained—things we still might study—but only occasionally were there informal attempts to understand causality via analyses of cases from diplomatic history. These analyses, however, were typically inconsistent, rarely going beyond single analogies.

The carnage of World War I produced the first real impetus towards understanding international relations via more scientific methods. In order to make sense of the enormous human and material costs of the war, or perhaps to justify them, there was an effort to make World War I "the war to end all wars." Scholars began to do all they could to prevent another such war from occurring, by stressing the need to reach some understanding of why it had happened in the first place. So the modern study of international relations began with an emphasis on developing predictive and prescriptive theories.

The Realists Versus the Idealists

Initially, one group of theorists, the *idealists*, built on the public revulsion from the carnage of World War I to dominate the field of international relations, but a rival set of views was already in the background, and within 20 years a great debate arose. This proved to be only the first of several that have gripped the field. This first major debate pitted two camps, one tracing its

The Core Assumptions of Classical Idealism

1. Human behaviour can be perfected.
2. There exists a harmony of interests between people and between nations.
3. Therefore, war is never an appropriate way to solve disputes; instead, the underlying harmony of interests should be uncovered and emphasized.
4. If the correct laws and institutions guide behaviour, the good in humans can be evoked (thereby illuminating the harmony of interests between people and between states).

lineage back to the previous study of diplomatic history, the other proceeding from work in international law. Both sides were concerned with the possibility of another major war. Those who drew on legal studies approached the task by emphasizing the importance and utility of international law. Why are laws useful in domestic society? Because they influence the way people act: without laws in place, people would behave differently. Thus, if we vary the laws, we can change how people behave. Since laws guide behaviour, those who write the laws intend to make humans interact in more desirable ways (at least more desirable from the law-makers' perspective). Laws, in that sense, create better citizens. Those who stressed the potential for international law to create a more peaceful society of states became known as the *utopians*, or idealists, because they stressed the possibility of perfecting the behaviour of man and thus perfecting the actions of states.

The idealists stressed choice, rationality, and the potential or actual existence of a harmony of interests between individuals and, therefore, also between states. They would have put their argument this way: "can't any rational person see how futile war is, how pointless World War I had been, and therefore can't we all agree not to do it again?" They argued that there were ways in which the international system could be perfected or more desirable standards of behaviour achieved. Thus, idealism has always been very teleological (goal-oriented) and has continually emphasized the normative goal of international peace.

Early specialists who focused on historical patterns took a different stand. For them, war was something to be expected—it was the traditional way in which states had settled their most important disputes. *Realists*, as these scholars became known, stressed the importance of power in international relations, if not in all social interactions. They stressed continuity in states' behaviour, especially in the willingness to use power to resolve differences. They considered the utopians to be idealistic and unrealistic (note the pejorative connotations associated with those words today). In contrast to the assumptions made by the idealists that humans could be perfected through the creation and application of law, realists assumed that humans were basically selfish, greedy, and interested in dominating each other. Drawing on diplomatic history, realists argued that humans had been evil to each other quite often. (It is important to stress that this was a debate over assumptions, not facts—realists have no special claim to reality.)[1] Whereas the idealists could work with the public's distaste for war, realists took more time to develop their ideas. Indeed, it took the work of one realist, E.H. Carr, to display how realism was developing as a coherent counterpoint to idealism.[2]

Realism Emerges Dominant

Carr is remembered as one of the earliest proponents of realism. His observations of the international situation in the late 1930s reflected a sober assessment of idealism, but a careful reading of his work also yields insights into the problems of *classical realism*. Carr argued that idealists were overly optimistic about the ability of scholarship to change the world. Idealism stressed prescriptions and normative goals prior to developing an understanding of how things actually worked. As such it was doomed to fail. Of course, Carr pointed out how realism—as a foil to idealism— had its own weaknesses, the most important of which was its failure to develop normative goals, as well as its inability to present an emotional appeal to the public or to render moral judgements—all of which would ultimately undermine realism's ability to provide grounds for actions.[3]

Carr was writing in 1939; his assessment was based on some of the events he had already observed, such as the failure of legalistic attempts to prevent war in the 1930s. The League of Nations had been created with the express purpose of implementing international law to punish aggression, yet it seemed impotent in the face of fascism. The advent of World War II merely proved his point even more strongly and gave the realists control over the agenda of the field of international relations.

Early realists focused their arguments on human nature and the sorts of assumptions one should make about what drives human interactions. Reinhold Niebuhr, for instance, drew upon Christianity to argue that man was tainted by sin, and thus human behaviour could never be perfected. Like other realists such as Hans Morgenthau, Niebuhr also argued that man had a will to live, which drove humans to want to dominate their environment and each other.[4] Morgenthau rooted his version of realism in human nature and the desire for

The Core Assumptions of Classical Realism

1. Humans have a will to survive, which makes them selfish.
2. The will to survive means a will to dominate the environment, including other humans.
3. Since this creates competition to dominate, the will to survive creates a search for power.

power.[5] The will to survive becomes a will to power. These same assumptions were then translated into the affairs of states.

The realists gained ground in their debates with idealists by arguing that morality played no role in the foreign policies of other states (such as Nazi Germany or the Soviet Union). Therefore, the foreign policy of the U.S. or other Western democracies should be just as amoral when facing these threats. Much of this debate swirled around the issues of foreign policy in the late 1940s and early 1950s as much as on philosophical views of human nature. In the minds of these early realists, moral objectives were luxuries Western states simply could not afford.[6]

Realism changed as time went on. While realists maintain dominance today, they do not now have, nor have they ever had, universal appeal. Idealism fell out of favour in the early post-World War II era, but later paradigms emerged which took up some of its core arguments. Indeed, some of the rivals to realism are currently flourishing, but in the 1950s and 1960s realism clearly held sway.

The Cold War and the Evolution of Realism

In many ways, the decades of the 1950s and the 1960s were not just the time of realism's dominance, they were the golden years of security studies.[7] Because the U.S. and other Western powers were locked in an ideological struggle and an arms race against the Soviet Union, there were constant demands from governments for informed analyses of military and diplomatic strategies. These demands stimulated theoretical analyses of security affairs, and many of the brightest minds were drawn into the field.

Realism changed during these decades, in some of the ways which Carr's assessment had predicted. Without the rival idealists offering an attractive alternative, realists began to question the utility of their own assumptions. Kenneth Waltz argued in his book *Man, the State and War* that human nature was not a particularly useful assumption for constructing theories.[8] He argued that human nature was not set—humans were capable of both good and evil.

Moreover, no one was arguing that human nature changed. If it did not vary, how could it be useful for explaining specific acts? States could be thought of in the same way; they too were capable of acting for either good or evil purposes. Waltz's underlying argument was that the particularities of the situation influenced how humans (or states) behaved. He therefore proposed that it did not matter whether one assumed human nature to be basically good or basically evil; in certain situations, good people (or good states) acted the same as evil people (or evil states). Though it took some time for these ideas to gel into a coherent set of assumptions, realism was changing.

Another Great Debate—Behaviouralism and Realism Transformed

The second great debate in international relations, fought primarily among realists, concerned the research methods one should employ.[9] The debate occurred primarily in the 1960s and 1970s, though factions persist on both sides to this day.[10] Scholars disagreed over the best ways to uncover causality, the best methods for interpreting evidence, and the best ways to go about asking questions. On one side were the *traditionalists*, who argued for a continued emphasis on history and the study of particular historical episodes as unique events. On the other side there were the *behaviouralists*, who stressed the need to aggregate information in order to apply methods of data analysis (statistics) to interpret the evidence. This sort of debate still goes on in political science and occurs in other social sciences such as history (where the arguments are just beginning).

One of the most important aspects of realism as it developed was its emphasis on the notion of *sovereignty*, the concept that states hold the ultimate legitimate political authority. States enforce laws and do not have to answer to other political authorities, only to themselves. For realists, the fact that states respect no higher authority, and exercise political authority over other actors (whether individuals or groups), makes them the most important actors in international relations. When two sovereign actors have a dispute, how do they resolve it? If each respects no higher authority, they must settle the dispute between themselves. Each state can act as judge, jury, and executioner. And that means that to survive, or to achieve goals beyond mere survival, states have to have power for confronting other states.

These are some of the basic building blocks of realist theories. States, as sovereign entities, are assumed to be the primary actors in international relations. States are also assumed to be *rational* and unitary (in other words, the state acts as a coherent, single entity).[11] The international system, because it lacks an authority above the units (states), is anarchic. Realists use the term "anarchy"

Figure 1.1: Waltz's View of Causality in International Politics

change in structure

|

leads to

↓

change in state interactions

|

leads to

↓

a new outcome

not in the sense of chaos, but in the sense that there is no government superior to the actors in question. In such a system, states are under constant threat and, therefore, must do what they can to defend their own interests; hence, they must maximize power. Note that in this version of realism, there is no need to make an assumption about human nature.

Kenneth Waltz, in *Theory of International Politics*, lays out the basic points of realism in a slightly different way, which shows how realism continued to move away from its original focus on human nature.[12] Waltz says we can understand states' policies by understanding the system in which states operate. The key concept for Waltz is *structure*. Structure is a way of depicting the relations of the units, or the composition of the system. As he puts it, "units differently juxtaposed and combined, behave differently and in interacting produce different outcomes."[13] This thinking can be easily portrayed in a diagram.

According to Waltz, structure has three characteristics: an ordering principle, the differentiation of the parts, and the distribution of capabilities. The ordering principle refers to whether the system is hierarchical or anarchic. Domestic politics is hierarchical—the national government is usually dominant, with lower levels of government exercising authority over a specific range of topics and answerable to the authorities above; realists such as Waltz assume the international system to be anarchic. Differentiation of the units refers to the similarity in functions that actors perform. For instance, in domestic politics, different levels of government perform different tasks (though there can be some overlap); one level maintains roads, another level the health care system, another national defence, and so on. Waltz's point is that at the international level, states perform very similar functions—they each provide legal systems, defence, monetary systems, public infrastructure, etc. Thus, political units are alike, in that sense, but they are also rivals in providing these services and do not rely on each other. Units differ in their capabilities to perform such activities or functions well, and some states have greater capabilities than others.

Waltz's assessment of these three characteristics of the international system is meant to hold true for the modern period. Since it is useful to understand each element of his definition of structure in order to understand how we use structural realism, as his approach is known, it is useful to remember that the international system did not always have these same specific characteristics. It was the Peace of Westphalia in 1648, with its numerous treaties that ended the Thirty Years War in Europe, that first recognized states as sovereign. Prior to that, political units were organized in different ways. Many were linked hierarchically in two ways. First, units were linked through the old feudal system; there were kings, dukes, princes, barons, etc., with the king exercising authority over the dukes, the dukes over princes, and so on down the line. At the same time, much of Europe was also administered by the Catholic Church along hierarchical lines. The Catholic Church had its own power structure, and it existed alongside and within the same set of political bodies as the secular state, for there were political entities attached to the church. Bishops and abbots also ruled territory in those days, so they exercised not just religious but also civil authority.

The Peace of Westphalia began the recognition of a shift away from these dual hierarchical forms of international organization towards a more anarchic situation. Each state was to be considered equal and sovereign, rather than an element in a hierarchic structure. More interestingly, prior to 1648, sovereignty did not inhere to a political unit, but rather it was a characteristic of a person. This can still be seen in one of the meanings of the word *sovereign* in English: supreme ruler. Before the Peace of Westphalia, sovereign actors were kings, princes, bishops, and the like; afterwards, sovereignty was attached to the state. One should not, therefore, expect Waltz's specific assessment of the characteristics of the international system to fit premodern periods, because his assumptions would not be appropriate.

The first two aspects of structure, according to Waltz's definition, haven't changed that much since 1648. But in terms of the third trait, the distribution of capabilities, there has been tremendous change. The distribution of power is therefore the key variable on the causal side in *structural realism*. It is a characteristic of the system of states. To make the point another way, the distribution of power can only be understood through an examination of the units together, as a set, not by studying a single state. Few present-day realists talk much about human nature, but focus instead on how systemic factors constrain the behaviour of states.[14]

A basic notion we will see constantly resurfacing in realism is the *security dilemma*, a concept used to describe relations between sovereign states in the

The Core Assumptions of Structural Realism

1. States are the most important actors in international relations (but they are not the only actors).
2. States are unitary, rational actors.[15]
3. The international system is anarchic.
4. States, in order to protect their own interests in this environment, will seek to maximize their power.

context of international anarchy.[16] The fear of being dominated by one's neighbour causes each state to treat its neighbours as potential sources of threats. As a consequence of the anarchic environment, each state must prepare to deflect potential dangers. One state's attempt to enhance its security via power maximization, however, threatens other states. This creates a chain reaction. The irony is that all states make great efforts to ensure their security, but in the end they remain essentially insecure.

At the same time, definitions of security or national interest have always been controversial.[17] Because it was so difficult to come to any particular agreement on what national interest means, realists tried to evade this question by assuming that the goal of survival comes before all other goals; since power was necessary for survival, power was the most important goal. Others argued that power could be translated into other goals. Some realists, however, have softened their emphasis on states' desire for power. They modified realism by pointing out that citizens demand much more from their governments than merely national defence; for instance, they expect their states to provide a smoothly functioning economy, with full employment. A full list of citizens' expectations of the modern state would be quite long. Power is not always very useful for attaining these goals, so some realists (often called *neo-realists*) began to think of security (or survival) as only a minimal goal.[18] Once survival was ensured, other goals become important. Thus, instead of assuming that states maximized power, they assumed that states maximized utility. Utility is an open concept, which the neo-realists either defined by considering a state's past actions (discovering what the state had spent money and effort to attain, for instance), or left undefined.

Unfortunately, other modifications to realism have made the situation more confusing for most of us. Various authors, referring to themselves as realists, have introduced additional assumptions alongside the traditional elements of realism, which are often quite contradictory. For instance, Joseph Grieco, working along neo-realist lines, developed a "minimal" version of realism that turned to other factors to explain where states' interests come from.[19] Jack

The Core Assumptions of Neo-realism

1. States are the most important actors in international relations (but not the only actors).
2. States are unitary, rational actors.
3. The international system is anarchic.
4. States will seek to maximize their utility.

Snyder, a proponent of "defensive realism," has also used domestic politics to explain state goals[20]—causing some to argue that both had strayed so far from realism that they were really employing theories better categorized under a different paradigm.[21] Such arguments, relying so heavily on independent variables outside the core assumptions of realism, reflect the weaknesses of the paradigm.

Realism's Challengers

There are other definitions of the *system level* besides the one Waltz developed into structural realism. Hedley Bull, for instance, worked within the realist tradition but developed a set of arguments based on a different notion of the system.[22] Bull considers an international system to exist when a group of states see themselves bound by a common set of rules governing their relations (such as international law, diplomacy, international organizations, rules of war, etc.). It is important to appreciate how he brought in notions of community and interaction to this definition, making it quite different from Waltz's. Even in anarchy, features of society may play a role, constraining actors' behaviour.

The system level does not belong only to the realists. Radicals have their own views and their own theories, which often operate in a similar fashion to realism. Helen Milner, for instance, stresses the importance of the international system, but disagrees with some of Waltz's assessments of the characteristics of the international structure.[23] She highlights the differences in her views by elaborating arguments made by more radical theorists. For instance, she considers that Waltz's assumption that states are functionally undifferentiated may not be very useful if one is interested in questions of international political economy. Radicals such as Marxists may agree with Waltz that, politically, all states claim to perform the same functions, but in the international economy there is a great degree of specialization and, therefore, of differentiation. Different states provide different goods and services to the international economy. Whenever trade takes place, there is a division of labour. The Marxist critique of the *division of labour* in the domestic economy is that it creates

The Core Assumptions of Classical Marxism

1. Social classes are the most important actors in politics.
2. Classes act in their own material interest.
3. The expropriation of surplus value is exploitation.

classes. Classes are not in anarchy—they perform different functions and are organized hierarchically. So modern Marxists challenge Waltz's definition of the system, arguing in favour of competing assumptions, which will lead them to create rather different theories.

In *classical Marxism*, developed in the nineteenth century by Karl Marx and Friedrich Engels, states were not considered the most important actors. One of Marx's most profound contributions to the social sciences was his emphasis on social classes as the most important actors in domestic or international politics. Writing at the time of the Industrial Revolution, Marx was interested in how economic changes were transforming society and redefining social hierarchies. He argued that classes act in their own material interests. Most importantly, he believed that all economic output was ultimately produced by the labour of workers. Since workers did not enjoy all the earnings from their output (entrepreneurs, middlemen, and bosses kept large portions of any economic gains), some of the rightful earnings of the working class were being taken from them via market transactions. In fact, Marx was primarily criticizing the liberal analysis (the different versions of liberalism will be discussed below).

Classical Marxism was developed as a model of the domestic political economy; it was not designed to explain or predict state behaviour.[24] It was created as an alternative to liberalism, another paradigm established to model the domestic political economy. These two paradigms, liberalism and Marxism, actually have older roots than realism. (Defenders of realism would say that examples of realist thinking have existed for millennia.)[25] Eventually liberalism and Marxism spawned theories of international relations, and these compete with theories from the various versions of realism.

Just as realism has changed over time, so too has Marxism. For our purposes, we will concentrate on the two variants of Marxism most often used in international relations. The first was developed in the late nineteenth century by scholars seeking to explain European imperialism. Marx himself would have probably argued that members of the same class shared so much in common that their class interests overrode their national differences—a banker from England and a banker from France had more in common with each other than with workers from their own countries. Yet Marx and Marxists also believed that states acted in the interest of their capitalist class. When states competed

The Core Assumptions of Instrumental Marxism

1. Social classes are the most important actors in politics.
2. Classes act in their own material interest.
3. The expropriation of surplus value is exploitation.
4. States act in the interest of their national capitalist class.

against each other for territory in their imperialist policies of the late nine-teenth century, Marxists explained this competition in terms of the states act-ing in the interests of each country's capitalists against capitalists from other countries. This version of Marxism was made prominent by V.I. Lenin (who developed his theory as the basis for political action, which he then imple-mented by successfully leading the Russian Revolution), hence it was once termed Leninist, but now is more often referred to as *instrumental Marxism*. In many ways, then, this version of Marxism resembles realism, since it depicts states in conflict with other states. In it, however, states are interested in maxi-mizing the economic benefits of their own capitalists, not maximizing national power. The consequences of changing this single assumption are enormous, as we shall see in some of the cases.

Over time, however, problems arose with this version of Marxism. States began to develop and execute policies incompatible with the interests of their own capitalists, who were not gaining any direct benefits from the policies be-ing pursued. States taxed capitalists and instituted welfare policies to alleviate some of the problems workers faced. They carried out expensive policies inter-nationally which did not seem to have any economic pay-off, such as the U.S. involvement in Vietnam. Economically, Vietnam was not very valuable, yet the U.S. was willing to expend extensive resources to prosecute a war defend-ing South Vietnam against communism. Marxists resolved these shortcomings in their theories by altering their assumptions once again. Instead of assuming that states act in the interests of their own national capital class (and therefore against the interests of capitalists from other countries), some Marxists began to assume that states acted to protect the workings of capitalism itself. This helped explain why states might sometimes do things against the immediate interests of their own capitalists. It does present some problems with falsifi-ability, however, since any form of state policy might be considered compat-ible with this expectation. This version became known as *structural Marxism*, since it emphasized how states acted politically to maintain the overall political economic structure of capitalism.[26]

More recently, another form of analysis has sprung from Marxism. This approach mixes together different kinds of actors, for although it retains an

The Core Assumptions of Structural Marxism

1. Social classes are the most important actors in politics.
2. Classes act in their own material interest.
3. The expropriation of surplus value is exploitation.
4. States act to maintain capitalism, even if such actions are inconsistent with the interests of their national capitalist class in the short-run.

---

emphasis on classes, it perhaps stresses the role of states even more. It is also rooted in the work of historians and sociologists. It is called *modern world-systems*, because it analyzes the coaction of the international political and international economic systems in the modern capitalist era.

The Modern World-Systems Approach

The main argument made by Immanuel Wallerstein, who is often considered the originator of world-systems analysis, stresses how the emergence of capitalism required the creation of an international economy; the development of this international economy, in turn, had profound consequences for the evolution of domestic political economies.[27] Wallerstein was, of course, not working alone. He was building on similar types of analyses done by a group of historians in France led by Fernand Braudel (the *Annales* school), and by other Marxists such as Theotonio Dos Santos and André Gunder Frank, who were interested in the consequences of imperialism and international trade.[28]

Wallerstein's work is a blend of history, sociology and political science. It does not purport to develop an explicit theory of international relations to perform the tasks of theory as laid out in the earlier sections of this text. Instead, Wallerstein's arguments are really about the historical development of the international political economy. As such, the arguments provide a framework that other theorists have used to develop a number of specific theories. Generalizable arguments have been made, to illustrate how some patterns of activity recur.[29]

The practitioners of this approach depict the international system as a hierarchical structure. At the top are the core states, which are characterized by a combination of political and economic power. They are the most economically developed states, with the highest concentration of capital. Being economically developed, and therefore also rich, they are able to generate the most political power. They then use this political power to shape the international political economy, enhancing their political and economic dominance. Again,

The Core Assumptions of Modern World-Systems Analysis

1. The world is a structural whole, and is the appropriate unit of analysis.
2. The various parts of the system are functionally related, via the international division of labour.
3. States and markets are the products of underlying social (i.e., class) dynamics.

there are numerous similarities to the types of arguments realists make. These similarities have been perceived by some as a weakness, leading some Marxists to be highly critical of the modern world-systems approach,[30] which they see as diluting Marxism's traditional assumptions. Are classes still the most important actors? Does economic change drive political change? For these reasons, Marxist critics are often harsher on this approach than non-Marxists.

Marxism's Original Rival: Liberalism

Marx developed his arguments to criticize *classical liberalism*. In the mid-nineteenth century, liberalism was at its zenith, claiming that everyone would benefit from participation in markets. Economic advancement would include everyone—something Marx did not believe. Marx saw the impact of the Industrial Revolution, especially on the creation of an industrial working class, and concluded the working class was not benefiting from the economic changes Europe was undergoing.

Liberalism had its own start in international political economy in the late eighteenth century as a challenger to absolutism. Under absolutism, the monarch claimed absolute powers over the individual in the political and/or economic realm. At the international level, absolutism produced mercantilist policies. Mercantilism generated tremendous tax revenues for the state, but only by inhibiting the development of the international political economy. Liberalism developed different notions of how to think about the functioning of the national and international economy. Instead of emphasizing the role of the state and the importance of a positive balance of payments (as mercantilism had), liberalism aimed to free the individual both politically and economically from the state. It also promised that national wealth would be increased if individuals were free to compete against each other, as opposed to having the state interfere with the market. Similar results could be attained at the domestic and international level, according to the classical liberals.

The Core Assumptions of Classical Liberalism

1. Individuals (plus households or firms) are the most
   important actors.
2. Individuals are rational (and obviously unitary) actors.
3. Individuals maximize their utility.
4. Everything can be traded.
5. Individuals' indifference curves can be aggregated into
   social indifference curves.[31]

Among the most important classical liberals were Adam Smith and David Ricardo, though there were many others. Smith and Ricardo developed theories about international trade to illustrate mathematically that trade would normally benefit both parties in an exchange. These arguments will be explored in the later chapters on international political economy. What is important to note here is that these economic arguments were used as a basis for a variety of political theories. The core assumptions of classical liberalism highlight the differences between it and the mercantilism of the absolutist monarchies which had come before, but also underscore the emphasis liberalism has always placed on economic gain (in distinction from idealism, though there is obviously overlap between the two).

Because it was engaging mercantilism, liberalism always had both a domestic and an international aspect. Later theorists and policy-makers began to elaborate variants of liberalism which were focused much more on international political economy. Richard Cobden, a nineteenth-century British politician, developed a version intending to show that, if international economic relations were guided by liberalism, political benefits would result. *Commercial liberalism*, as this view is known, argues that free trade is not only beneficial to individuals in an economic sense, and therefore economically beneficial to states since states are merely agglomerations of individuals, but will also provide positive political spin-offs. If all states participate in free trade, they will learn to meet their desires through exchange. Trade will benefit all sides and therefore undercut the sources of conflict between states. In short, free trade is the route to international peace.

These ideas so infused the thinking of British policy-makers in the early 1800s that the British government was seriously considering how to devolve the British Empire. While the Empire was not dismantled, commercial liberalism remained. Sir Norman Angell, writing in 1912, made precisely these same sorts of arguments just prior to World War I.[32] The concepts can also be found in the writings and practices of Cordell Hull. Hull was a Congressman in the

The Core Assumptions of Commercial Liberalism

1. Individuals (plus households or firms) are the most important actors.
2. Individuals are rational (and obviously unitary) actors.
3. Individuals maximize their utility.
4. Everything can be traded.
5. Therefore, trade is the route to cooperation and peace.

U.S. House of Representatives and then later Secretary of State in Franklin D. Roosevelt's administration in the 1930s. He observed the economic blocs created by Nazi Germany and Imperial Japan, and understood that the erection of barriers between economies would eventually lead to war. If countries were trying to create industrial economies that could survive without trade altogether, how would these countries' resource needs be met? Industrial states require a variety of resources such as oil, minerals, and ores, which Germany and Japan lacked. As Hull feared, these countries sought these raw materials through military conquest rather than through trade. In Hull's view, a smoothly functioning international economy based on liberal principles offered a clear alternative to wars between the major powers.

Another Version: Republican Liberalism

A rival view of liberalism had always existed alongside the classical and commercial versions, which had been founded on economic issues. These other theories placed greater emphasis on political liberalism. Though Woodrow Wilson is the most famous modern proponent of *republican liberalism*, the roots lie in the writings of Immanuel Kant. Kant theorized about the international relations over 200 years ago; at the time, there were no true democracies and only a small number of republics. Kant's arguments emphasized that republican states behaved differently towards each other.

According to republican liberalism, what shapes national policies is whether or not political liberalism is established within countries. Where individuals have a say in the formulation of national policy, national policy will be peaceful and will pursue the creation of wealth. This characteristic behaviour is tempered by the demands of national security whenever a republic confronts a non-republican state. When two or more republics interact, they create an international community. Such ideas are mirrored in the works of many scholars. The idea that democratic states behave differently in their own interactions is quite popular, because modern democratic states have rarely if ever

The Core Assumptions of Republican Liberalism

1. Individuals are the most important actors.
2. Individuals are rational (and obviously unitary) actors.
3. Individuals maximize their utility.
4. National self-determination, where individuals can express their preferences, is the route to international peace and understanding.

engaged in wars against each other. Today's arguments stress how democratic states practise particular norms, which constrain the ways in which these states behave.

Another reason these ideas have recently gone through a great resurgence is that democratic practices are much more widespread than ever before. Many countries have gone through dramatic changes of government since the early 1980s. Developing countries and former members of the Soviet bloc alike have transformed themselves into democracies. They have also, by and large, liberalized their domestic economies. Based on the theories of how democracies behave and the growth in the number of democracies in the system, several scholars and policy-makers expect the future to be extremely peaceful.[33] The current popularity of such arguments illustrates that alternatives to realism are alive and strong.[34]

The Successors to the Idealists—Complex Interdependence

It is worth noting that idealism never disappeared entirely. Just as realism evolved over time, so did idealism. It also has something to say about system-level theories, arguing that the international system is characterized by a high degree of interdependence. This point is extremely important when we consider the integration of economies. Whereas realists use the notion of sovereignty to divide states into separate entities, idealists have always seen linkages between states and between the people within states. An important reason for the advent of these linkages is the nature of technological advance. As technology improves, the world becomes "smaller" in the sense that we know more about other peoples, other cultures, and political events elsewhere. This flow of information and communication is important to modern idealists (or transnationalists as they are also referred to), for it helps connect issues. Also, as the economy becomes more advanced, it builds greater linkages with other economies, which mean that events in one country or one economy have an effect on events elsewhere. *Interdependence* can be defined as a situa-

The Core Assumptions of Complex Interdependence

1. States are not always the most important actors in international relations.
2. States are not rational unitary actors, but are composed of many different groups, bureaucracies, individuals, and firms.
3. States are under pressure to do much more than ensure survival of the country, so they have many different goals, and power may not be the most important.

tion where changes or events in any single part produce some reaction or have a significant consequence in other parts of the system. Others have defined interdependence as the mutual contingency of policies; as linkages increase, interdependence increases, so states therefore have to communicate with each other more often in order to coordinate their actions.[35]

The notion of interdependence was used by idealists to challenge realists' ideas respecting the security dilemma, since they were really saying that state A's welfare depended on state B's welfare and vice-versa. Threatening another state was only threatening one's own interests. This was a reassertion of the notion of the "harmony of interests." Theories of technological advance and interdependence quickly became more than just a system-level approach though, because they suggested the importance of other actors besides states. Governments might coordinate their activities through international organizations; these inter-governmental organizations (or IGOs, such as the U.N.) might take on a life of their own. Groups mattered at the domestic level because they influenced government policy and might develop international linkages of their own, independent of governments. Some might coalesce into their own organizations. These non-governmental organizations (or NGOs, such as Greenpeace) have grown in number and power in recent years. Firms mattered because they were increasingly using technology (in terms of transportation and communication) to become multinational. Moreover, these other actors often became transnational or multinational because they wanted to evade government policy. As their character changed, they sought to alter government policy in new ways. So, while some transnationalists focused on the level of state interaction (because they were still interested in explaining state policy), they increasingly moved beyond that.

Complex interdependence has the obvious advantage that it can incorporate a vast array of different actors and causal forces.[36] This breadth is both a strength and a weakness. By including so many possible actors and allowing for states to have so many different goals, complex interdependence provides little guidance to theorists. Which actors are the most important to consider? Which can be safely ignored? Does one need to look at all actors of all types at all times? The complex interdependence model serves an important purpose in criticizing structural realism, but it is unclear in how it offers a rival theory. Complex interdependence simply leaves too much open to interpretation.

International Political Economy Reborn

The politics behind international economic relations had already been studied by economists (Smith, Ricardo, etc.) and by political activists (Hobson, Lenin, etc.), but mainstream international relations had in fact left these issues by and large to the economists in the decades after World War II. This mirrored the separation of economics and political science in academia, but it also reflected the every-day functioning of the real world. When people in the industrialized Western countries began to ask why some policies turned out the way they did, or wanted to offer policy prescriptions about economic relations, they largely engaged in debates completely within an economic framework. Such debates were typically devoid of political issues. Economists' predictions were adequate for many questions, even in the absence of an analysis of the politics of the questions posed.[37]

Eventually, however, some of the predictions became less accurate. Models that had performed well in the past began to lose their efficacy. Monetary affairs were thrown into disarray by pressures on the U.S. dollar. The value of currencies had been fixed under the Bretton Woods accords, yet the relationships between currencies (and between each currency and the reserves held to support its value) no longer made sense. Market forces and government policies now clashed. The fixed exchange rates could no longer be maintained—what should happen? Should rates merely be fixed at new levels, or should currency markets set the rates? Economists were divided. National interests were divided, too.

Direct political interference in the international economy also emerged. The Organization of Petroleum Exporting Countries (OPEC) embargoed the sale of oil, and, by doing so, achieved two goals: it increased the price of oil (and thus its members' own revenues) and showed support for the Arab states in their political confrontation with Israel. This was a clear example that politics could disrupt the international economy. A much broader political challenge, drawing from more radical perspectives, was mounted in the 1970s as well. Some mainstream economists, such as Raoul Prebisch, had endeavoured to show how an international economy based on liberal markets tended to leave the economically developing countries further and further behind the industrialized nations. Prebisch advocated greater management of international economic affairs as a corrective to the workings of the market. Marxists extended the argument in dependency theory. They argued that such markets were clearly exploitive, and therefore the less economically advanced countries should withdraw from them; political challenges to the capitalist international economy were necessary. Fuelled by such analyses, representatives from less economically developed countries gathered together and, working through the various agencies and bodies of the U.N., used their numbers to vote for changes in the ways the international economy works. Their demands ranged from calls for increased foreign aid from the industrial states to rearranging global trade relations.[38]

Such changes in the real world and the re-evaluation of theories and models forced scholars to appreciate the role politics had always played in the workings of the international economy. Many began to think about how certain U.S. foreign policies had created an environment where the economic relations between the Western countries could operate largely without political interference. As political scientists had always understood about the domestic economy, a seemingly apolitical economy is the result of rigorous political construction. The apparently apolitical domestic economy of the U.S. or Canada can exist only because of political actions that provide a foundation for it. Contracts must be enforced by courts and police; a currency which must be managed must exist (and be accepted by all) to allow for smooth market transactions and for savings and investments to take place; communication and transportation networks must be constructed and regulated; and so on. Some of these same political functions were necessary for the apparently apolitical post-World War II international economic relations between the Western powers. When the U.S. seemed unable or unwilling to provide the necessary leadership in providing the political underpinnings the international economy required, it failed to function as well as it had.

In short, the rapid changes in the world not only raised new questions for scholars, but also undercut our faith in existing models and theories. In this environment, the subfield of international political economy (IPE) blossomed. IPE was developed to confront these very questions, which were largely outside the realm of mainstream international relations. In order to answer them, international political economists began to incorporate more analytical techniques from economics and explored the connections between international relations and other fields in political science (particularly comparative politics) more deeply than ever before.

This is not to say that security studies died or even withered. In the 1980s, security studies (perhaps sparked by the ideas and methodologies so prominent in IPE) experienced a renaissance. In the 1990s, with the end of the Cold

War and new subjects rising to confront specialists in international relations no matter what their expertise, we have seen greater recognition of the interaction between economic and security affairs. Economic factors seem so prominent in many different events nowadays, ranging from explanations of the Soviet Union's collapse to the political integration of Europe. The terrorist attacks of September 11, 2001 both called into question existing ideas about the meaning of security and reasserted old notions about the primacy of power.

In the 1970s, though, the key questions challenging the new subfield of IPE mostly had to do with evolving characteristics of the international economy. To describe IPE's characteristics, scholars developed the concept of *international regime*.[39] An international regime can be defined as a set of "principles, rules, norms and decision-making procedures around which actors' expectations converge."[40] In short, a regime is a set of prescriptions and proscriptions for state behaviour. Regimes can vary considerably. Sometimes the rules are implicit; at other times they are laid out in explicit detail in a treaty. Sometimes regimes cover a very narrow subject; in other instances they are quite broad. The concept is an extremely useful one not only because it is very flexible, but also because it gives us a method for describing IPE practices. Not everyone finds the concept equally useful; dependency theorists had always focused more explicitly on the international division of labour, for instance, and many people still preferred theories aimed at explaining individual state's policies rather than IPE traits.

In the early 1970s, IPE regimes seemed to be in flux. The rules and practices governing monetary relations had already given way—but to what? What new rules were likely to emerge? How much would the rules governing trade change? Would the developing countries succeed in their efforts to alter several economic regimes in some fundamental way? Scholars and policy-makers alike were unsure. The efforts to address these questions resulted in a new paradigm, one based primarily in IPE: *institutionalism*.

Explaining Changes in International Regimes: Institutionalism

Institutionalism was inspired by the observations and arguments made by scholars of IPE in their work on international regimes. Realists had always explained the creation and persistence of international rules and practices as an outcome of the exercise of power. The realist belief was that it took the concentration of power in the hands of a single actor to create some semblance of order in the international system. (These arguments fall under the rubric of *hegemonic stability theory*, to be discussed later.) According to realists, once power becomes decentralized that semblance of order is lost. In the early

The Core Assumptions of Rationalist Institutionalism

1. Actors are self-interested, rational utility maximizers.
2. International regimes can facilitate the making of agreements by actors.
3. Actors are interested in the pursuit of goals which are not always zero-sum in nature.

1970s, economic order seemed to be breaking down as the U.S. fell in power relative to West Germany, France, and Japan. Realists expected international practices to become increasingly disordered as time went on.

By the early 1980s, it was clear that even though the U.S. continued to decline economically relative to other states, and was certainly weaker than it had been a decade before, few international regimes had fallen apart. This sparked realism's opponents to develop rival explanations. Robert Keohane drew on the literature on domestic institutions to argue that regimes providing useful purposes would be maintained by the participants—without the sanctioning of a hegemonic power.[41] As long as the regimes delivered benefits to the participants, the participants would have reasons to maintain those regimes, and there would be no need for a hegemonic leader. From these arguments, originally formulated to explain why regimes persisted despite changes in the distribution of power, institutionalists were able to create theories explaining other examples of coordination and cooperation. They soon turned their focus to questions concerning the emergence of international regimes.

Institutionalism based on the rationalist perspective (or *rationalist institutionalism*) explains the creation and persistence of international institutions by viewing them as mechanisms for actors (most often states) to ensure that their joint activity leads to outcomes they prefer.[42] Art Stein analyzed such actions as two sorts of problems: dilemmas of common interest and dilemmas of common aversion. An example of a dilemma of common interest is a collective good, and it requires the actors involved to engage in collaboration in order to reach a specific preferred outcome. Dilemmas of common aversion, such as the avoidance of an accident, require the interested actors to coordinate their activities; that is, they simply want to avoid one (an accident) out of many possible outcomes.[43] Institutions matter because they help actors achieve their joint interests.

Keohane himself has pointed out how this early institutionalism was based on rational calculation, but a second form of institutionalism, a "reflective" approach, also exists. This second approach (also referred to as a "sociological approach") emphasizes the importance of subjectivity and the embeddedness

of existing international institutions and regimes.[44] Rationality is always contextual, and the structural realists sometimes assume too much to be already
established and fixed. Existing institutions and norms shape the ways in which
preferences—including the desire for power itself—are defined. The institutionalists using a reflectivist approach stress that regimes are rarely the product
of purely rational design, "but rather emerge slowly through a less deliberative
process, and that they are frequently taken for granted by the people who are
affected by them." In their view, utility maximization is not such a clear-cut
issue when international institutions or international regimes are forming.[45]
Reflectivist institutionalism, therefore, poses a more straightforward challenge
to realist thinking.

One realist, Joseph Grieco, has engaged the institutionalists in a debate by
providing a sketch of the basic assumptions of institutionalism. In short, he
identifies assumptions which are reminiscent of those at the core of complex
interdependence: states are not the single most important actors in the international system; states are not unitary actors but rather are agglomerations
of different agencies and actors each exercising a different form of authority; furthermore, power is not the ultimate goal for states, since other forms
of interaction may matter more in the modern world and because states are
expected to do much more than simply defend the national territory and interests.[46] This set of assumptions is compatible with more than one argument.

Keohane himself sketched out the most important assumptions of rationalist institutionalism in his journal articles and in *After Hegemony*.[47] Instead of
emphasizing non-state actors, he not only continues to assume that states are
the key actors, but also that they are self-interested, unitary actors. Moreover,
he also assumes that the international system is anarchic. Because power is
not the only goal of state action, however, the interaction of states can take on
forms quite unexpected from the structural realist perspective. Power is relative; when one state has more, another has less, and thus we refer to this type
of situation as "zero-sum." Any increases in one side's power must involve
decreases in the other's, so that the changes cancel each other out (i.e., the sum
of the changes is zero). But when other goals are at stake, such as wealth, the
situation may be quite different. Trade involves voluntary exchanges where
each side intends to gain, hence the interaction is positive-sum. Cooperation
is not only possible, but it is likely whenever these egoistic actors see potential
joint gains from cooperation. As Keohane puts it, "regimes are valuable to
governments where, in their absence, certain mutually beneficial agreements
would be impossible to consummate."[48] Regimes are created in this perspective, not as exercises of power, but as devices to further coordination (as noted
above), and hence can be constructed voluntarily by their participants.

Both versions of institutionalism, therefore, provide a framework for developing hypotheses about strategic interaction and seek to explain examples of cooperation as well as competition. These hypotheses attempt to explain systemic outcomes, not the specific foreign policy of a state. The debates between structural realists and most institutionalists have centred, therefore, on which has a better explanation for the way in which international institutions or regimes have evolved.

Another "Reflective" Paradigm: Constructivism

Institutionalists have had a harder time producing a plausible explanation for the creation of regimes, which is why the reflectivist approach has garnered more attention of late. The logic of regime persistence should also fit for regime creation, yet when one looks more closely at the historical record, it is hard to separate out the role of state power. Keohane was careful to make his specific arguments about the evolution of international regimes *after* hegemony had ended, though he hoped to use that information to make inferences about regime creation. Yet other rivals of structural realism have emerged, ones that look more intensely at the creation of norms and practices at the heart of regimes. These theories, generally referred to as *constructivism*, come from a similar "reflective" background as does institutionalism. Constructivism also incorporates the role of ideas as a causal factor, in a way completely unlike other paradigms.[49]

Just as institutionalism represents a reaction to realism, so does constructivism. Structural realism intentionally makes an abstract simplification by separating structure and process. In structural realism, process flows from structure. Constructivists pose questions about the blurring of structure and process. Is process only the outcome of structural constraints, or is structure affected by process? The clearest way to illustrate this problem is to discuss alliances. Structure is determined by the distribution of capabilities. This distribution of capabilities influences the way states act: perhaps to form new alliances. The new alliances create a new distribution of power. Structure has therefore changed, if only in a minor way.[50]

Constructivism is potentially quite powerful. According to Alexander Wendt, the principles of self-help and power politics identified by realists were socially constructed. They are institutions that have evolved, not essential features of an anarchic situation.[51] In other words, Wendt offers a different way for understanding realism and thus for explaining outcomes consistent with realism. Yet constructivism offers to do much more. Key concepts, such as interests, have no meaning, argue the constructivists, until the actor's identity has been established. Interests can never be assumed devoid of social context.[52]

The Core Assumptions of Constructivism

1. Interests and preferences are socially constructed, and hence are flexible rather than enduring.
2. Ideas are important as forces shaping preferences, identity, etc.
3. Rationality is always contextual.

Constructivism represents a broad assault on theories and paradigms based on assumptions intended to cover many types of situations. Constructivists, therefore, do not aim to create theories as generalizable as those created by realists, for instance. This doesn't mean the constructivists have an easy task ahead of them. They seek to understand the codetermination of structures (or institutions) and process. Perhaps for this reason, analyses of empirical examples using this approach are not very numerous and are often plagued by problems of identifying cause and effect.[53]

In some senses constructivism merely harkens back to some of the beliefs of the early idealists. By emphasizing how the structure of the international system and even the nature of the actors themselves are malleable, constructivists provide a picture of the future with many possibilities. By utilizing education, by introducing new ideas or new points of view, they believe the interests of actors can be redefined, and thus actors' behaviour changed.

International Relations and the End of the Cold War

This is an exciting time to be creating and refining theories of international relations. The world has recently changed in unanticipated and interesting ways, not unlike the early 1970s. Policy-makers and theorists alike confront new questions as well as old, enduring ones.[54] Among theorists, some continue to argue that nothing has really changed, while others believe it has changed fundamentally.[55] Either way, IPE will play a fundamental role in how international relations develops in the near future. The source of much innovative work in the past two decades, IPE has also had a tremendous impact more broadly: it has infused security studies with new and interesting ideas,[56] has played an important role in current debates over definitions of security, and has become intertwined with comparative politics.

The sorts of questions we confront fall into two broad categories. On the one hand, specialists in IPE have always been interested in the ways in which international regimes persist, evolve, or fall apart. What causes an international regime to change? Why do some change at a faster pace than others?

Figure 1.2: The Evolution of Paradigms

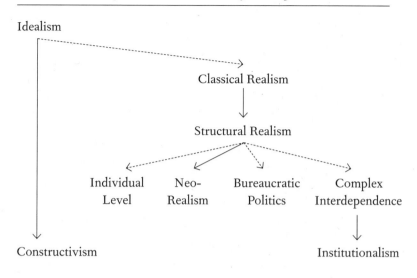

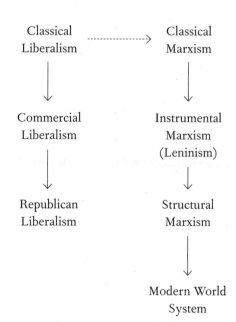

Broken lines denote negative relationships (where a paradigm is spawned in opposition to another), solid lines denote positive relationships (where one is an evolution of another).

Why do some seem to perform well, while others do not? Our paradigms have largely been constructed to answer these sorts of questions. Another set of questions pertains to the ways in which individual states behave. Why does a state choose to change its foreign economic policies? Why would it change its policies at one point in time rather than another? While these sorts of questions are related to those above (because any international regime worth talking about guides state behaviour in some fashion, and a change in the behaviour of a single state often produces changes in an international regime), they remain different. In addressing such questions, we can associate particular qualities of theories with models or theories from different levels of analysis, as detailed in the next chapter.

Notes

1. On this point, see Martin Griffiths, *Realism, Idealism, and International Politics: A Reinterpretation* (New York, NY: Routledge, 1992).

2. E.H. Carr, *The Twenty Years' Crisis, 1919-1939* (1939; New York, NY: Harper, 1964).

3. Carr 89.

4. Michael Doyle has referred to this as Fundamentalism, where human beings' psychological and material needs create a drive for power, and power is both a means to goals, but an important goal in itself. See "Thucydidean Realism," *Review of International Studies* 16 (July 1990): 223-37.

5. Hans Morgenthau, *Scientific Man vs. Power Politics* (Chicago, IL: University of Chicago Press, 1946).

6. Moreover, many of these early realists (such as Morgenthau or Carr) saw moral goals in international affairs as mere smokescreens for actual material or power interests.

7. See the contribution of Peter Katzenstein in "The Role of Theory in Comparative Politics: A Symposium," *World Politics* 48,1 (October 1995): 10-15, for a recent brief discussion of "great debates" in International Relations.

8. Kenneth Waltz, *Man, the State and War* (New York, NY: Columbia University Press, 1954).

9. Morton A. Kaplan, "The New Great Debate: Traditionalism versus Science in International Relations," *World Politics* 19,1 (1966): 1-20.

10. One of the recent versions of this argument has centred on the correct method for analyzing deterrence success and failure. See Christopher Achen and Duncan Snidal, "Rational Deterrence Theory and Comparative Case Studies," *World Politics* 41 (January 1989): 143-69.

11. The assumption of rationality contains three conditions: first, the actor is assumed to have perfect information—it is assumed the actor knows all its options all the costs and benefits (the ramifications) associated with each option; second, the actor must understand the causal effect of each possible choice; third, the actor must be able to rank its choices, which requires that it be able to relate what it values into some sort of schedule of preferences.

12. Kenneth Waltz, *Theory of International Politics* (Reading, MA: Addison-Wesley, 1979).

13. Waltz, *Theory of International Politics* 81.

14. See Doyle.

15. All rational actor models assume that choices are made beginning with perfect information (that the actor knows all its possible choices, as well as all the costs and benefits associated with each), that the actor then assesses all the costs and benefits involved with each choice, that it knows its own preferences, and that it can then select the proper choice for attaining its highest preference. Assumptions of rationality are critical for all models that treat actors as purposive.

16. See Glenn H. Snyder, "'Prisoner's Dilemma' and 'Chicken' Models in International Politics," *International Studies Quarterly* 15 (March 1971): 66-103; and Robert Jervis, "Cooperation under the Security Dilemma," *World Politics* 30 (January 1978): 167-214.

17. The best discussion of this problem can be found in Arnold Wolfers, "National Interest as an Ambiguous Symbol," *Discord and Collaboration* (Baltimore, MD: Johns Hopkins University Press, 1962) 147-65 (originally published in *Political Science Quarterly* 67,4, December 1952).

18. For a broad discussion of the possible meanings of the term "neo-realism," see Robert Keohane (ed.), *Neorealism and Its Critics* (New York, NY: Columbia University Press, 1986).

19. Joseph Grieco, "Anarchy and the Limits of Cooperation," *International Organization* 42,3 (Summer 1988): 485-507.

20. Jack Snyder, *Myths of Empire* (Ithaca, NY: Cornell University Press, 1991).

21. Jeffrey W. Legro and Andrew Moravcsik, "Is Anybody Still a Realist?," *International Security* 24,2 (Fall 1999): 5-55.

22. Hedley Bull, *The Anarchical Society* (London: Macmillan, 1977).

23. Helen Milner, "A Critique of Anarchy," *International Politics: Enduring Concepts and Contemporary Issues*, ed. Robert Art and Robert Jervis (New York, NY: HarperCollins, 1996) 70-80 (originally published as "The Assumption of Anarchy in International Relations," *Review of International Studies* 1991).

24. For instance, Marx himself wrote very little about one of the most important aspects of international politics in his time: imperialism. His thoughts on imperialism are primarily found in letters and in his accounts of British imperialism in India written for the *New York Daily Tribune*. It remains clear, of course, that he thought of class as superceding nation-state; one has only to look at his address to the First International in October 1864.

25. Many realists cite the works of Hobbes, Machiavelli, and even Thucydides to support this position.

26. A well-known off-shoot of this approach is *dependency theory*, which will be discussed in later chapters.

27. See Immanuel Wallerstein, *The Modern World-System*, Vol. I-III (New York, NY: Academic Press, 1979, 1992, 1984); and Robert Gilpin, *The Political Economy of International Relations* (Princeton, NJ: Princeton University Press, 1987) 67-72.

28. Braudel's most important works include *Civilization and Capitalism, 15th-18th Century*, Vol. I-III (New York, NY: Harper and Row, 1974, 1980, 1989); Dos Santos wrote a pioneering article on dependency, "The Structure of Dependence," *American Economic Review* 60,2 (May 1970): 231-36; and André Gunder Frank wrote a large

book exploring dependency in the Americas, *World Accumulation, 1492-1789* (New York, NY: Monthly Review Press, 1978).

29. See for instance, the works of Christopher Chase-Dunn, Albert Bergesen, Terence Hopkins, etc. A helpful overview can be found in Christopher Chase-Dunn, "Comparative Research on World-System Characteristics," *International Studies Quarterly* 23,4 (December 1979): 601-23.

30. Most notable has been Robert Brenner's "The Origins of Capitalist Development: A Critique of Neo-Smithian Marxism," *New Left Review* (1977): 25-92. See Robert A. Denemark and Kenneth P. Thomas, "The Brenner-Wallerstein Debate," *International Studies Quarterly* 32,1 (March 1988): 47-65.

31. Social indifference curves refer to an indifference curve representing society as a whole. As such, this assumption essentially eliminates the problems of moving from numerous individuals' wants to those of a society—even though there are many different ways to do this, which in fact alters the results, as comparative politics shows!

32. See Norman Angell, *The Great Illusion* (New York, NY: Putnam's, 1910). Angell argued that war between industrialized nations was obsolete, due to economic interdependence. Specifically, he tried to show that war "did not pay" and that perceived economic gains from victory in past wars were quite illusory. His works were widely read in the years after World War I, so much so that in 1933 he received the Nobel Peace Prize.

33. See the recent work of Bruce Russett and several collaborators, including *Grasping the Democratic Peace* (Princeton, NJ: Princeton University Press, 1993); and also Francis Fukuyama, "The End of History?," *National Interest* (Summer 1989): 3-18.

34. See the review article by Steve Chan, "In Search of the Democratic Peace: Problems and Promise," *Mershon International Studies Review* 41,1 (May 1997): 59-91. See also Charles Lipson, *Reliable Partners: How Democracies Have Made a Separate Peace* (Princeton: Princeton University Press, 2003).

35. Robert Keohane and Joseph Nye, *Power and Interdependence* (Boston, MA: Little Brown, 1977).

36. Complex interdependence was initially developed by Robert Keohane and Joseph Nye in an article, "The Role of Transnational Forces," *International Organization* 25 (Summer 1971): 721-48.

37. Economists had not solved all their questions, of course. Explanations for patterns of trade and investment among the most economically developed countries remain a matter of contention to this day. See the discussion in the chapter on trade.

38. For the response of one American realist to these challenges, see Stephen Krasner, *Structural Conflict: The Third World Against Global Liberalism* (Berkeley, CA: University of California Press, 1985).

39. There have always been other ways to discuss the characteristics of the international political economy, such as the international division of labour.

40. Stephen Krasner, *International Regimes* (Ithaca, NY: Cornell University Press, 1983) 1.

41. See Robert Keohane, *After Hegemony* (Princeton, NJ: Princeton University Press, 1984).

42. See the description in Lisa Martin, "An Institutionalist View: International Institutions and State Strategies," *International Order in the Twenty-first Century*, ed. John A. Hall and T.V. Paul (New York, NY: Cambridge University Press, 2001).

43. Arthur A. Stein, *Why Nations Cooperate* (Ithaca, NY: Cornell University Press, 1990).

44. Interestingly, John A. Hall, a sociologist, has noted that the rationalist versus reflectivist debate now going on in political science has had its parallel in sociology in the competition between the "idealist" and "materialist" approaches. See John A. Hall, "Ideas and the Social Sciences," *Ideas and Foreign Policy*, ed. Judith Goldstein and Robert Keohane (Ithaca, NY: Cornell University Press, 1993) 32.

45. Robert Keohane, "International Institutions: Two Approaches," *International Studies Quarterly* 32 (December 1988): 389.

46. Grieco uses the term "neo-liberal," but since the only liberal aspects are in the normative goals which this approach seems to contain, I will abandon the "neo-liberal" reference. See Joseph Grieco, *Cooperation Among Nations* (Ithaca, NY: Cornell University Press, 1990) 4-6.

47. The most important article would be Robert Keohane, "The Demand for International Regimes," *International Organization* 36,2 (Spring 1982): 141-71.

48. Keohane, "The Demand for International Regimes" 150.

49. For a recent volume exploring the role of ideas as causal factors, see Judith Goldstein and Robert Keohane (eds.), *Ideas and Foreign Policy* (Ithaca, NY: Cornell University Press, 1993).

50. David Dessler, "What's at Stake in the Agent-Structure Debate?," *International Organization* 43,3 (Summer 1989): 462.

51. Alexander Wendt, "Anarchy is What States Make of It," *International Organization* 46,2 (Spring 1992): 395.

52. A fine example of constructivist argument, comparing its views with realist theories, can be found in Yakub Halabi, "The Expansion of Global Governance into the Third World," *International Studies Review* 6 (2004): 21-48.

53. One of the main efforts to provide such an empirical basis for Constructivism was the special issue of *International Organization* 46,1 (1992). Since then, another special issue has addressed the legalization of world politics with a view to linking changes in ideas and norms to substantive shifts in law. See *International Organization* 50,3 (Summer 2000).

54. See David A. Baldwin, "Security Studies and the End of the Cold War," *World Politics* 48,1 (October 1995): 117-41.

55. For one proponent of the view that nothing has changed, see John Mearsheimer, "Back to the Future: Instability in Europe after the Cold War," *International Security* 15 (1990): 5-56.

56. For example, see Jonathan Kirshner, *Currency and Coercion* (Princeton, NJ: Princeton University Press, 1995); Joanne Gowa, *Allies, Adversaries, and International Trade* (Princeton, NJ: Princeton University Press, 1994); or Edward D. Mansfield, *Power, Trade and War* (Princeton, NJ: Princeton University Press, 1994).

Additional References

Baldwin, David. "Power Analysis and World Politics" *World Politics* 31,2 (January 1979): 161-94.

Bull, Hedley. *The Anarchical Society*. London: Macmillan, 1977.

Carr, Edward H. *The Twenty Years' Crisis, 1919-1939*. New York, NY: Harper and Row, 1964.

Dessler, David. "What's at Stake in the Agent-Structure Debate?" *International Organization* 43,3 (Summer 1989): 441-73.

Doyle, Michael. "Thucydidean Realism." *Review of International Studies* 16 (July 1990): 223-37.

Kaplan, Morton A. *System and Process in International Politics.* Huntington, NY: Robert Krieger, 1975.

Keohane, Robert (ed.). *Neorealism and Its Critics.* New York, NY: Columbia University Press, 1986.

Keohane, Robert, and Joseph Nye. *Power and Interdependence.* Boston, MA: Little, Brown, 1978.

Kuhn, Thomas. *The Structure of Scientific Revolutions.* New York, NY: Cambridge University Press, 1962.

Morganthau, Hans J. *Politics Among Nations.* New York, NY: Knopf, 1978.

Wallerstein, Immanuel. *The Modern World-System I.* San Francisco, CA: Academic Press, 1979.

Waltz, Kenneth. *Man, the State, and War.* New York, NY: Columbia University Press, 1954.

—. *Theory of International Politics.* Reading, MA.: Addison-Wesley, 1979.

Wendt, Alexander. "Anarchy is What States Make of It." *International Organization* 46,2 (Spring 1992): 391-425.

CHAPTER 2

The Levels of Analysis— System-Level Arguments

Grouping theories together by levels of analysis is one useful way to understand how theories differ. In particular, it can be the most useful way to group together those theories seeking to explain states' behaviour. Why would a state suddenly change its policies? What explains why new policies mirror or diverge from past policies? Organizing theories by levels of analysis emphasizes one assumption embedded in theories: at each level, one actor is assumed to be more important than others.[1]

System-Level Theories and the Concept of Power

System-level theories concentrate on characteristics of the international system, and most often the system's structure, to explain state behaviour. Structural realism is an excellent example of this sort of argument. To be even more specific, structural realists use the distribution of power to explain state behaviour. Different distributions of power among the sovereign states in an anarchic environment drive them to act differently.

Before examining the role the distribution of power plays in the system, we should first consider the meaning of the notion of *power*. Power is a central concept in all political science, but it is often very poorly defined. Jeffrey Hart has identified three different definitions:[2] (1) power over other actors, (2) power over resources, and (3) power over events and outcomes. In his deliberations, Hart considers the third definition to be the most useful, because, ultimately, it encompasses the other two. It is general enough to capture examples of coercion, where one state may exercise power over other actors or expend resources, but it also includes examples of cooperation. This definition of power in international politics as power over outcomes is very useful for describing past events, but how useful is it for building predictive theories? For our most pressing task—creating predictive theories—this definition of power will not be of much help, for we cannot recognize power, defined along these lines, until after the event has already occurred.

Robert Dahl has given political science one of its oldest and most durable definitions of power. Power, according to Dahl, is control over actors,[3] and it appears in three ways: (1) control over actions (getting an actor to do something which he/she otherwise wouldn't do—perhaps the oldest most durable definition of power, but clearly a limited definition since it only pertains to coercion), (2) control over the agenda (that is, control over which issues are debated, which decisions will be taken, and when), and (3) control over preferences (the ability to influence what other actors desire—as through advertisements; this has been referred to as ideological or cultural power). Again though, as in the previous definitions, we can usually only recognize power after it has been used.

The problem with each of these examples and with most other definitions of power is that each tends to be descriptive and cannot be easily applied if we are interested in including power as an element in a predictive theory. That is, we are usually asking questions such as "how much power is necessary to control another state's actions?" This question underscores an obvious point, yet one deserving important consideration: power is relative. A measure of power only takes on meaning when placed in a framework of comparison. Is Russia powerful? Against Azerbaijan, the answer is yes; against an alliance combining Azerbaijan, the U.S., China, and others, the answer is no. Of course, even here we get into problems of comparison, because measurements of power are often like comparing apples and oranges. During the Cold War, some experts described the Soviet Union as powerful because that country fielded very large armed forces equipped with thousands of tanks, hundreds of aircraft, etc. When the Cold War ended, and experts from the West could analyze Soviet equipment and training intently, it turned out these forces were not so powerful after all. Comparing military units straight up had been misleading. Numbers alone do not tell the whole story.

This problem of measurement is complicated by the intangible aspects of power, which are beyond the quality of resources. Ray Cline tried to develop a formula to measure potential power capturing easily measured factors, but also introducing its intangible dimensions.[4] He argued that potential power (Pp) equaled the critical mass of population and territory (C), plus economic capabilities (E), plus military power (M), multiplied by the country's strategy and will to use power (S and W). The resulting formula looked like this: $Pp = (C+E+M) \times (S+W)$. This formula is an interesting attempt to incorporate tangibles and intangibles in the same equation. It is not clear how one would measure the intangibles (other than in an arbitrary fashion), but the formula was meant to capture such situations as the Vietnam War, where the seemingly more powerful country lost. Cline would argue that the strategy and will (i.e., S+W) of the U.S. were so low as to approach zero and therefore nullified any advantage in quantifiable resources. But again, we can only assign weights to these variables representing strategy and will after the fact, so this may not be much of an advance on other definitions of power. Simply put, it is hard for political scientists to escape this fundamental problem of defining power.

Power and Structure

As mentioned above (and in Chapter 1), structural realists often look at the distribution of power, however poorly defined, to create theories about how states will behave. In a situation where states are sovereign actors in an anarchic environment, the stronger powers will be able to enforce their wishes on the weaker ones—but how, then, will the stronger powers behave? What does this mean for our traditional concern about the risk of war? What does this mean for structural realists' theories about the operation of IPE?

When realists talk about the system level, and especially when they are employing structural realism and therefore want to talk about how structure shapes behaviour, they define structure in terms of the distribution of capabilities. The simplest way to do that is to identify the number of major powers or poles in the system. The various sorts of structures are easily imagined: first, a *unipolar* distribution is possible—a system with a single major power. In such a system, according to the realists, that one powerful actor would simply eliminate its rival states. While we have never seen such a structure before, we can use these realist assumptions to construct a theory about what we expect would occur. We can even loosen up this argument a bit to consider a system where one state has greater capabilities than the others, but not so much more power that it could actually eliminate the other states. Such a structure is described as *hegemonic*, that is, dominated by a single actor. This single actor may not be able to take complete control over the other states, but it would certainly be able to influence events towards its own desires. This is a more practical version of the structure with a single pole, and some scholars consider the current distribution of power to be hegemonic, with the U.S. as the only pole.

A second possible distribution of power is *bipolar*, where there are two poles, or two strong states, or even two strong alliances. We can find such distributions occurring at different times in history. Such a system may have existed among the Greek city-states, when Athens and Sparta each led powerful alliances. Prior to World War I, two alliances faced off against each other (the Triple Entente, composed of France, Russia, and Britain, versus the Triple Alliance made up of Germany, Austria-Hungary, and Italy). A more recent example of a bipolar system occurred after World War II, when the U.S. and the Soviet Union combined scientific knowledge, technology, industrialized economies, and continental resources to emerge as superpowers and become the leaders of rival alliances (NATO and the Warsaw Pact respectively).

A third possible distribution of power is *tripolar*, where three states hold considerably more power than other members of the system. Since analysts disagree over measurements of power, some see tripolar distributions where others see bipolar ones. Some argued that in the 1970s the system could be characterized as tripolar, given the rise of the People's Republic of China as an independent actor with nuclear capabilities. Others argued that this was not the case, since the Chinese could not project their power very far. (They had nuclear missiles, but they could not deploy their troops far beyond their own borders because of their limited supply system and weak navy.) Nevertheless, as long as China could threaten the Soviet Union, we could say that the structure was indeed tripolar.

After tripolarity, we begin to talk of *multipolar* structures, systems characterized by many poles. We can thus talk about several different structures and changes from one to another (as when states in a multipolar situation line up into two separate alliances). Realists take this information about structure, combine it with their assumptions, and create theories about how states will behave differently in the different structures. This will become clearer if we consider a practical application. The most obvious is to return to the main question separating the realists and idealists—how do we prevent another major war from occurring? Instead of turning to international law and international institutions (such as the U.N.), the realists say the answer to finding a stable peace has to be found in the distribution of power. That means elaborating some theories about which of these various types of systems are more peaceful and stable.

Waltz argued in the 1960s that bipolarity produced a stable and peaceful system, because states are rational, power-maximizing units, and, since power is relative, states will do their best to match any increases in their neighbours' power in order to lessen possible threats.[5] In a bipolar system, each of the major powers has only one other state to fear and therefore has only one country to focus on in this competition. A balance of power will occur, and both states will strive to maintain this balance. In such a situation, each of the major powers will also be able to control and constrain its allies (who by definition are all weaker than either superpower). This element of control, plus the element of competition, led Waltz (in 1964) to predict that a bipolar distribution of power would create much verbal jousting and posturing, arms races between the two top powers, and other forms of competition, but would limit the chance of war breaking out.

Richard Rosecrance, on the other hand, argued that bipolarity was dangerous.[6] Using the same assumptions, he felt that bipolarity makes international affairs a zero-sum situation for the two major powers. Since power is relative, any gain by one automatically means a loss for the other. The situation is dangerous because every possible source of power is contested, no matter how small. Conflicts are likely to erupt over the most minor of issues. In a multipolar world, by comparison, alliances are constantly shifting, and each of the major powers is unsure which of the others poses a threat; conflicts therefore spring only from large issues. In a multipolar world, small changes in potential sources of power don't matter very much, but in a bipolar world every issue is contested.

Rosecrance reached these conclusions largely through an *inductive* approach—that is, through an historical analysis of past distributions of power. He studied the outcomes associated with different distributions of power from 1740 to 1960. He noticed that the international system had experienced a great number of different distributions of power. In previous periods characterized by bipolarity, such as the one that developed from 1890-1914, the distribution of power apparently created rivalries that eventually led to war. On the other hand, he found that peace and stability were associated with other distributions of power, particularly multipolar ones. Before we debate the various merits of the theories developed by Rosecrance and Waltz, remember what theories are supposed to do for us. Not only should they provide descriptions and make predictions, they should also guide our policy prescriptions. Consider the utility of these theories in terms of advising policy. Is it practical to say peace will come through a multipolar system? How can statesmen end bipolarity? Is it possible to follow a policy prescription calling for the distribution of power to be altered? This is perhaps possible, for U.S. statesmen may have opened diplomatic relations with the People's Republic of China in the 1970s for precisely this reason.

Theories can be based on other characteristics of the international system or structure besides the distribution of power. For instance, Rosecrance developed another notion, that of a *regulator*, or coping mechanism.[7] His insight is derived from a piece of mechanical equipment found in some engines. A regulator is a device that maintains the smooth operation of the engine; for example, a valve on a steam engine allows pressure to escape from the boiler, thereby preventing explosion. In terms of the international system, a regulator is a device or resource that keeps the system on track. Rosecrance found that diplomats had different sorts of tools for keeping the system peaceful and stable at different times. In the pre-World War I period, the most important regulator was the use of non-European regions as resources for compensating the European powers. Rivalry among the European states was contained because whenever a European state made gains within Europe, its rivals could be sated by granting compensation in the form of territory in Africa or Asia. Thus, no one state was terribly unhappy, and no one state could get an enormous advantage over the others. This regulator worked as long as there was plenty of colonial territory available (i.e., tracts of land unclaimed by one of the major powers). When almost all of Africa and Asia had been divided among the European powers, compensation became more difficult, and the nature of European competition changed. Alliances were created, and the multipolar situation moved to bipolarity as two armed camps formed.

The distribution of power can also be used to explain particular outcomes in IPE. If power is shared between many countries, the competition engendered in an anarchic environment might well cause them to pursue protectionist trade policies, since each would fear falling behind the others. If there were two powerful states or alliances, and power was distributed roughly equally between them, then we might find a parallel division in the international economy, since we expect to find economic competition mirroring political competition. A unipolar distribution of power means that the single powerful state (or alliance) has the ability to structure international economic relations in the ways it desires.[8]

Economics and Power: The Concept of Power Transition

When Waltz discussed the nature of bipolarity, he noted that the two poles could try to match each other's power through two different strategies: one internal and the other external. Developing power through internal activity requires the dedication of greater economic resources or wealth to the realization of power and/or influence in the international sphere. This usually requires a lengthy period of time and was not always possible in the days when all economies were based on agricultural activity. Economies were slow to change then, so internal sources of power were difficult to modify. Another method, tapping into external resources, is to form alliances. Bringing together a group of states into an alliance, so that their individual powers are united as a single force, can change the distribution of power quite rapidly. Of course, under special circumstances, internal measures can develop a country's power just as rapidly. When a country undergoes industrialization for the first time, its ability to convert resources into power changes dramatically.

During different historical periods, the appeal of these strategies for maximizing one's power has changed. When the Industrial Revolution occurred in Britain, it enabled that country to convert its internal resources more rapidly into military power. This meant that Britain was able to dominate some of its rivals in terms of power—at least until these other powers began to industrialize too. When rapid internally driven change in a country's strength alters the systemic distribution of power, we get what A.F.K. Organski labelled a *power transition*.[9]

Organski argued that as the "power gap" between two states narrows, war becomes more likely, since the newly strong state will try to alter the old relationship between the two countries. This illustrates an important aspect of realist thinking, for one can infer from this logic that when power is distributed unevenly, the more powerful country will also be more satisfied with the status quo. The weaker state is assumed to be less satisfied. As the weaker state gains power, it is able to voice its dissatisfaction with the situation. Organski developed several other themes, but here we are only interested in his views on the consequences of different distributions of power in the system.

The Many Meanings of Balance of Power

The term *balance of power* has meant a lot of different things to different people. Ernst Haas, in a survey of the literature in international relations, uncovered eight separate meanings to the term. On the one hand, it can mean (1) any distribution of power (it doesn't matter if power is evenly distributed or not). Others use the term to mean (2) an exact equilibrium, or perfectly even distribution of power. Some have used the phrase to mean (3) hegemony, or dominance, or the attempt to gain a position of dominance. Still others have employed the term to mean (4) stability in the distribution of power (i.e., that there have been no changes in how power is distributed among countries). Some even take "balance of power" to imply a concert among the major actors.

Haas found that still others used the term "balance of power" to refer to the opposite, that is (5) that the balance of power results in instability and war. Some used the phrase to refer more generally to (6) power politics or to (7) a universal law of history (that in international relations, a balance of power will be attained), while others refer to "balance of power" as (8) a plan of action or policy prescription for decision-makers. Some of Waltz's ideas are covered by the seventh definition, for Waltz believes that sovereign states in a situation of anarchy will attempt to balance power as the means for individual states to survive. This does not mean that Waltz always expects balances to be achieved, but rather that he expects states to strive constantly to create a balance of power.

Waltz and others have used this idea to talk about why the system's structure has remained so similar over time, except for changes in the distribution of power. States surrender their sovereignty only if forced to do so—as in a unipolar system. Yet we have never seen a truly unipolar system in modern times. Waltz and others have argued that this is because whenever one state strives to attain a position of unipolarity or dominance over all others in the system, the other states have banded together to balance the power of the potentially dominating state and thereby thwart that state's ambitions.[10] In such situations, countries with few common interests will form alliances to deal with this common threat. As long as states value their autonomy and sovereignty, domination by a single state seems very unlikely.

While Waltz argues that in an anarchic environment, sovereign states will produce balances of power, he cannot tell us how that balancing will take place. Will states seek to create alliances, or will they attempt to increase their power through internal measures? To underscore this point, let us consider how Waltz's theory makes a trade-off between the various qualities a theory may have. The theory seems precise in its predictions and descriptions of state behaviour; it is clearly generalizable, for it is meant to be applied to all states in the modern period. It is quite vague, on the other hand, when one tries to understand just what is or is not "balancing." This makes it difficult to ever falsify this theory; moreover, there is no clear time reference either—how long does it take a state to recognize the need to balance? Several different forms of behaviour fit this prediction, from forming alliances to building up one's own military in isolation. Even though Waltz's theory may be logical and generally correct, it may not give very solid predictions about what states will actually do in terms of policy.

Thinking of International Politics as a System

Morton Kaplan, writing in the late 1950s, analyzed international relations in terms of a mechanical system and in so doing developed a prescription for action to stabilize the international system.[11] Kaplan developed six recommendations for maintaining a balance of power. (1) Build up your power, but prefer negotiations over fighting. (2) Fight, rather than surrender to rivals. (3) Stop fighting before you eliminate a major power. (4) Oppose any state that tries to dominate the system (a state which strives to attain unipolarity). (5) Oppose any state or ideology that seeks to subordinate the nation-state. (6) Accept any partner into your alliance (even recent enemies—and allow defeated powers to reenter the circle of major powers). Such a system may be stable, but it would not be peaceful. Kaplan's model may also be problematic, for he mixes together descriptions and policy prescriptions.

What we find in Kaplan's work, but not in the writings of Waltz, is some notion that policy choices shape the use of balance of power to maintain or manage the system. Kaplan based his model upon theoretical conjectures but also upon prior diplomatic practices. Between the 1700s and World War I, multipolar systems appear to have been more stable, though not always peaceful. In the eighteenth century, there were numerous wars, but these were limited affairs. Kaplan looked at the diplomatic practices prevalent in those days and found that major states did not try to eliminate other major states. Alliances were formed to prevent the domination of Europe by a single power (Napoleonic France); in the wake of those wars, statesmen agreed that a five-power system was more stable, and a multipolar system would be the best way to provide peace and security. Defeated powers were therefore allowed to recover quickly and to reenter the diplomatic scene.

The treatment given defeated powers was very deliberate. After the 20 years of warfare associated with the French Revolution and Napoleon, the statesmen (such as Castlereagh, Talleyrand, and Metternich) who rebuilt Europe did so around a set of principles specifically designed to create a stable, peaceful system. The management of the system was to be through a conscious coordinated effort, known as the *Concert of the Great Powers*. There were formal negotiations to compensate actors, and efforts were made to deal with threats before they became vital issues. Non-systemic factors were also important in this case. All five major powers were concerned with smooth domestic governance and feared revolutions in their own countries, and all five were satisfied with the international status quo.

The Concert of the Great Powers broke down when some became less satisfied with their position in the international system. For example, the unification of Germany created a strong power with accordingly strong ambitions. Bismarck, the statesman guiding the new country's foreign affairs, sought to isolate Germany's most feared opponent: France. Thus, through secret treaties, Germany was actually able to create not a balance of power, but a secret coalition of four states opposing France (the four being Germany plus Italy, Austria-Hungary, and Russia). This distribution of power lasted until Bismarck was removed from office (1890) and his replacements began to simplify Germany's relationships. Where Bismarck had created relationships giving Germany a free hand, his successors alienated Russia, giving France the opportunity to build a rival alliance.

The bipolar post-Bismarck European system proved dangerous because bipolarity heightened the competition between the two sides. Each side feared losing allies, which would mean a gain in the strength of the other side. When Germany's most important ally, Austria-Hungary, decided to augment its power by asserting control over Bosnia, its policy clashed with that of Serbia, an ally of Russia. In the ensuing crisis, each weak power was able to ask for and receive support from stronger allies. Serbia asked Russia for help, which Russia felt it had to give or risk losing an ally; the Germans similarly felt compelled to give Austria-Hungary help against the Russians, otherwise lose one of its important allies. The French became involved as well, for they could not afford to lose their most important ally, Russia. Bipolarity meant that each alliance was very reluctant to see any alliance member weakened. Since everyone knew the various linkages, as soon as the Austrians decided upon war with Serbia, the Germans attacked France. Clearly, what had been set up as a peaceful stable system a century before with the Concert of the Great Powers had developed into an unstable and dangerous situation. The result was World War I.

One way of modelling the relationship between the distribution of power and war is to think about the conclusions drawn from these different theories and historical examples and then to display them graphically. There may be a high chance of war if there are two major powers, but this lowers when there is tripolarity, and then goes back up with multipolarity. In the strictest terms, from the eighteenth century to the late nineteenth century Europe could best be described as multipolar, for power was distributed among four to seven states during this time. Yet, because of the attitudes or policies of statesmen, the results were quite different from one period to the next. In the 1700s, something like the balance of power described by Kaplan occurred. Wars were frequent, but of a limited nature. Napoleon tried to form a unipolar system but was blocked by a coalition of the other major powers. The Concert of Great Powers established after the defeat of Napoleon created a very different situation from the 1700s, for very few wars occurred. The Bismarckian period saw the creation of an unbalanced coalition aimed at France, which then turned into a more balanced bipolar system via the creation of alliances. But note that the structure of the system, as defined by Waltz, did not change very much, save for the rise of a united Germany in the late 1800s. So what else did change?

Status Inconsistency

What we might want to add to the purely structural discussion is a notion of whether states support or accept the status quo. As mentioned earlier, structural realism suggests that the strong states get what they want, and the weak do not; the distribution of power is used to define both states' capabilities and their interests. Yet strong states sometimes appear to be dissatisfied with the international system. Another way of looking at this question is through *status inconsistency*. Sociologists have used this notion to argue that expectations are formed by individuals about their roles in society in one facet of life, but often this fails to match up with other parts of life. When this happens individuals can respond with frustration, unhappiness, and even violence or aggression. A member of the clergy can provide an excellent example of status inconsistency. As a person holding a position of clear ethical standing in the community, a clergy member is normally given great respect. At the same time, members of the clergy normally do not earn large salaries and thus typically face economic hardships. Social status and economic status in this instance are quite inconsistent, and this inconsistency can lead to emotional distress or difficulty in relations with other people.

This argument has been transferred to the international level, to talk about states that have risen in power, but not in status. Historians write about the "German problem" prior to World War I.[12] Germany was newly powerful, but lacked the recognition due a great power—it wanted all the trappings of a nineteenth-century imperial power, including colonies, a navy, and so on. In an effort to attain such things, Germany disrupted international affairs and challenged the international status quo. Similar arguments were made about the Soviet Union, especially in the late 1960s and early 1970s, when the Soviets were building up their navy, getting much more involved in Africa, trying to insert themselves into the Middle East peace process, and so on. It might not be such a threat to peace to have states with status but no power, but it is perhaps quite dangerous to have the opposite mix, for such states have the willingness and ability to use force to alter the situation. Stability and peace can then only be ensured through negotiations or deterrence.

Balancing versus Bandwagoning

Perhaps the balance of power approach is flawed or needs something added to it. Although we have examined different arguments as to why and how balances occur, we still have little insight into how it occurs. The threatened state is supposed to gather together other threatened states, each weak individually, and unite them in an alliance with enough power to defend themselves as a group. In practice, however, weak states sometimes do the opposite. Waltz says balancing occurs in the international system since states are trying to keep their security and independence, yet what could be happening when we see states joining the stronger side? This is referred to as "bandwagoning," because a similar practice is found in domestic politics. Before an election, political parties select a leader. During the leadership competition, the various candidates compete quite fiercely, but then once one begins to emerge as the likely winner, the others quickly change their tune. They are said "to jump on the election bandwagon," because they want their party to win the election, plus they may wish to play a role in the future government. Hence, they begin singing the praises of the leader they were recently campaigning against. Keep in mind, however, that this describes a different kind of political situation than international relations.

Stephen Walt, who first gave bandwagoning in international relations serious analysis, agrees with Waltz that some states balance power in order to ensure their security. But Walt goes on to add that some very weak states may find bandwagoning much more attractive.[13] If a very weak state were to join the weaker side, it might not tip the scales in the balance of power between the two sides. If the actions of this very weak state might not make any difference in determining which side would win, joining the weaker side would not mean achieving a balance. Why join the side that is likely to lose? A very weak state might be better off allying with the stronger side, and thereby at least be included among the victors.

Walt's notion of bandwagoning is a good example of a system-level argument, because it illuminates the conditions under which states will balance or when they will bandwagon. The key factors in a state's strategy are the relative strengths of the two sides and its own strength. (Notice how this draws on the distribution of capabilities.) What is perhaps missing in Walt's analysis, which Kenneth Waltz would be quick to point out, is that when a weak state joins a powerful alliance, it gives up its freedom of action—other members of the alliance are unlikely to listen to it, and the stronger members may well be able to compel this weak state to concede its own sovereignty. The bandwagoner may be thrusting itself into a situation of dependence, a concept that will be developed later.

Hegemony

Another theoretical interpretation of the necessary systemic ingredients for peace argues that peace and stability occur in hegemonic or dominated systems. Theorists ranging from Robert Gilpin to George Modelski or Immanuel Wallerstein have written that imbalances of power lead to peace, because when there is a recognizably dominant power, it can provide order through the issuance of threats or the promise of benefits.[14] (If the hegemonic power is truly strong, it doesn't have to resort to war to achieve its goals, since no weak power would be foolish enough to resist.) As balancing occurs, other states have the possibility of combating the hegemonic country's demands, challenges occur, and great wars result. When a hegemonic power exists, it can dominate the scene and create international relationships to its liking.

This may sound antithetical to the balance of power school, especially when we see that these hegemonic theorists cite the same historical evidence (though they obviously give it a different twist). Britain provided international order in the 1800s, and the unfortunate rise of Germany led to that country's arms race with Britain and, eventually, to World War I. After World War I international relations were chaotic because no leading country emerged, though the U.S. might have had the capabilities if it had asserted itself. After World War II, when the U.S. finally did assert its power, it provided order (if only to Western countries).

We can see that this theory has an economic bias to it, in that it has been used to describe order in economic relations. In security terms, it is not clear that there has ever been a period when the international system could be described as hegemonic. In economic terms, however, there have been occasions, such as when Britain went through the Industrial Revolution or when the U.S. emerged from World War II, when one country has commanded a huge economic lead over all others. In economic terms, then, we can identify hegemonic states. The relationship between hegemonic states and international regimes will be one of the key system-level themes to be explored below, since it is at the heart of the realists' explanations for the evolution of IPE. Realists relate changing distributions of power with changes in international regimes; some Marxist arguments parallel the realists' views, though they are based on rather different assumptions about motivations, which provide ways to keep their arguments distinct; and of course there are a host of alternative views—from liberals, institutionalists, and constructivists, as well as from those who operate at other levels of analysis.

As for the relationship between the distribution of power and major power war, the real disagreement comes down to how one interprets certainty and uncertainty. How should we consider the way states deal with risk? There is a logical plausibility to rather opposite views. Where there is a balance of power, there is uncertainty as to whose threats are more potent. If a state is averse to taking risks, it will not endanger itself fighting a war it is unsure of winning. If, on the other hand, running risks is acceptable, then war settles the issue of which state is actually stronger and determines which should back down in a dispute. Where one side has a clear advantage (i.e., if an imbalance exists), a risk-averse weak state will obviously back down. War involves more risk for the weaker power and thus is a less rational course of action for that power unless it is very risk-acceptant. Would certainty make threats more effective? Does certainty therefore reduce the possibility of war, or does it encourage states into taking risks? Even states identified as possible hegemonic powers have not always won the wars they fought. The example of the U.S. in Vietnam stands out—as noted previously, intangibles do matter, such as the willingness to pay the costs of victory. In any war, no state can ever know with complete certainty which side is going to win.

As will be detailed later, hegemonic distributions of power are often related to certain developments in IPE. Free trade and stable monetary orders appear to occur when capabilities are concentrated in the hands of a single powerful state. Realists would argue that such stable relations are the result of the actions and interests of the single hegemonic state. (*Hegemonic stability theory*, as this realist argument is known, will be presented in more detail in Chapters 7 and 8.) Thus, systemic characteristics such as anarchy or the distributions of power matter for how one explains changes in IPE.

The Security Dilemma

The notion that equal distributions of power are dangerous, because they make all states insecure, brings us back to the security dilemma (discussed in Chapter 1). In an anarchic environment, where we cannot be sure who our friends are (or will be), one state's attempts to enhance its security via power maximization threaten other states. This causes these other states to increase their own power, creating a continuous chain reaction as all states strive to outdo the others. Though all states make great efforts to attain security, they remain essentially insecure.

We can model the security dilemma using game theory. Let us take two states, A and B. Each state has a choice, to arm or not to arm; their combination of choices make for four possible outcomes, and we can rank each state's preferences for one outcome versus the others. The final outcome is determined by the decisions each actor makes. In this case, each actor has a dominant strategy—that is, each actor is better off making the decision to arm regardless of the decision of the other actor. Consider the boxes in the diagram. If A decides to arm, but B is disarmed, then A receives its highest preference (and 4 > 3, the result for A if it had chosen to be disarmed as well). If B decides to arm, then A would at least avoid its worst outcome (where it would be disarmed, but B armed; in this case, 2 > 1).

Game theory is useful, because it vividly illustrates how outcomes are the result of joint decision-making; the results come from the strategic interaction of the two sides. In this case it represents the *prisoners' dilemma*, an example of the failure of two actors to recognize their harmony of interests. In this particular game, each player's dominant strategy drives it to make a decision, which when taken together leaves both worse off than they could otherwise be. In the security dilemma interpretation, a player always attains a higher preference by arming, regardless of the actions of the other player. In the prisoners' dilemma game, the result of both players' choices is that both are worse off than if they could coordinate their activities. With coordination, the two players could presumably reach the outcome where both are unarmed—which they would both prefer to the outcome where they are both armed. Realists use this game to underscore how situations can drive actors to socially suboptimal outcomes.

Factors Influencing the Security Dilemma

The security dilemma may be a bit of an oversimplification. After all, desires to raise defence levels may not threaten one's neighbours. Country A may simply build extensive fortifications, for instance, which do not enhance its ability to assault country B. This has led some scholars to try to categorize

Figure 2.1: The Security Dilemma

A's HIERARCHY OF PREFERENCES:
highest = to be armed, but have B unarmed (4)
next highest = both unarmed (3)
low = both armed (2)
lowest = be unarmed, when B is armed (1)

B's HIERARCHY OF PREFERENCES:
highest = to be armed, but have A unarmed (4)
next highest = both unarmed (3)
low = both armed (2)
lowest = be unarmed, when A is armed (1)

		B	
		DISARM	ARM
A	DISARM	3 , 3	1 , 4
	ARM	4 , 1	2 , 2

different kinds of weapons and weapon systems, to sort out offensive and defensive weapons. Advances in technology or changes in the style of warfare can tilt military abilities in favour of the offence or the defence, which can make the security dilemma more urgent or less urgent.[15]

According to Robert Jervis, a variety of factors, such as technology, geography, military doctrines, and strategies, may influence military capabilities. When these factors make offence dominant, it is easy for attacking forces to defeat defensive forces; in such a situation, the risks of the security dilemma are doubly apparent. Each state is vulnerable to attack. When the best defence is a good offence, it makes sense for each side to want to attack first whenever there is a dispute, because whoever attacks first has the better chance of winning.[16]

In a system where defences are more powerful than offences, attacking forces are unlikely to achieve victory, and states are more secure. Going to war is less likely to achieve positive gains, so states will resort to war less frequently. Such a situation is likely to be more stable and peaceful. The difficulty, of course, lies in recognizing what sort of situation we are in. Which weapons are dominant? Which weapons are offensive, and which are defensive? A fort

Figure 2.2: Offence, Defence, and the Security Dilemma

	OFFENCE DOMINATES	DEFENCE DOMINATES
POSTURES NOT DISTINGUISHABLE	Twice as dangerous	Security dilemma exists, but it is solvable
POSTURES DISTINGUISHABLE	Security dilemma exists but aggression possible	Twice as stable

is usually considered defensive, since it is immobile; so is a gun permanently installed in a fort. Being immobile makes it an easy target, so most guns are no longer placed in forts, but are either wheeled or placed on tracks. Are mobile artillery pieces offensive or defensive? Iraqi tanks were offensive when they were driven into Kuwait, but defensive once they were dug into bunkers; any assessment of today's military hardware depends not on the qualities of the weapons themselves but rather on the way the weapon is used.

Historically it is hard to find a period when offence or defence was truly dominant. There is always some mix. What may be more important is which one people believe to be dominant. This creates an opening for the role of ideas. As Jervis discusses, where weapons are easily identifiable as offensive or defensive, and when one type of weapon does dominate, it has important consequences for the security dilemma.[17]

Geopolitics

Related to the notions of offence and defence are questions about geography. Some states are blessed with features that naturally enhance their security. Island countries such as Britain or Japan rely on natural barriers, plus a navy, to stay aloof from other powers—what the British called "splendid isolation." The Japanese were able to cut themselves off from outside contact for several centuries. Other forms of terrain matter, too, for defence. Mountainous areas are more easily defended, so the Swiss, for instance, have adopted a "porcu-pine" strategy. Rather than enter into alliances, they have tried to stay neutral for the last two centuries. This neutrality has been based on military training for a large part of the population, but also depends on Switzerland's moun-tainous topography. The Swiss have taken the attitude that if others choose to invade, they will simply resist so fiercely that the aggressors would never benefit. Many say the terrain of the former Yugoslavia fosters the same kind of defence, thereby explaining the reluctance of outside forces to intervene on the ground during the Yugoslav civil wars.

Other countries may have geographic weaknesses, which heighten their security dilemma. Israel's small size makes it more fearful of an offensive action by one of its neighbours. Therefore, Israel has been more likely to engage in preemptive strikes against any perceived threats; it has also adopted an offensive military strategy to ensure that any fighting is done within its neighbours' territories rather than its own. Located in the middle of Europe and lacking natural borders to the east and west, Germany has found itself with too many threatening neighbours at times. To avoid fighting a war on two fronts, Germany has adopted particularly aggressive strategies such as the Schlieffen Plan in 1914. Climate might be another factor to consider; after all, bad weather saved the Russians from Napoleon in 1812 and from Hitler in 1942.

Geopolitical arguments have died out to a great extent in the last 40 years because technology has changed, and as technology changes it affects the way we view geography, especially the way geography interacts with military issues. Originally, Alfred T. Mahan argued that the strongest countries were those with the most powerful navies.[18] In the late 1800s, when Mahan was writing, naval force was the fastest way to project power around the globe. Then, however, as railroads were extended and developed, land transportation became as rapid as ocean travel. Eventually it became clear that it was in fact faster to move troops by rail from Asia to Europe (or vice-versa) than by ship, because the ships had to go much longer distances, and Mahan's ideas fell out of favour.

This change in technology sparked Halford Mackinder to theorize that the most important area of the world geopolitically was what he termed the *Heartland* of Eurasia.[19] Whoever controlled this area (spanning from Central Europe right across Siberia) would not only control resources but, via railroads, would be able to pivot military forces rapidly and thereby threaten and/or control all the rest of Europe and Asia. Mackinder argued that other states must prevent a single power from dominating the Heartland. This point of view was challenged after World War II by an American, Nicholas Spykman, who argued that it was the *Rimland* around the edge of the Eurasian land mass that was most important, not because of lines of transportation and communication (which now seemed less important because of the advent of air transport and missile technology), but because economic activity happened to be concentrated in the Rimland (i.e., in Britain, France, Italy, Germany, and Japan).[20] In the context of the 1940s, Spykman argued that the U.S. needed to

Figure 2.3: Boulding's Loss of Strength Gradient

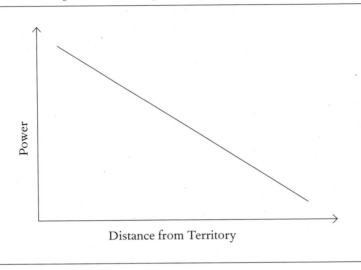

ensure that potential enemies (the Soviets, Nazis, or others) did not dominate the Rimland.

The overall point is that geopolitics seems to matter less as technology improves. Technology affects our ability to overcome physical barriers and therefore alters the implications of geography. The advent of aircraft ended Britain's splendid isolation. But the creation of new weapons brings us back to some questions about offence and defence, for offensive weapons have ranges—they can project power different distances. When transportation technology was poor, it was difficult to apply force long distances away. For instance, if the British wanted to deploy forces into Afghanistan in the 1800s, they had to transport troops from Britain to India (with the ship stopping to take on coal, water, and other supplies at several points along the way, with each station along the way manned and defended), then land them in India, put them on trains up to the Northwest Frontier (the trains having to be supplied and protected as well), then march them through the Khyber Pass, again keeping them in constant supply via a chain of stations and forts. It might take thousands of soldiers and sailors, dozens of ships and trains, to get 100 infantrymen from Britain into Afghanistan.

Kenneth Boulding tried to model this situation with his idea of a "loss of strength gradient." The notion was that due to the limits of technology, a country's ability to project power fell the further one moved away from the country's home territory.[21]

But, as technology improves, how does this gradient change? The slope of the line depends on the level of technology. If technology improves, this line will flatten out. Advances in sea transport, aviation, ground transportation, and communications all serve to smooth out this strength gradient. Nonetheless, as wars in the Persian Gulf have illustrated, it can still be very difficult to deploy and sustain large numbers of troops in distant lands.

In a similar vein, Rosecrance has argued that states make a choice in how to pursue gains in the international arena.[22] States may try to attain benefits from other states via coercion, or they may try economic exchange. Improvements in technology have radically altered that choice in recent decades, according to Rosecrance. Instead of finding it easy to militarily seize and occupy territory, even the most powerful countries have difficulty holding land where the populace resists. Meanwhile, when it comes to economic transactions, improved communication and transport means that the gains from trade are higher and higher. Wise states, in this view, will abandon the use of coercion and instead pursue international economic competition. In short, the same sort of logic applies to both security and international political economic issues.

Interdependence as a Systemic Concept

Theories can be built around other conceptualizations of the system and systemic characteristics, as noted in Chapter 1. The discussion above has been largely around realists' views of the system. Liberals and institutionalists point out that the system must have other characteristics besides those the realists speak of, because states act in ways that realists would not expect. Realists do not expect states to rely upon each other unless they must, yet states do rely on each other, especially if we consider their economic relations.

The theorists of complex interdependence argue that the world has been transformed in recent decades. Because of various economic, political, and societal changes, international relations are different because, even though states may make claims to sovereignty, they are largely penetrated by actors who move across many different states. These actors vary from multinational corporations to international non-governmental organizations (NGOs) such as Greenpeace. Today when states develop policies, they must take into account the variety of actors and forces exerting pressure on them—and such actors and pressures are more than just other states seeking to maximize power.

This highlights another area of dispute among theorists exploring system-level explanations, one which was first raised in a serious fashion by those arguing that complex interdependence is a better characterization of the international system than classical realism: states have many other goals besides simply maximizing power. Proponents of complex interdependence suggested that in fact states often place other goals above power maximization—states may spend a large part of their budgets on defence, but that is not the only thing they spend money on. In fact, defence is not even the fastest growing portion of most countries' budgets, and everyone understands that citizens demand much more from their governments than ever before. Compared to the turn of the century (when defence was one of the state's primary goals), most citizens expect their state to provide a stable growing economy, promote certain types of social improvement (be it in the areas of health care, education, equality of living standards, or whatever), regulate the environment, and so on.

One response among theorists has been to examine the ways in which security is being redefined. Another has been to modify some of the core assumptions in structural realism; as we saw in Chapter 1, neo-realists simply adjusted their assumption about the goals of state activity in a way that would allow them to talk about security but also other aims as well. Another response has been to discuss how these other priorities are set, and this often means exploring non-systemic factors, perhaps most especially differences in the ways interests become organized and express themselves politically within different domestic political institutions. In short, such criticisms of structural realism have forced many theorists to take a closer look at non-systemic arguments.

Marxist Conceptions of the System— The Modern World-System

Another point of criticism made by the complex interdependence theorists has been to question the realists' assumption about anarchy. Not all realists have assumed that international relations lack any sort of organization (see Bull in particular), but for the most part they have stressed that states perform similar functions and are independent and sovereign actors. Interdependence, on the other hand, is a concept borrowed from economics; it is often used to describe relationships resulting from specialization in economic activity. In other words, interdependence comes from different actors performing very different tasks but integrating their activity in such a way that they can combine the results into more profitable ends than they could otherwise achieve. This sort of thinking lies at the heart of economists' understanding of how international trade is undertaken.

Since the proponents of complex interdependence were largely drawing from a traditional economics background, they tended to consider this specialization to be a trade-off between increasing vulnerability (since each actor came to rely on others) and benefits (since greater economic output was the result). Marxists and other radical theorists, on the other hand, used this same criticism to challenge the realists but put a much more negative spin on the resulting economic relationships. According to Marxists, not only was the international system characterized by states performing different functions, these functions reflected a division of labour. This division of labour is organized in a hierarchic fashion, similar to the way one conceptualizes the relations between classes within society. On the top are the richest states, with the most autonomy and the most power; below are middle-level states with less range to manoeuvre and more vulnerability; and then at the bottom are the states that are largely exploited economically by the other states and, thus, are the most vulnerable.

Summary: The Qualities of System-Level Theories

Finally, we need to consider the list of qualities of theories and evaluate the characteristics of systemic theories. Are they accurate? Some are, relatively, some are not—we will have to reserve judgement until we take into consideration specific theories. But certainly we can say that system-level theories are very generalizable (that is, they can be applied to a wide variety of cases, since they are meant to apply to the behaviour of all states). And they tend to be parsimonious—simple and short but asserting many predictions. So whether or not they are accurate, we can say that as a group, system-level theories are parsimonious and generalizable.

Also, remember that system-level explanations can be built together, so that perhaps some notion of the structure taken from Waltz can be complemented by the existence (or lack thereof) of a regulator (taken from Rosecrance) or international regimes, or of some notion of a state's satisfaction with the status quo, in order to explain why some systems are stable and peaceful when compared to others. Remember, too, that we have spent most of our time discussing realist theories at the system level, but there were others mentioned: radicals look at economic connections, some idealists or liberals talk about affection, about community or morality playing a role at the system level.

One way of thinking about the limitations of system-level theories is to find two states located in similar structures and see if they are acting similarly. This was precisely the tactic taken by Peter Katzenstein[23] when he edited a set of articles comparing how each of the industrialized states responded to the Arab oil embargo. While they all responded with the same general goal in mind (all tried to secure sources of energy), they chose very different policies to attain this goal. France and Japan invested heavily in government nuclear programs, other states tried to be friendlier to the Arab states, while some (most notably the U.S.) became more hostile to OPEC. System-level arguments may tell us that each state will want more secure sources of energy, but such arguments may not tell us how different states go about pursuing their goals. For more detailed arguments and explanations, we may need to turn to the lower levels of analysis.

Notes

1. It is worth noting, however, that the systemic and state levels both focus on the state as the key actor, though the systemic level considers how states are arranged.

2. Jeffrey Hart, "Three Approaches to the Measurement of Power in International Relations," *International Organization* 30,2 (Spring 1976): 289-305.

3. Robert Dahl, "The Concept of Power," *Behavioral Science* 2,3 (July 1957): 202.

4. Ray Cline, *World Power Assessment* (Boulder, CO: Westview, 1977).

5. Kenneth Waltz, "The Stability of a Bipolar World," *Daedalus* 93 (Summer 1964): 881-909.

6. Richard Rosecrance, *Action and Reaction in World Politics* (Boston, MA: Little, Brown, 1963).

7. Rosecrance, *Action and Reaction* 220-21.

8. See a similar discussion in Stephen Krasner, "State Power and the Structure of International Trade," *World Politics* 28,3 (April 1976): 317-47.

9. A.F.K. Organski, "The Power Transition," *World Politics* (New York, NY: Knopf, 1958).

10. This thinking is laid out most clearly and in most detail in Charles Doran, *The Politics of Assimilation: Hegemony and Its Aftermath* (Baltimore, MD: Johns Hopkins University Press, 1971). The same thinking emerges in the work of analysts using the modern world-systems approach; see Christopher Chase-Dunn, "Interstate System and Capitalist World-Economy: One Logic or Two?," *International Studies Quarterly* 25 (March 1981): 19-42.

11. Morton A. Kaplan, *System and Process in International Politics* (Huntington, NY: Robert Krieger, 1975).

12. David Calleo, a political scientist, reviewed this and several other explanations for Germany's foreign policy prior to World War I. See David Calleo, *The German Problem Reconsidered* (New York, NY: Cambridge University Press, 1978).

13. Stephen M. Walt, *The Origins of Alliances* (Ithaca, NY: Cornell University Press, 1987).

14. Gilpin has discussed hegemony in two books: *U.S. Power and the Multinational Corporation* (New York, NY: Basic Books, 1975) and *War and Change in World Politics* (Cambridge: Cambridge University Press, 1981); Modelski's arguments were laid out in most detail in *Long Cycles in World Politics* (Seattle, WA: University of Washington Press, 1987); and Wallerstein's arguments appeared in the three volumes of *The Modern World-System* (New York, NY: Academic Press, 1974, 1980, 1989), discussed below.

15. See George Quester, *Offense and Defense in the International System* (New York, NY: John Wiley and Sons, 1977), and Robert Jervis, "Cooperation under the Security Dilemma," *World Politics* 30,2 (January 1978): 186-214.

16. As an example, the geographic position of Israel and the speed of modern military equipment have combined to encourage Israel to strike first on more than one occasion.

17. Jervis 186-214.

18. Alfred T. Mahan, *The Influence of Seapower on History, 1660-1783* (Boston. MA: Little, Brown, 1897).

19. Halford Mackinder, "The Geographical Pivot of History," *Geographical Journal* 23 (April 1904), and also his *Democratic Ideals and Reality* (New York, NY: Norton, 1962).

20. Nicholas Spykman, *America's Strategy in World Politics* (New York, NY: Harcourt Brace Jovanovich, 1942), and his "Geography and Foreign Policy, I," *American Political Science Review* 32 (February 1938): 213-36.

21. Kenneth Boulding, *Conflict and Defense* (New York, NY: Harper and Row, 1963).

22. Richard Rosecrance, *The Rise of the Trading State* (New York, NY: Basic Books, 1986).

23. Peter Katzenstein (ed.), *Between Power and Plenty* (Madison, WI: University of Wisconsin Press, 1978).

Additional References

Bull, Hedley. *The Anarchical Society: A Study of Order in World Politics*. London: Macmillan, 1977.

Gilpin, Robert. *U.S. Power and the Multinational Corporation*. New York, NY: Basic Books, 1975.

———. *War and Change in World Politics*. Cambridge: Cambridge University Press, 1981.

Keohane, Robert, and Joseph Nye. *Power and Interdependence*. Boston, MA: Little, Brown, 1977.

Lake, David. "International Economic Structures and American Foreign Economic Policy, 1887-1934." *World Politics* 35,4 (July 1983): 517-43.

Morgenthau, Hans. *Politics Among Nations: The Struggle for Power and Peace*. New York, NY: Knopf, 1978.

CHAPTER 3
Theories from the National or Domestic Level

Some critics of system-level analyses argue that they "black-box" the state; that is, system-level theories consider all governments to have the same goals and to think and act in the same manner. Those assumptions serve to clarify situations and to reduce complexity. As such, they promote abstract theorizing, but some theorists consider them oversimplifications. The latter have argued that a theory of domestic politics was needed in order to compensate for two things systemic theories tend to lack: (1) an elaboration of social purposes—what is it states are trying to do besides simply survive; and (2) a better understanding of why states react differently to similar stimuli (as explored in Katzenstein's *Between Power and Plenty*).

The Variety of Theories at the National or Domestic Level

These domestic-level or national-level arguments can be lumped into various categories, with emphases on very different factors: (1) political culture (i.e., is a nation-state imbued with a militaristic culture? is it peaceful? tolerant?); (2) regime-type (the most popular of which at the moment is that democracies don't fight each other; another one is that dictatorships are more likely to be aggressive); (3) ideology (do communist states have different goals than other states? do Islamic republics such as Iran or the Sudan behave differently than other states?); (4) domestic political stability (when a society is unstable at home, do leaders have an interest in fomenting trouble abroad in order to distract the public? Or does domestic instability weaken a state and paralyze its foreign policy?) In addition, a wide variety of theories in IPE build on (5) the economic characteristics of countries. (Are capitalist countries more imperialistic than non-capitalist countries? Are high-technology countries more demanding of their neighbours in terms of what they need and therefore engage in greater trade?) While this list is hardly exhaustive of the different types of theories one can find among domestic-level theories, most examples fall in one of these subcategories.

Culture and History

If we start at the top of the list, recognizing that the subcategories are in an arbitrary order, consider *culture* as a possible causal factor. Culture is a difficult concept to make use of, especially if one is interested in constructing predictive theories.[1] On the one hand, most people agree culture exists; it is passed on from generation to generation within a society, and it definitely has meaning across individuals and across time. In the past, however, theories of foreign policy employing cultural factors too often promoted stereotypes. Any meaningful argument employing culture as a causal variable must be wary of this danger. At the same time, cultures differ, peoples from different lands may have very different values, and they may have different perspectives on many issues (including foreign policy).

One example of a culturally based theory is the argument that the U.S. lost the war in Vietnam because Americans valued life more than the Vietnamese. When the war escalated and casualties on both sides increased rapidly, the Americans conceded they could not win. This argument is bolstered by some pieces of evidence. For instance, the North Vietnamese lost a much higher proportion of their population in battle than just about any other example for which accurate figures exist—perhaps up to 4 per cent of the prewar population of the North. During the war, General Giap of North Vietnam was supposed to have proclaimed "life and death don't matter." Yet this particular example hardly makes sense, since it is not placing life in perspective with other values. It may not have been so much that the Vietnamese didn't value life as much as Americans, but rather that the Vietnamese valued other things more highly than the Americans (e.g., the political future of Vietnam) and therefore were willing to make sacrifices the Americans weren't prepared to match.

Another problem plaguing cultural theories is the slow manner in which culture changes. Since foreign policy is constantly changing, it is difficult if not impossible to use cultural arguments to explain these rapid changes in behaviour. Culture can only be appealing for developing explanations of consistent behaviour. Due to this weakness and the inherent susceptibility of such theories to slip into stereotyping, cultural theories are no longer employed very often. That said, it is still very important to understand how culture shapes values from one country to another for the successful conduct of diplomacy. If you want to threaten a state, but you misunderstand what that other state or society values, then your threat could easily be misdirected. The same holds for delivering rewards. If you do not understand what the other state values, it may be difficult to structure positive incentives to bring the other side to behave as wished. While cultural theories are no longer often used by political scientists, you can see how being sensitive to cultural differences may be important for making any theory or policy more effective.[2]

The fact that the attacks on the U.S. on September 11, 2001 were executed by Islamists may seem to highlight cultural sources of conflict. This is only partly true. For one thing, Islam has many different versions and variations. Few endorse the use of violence against innocent civilians under the logic given by Osama Bin Laden. Indeed, I have referred to the terrorists as Islamists, for their beliefs are more of a political ideology than a religious sect. As well, the U.S. worked closely with states with Islamic populations both before and after the attacks, as illustrated by the alliances the U.S. relied on to defeat the Taliban in Afghanistan. Understanding Islam is critical for understanding the beliefs of Bin Laden and his followers, but Islam by itself does not explain the conflict.[3]

The Ideological Characteristics of States

We can therefore examine how *ideology* can be an important factor in explaining or predicting state behaviour. As a professor, Henry Kissinger developed arguments based on ideology in order to develop a theory binding together the goals of foreign policy with other typical characteristics.[4] Kissinger identified three functions of ideology and linked each function to specific aims; from there he theorized about the foreign policies that would be generated. First, ideologies provide images of what the world should look like. When different countries have different ideals, Kissinger reasoned, they are more likely to come into conflict. Kissinger argued that this effect was proportionate—when the countries were very distant ideologically, their conflict would be greater. Second, ideologies provide conceptual frameworks for understanding the world. They may colour the analysis of decision-makers, since they provide the lens through which the actions of other states are interpreted. Thirdly, since ideologies provide positive goals for nation-states, they establish the ideals states work towards, thereby establishing the goals of foreign policy beyond mere survival.

By viewing states along these lines, Kissinger could group them into three broad categories. The first contains the democratic, economically advanced states we generally label the West. This group consists of Western Europe, Canada, the U.S., and Japan. In these states the leadership is very pragmatic and highly bureaucratized. They approach foreign policy as a set of problems to be managed, a series of problematic episodes that have rational solutions. This means they are more likely to fit our notions of rational, unitary actors as developed by system-level theorists.

A second category of states, however, acts very differently. This second set consisted in Kissinger's time of the Soviet bloc. The leaders of these countries were guided by Marxist-Leninist ideology according to which objective factors are the guiding forces in the development of mankind—with a world socialist revolution at the end, of course. These states' policies were very goal-oriented and very much focused on achieving the end of global revolution.

The third category of states Kissinger called the charismatic revolutionary countries, because at the time he was writing many Third World countries were ruled by very popular nationalists. The popularity of such leaders was often due to the critical role they played in the country's political formation or independence. These countries were considered revolutionary, though, because they tended to challenge the international status quo.

This approach provides a simple way to think about the manner in which different countries formulate and pursue foreign policy goals. It also provides a better sense of what it is that states might fight over beyond mere survival. Moreover, the information deduced from Kissinger's arguments can be used to create new arguments. For instance, this framework can be used to reach a better understanding of why some states ally together. Kissinger used it to build more sophisticated theories about how states from the three groups interact. The bureaucratic/pragmatic states are obviously oriented to the status quo and managerial. That also means they are primarily reacting to other states' policies, rather than seizing the initiative. The other states have the advantage, therefore, in that they set the agenda through their own actions. The results worried Kissinger, for it meant that the choice of issues would not be determined by the West but by states seeking to alter the status quo. These states, either the charismatic revolutionary states, which hoped to alter the status quo, or the Soviet bloc, would also dictate the time when various issues arose.

These same ideas can be used to examine the war the U.S. has declared against terror. The terrorists are clearly motivated by a revolutionary ideology; they have the initiative and are able to strike when and where they choose. This gives them tremendous advantages over the Western states they oppose. The U.S., despite its development of strategies of preemption, must still determine when and where to preempt, and must get others to accept the legality and rationality of such a strategy. Thus, Kissinger's depiction of the world, although it was developed to describe the Cold War era, may provide useful insights into the future.

Theories of "Lateral Pressure"

Other state-level or society-level arguments are based on the variations in the economic attributes of states. Like Kissinger's arguments raised above, these factors can be used to deduce variation in states' goals. Robert North created

Figure 3.1: Population, Technology,
and the Level of Demand for External Inputs

		Population	
		HIGH	LOW
Technology	HIGH	High Demands	Medium Demands
	LOW	Medium Demands	Low Demands

such an argument by looking at three characteristics of states.[5] First, North said that states with larger populations require greater volumes of resources to satisfy their needs. Likewise, states that were economically advanced, and possessing advanced technology, would consume more resources. These states would need to extract greater amounts of resources from other countries. A simple assessment allows one to identify which states would place the highest demands for resources on the international system.

While this simple framework helps to establish the sorts of demands states or societies would have, to understand how this influences their foreign policy we must introduce a third factor: their domestic supply of resources. Some states, such as Brazil, Canada, Australia, Russia, or the U.S., possess vast resources at home. Even though they may have a technologically advanced economy, or large populations, they are able to meet many of their own needs. Countries with high needs and very few or limited domestic resources, on the other hand, will have to look internationally to satisfy their demands. North argued that these countries are more likely to cause trouble for the international system.

As an example, let us examine the role Japan played in the international system in the twentieth century. Japan is very densely populated, its economy is very advanced and industrialized, but it is not very rich in resources. Japan fits the case of a potentially disruptive member of the international system, for the country should have intense needs for foreign resources. What this particular state-level analysis doesn't tell us, however, is how Japan will go about filling its requirements. North's argument tells us only that Japan's international relations will be important for that country's economic survival. Trade is one route for meeting its needs. When trade fails, though, as in the

1930s (when other countries placed barriers against imports and/or joined exclusive trade blocs), a country with high resource needs such as Japan may be driven to imperialism to satisfy its demands. To complete this picture, one needs a sense of the international economic environment.

The Domestic Economic Sources of Imperialism

Another well-known argument based on domestic economic factors was developed by Hobson and Lenin at the beginning of the twentieth century.[6] Hobson and Lenin (and others) wished to explain the resurgence of European imperialism in the late nineteenth century. They both based their arguments on the development of capitalism within Europe, arguing that capitalism could only survive by paying workers extremely low wages. If the workers weren't exploited, businesses would collapse, causing the capitalist economy to crumble. Using Marxist economic theories, they believed that this exploitation was reaching its maximum. As technology progressed, workers' wages declined: machinery did more work, labour less. But in Marxist analyses firms relied on the exploitation of labour for their profits, so when labour's input fell, firms could not exploit labour as much. The Marxists expected firms' profits to fall over time, and in fact firms' profits did decline in the economic downturn of the 1870s. In response to this fall in profits, firms formed monopolies or cartels in order to control and reduce competition. Even though such actions bolstered profits somewhat, the Marxists expected such processes to continue. As the firms reduced workers' wages further, the workers' ability to buy goods had to fall. This in turn put further downward pressure on profits. Firms would then respond by looking for export markets. After developing markets abroad they might even begin international investments. Firms would be especially interested in economically underdeveloped areas, where the capital invested would not face very high competition and would therefore make high profits. But investments in such areas needed protection, so the capitalists urged their own governments to seize political control of these other territories. Thus, according to Hobson and Lenin, capitalist countries were being driven by their own domestic economic failures to engage in *imperialism*.

Hobson's version was produced earlier, with Lenin apparently borrowing some of his reasoning. Lenin did add a few critical steps. He asked "what happens when capitalist imperialism covers the globe? How would the capitalist countries deal with their problems then?" They could only gain new markets or new areas for investment by taking them away from other imperialist powers. Of course, critics of Lenin's views have developed numerous counter-arguments, and Lenin's evidence has largely been contradicted over time. Underconsumption has not become much of a problem since most people in industrialized countries live better than ever before; investment has been concentrated in the other economically developed countries, not the economically underdeveloped ones; and, also, one can see that the places which received the most investments were not necessarily colonies, but were often other major powers. Nonetheless, Lenin's argument has been extremely popular ever since it was written nearly a century ago.

It is important to note that Lenin and Hobson both assumed that the state is dominated by its capitalist class. (See the difference between instrumental and structural Marxism in Chapter 1.) Capitalists of one country were in competition with capitalists from other countries; workers on the other hand shared interests with other workers, no matter what country they were from. (Thus, the authors retained their belief in that final recommendation of the Communist Manifesto: "Workers of the world unite!") Today, we have many reasons to question these assumptions, since capitalists may turn out to be very cosmopolitan (via multinational companies), yet workers be very nationalistic. These examples illustrate how theories of international relations can be based on the economic characteristics of states, while the understanding of those characteristics can vary widely—not simply just among Marxist theories, but among different types of non-Marxist economics as well.

Theories Based on Regime-Type

Rather than classify a state on the basis of its economic traits (and consider the consequences of the economy for the formulation and pursuit of goals), we can execute the same sort of argument but emphasize states' political characteristics instead. A simple version of this type of argument bases its understanding of states' foreign policies on the form of regime-type. These theories have a long tradition. Some people have argued that authoritarian regimes are dangerous, for instance, because they use coercion at home and therefore have a propensity to use violence in all situations. Democratic regimes, on the other hand, have domestic politics characterized by tolerance, diversity, pluralism, and compromise. These same attitudes and policies may carry over to democratic regimes' behaviour in the international realm. Totalitarian regimes are the opposite—they tolerate no rival viewpoints and never compromise; if those attitudes are carried over into the international realm, conflict between states is more likely.

Theories about the behaviour of totalitarian states focus on that defining feature: the state totally controls the flow of information, of education, of social life, etc.[7] A totalitarian state whose society is penetrated by ideas or information from a neighbouring state may seek to maintain its monopoly over information and ideas by lashing out, seeking to knock out the external source of rival views.

This may be the only way for the state to defend its total control of domestic society. (An example is the concern expressed in Soviet policies towards the states along its southern borders after the Islamic Revolution in Iran. Another employs the same logic to explain Saddam Hussein's invasion of Iran.)

In contrast, classical theorists such as Immanuel Kant have argued that democracies are more peaceful, or at least they are more peaceful among themselves, because they have greater respect for law, tolerance, and compromise.[8] Other scholars have noticed how peaceful democracies are with each other but argue that the key difference is that democratic institutions constrain decision-making by political leaders. Democratic governments must do things that are popular with their citizens. The majority must be convinced that a policy is worthwhile if it is to be pursued with any success. Those who actually do the fighting and dying—the citizens—are more likely to resist war as a way to resolve disputes if they are given a say in the decisions.

Liberalism and Theories of the Behaviour of Democratic States

The belief that democracies are more peaceful than other sorts of states has surfaced a number of times, most notably with Woodrow Wilson's diplomacy during World War I and then later again during the Cold War. In the last two decades, statistical studies have produced a startling confirmation of these ideas: given strict definitions of democracy and war, no two democracies have ever engaged in a war against each other.[9] Since the number of democratic regimes rose rapidly in the late 1980s and early 1990s thanks to the debt crisis (which discredited so many authoritarian regimes in the developing world) and the breakdown of the Soviet bloc, these issues suddenly became of terrific import. At least one writer heralded these changes as "the end of history" since all the major powers were adopting democratic institutions.[10] In a world of liberal democracies, war should be unlikely, and ideological conflict should also disappear.

The current fascination with "the democratic peace," as it is now referred to, is actually a qualified version of earlier arguments. Originally, arguments were made claiming all democracies were peaceful towards all other states. (The statistics, however, show that democracies engage in warfare as often as other types of regimes—they just refrain from engaging in war with each other.) Woodrow Wilson spoke of "making the world safe for democracy," since he believed other states were largely responsible for starting wars. In his thinking, the best way to achieve world peace was to convert all states to democratic practices.[11]

On the other hand, one theorist, Theodore Lowi, has turned this statement on its head.[12] Lowi argued that democracies were actually more dangerous to their neighbours than were other states. He based this argument on his observations of democratic practices and of how such patterns might affect the formulation and execution of foreign policy. Leaders in democracies have to persuade their public of the efficacy of policies, so, in order to get approval, they often oversell their policies. Because it is difficult to get public support and construct a majority, leaders in democracies often take a small event and blow it out of proportion—they may create an international crisis. This kind of overselling, especially of threats, can be found in the foreign policies of many democracies but was most apparent in U.S. foreign policy during the Cold War. The Bush Administration used the threat of Saddam Hussein developing weapons of mass destruction to justify the invasion of Iraq, clearly exaggerating the threat posed to the U.S. or other countries.

An example with greater consequences is the incident that led the U.S. Congress to pass the Gulf of Tonkin Resolution. U.S. naval forces were patrolling off the coast of North Vietnam in 1965, trying to intimidate North Vietnam into ending its support of the Viet Cong in the South. During one dark night, the U.S. forces believed they were under attack. President Lyndon Johnson used this incident to persuade Congress to support his administration's desire to send more forces to Vietnam and to engage the North Vietnamese and Viet Cong more directly. Congress approved the use of force in response. It has never been clear whether the U.S. forces were actually attacked, or whether the sailors were simply nervous and misinterpreted the situation, but Johnson was able to use this event to build support for the use of military force.

Lowi argued that this tendency to oversell policies drives democracies to take extreme positions. During wars for instance, democracies tend to ask their enemies for unconditional terms. They often engage in crusading wars, where they aim not simply to win but rather to convert their opponent into a democracy (which usually means the opposing leadership has to be eliminated). Many observers believe the conservative advisers to President Bush persuaded him to engage in this sort of campaign in Iraq, as a way to alter regional politics in the Middle East. Lowi notes that totalitarian regimes don't have to engage in overselling since they can change public opinion more rapidly and easily. Also, such regimes can move without the support of the majority; they have a greater ability to ignore public opinion or at least block access to information and therefore reduce criticism of their policies.

Lowi also pointed out that the policies of democracies could be difficult for other types of states to anticipate since democracies do not act consistently. He identified how one particular aspect of democracies—internal political competition—may confuse other countries' decision-makers. Overcoming such internal divisions takes time, as does the construction of a solid consensus behind a specific policy; democracies simply move slowly. When a non-democratic country is engaged in diplomacy with a democracy, and sees the democracy racked with internal divisions and likewise slow to act, the non-democratic country may believe that striking quickly and decisively to achieve a limited goal will succeed before the democracy can muster a reaction.

Many people believe this is exactly the sort of interaction and calculation that went on in the Iraqi decision to invade Kuwait. The Iraqis may have thought they could seize Kuwait before the U.S. responded. The miscalculation came in the failure to recognize that democracies can also move quickly once a crisis begins. Normally, democracies move slowly and must contend with domestic rifts, but in a crisis the *rally-round-the-flag effect* may result. Everyone is asked to pull together and fulfill their patriotic duty by falling in behind their leaders. (Naturally, some leaders may try to create this effect by engineering international crises via overselling.) This inconsistency (slowness in everyday decision-making, but speed during crises) means that other states miscalculate and get themselves into conflicts with democracies that they did not intend.

Liberalism in International Relations: The Importance of State-Society Relations

An important aspect of these arguments, which is perhaps more subtle but also more useful, is to consider ways in which state-society relations vary. We have many notions of the state in political science and how it is constrained by or linked to society. On one extreme we can think of the state as being totally dominated by certain social actors. Lenin and some other Marxists contend that the state is merely the instrument of the capitalist class. The theory of totalitarian states discussed earlier assumes that the state is largely independent of society and can do pretty much as it pleases.

These two positions are extremes, and if we imagine them as end points on a spectrum, most states fall somewhere in between. This affords us some ways to identify differences among democracies, for instance, since some states are stronger versus other social actors while others are weaker. Stephen Krasner talks of how insulated the key decision-makers are from societal pressures as one way to identify stronger or weaker states.[13] An example of a state which is weak against its society is the U.S. The U.S. government is open to pressure from societal actors at many points—special interests can lobby Congress, appeal to the President and his advisers, take action in the courts, battle for public opinion directly, and so on.[14]

Many theorists of U.S. politics view the U.S. government as a broker between these interest groups, trying to please as many as possible. Policy reflects the struggles between these various interest group pressures. Other democratic governments are not so penetrated by societal actors. A country like Japan has a state composed of rather insulated decision-makers—many policies are set by bureaucrats operating inside the government, unaffected by elections or public opinion. If few groups have access to these key bureaucratic decision-makers, the decision-makers can come up with policies and pursue them in a more consistent manner. We would expect those policies to have a single goal since they would not reflect the views of a wide variety of groups (as U.S. policy does). We can also examine some of the variation in policy instruments that different democracies wield: Canada or the U.S. relies on macroeconomic policy to guide the economy, which means treating actors the same way (i.e., everyone faces the same change of interest rates in the market), whereas in other countries such as France or Japan the government doesn't have to work with such broad instruments (i.e., they can more selectively affect interest rates so that one company may be able to borrow money at much cheaper rates than another).

Regime Tools and Policy Instruments

Katzenstein's edited volume *Between Power and Plenty* explored these differences in policy instruments as part of a possible alternative to system-level theories. The authors in that volume each took an industrialized country that appeared to be similarly located in the international system and examined how each reacted to a similar problem (the OPEC oil embargo). The variation in policy responses illustrates differences in the states' strength *vis-à-vis* their societies, and illuminates the different policy instruments each state had at its disposal at the time. Faced with the international oil shortage, each country needed more energy, yet they each responded to this problem in a distinct way.

Those states with governments considered relatively strong versus their own societies, France and Japan, acted quickly, decisively, and with a single-minded purpose. They sought a new form of energy which would be under the state's own control, so they both embarked on massive programs to build nuclear power plants. This was meant to free them from the threat of future embargoes. In the U.S. case, where the state is relatively weak compared to its society, the state's response was much slower and much more muddled; there were all kinds of interest groups (ranging from environmentalists to oil companies) lobbying the government, each arguing for a particular solution. When the government tried to satisfy every group, the policy became a mishmash that culminated in very limited results.

Figure 3.2: The Interaction of State and Societal Centralization

neither state nor society centralized	society only centralized	state only centralized	state and society centralized
U.S.	Italy Germany	Britain France	Japan

To display this variation in response, Katzenstein developed a grid, mapping out the relationship between the relative strength of the state and the relative strength of society, and the policy response selected. Where the state is strong and society weak, policy reflects the state's wishes, and where it is the other way around policy reflects society's wishes.[15]

It is important to note that the policy instruments available to the state only provide half the information in this calculation. Societal inputs are also used. This mix of state characteristics and societal inputs is probably the most common form of model or theory one finds in IPE. Because societal splits rooted in economic issues are easily identified (thanks to elaborate models developed in economics which we can easily borrow), political scientists can use this information to discuss political competition over foreign economic policy. Information on the governmental structure is then needed, since domestic political institutions frame the political competition between groups.

Figure 3.3: A Typical Domestic-Level
Argument in International Political Economy

societal groups →organization →domestic politics →state institutions →policy

It is safe to say that such theories are much more common in international political economy than in security studies, precisely because of the nature of the issues at stake. Economic policy creates domestic divisions that are more clearly observed. The cleavages within societies created by security issues, on the other hand, are much more difficult to predict or explain.

Foreign Policy Consequences of Domestic Disturbances

Another important national-level argument looks at domestic society's stability as a determinant of the likelihood the state will adopt an aggressive foreign policy. In this view, war is the result of policy decisions made by an elite. The elite may be responding either to international pressures or domestic social pressures, but this view is interesting in that it seeks to understand state policy not in terms of "national interest" but the interest of the elite. Elite decision-makers may choose one policy over another to satisfy their own needs, regardless of the interests of the rest of society or the state as a whole. After all, if a weak state is told by a strong society what to do, who tells a strong state what to do? If an elite is concerned with its own interests, then it may be worried about its own position within the domestic political system. From this starting point, two very logical but opposing theories emerge.

The first is known as *externalization*. Externalization occurs when a society is becoming unstable, and in order to reconsolidate their control, elite policy-makers instigate an international incident, crisis, or conflict, to divert the population from domestic problems or domestic differences.[16] This logic has been immortalized in the movie *Wag the Dog*. The movie's theme mirrored reality when President Bill Clinton ordered strikes on suspected Islamist terrorists bases, just as Congress opened impeachment proceedings against him. According to the theory, the policy-maker hopes to create greater domestic cohesion by identifying an external enemy, enabling it to capture the rally-round-the-flag-effect. The logic of the other theory relating domestic turmoil and foreign policy runs in the opposite direction. Whereas externalization theories argue that domestic instability may drive the elite to adopt more active foreign policies (leading to more foreign engagements), an opposite view also exists: in countries with domestic instabilities, the elite may be so preoccupied with settling internal problems that it cannot manage foreign affairs effectively. Instead of becoming more externally oriented, this theory suggests that domestic turmoil can lead a state to reduce its foreign relations. A good example is the Soviet Union in the 1920s, when its elite was preoccupied with the attempt to transform its economy. Another is the U.S. in the 1930s, when the Great Depression forced the government to concentrate its efforts on domestic issues. As a consequence, the U.S. largely ignored international developments such as the rise of Hitler in Germany or Japanese aggression in Asia.

These two theories present the connection between domestic instability and international policy or conflict very differently. The key question is whether one believes engaging in international conflict will lead to more domestic cohesion and stability or not. The evidence is quite mixed. In 1870, Bismarck used a war between France and Prussia to get Prussia's German allies to agree to unify, creating a single country. In 1905, the Russians hoped that war with Japan would reduce pressures for political reform and consolidate the Czar's control. Instead, the war put so much pressure on the economy and society that appeals for political reform were accelerated.

In more recent times, the Vietnam conflict clearly split the American society quite deeply—the scars are still visible. Much of the bitterness in the 2004 presidential campaign originated in the different stances each candidate held on that war. But in the Gulf War, the first President Bush got the highest approval ratings any president has ever received since polls have been taken, and this was definitely caused by the rally-round-the-flag effect, since his approval rating dropped afterwards. So even in the same country within a short span of time, the relationship between domestic politics and the identification of external enemies isn't clear or consistent. Success in the crisis or conflict may be a key factor of course—quick, decisive actions seem to pay off.

Summary: Evaluating National-Level Theories

When evaluating the state- or national-level of analysis, we find a wide variety of theories. Each builds on specific characteristics of states or societies to predict variation across states' policies. In contrast, system-level theories suggest similarity between foreign policies when states are placed in similar situations. They also tend to assert uniformity in states' goals. Domestic-level theories lead us to expect to see more variation in policy because different kinds of states want different things. State-level theories are picking up on more details, and they tend to make more specific descriptions and predictions than system-level theories.

At the same time, this specificity comes at a cost. Because state-level theories typically employ more information than system-level theories, they have different characteristics. They make use of more details, and hence tend to be more descriptive. Because they utilize more details, they may seem more accurate in analyzing historical situations. That doesn't necessarily mean they provide better predictions—we would have to compare specific theories to reach that conclusion, and there are plenty of poorly constructed domestic-level theories.

More important for our considerations, state-level theories are not as generalizable as system-level theories. System-level theories are meant to work for all states. We can use theories on balancing or bandwagoning to make a prediction about any state's foreign policy, but cannot do the same thing with most state-level theories—an argument about capitalist countries engaging in imperialism is not applicable to Vietnam's invasion of Cambodia or the Soviet Union's invasion of Afghanistan. And many state-level theories include details in them that make them useful only for a specific, limited subset of cases.

If we turn to the last characteristic of theories, parsimony, we find that system-level theories are fairly parsimonious compared to state-level theories. The trade-off is that system-level theories usually provide somewhat vague predictions. We need more information to utilize state-level theories, but hopefully what we lose in parsimony when we bring in more details, we gain in accuracy. Again, we may have to consider some specific theories to evaluate how such a trade-off is made.

Notes

1. John A. Hall, however, points out that many of the past uses of culture can now be found in our use of the concept of ideas or beliefs as a causal factor. See John A. Hall, "Ideas and the Social Sciences," *Ideas and Foreign Policy*, ed. Judith Goldstein and Robert Keohane (Ithaca, NY: Cornell University Press, 1993) 43-48.

2. One important exception would be Samuel Huntington's *The Clash of Civilizations and the Remaking of World Order* (New York, NY: Simon and Schuster, 1998). Huntington's work has not won broad support among theorists, however.

3. For an interesting overview of recent works on the subject, see the review by Daniel L. Byman, "Al-Qaeda as an Adversary: Do We Understand Our Enemy?" *World Politics* 56 (October 2003): 139-63.

4. Henry Kissinger, *American Foreign Policy* (New York, NY: W.W. Norton, 1969).

5. Robert C. North, "Towards a Framework for the Analysis of Scarcity and Conflict," *International Studies Quarterly* 21 (December 1977): 569-91.

6. Excerpts from both Hobson's "The Theory of Underconsumption" (1894), and his larger work *Imperialism: A Study* (1902), as well as from Lenin's *Imperialism* (1916) have been reprinted in numerous texts. One set can be found in D.K. Fieldhouse, *The Theory of Capitalist Imperialism* (London: Longmans, 1967), which also contains other contemporary writings.

7. For an example, see Ivo K. Feierabend, "Expansionist and Isolationist Tendencies of Totalitarian Political Systems: A Theoretical Note," *Journal of Politics* 24 (November 1962): 733-42.

8. Immanuel Kant, *Perpetual Peace* (New York, NY: Columbia University Press, 1939).

9. For a taste of these early findings, see Steve Chan, "Mirror, Mirror on the Wall ... Are the Freer Countries More Pacific?," *Journal of Conflict Resolution* 28,4 (1984): 617-48; Michael Doyle, "Liberalism and World Politics," *American Political Science Review* 80,4 (1986): 1151-61; and Erich Weede, "Democracy and War Involvement," *Journal of Conflict Resolution* 28,4 (1984): 649-64. There was an explosion of such work in the early 1990s.

10. Francis Fukuyama, "The End of History ?," *National Interest* (Summer 1989): 3-18.

11. See Ray S. Baker (ed.), *Woodrow Wilson and World Settlement* (Garden City, NJ: Doubleday, Page and Co., 1922).

12. Theodore Lowi, "Making Democracy Safe for the World: National Politics and Foreign Policy," *Domestic Sources of Foreign Policy*, ed. James N. Rosenau (New York, NY: Free Press, 1967) 295-331.

13. Stephen Krasner, *Defending the National Interest* (Princeton, NJ: Princeton University Press, 1978) 55-61.

14. For this point, see Krasner 61-70.

15. Peter Katzenstein, "Conclusion: Domestic Structures and Strategies of Foreign Economic Policy," *Between Power and Plenty*, ed. Peter Katzenstein (Madison, WI: University of Wisconsin Press, 1978) 324, Table III.

16. For example, see Arno Mayer, "Internal Causes and Purposes of War in Europe, 1870-1956," *Journal of Modern History* 41 (September 1969): 291-303.

Additional References

Gourevitch, Peter. "The Second Image Reversed." *International Organization* 32,4 (Autumn 1978): 881-912.

Katzenstein, Peter (ed.). *Between Power and Plenty*. Madison, WI: University of Wisconsin Press, 1978.

Lake, David. "International Relations and Internal Conflict: Insights from the Interstices." *International Studies Review* 5,4 (December 2003): 81-90.

Milner, Helen. "Trading Places: Industries for Free Trade." *World Politics* 40,3 (April 1988): 350-76.

Rogowski, Ronald. *Commerce and Coalitions*. Princeton, NJ: Princeton University Press, 1989.

Russett, Bruce. "Reintegrating the Subdisciplines of International and Comparative Politics." *International Studies Review* 5,4 (December 2003): 9-12.

CHAPTER 4
Bureaucratic Politics

Dropping down another step in the levels of analysis, we begin to examine theories that emphasize individuals as the key actors in international relations. There are two very different ways of thinking about individuals in foreign policy decision-making. One treats each individual as a unique entity, so that any foreign policy decision can be understood or predicted only if we knew who the particular decision-maker is and how that person thought or behaved. This approach emphasizes the idiosyncratic features of individuals—the things that make one person different from another. Those theories will be examined in the next major section of this chapter. The other way to consider the role of individuals, however, is to view them as actors constrained by the offices they hold. Their positions on policy are formed by the roles they play within domestic politics. The models we are building are actually about positions, roles, or offices rather than the particular characteristics of any one individual.

The Importance of an Individual's Role

These theories are based on the assumption that duty and obligations— defined by the role one plays—determines how individuals behave. Thus, the responsibilities of office shape how individuals formulate and execute foreign policy. This level of analysis was developed after analysts experienced frustrations with system-level arguments. Since realist system-level arguments assume states are unitary actors, the array of policies a single state adopts should fit together into a rational package—the entire range of policies should be coherent and aimed at similar goals. Yet, when we look at any country's policies, we often see conflicting schemes enacted at the same time. Such contradictory actions are incompatible (and therefore inexplicable) with the assumption that a single rational actor is at work. Some of the best examples can be found in domestic affairs; consider how the U.S. government handles cigarettes: the government subsidizes the production of tobacco, then turns around and spends money to dissuade people from smoking![1]

Foreign policies often have the same element of irrationality when one considers the entire range of policies a country pursues at any one point in time. In order to understand how such a confusing mix of policies has come about, practitioners of the bureaucratic politics approach drop the assumption that the state is a unitary actor and replace it with one that says the state is composed of disparate groups or organizations. It is assumed that each of these organizations has its own goals and is independent enough to determine a portion of policy output. When taken together, these varied goals and policies may work well or may simply undermine each other. Some of the best examples come in the area of defence procurement, such as the U.S. military's purchasing of aircraft.

From an overall point of view, a single rational decision-maker might be able to establish the specific number of aircraft necessary to defend the U.S. This number would undoubtedly be lower than the actual number of planes and helicopters the U.S. military actually operates. The result must be somewhat wasteful of scarce resources, since the government could spend the money in other ways. To understand why we observe this excess expenditure, we can apply the bureaucratic politics model; the approach focuses on who decides which aircraft (and how many) to buy. The U.S. military is not a monolithic organization but is made up of four services, or branches: the Air Force, the Navy, the Army, and the Marines. So who decides how many aircraft to procure? One might think it would be the Air Force, since the Air Force should be responsible for military applications of aircraft. But that is merely the beginning of the armed forces operating in the air—the Navy has its own planes and helicopters, and not just for attacking other naval forces, or operating from carriers, but for attacking targets on land, too. And even though the Marines are really part of the Navy, they purchase and operate their own planes and helicopters as well. Which of these branches has traditionally operated the most helicopters? None of the three mentioned so far, but rather the U.S. Army. The Army wants to operate its own air support under its direct command. Since the Army isn't allowed to buy planes (that is the Air Force's duty), it procures helicopters—even though helicopters may not perform as well as fixed-wing aircraft and require much higher maintenance.

The result of this is an overabundance of some types of weaponry and overlapping responsibilities. From an overall perspective, it is wasteful and inefficient. Yet this is the outcome of the decisions made within the Pentagon. The heads of each branch of the military are not necessarily thinking about what is best for the country but, rather, are thinking in terms of what is best for his or her service: the head of the Navy argues strongly for everything the Navy wants, and so on. The individual's goals in this model are established by the role he or she plays, by the office he or she holds.[2]

This sort of thinking was first developed by Graham Allison in his analysis of the Cuban Missile Crisis.[3] Allison set out three rival models for interpreting the Crisis. (This is the same sort of practice we employ in the cases in Part III.)

He labelled the three prototypes Models I through III. Model I was a standard system-level argument (assuming the state to be a single, unitary, and rational actor), which Allison felt didn't work well. His Model III is the prototype for *bureaucratic politics*. Model III worked better in Allison's estimation, because it saw policy as the result of internal bargaining among bureaucrats within each government—foreign policy was the result of different actors (each with his or her own goals in mind) struggling amongst themselves over their country's foreign policy.

Theorists using the bureaucratic politics approach point out that particular decision-makers see the problems of foreign policy differently, depending upon their responsibilities and goals. They therefore are likely to offer different solutions to problems or to suggest alternative policies. A good example comes from American decisions regarding the possible development of an anti-ballistic missile (ABM) system in the 1960s.[4] It was rumoured that the Russians were already well along in creating such a system, and the U.S. president at the time, Lyndon Johnson, saw this as a problem. He didn't particularly see it as a threat to the U.S., but rather he thought the Russians' policy demanded a reaction, lest he leave himself open to domestic critics in a reelection year. Johnson didn't require that a substantial effort be made to match the Russians; he needed a symbolic effort.

Johnson handed the issue over to his staff. His advisers viewed the problem quite differently: they were concerned that any new arms program would upset U.S.-Soviet relations and didn't want the Russians to feel threatened. Due to such concerns, the advisers suggested that any American ABM system be limited and perhaps even imperfect. A vast missile defence system, operating with high levels of efficiency, would negate the Russians' ability to threaten the U.S. In so doing, it would undermine the Russians' ability to deter the U.S. from launching its own first strike. This was potentially destabilizing, since it would surely frighten the Soviets. These advisers therefore argued for a system that would only protect U.S. missiles, thereby ensuring the U.S. held a potent retaliatory force and enhancing its deterrent. But this meant building a small ABM system that would not even defend U.S. cities. What would the voters think?

And, of course, there was dissension among other actors involved. Each of the armed services wanted in on any new large defence program, so they bickered over who would operate the ABM system. If the system was to protect cities, the Army argued that the project fell within its domain. The Air Force replied that missiles were its responsibility, so it should operate the system. Congress viewed things through a completely different lens and was concerned not simply with who would operate the system, but which private contractors would be hired to build it, how much it would cost, and so on.

In short, each of the prominent decision-makers envisioned a very different ABM system. In the end, no ABM system was ever constructed, though testing was undertaken.

Bureaucratic Goals

The example illustrates how each of these individuals—the president, his advisers, the head of the Army, the head of the Navy, the congressmen—were acting rationally, but each was pursuing a goal specific to his or her job. Since this model focuses on organizations or bureaucracies as the key actors, one must turn to these bodies to identify the goals identified with a particular role. In an important book expounding on the bureaucratic politics approach, Morton Halperin and Arnold Kanter identify five goals of organizations.[5] The first is to defend the bureaucracy's essential mission or purpose. One must continually prove to others that one's organization has important responsibilities and deserves to exist in the future. The second goal refers to defending and/or extending the organization's domain, or bureaucratic "turf." This means decision-makers must not only be proving that their bureaucracy plays an important role, but that no other bureaucracy can do the job as well. Time and energy is spent defending areas of responsibility from encroachment by others. The third goal is maintaining the organization's autonomy—defending its independence and ensuring that no one else will gain dominance over the organization. The fourth goal is maintaining morale within the organization, which is important for making sure the organization functions well. The fifth goal is, of course, making sure the organization's budget grows.

Information is required for any bureaucratic politics argument to work well. One must know who the key decision-makers are and which interests they are reflecting. This is important, for not all governments are organized in the same way. Consider the structure of the Canadian military, for example. It is much more unified than the American military, so we might expect it to reach different policy decisions. In fact, Kim Nossal has argued that the bureaucratic politics model doesn't work very well for Canada, or probably for many other countries, for it was developed in the U.S. and reflects the divided and bureaucratic nature of the government there.

One should also remember that the organization of government can be changed. Different presidents in the U.S. organize their cabinets differently. If the goal is to change policy outcomes, what in fact does the bureaucratic politics model prescribe? Changing the bureaucratic structure will produce different policy. In the U.S., for example, there used to be a cabinet position titled the Secretary of Health, Education and Welfare. But to show a greater effort aimed at education, a separate Department of Education with its own secretary was created, and the rest of Health and Welfare was renamed Health and Human Services. When Ronald Reagan wanted to deregulate the production of energy, he dismantled the Department of Energy. The intention was to decrease the role of government to allow the market to determine energy policy instead.

After the attacks on September 11, 2001, questions were raised about the collection and interpretation of intelligence. Investigations by Congress and other agencies illustrated that different parts of the U.S. government were aware of bits of the threat before it hit, but that no one had a handle on the overall situation. Therefore, many have called for the creation of a new cabinet-level post, an "intelligence czar" who can monitor all sources together and coordinate the activities of the various bureaucracies. This also underscores the idea that the U.S. wishes to place greater emphasis on gathering intelligence.

When a brand new bureaucracy is set up, it must fight to establish its own turf. When it was argued that the U.S. could do more to support arms control efforts, it was decided that a separate arms control agency should be created, since, if there was an organization within the executive branch pushing for arms control measures, results would follow. There was a big fight over whether this agency would belong to the State Department or the Department of Defense. A similar struggle occurred when the U.S. decided to create a high-level trade negotiator—would the post be assigned to the State Department or the Department of Commerce? That position, the Special Trade Representative, wound up belonging to neither. Shifting posts, reassigning duties, and creating and dismantling agencies and offices are all signs that someone believes that bureaucratic structures do make a difference for policy outcomes.

Bureaucratic Organizations and the Execution of Policy

These examples illuminate how the bureaucratic politics or *"role"* approach works (in explanation, description, and prescription). In particular it is good for analyzing events and outcomes that system-level arguments fail to explain, especially those situations where a country's foreign policy appears to include contradictory elements. The key insight is that the policy is the result of differing viewpoints: even when the policies fit together, they may not seem rational from an overall viewpoint, which can only be understood as the result of pushing and pulling among different decision-makers.

Bureaucracies and organizations matter in another aspect of foreign policy; we have already seen how roles affect decision-making, but even after decisions have been made the characteristics of organizations and bureaucracies determine how foreign policy is executed. This was another key insight Allison uncovered in his analysis of the Cuban Missile Crisis. Organizations played a significant role in that Crisis when it came to the conduct of foreign policy. The only way Allison could make sense of how well messages were sent and received, and therefore assess the ability of the two sides to communicate and to interact, was to disentangle the effect of *organizational processes*. Here again we have a way to explain why policy did not appear to be driven by a single rational actor. Though policy may be rationally formulated by those in charge of foreign policy (in this case, the president and his advisers), bureaucracies and organizations may not be able to carry them out as originally intended.

Organizational process also shaped the outbreak of the Crisis. In order to threaten the U.S. with more missiles, the Soviets were interested in shipping their medium-range missiles to bases in Cuba in range of U.S. targets and to do so undetected. The Soviets understood the provocative nature of their actions and knew that if the U.S. discovered the missiles before they were ready to fire, the U.S. might well launch air strikes when the missiles were most vulnerable. Thus, they took very special precautions, loading troops and equipment on regular freighters and ordering all troops to stay below decks for the entire voyage from the Soviet Union to Cuba. The troops and their equipment were unloaded at night and moved about only in secrecy. All of this was done without U.S. knowledge. Yet, when the Soviets began setting up their launch sites, the U.S. knew exactly what they were doing. The bases were laid out in a very distinctive pattern, which U.S. intelligence analysts recognized immediately, since they had seen exactly the same patterns in aerial photographs taken over Eastern Europe and the Soviet Union. The Soviet engineers had done nothing differently! When the Soviet missile troops got to Cuba, they simply followed the instructions in their manuals. Despite all the efforts to maintain secrecy, organizational practice blew the operation, and a major crisis resulted.

The point to take from this example is that organizational routines—the kinds of things groups practise over and over again, the way the members of the organization are trained, and so on—constrain the ability of organizations to act. Even if a perfect plan can be formulated, even if decision-making is quite rational, organizational constraints such as *standard operating procedures* (SOPs) can force things to go awry. These constraints can easily cause a policy to fail or at least to appear as irrational.

Allison found evidence of such problems in the execution of U.S. policy in the Cuban Missile Crisis. While U.S. intelligence identified the missile sites early, its following actions were far from perfect. Allison uncovered evidence of a bitter turf war between the Air Force and the Central Intelligence Agency (CIA) over which agency should provide the air reconnaissance photos of Cuba that the president wanted. The CIA had the right kind of spy planes (U-2s, which flew higher than missiles could reach them in those days), so it claimed it should do the job. The Air Force countered that it was better suited to perform this mission—what would the world think if a U-2 was shot down or crashed? Wouldn't it be much better if there was a man in uniform on board, rather than a civilian? While the two sides argued, precious time was lost, and no photos were taken. Finally, the situation was resolved by training Air Force pilots to fly the CIA's planes, but this took even more time.

All these examples are invaluable for illustrating how, in practice, the formulation and execution of foreign policy is affected by internal decisions. Each highlights how the process of decision-making shapes how policy is determined, and how the range of choices decision-makers select from are limited by what the state's bureaucratic organizations are capable of doing. This also shows how choices made rationally may get implemented in a different way, so that policy doesn't appear to be rational in the end.

Is Bureaucratic Politics a Phenomenon Specific to U.S. Policy-Making?

You may have noticed that many of the examples provided so far have drawn from U.S. foreign policy. Allison's original work on the Cuban Missile Crisis focused very intently on U.S. policy, so these classic examples were cited to present his reasoning. Moreover, many of the applications of bureaucratic politics have been focused on the security relations between the U.S. and the Soviet Union. Some Canadian researchers believe that this approach suits analysis of U.S. foreign policy but that it is less well-suited for applications to other countries, especially those with parliamentary systems, such as Canada, which appear to have fewer of the internal differences spawned by the U.S. system of checks and balances. The bureaucratic politics approach can be applied successfully elsewhere, but it is worth noting some of the difficulty researchers confront when doing so. Detailed information is needed in order to know who is invited to participate in decision-making and which bureaucracies they represent.

It was always somewhat difficult to create bureaucratic politics arguments about the former Soviet Union's foreign policy because we didn't have enough information about just who was making which decisions. We could guess that the Soviets also suffered from some of the signs of bureaucratic politics, such as overspending on their military. Yet it was hard to develop any detailed predictions, because we didn't know who was involved in which decisions or often even who was running particular bureaucracies. A major part of the analysis concerned identifying who was holding what job and who was involved in policy-making circles. A whole new field developed: "Kremlinology." Kremlinologists were experts who analyzed photos or other information coming from the Soviet Union, gleaning whatever possible insights they could by learning who was standing next to whom at the last parade or funeral. It was always easier to apply this approach to the U.S., and especially to past policy decisions, because that information was so much easier to attain. Now that the Cold War has ended, we can go back and examine past Soviet policy in much greater detail.[6] For instance, the inability to establish precisely how many nuclear weapons the Soviets constructed reflects how the various branches of the Soviet military struggled to include nuclear weapons in their bureaucratic turf. The information requirements simply make it difficult to apply the bureaucratic politics approach to countries with closed governments.[7]

It is astounding to think about what kind of information we must have to answer questions such as "Who is important? Which organizations matter? How do organizations compete? But, more importantly, how is competition resolved?" Possible answers to this last question can be surprising. In Japan in the 1930s, the civilian government had been ousted. The military ran things, but the military was divided between the Army and the Navy. The Army thought Japan's true interest lay in invading China, in order to obtain necessary material resources for the Japanese economy. This policy also naturally handed the most important responsibilities to the Army. The Navy, on the other hand, was worried about oil supplies for its fleet, so it wanted Japan to occupy much of Southeast Asia, including Indonesia. This policy gave the highest responsibilities to the Navy. How did they resolve this difference? At one point, the Navy was certain it was going to be attacked by the Army, so all Navy offices were protected by sandbags and armed guards. As it turns out, the Japanese decided to pursue both policies: conquer China and also attack to the south. The policy results were not very rational, since Japan chose to launch a large-scale ground war and take on the world's foremost naval power at the same time. Success in either effort alone would have been unlikely, but by attempting to do both, Japan was doomed to defeat.

In this particular example, as in some of the others mentioned above, policy was decided on simply by letting each organization do what it wanted. Sometimes compromises do occur (as when Air Force pilots operated the CIA's planes in the Cuban Missile Crisis), and the end result can be fairly close to what we might expect if a country really did act in a unitary and rational manner. A major weakness of the bureaucratic politics approach is the inability to predict how these disputes are resolved. The approach gives us tremendous insight in what the different actors are likely to be arguing about, but how will policy be set in the end? If we work backwards and use this approach to provide descriptions of past events, the model is very strong—it incorporates so many details, the interpretations can be very persuasive. But for predictions we confront some serious problems. Moreover, the informational requirements mentioned earlier make the model less than parsimonious. Once a model specific to one country has been created, it may not be very useful for examining decision-making elsewhere, since decision-making structures vary widely. These are the strengths and weaknesses of the approach.

Bureaucratic Politics and IPE

One might also note that most examples of bureaucratic politics are drawn from the realm of security affairs. The approach seems to find little favour in IPE, though there are major exceptions.[8] This is partly because so many of the key questions confronting scholars in IPE concern the development of IPE as a whole (rather than a particular country's policy decisions—though these two are related matters). Also, scholars in IPE have powerful alternative arguments at the state level. Whereas security specialists may look at bureaucratic actors who have rather amorphous constituencies, IPE scholars draw on the vast array of economic models identifying rather specific interest groups within society. It is useful to draw on both sets of arguments by reflecting on the links between bureaucracies and societal groups.

As an example of such a more balanced approach, let us consider how international monetary policy is typically made. Responsibilities for such policies usually fall in the realms of two separate bureaucracies: a central bank and a treasury (a finance ministry). A central bank is normally given a measure of independence and has the responsibility for managing the national currency. A treasury usually has to worry about financing the government's budget, though it may also have powers in terms of regulating and managing the country's financial system. Since these two agencies have overlapping "turfs" but different bureaucratic missions, the way they interact can therefore have a powerful impact on the way policy is formulated. Moreover, a minister of finance is usually dependent on public support to remain in office, and a central bank only maintains its independence because other public authorities have conceded it, so there are ample opportunities for domestic interest groups to exert pressure on each of these bureaucratic actors.[9]

Challenges to the Bureaucratic Politics Paradigm—The Individual versus the Role

If the necessary questions regarding the participants in decision-making can be answered, the bureaucratic politics approach usually provides a powerful description of the policy selection. But how about prediction? This approach can be used to say that foreign policy is not likely to reflect the rational calculation of a single actor, but then what will future decisions look like? We have to be able to predict who will be involved in the next decision, as well as what point of view they will have. Robert Art wonders whether we can do this consistently—he claims practitioners of the bureaucratic politics approach waffle on this point.[10] Art questions whether we can separate idiosyncratic factors out from those deriving from the role a person plays. The bureaucratic politics model says that all Canadian external affairs ministers should act the same, because their positions in the bureaucracy are the same. But how do things like experience, attitude, or personality fit into the equation? Put differently, Art wonders whether someone does something because of their position or because of who they are as a person and argues that the theories applied in this area should specify evidence differentiating the two. The alternative is to argue that the individual's experiences and personality shape their decision-making more than the constraints imposed by the role they are playing. To understand more of these alternative views, we next examine the idiosyncratic features of individuals and their potential impact on decision-making.

Notes

1. The assumption of rationality contains three conditions: first, the actor is assumed to have perfect information—it is assumed the actor knows all its options and knows all the costs and benefits (the ramifications) associated with each option; second, the actor must understand the causal effect of each possible choice; third, the actor must be able to rank its choices, which requires that it be able to relate what it values into some sort of schedule of preferences. In this instance, the evidence suggests an inability to rank preferences.

2. It is interesting to note that Canada has attempted to integrate its armed forces, in part to overcome some of the inter-service rivalries which plague most militaries. The degree of success Canada has achieved is debatable, however.

3. Graham Allison, "Conceptual Models and the Cuban Missile Crisis," *American Political Science Review* 63 (September 1969): 689-718; also Graham Allison, *The Essence of Decision* (Boston, MA: Little, Brown, 1971).

4. Morton H. Halperin, "The Decision to Deploy the ABM: Bureaucratic and Domestic Politics in the Johnson Administration," *World Politics* 25,1 (October 1975): 62-95.

5. Morton H. Halperin and Arnold Kanter, *Readings in Foreign Policy: A Bureaucratic Perspective* (Boston, MA: Little, Brown, 1973).

6. In fact, one of the most interesting aspects of such research was a gathering together of the surviving participants from each side in diplomatic wrangling of the Cuban Missile Crisis.

7. See Matthew Evangelista, *Innovation and Arms Races: How the United States and the Soviet Union Develop New Military Technologies* (Ithaca, NY: Cornell University Press, 1988).

8. The works of I.M. Destler (and his later collaborations with C. Randall Henning) provide excellent examples of just how powerful the approach can be. An excellent

example would be *Making Foreign Economic Policy* (Washington, DC: Brookings Institution, 1980).

9. This sort of argument—mixing bureaucratic politics with sectoral interests—is laid out in Mark R. Brawley, *Afterglow or Adjustment?* (New York, NY: Columbia University Press, 1999).

10. Robert Art, "Bureaucratic Politics and American Foreign Policy—A Critique," *Policy Sciences* 4 (1973): 467-90.

Additional References

Allison, Graham. *The Essence of Decision: Explaining the Cuban Missile Crisis.* Boston, MA: Little, Brown, 1971.

Bendor, Jonathon, and Thomas Hammond. "Rethinking Allison's Models." *American Political Science Review* 86,2 (June 1992): 301-22.

Levy, Jack. "Organizational Routines and the Causes of War." *International Studies Quarterly* 30,2 (June 1986): 193-222.

Welch, David A. "The Organizational Process and Bureaucratic Politics Paradigms: Retrospect and Prospect." *International Security* 17,2 (Fall 1992): 112-46.

CHAPTER 5

Theories Based on the Idiosyncratic Characteristics of Individuals

Whereas theories of bureaucratic politics were based on the assumption that foreign policy is the result of decisions made by individuals whose actions can be understood by examining their responsibilities or duties, the individual level of analysis builds causal theories by exploring decision-makers' idiosyncratic features. That is, instead of focusing on the positions of foreign policy decision-makers to understand what ideas or policies the individuals will put forth and support, practitioners of the individual level usually focus on attributes specific to each individual.

The notion here is that while role or other constraints derived from bureaucratic structures matter for some part of the explanation (especially in specifying who is worth analyzing, since it explains who should be involved in foreign policy decision-making), other factors influence what those decision-makers are likely to do. Naturally, it is the prime minister and the minister for external affairs who are likely to have the most say about foreign policy, but why should we assume that all executives or cabinet members think alike? Idiosyncratic features—individual personalities, beliefs, psychological make-up, experiences—may influence their decisions much more than their roles.

Perception and Misperception

An interesting point with which to begin our analysis involves the different ways people perceive events. In the theories drawn from the other levels of analysis we have assumed that there is an objective reality, discernible to all relevant parties, with which decision-makers interact. Yet in real life, different people may look at the same event or incident and perceive it quite differently. Since a single stimulus can be interpreted or perceived differently, we naturally expect variations in the way people react to the stimulus.

Figure 5.1: Modelling the Role of Perceptions

stimulus → perception / interpretation → decision

This thinking questions the utility of the assumption about rational calculations, because instead of assuming that individuals objectively identify all possible responses to the stimulus and evaluate them objectively, this approach assumes that individuals have predilections for certain kinds of responses. By examining those predilections, scholars hope to be able to explain and/or predict the way individuals will react to similar stimuli at other points in time.

Rejection of the assumption of rational calculation is not unreasonable. For truly rational calculation to occur, several conditions must hold. The decision-makers are assumed to have perfect information—they are assumed to know all their options and to know all the costs and benefits (the ramifications) associated with each option. That also means they must understand the causal effect of their choices. Neither of these conditions is ever met in reality. The assumptions could still be of value, however. (Remember how we evaluate assumptions: not by a true/false test, but rather by their consequences for the quality of our theory.) A third condition for the rational actor model is that actors must be able to rank their choices, for they must be able to relate what they value into some sort of schedule of preferences. This is an easy task in and of itself, but can be achieved only if the prior two steps are fulfilled accurately. If the first two conditions are not met, then neither can the third, except by accident. Since decision-makers are unlikely to ever conduct rational calculation under these conditions, the proponents of the individual level of analysis argue that other factors shape decision-making. These other factors are usually components of personality or decision-making styles that provide the individual with "short-cuts" for reaching conclusions in policy-making.

Belief-Systems

The proponents of individual-level analysis argue that there are valuable alternatives to the assumption that actors are truly rational. Their most persuasive argument is to pose the question: do decision-makers seem to be taking the steps necessary for rational calculation? One way of examining these predilections to respond in a non-rational manner is to explore the *belief-systems* leaders have. Decision-makers often hold sets of beliefs (sometimes grounded in ideology, sometimes in personal experience) which force them to interpret or perceive other countries' actions in particular ways. These belief-systems may cover things such as the ways in which foreign policy is supposed to be conducted, what the proper goals of foreign policy should be, what is considered diplomatic and tactful (as well as what isn't), what is peaceful, what is aggressive, and so on.

Decision-makers rely on belief systems when confronting problems associated with the failure to achieve the conditions necessary to execute rational decision-making, as well as when dealing with stress.[1] If it is difficult to live up to the standards of the rational action model in practice—because there is always some uncertainty or lack of information about some options or of the consequences of such actions, and so on—belief systems offer a short-cut in decision-making. Stress, caused by fear, guilt, shame, or some other emotion, can also cause confusion, reduce the evaluation of alternative policies, or terminate the search for information.

Alexander George developed the idea of *value-complexity* to describe situations where policies may entail trade-offs in values the decision-maker would rather not face.[2] Instead of making a tough decision, one leaving the decision-maker with a certain sense of failure, decision-makers can respond to these difficulties in a variety of ways, often determined at least partially by their belief systems. When faced with value-complexity or lack of information, decision-makers may make a complex picture simpler by discounting information they don't want to deal with, ignoring some information altogether, or forgetting previous bits of information that were confusing. The number of techniques found in real-life examples is endless, but the point is always the same: to alter the perception of reality in such a way as to negate the difficult decision. Some of the best examples of this sort of behaviour come from the actions of John Foster Dulles, who served as the U.S. Secretary of State in the Eisenhower Administration. Dulles thought the Soviet Union presented a threat to the U.S. due to the evils inherent in Communist ideology.

Dulles's beliefs drove him to perceive and interpret Soviet foreign policy as rooted in evil and thus a constant threat to the U.S. and its allies.[3] Whenever friction with the Soviet Union developed, Dulles tended to assume the worst. He would portray a random Soviet act as the beginning of (or perhaps merely an integral element of) some sinister plot. If intelligence came in with photos showing a large ship under construction in a Russian port, Dulles would immediately declare he saw a warship being built, even though rationally speaking there wasn't enough detail to determine whether the vessel in question was a warship or just a freighter. Other U.S. analysts would try to give a more accurate assessment of the same information, and thus a debate would start.

In these debates, the group reached a resolution only if they first attained a consensual understanding or interpretation of the information they have received. Anyone entertaining another point of view brought in whatever supporting evidence they could muster. But Dulles ignored any evidence that undermined his predetermined conclusions, or at least he would attack its credibility. Sometimes he even reinterpreted evidence in order to put his own spin on it. Therefore, even when the Soviets did something apparently complying with U.S. wishes, Dulles would question their intention—perhaps they're only being nice because they want to lull us into letting our guard down. Vigilance was never required more than when the Soviets were supposedly quietly minding their own business. You can see how this sort of belief system could have played a role in generating (and then maintaining) the Cold War.

Responding to Uncertainty

Uncertainty can also undermine rational calculation. When uncertainty becomes a problem, there are several ways to deal with it. Procrastination can occur as a result of calculation—that is, one can decide that the best thing to do is to wait for more information to come in before making any decision—but it can also be what we call *defensive procrastination*. Defensive procrastination can occur when people refuse to deal with a problem in the hopes that the problem will resolve itself. The decision-maker weighs the alternatives, doesn't make up his or her mind, doesn't act, but instead hopes the problem will simply go away.

Another concept describing how evidence is incorporated with beliefs during decision-making is *bolstering*. Bolstering occurs when decision-makers stop engaging in the broad search for information and, instead of exploring the full range of policy options, choose instead to intensify their quest for information that supports the choice they have already made. Someone like Dulles would not look at all the information available to him, but would order aerial reconnaissance or send out spies to look for the evidence he wanted to find. We refer to this as bolstering because the effort is to support a position already determined, rather than make a rational judgement.

How are Decisions Made in a Crisis?

There is another angle to consider when thinking about how individual-level factors may lead foreign policy to deviate from expectations derived from a system-level analysis. This focuses on how situations affect decision-makers and their decisions. *Crises* have an impact on the decision-making process, and this change in the process affects the final results. There are several ways to define a crisis, but most definitions include (1) a high threat to something the decision-makers value very highly; (2) surprise—are decision-makers caught off guard?; (3) the need for a quick response—do decision-makers have a limited time-frame in which to react?; and some authors and scholars include (4) fatigue as a key factor in the crisis (though this may be quite secondary).[4]

Again, the main point is that these factors cause decision-makers to act in ways that pull them away from rational decision-making. Their actions are thus inconsistent with the expectations generated by arguments based on the assumption of rational action in any of the forms previously discussed. Decision-makers under stress caused by the high threat or the need to act quickly tend to limit their choices unnecessarily. They don't give full consideration to the complete range of choices they actually have. They also often exhibit increased cognitive rigidity; they tend to rely on things they believe to be true, without questioning whether or not this is the case in this particular instance. They become less tolerant, less creative, and rely much more on previous historical examples or stereotypes.

Crises exhibiting high threat, surprise, and the need for a quick response can also cause decision-makers to be myopic—the decision-makers think only about short-run consequences and only focus on one or two issues. Consider the way George Bush Senior and his advisers dealt with the first Gulf War, or how George W. Bush and his team handled the invasion of Iraq. In the first instance, the president and his people were so focused on the diplomatic and military effort to compel the Iraqis to leave Kuwait that they never adequately thought through the ramifications of their policy if it actually was successful. What should happen if the allies decisively defeated the Iraqi army? The Bush Administration handled things well (at least from their viewpoint) up to the end of the conflict, but then they were unprepared for the next stages, leaving confusion over the terms of the armistice. The weakness of the settlement, plus the continued survival of Saddam Hussein's regime, set the stage for the ongoing conflict in the region in the 1990s. When the U.S.-led coalition invaded Iraq in 2003, again many thought the foreign policy decisions short-sighted. The U.S. needed few allies to topple Hussein's regime, but to succeed in its goals afterwards, such as the political and economic transformation of the country during the occupation, assistance from other major powers was sorely needed.

Finally, researchers have observed that some decision-makers in a crisis will deny their own control over events, instead shifting full responsibility to their opponent. These decision-makers may believe their own hands are tied, that their own choices are extremely limited, whereas their opponents have a full range of choices. For all these reasons, scholars have seen that the assumptions made by the rational-actor, system-level theories concerning foreign policy decisions are not representative of decision-making practices during a crisis.

The popularity of individual-level theories began back in the 1940s and early 1950s. It was difficult for most people to understand the outbreak of World War II without discussing the particular personalities of the leaders of certain countries.[5] Would World War II have occurred if Germany had been led by someone other than Adolf Hitler? Because Hitler was mentally unbalanced, German foreign policy in the late 1930s was unbalanced, too. To understand German foreign policy, theorists and historians argued, you had to understand how Hitler thought and acted. Similar arguments were made about Soviet foreign policy in the 1940s and 1950s, with the beginning of the Cold War. If Stalin determined Soviet foreign policy, and Stalin was not rational, then what motivated Stalin's actions? How did he think? If one believed Stalin was paranoid, would Soviet foreign policy reflect his paranoia? To enter debates about the sources of Soviet foreign policy, one had to understand Stalin and his personality.

Typically, we view the foreign policy of a totalitarian or even an authoritarian state as an extension of the leader's personality. Since the society of such a state appears to be dominated by the particular individual who leads the state (think of recent examples, such as Iraq or Libya), it is easy to see why the country's foreign policy would be shaped by the leader's personality as well. Moreover, we often see patterns in the personalities of the leaders themselves. To have placed oneself in a position of dictatorial control over an entire country, it is probably correct to assume the leaders (people like Saddam Hussein or Muammer Khaddafi) were willing to use brute force to eliminate their domestic rivals. Such attitudes about the correct way to resolve political differences could well be transferred to the international arena, leading us to expect these states to pursue policies exhibiting intolerance and violence against external enemies.

There are potential problems with this sort of approach, however. One challenge comes from explaining changes in foreign policy. If we say the reason Iraq has a belligerent foreign policy is because Iraq's leader is belligerent, but the leader has been in power many years, why is Iraq belligerent only part of the time?[6] Personalities are usually considered to be fairly fixed—they take long to form and do not suddenly switch in the span of a day or two. Yet foreign policies can change quite rapidly. How then are the two related? If one considers the differences in the rate of change in the causal variable and the rate of change in the dependent variable, then the relationship between the two may not be as strong as initially suspected. This may be resolvable, however, if we can evaluate some connection between stimulus and response, filtered through beliefs, or we consider some way in which the personality traits are triggered by environmental factors.

More commonly, the problem with focusing on personalities as a causal factor behind foreign policy is that the argument becomes circular, because it is unable to separate out cause and effect. Just how does such a problem arise? Someone argues that a certain leader is overly aggressive and uses this to explain why a particularly aggressive foreign policy was chosen. What is

Figure 5.2: A Circular Argument

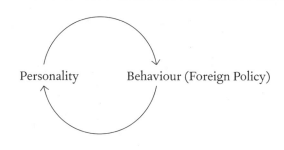

the evidence that this leader is overly aggressive? The foreign policy itself is overly aggressive. Circular arguments are impossible to falsify. If they can never be proven wrong, the theorist has a problem. The natural response for theorists has been to introduce further steps into the equation, as evidence of behaviour in other areas or as sources of the personality traits. If the theorist can understand how a leader's personality is shaped in the first place, then these factors can be seen as the underlying cause of the foreign policy. Evidence of the source of the personality, and of the personality's impact on other decisions, could allow us to create a falsifiable theory about foreign policy. The sorts of information which theorists have brought into play range from minute factors developed by psychologists to life experiences quite broadly defined.

Lest one get the impression that this approach is applicable only to the study of decisions made by leaders of totalitarian countries, or ones who we suspect have an apparent psychological disorder, we should remember that this approach is intended to be a full rival to those already presented. We should be able to look at the leaders of any state and employ these arguments to examine any kind of behaviour. In fact, some of the best early work on the personalities of leaders and how they related to foreign policy outcomes was done on Woodrow Wilson.[7] As U.S. president during World War I, Wilson played an important role in the diplomacy of the war and in the peace deliberations afterwards. Wilson had his peculiarities, so he was a good candidate for this kind of study. The work focuses on his childhood and how his upbringing shaped his adult personality, which in turn affected the way in which he handled foreign policy in this very crucial period of history. This analysis therefore hangs on debates surrounding the roots of his personality.

Wilson's parents were very strict. His mother, in particular, was very protective of him as well. She wouldn't let him go to public school and mix with other children until his later teens, so his early schooling was completed at home. His father was a religious minister. Both parents were apparently very righteous—dead certain about their beliefs—and they transferred this rigid attitude to their son. Also, because he was kept away from other children, Wilson didn't necessarily learn to interact and to share or to learn to compromise. Nonetheless, Wilson was very smart and a great orator; he was successful at Princeton University, where he served as a professor and then later as president.

From there he entered politics and again was very successful, eventually being elected president of the U.S. But as president, those aspects of his personality formed by his childhood and his relationships with his parents came back to haunt him. As part of U.S. foreign policy, he wanted to remake the world; World War I gave him the opportunity to make changes.[8] His ideas shaped the Treaty of Versailles, which established such notions as the right to national self-determination and the need to spread democracy. But then it came time for countries to ratify the agreements, which included joining Wilson's most ambitious project, the League of Nations. Although Wilson had been chief architect of this international institution, many Americans were not interested in having the U.S. become a member. Americans who were bitter over the role the country had played in World War I were reluctant to support an organization that proposed to tell states what they could or could not do. Eventually, after debates in the Senate (which must ratify all treaties under the U.S. Constitution), it was apparent to all that U.S. membership in the League of Nations would be achieved only if certain reservations were introduced. Wilson refused to accept the compromise hammered out in the Senate, as we might have predicted, given his personality. As a result, the League of Nations began without the dominant economic power of the day as a member.

Similar analyses have been done on other leaders, focusing on relationships with parents, childhood factors such as illness (it has been argued that weak or sickly boys grow up to be men who overcompensate for their physical problems with "macho" personalities), and so on. For most theories found in psychology, we can find an application or case in foreign policy analysis. Another way of examining the sources of personality or belief systems is to explore the relationship between life experiences and behaviour. More interestingly, we can explore how big events shaped the experiences of an entire group or generation and therefore shaped how that generation perceives foreign policy issues.

Generational Arguments

Many journalists implicitly executed this sort of analysis when Bill Clinton was first elected president. He was, after all, the first "baby boomer" in the White House, and journalists attempted to use that information to predict how his administration would differ from those of his immediate predecessors. The previous presidents, from the first George Bush right back to Kennedy and Eisenhower, were men who as young adults had seen the U.S. rise from the Great Depression of the 1930s, be attacked at Pearl Harbor, and then emerge from World War II as a world power. The U.S. had swung from isolationism to engagement in foreign affairs on a global basis in the span of two decades. The experiences these men faced in their late teens and early twenties were largely linked to military service. They (and many of their advisers) had witnessed momentous changes in the world. They had confronted Nazism, seen their country become the victim of a surprise attack, and survived a world war—often having lost close friends and family members in that war. All these things shaped this generation's view of external affairs and of the proper U.S. foreign policy in particular.

Presidents from these generations rejected isolationism as short-sighted. In the 1920s and 1930s, the U.S. had turned its back on the world's many problems and instead had focused on domestic problems. Yet the world's problems grew larger and larger until they arrived at the U.S.'s own doorstep. Thus, this generation could only view isolationism as a mistake. Likewise, they believed that appeasement of totalitarian dictatorships was wrong—in the 1930s, when Hitler said he wanted only the German-speaking parts of Czechoslovakia and Austria, Britain and France had not resisted. Instead, they thought that conceding to such demands would satisfy the German chancellor. After Hitler launched the war, the lesson this generation drew was that appeasement only fuelled the appetites of totalitarian dictators. They considered appeasement a flawed policy in all instances. When these leaders faced the Soviet Union, they resisted any and every move the Soviets made and conceded nothing.

The impact of World War II made these leaders focus much more of their attention on the potential threat posed by totalitarian dictatorships and, of course, on the danger of another world war starting. World war was something painfully real to them. But how does this compare with the "baby boomers" now in the White House? They grew up thinking of the U.S. as a world power. Their most powerful political experience concerning international affairs was watching their country divided and frustrated over the war in Vietnam. Instead of seeing a world remade by the U.S. and its allies, they saw a world unravelling despite U.S. power. Rather than seeing a U.S. that surged ahead of other powers militarily and economically, they saw one losing its lead or perhaps even falling behind economic and political rivals. They grew up not with the threat of World War III, but with the risk of small-scale but bloody wars such as those fought in Korea or Vietnam. Undoubtedly, the attacks on the Pentagon and World Trade Center will be the central events defining the beliefs of another generation.

We can do a similar generational analysis of the last Soviet leaders; in fact, some analysts believe the changing over of Soviet leadership from one generation to the next was pivotal in the break-up of the Soviet Union.[9] The former leaders were those who had lived through the Revolution and the Russian Civil War, or at least through the Nazi invasion and World War II. Their perspective was of a hostile outside world, ready to attack the Soviets whenever the country was vulnerable. Eventually a younger generation took the reins of power, people like Mikhail Gorbachev. These individuals had only dim memories of World War II. Instead, their belief-systems were shaped by the period of Soviet military power but economic stagnation. Their view was of a country striving to succeed in the foreign affairs realm at the cost of driving their society into the ground. A similar but perhaps even more persuasive analysis could be done on the generational shifts in the leadership in China, where some of the original revolutionaries have held power for a very long time.

At least one scholar, Michael Roskin, has used this sort of generational analysis to explain the cyclical nature of U.S. foreign policy.[10] One generation pursues a very active foreign policy, but the generation just coming of age at that time sees the problems associated with such active engagement. Once that second generation assumes positions of power, it turns its back on the world. The problems created by isolationism, in turn, affect the third generation, encouraging it to pursue a more active foreign policy once it takes power. Woodrow Wilson got the U.S. involved in World War I, but the next generation chose to be isolationist. Isolationism did not prevent U.S. involvement in World War II, so the next generation became much more outwardly oriented, trying to take a proactive policy stance. This global involvement brought on the Cold War, plus the Korean and Vietnam Wars. Roskin expected this cycle to continue. The journalists writing in 1992 made much the same sort of argument about Clinton and the "baby boomers" entering office. They expected the Clinton Administration to turn its back on the world and become more isolationist—and certainly Clinton and his staff struggled with decisions to intervene in the civil wars in the Balkans or in Africa. Surely Roskin would go on to look at September 11, 2001 as a key event swinging the U.S. back to greater involvement in the world.

What is the glaring weakness of this argument? Not everyone in a generation has the same experiences, and not all the members of a generation think alike. One of the key points in the 2004 presidential election centred on the different experiences of George W. Bush and John Kerry during Vietnam and the ways these experiences shaped their views on the utility of war. Moreover, all the foreign policy decision-makers in one country are rarely of the same generation at any one given time—generations do not follow neatly one after another either.

Interpersonal Generalization Theory

Another way to introduce other evidence about decision-makers' personalities is known as interpersonal generalization theory. In this theory, an individual's interpersonal relations are analyzed to provide insight into how he or she is likely to handle his or her country's relations with other states. Someone studying Lyndon Johnson would discover that he was very hard on his advisers and his administrative staff. He excelled in Congress because he was good at mixing bullying tactics with appeals to get people to agree with his point of view. He used to call in his staff individually and berate them as a way to get them to work harder and to defend their points of view. So his personality can be modelled on the base of how he treated the people around him, and that can be used to build an argument about how he would conduct foreign policy.

Franklin Roosevelt exhibited very different interpersonal relations. He was a master at engineering compromises, which enabled him to guide legislation successfully through Congress. He brought some of these same interpersonal skills with him when he engaged in diplomacy. Indeed, many theorists and historians have argued that a number of the problems of the post-World War II era in Eastern Europe resulted from the mismatch of Roosevelt's interpersonal skills with Stalin's. In the negotiations between the two men, Roosevelt kept offering concessions regarding the postwar Soviet role in Eastern Europe in order to create compromises. What kind of interpersonal skills did Stalin have? He was not known for his ability to compromise or to make concessions, and he did little of either in the Yalta negotiations.

Summary: Appreciating the Differences in Individuals

What are the strengths and weaknesses of the individual-level theories focusing on personality or psychological make-up? Well, as already noted about the generational arguments, identifying a generation level can be difficult. Moreover, it is usually incorrect to assume that everyone from one generation will think alike. Leadership does not shift in smooth patterns with one generation succeeding another, either. Any analysis of a generation's viewpoint will depend upon who within that generation becomes the focus of attention.

A similar set of problems may weaken theories about the ways in which personality drives an individual's foreign policy decision-making. Case selection can be a problem, as well as establishing consistency across cases.[11] The danger with many of these theories is that they are inductive and thus require greater care in case selection. Because the cases are often not viewed systematically, one leader's childhood is often not compared with others. To a large extent, these theories are only as convincing as the underlying arguments about personality, which are usually drawn from disciplines far removed from political science. When working at this level, one must be careful to construct theories we can test properly with a wide selection of cases. Any theory based on idiosyncratic characteristics of individuals should stand up to the other qualities we expect theories to have: they should exhibit generalizability, consistency across cases, and should be falsifiable. If the theory is unable to meet these criteria, how will we ever be able to move away from mere description and make it clearly predictive?

At least the policy prescriptions which flow from this type of theory are clear: do not allow certain personality types to hold positions of leadership. That means perhaps screening one's own candidates for leadership, or in the case of another country's leadership, the theories could lead to the recommendation that one should change the leader in order to change that country's policy. One country could promote such change in another country by fomenting a coup there, or war itself might be required. Those were the preferred options of the Bush Administration as it confronted Saddam Hussein's Iraq. Another question to ponder is whether these theories are rivals to the others already discussed or complements? For example, bureaucratic politics arguments are good for explaining foreign policy events that are inexplicable from the perspective of system-level theories. Those two theories are based on such different assumptions that they can be seen only as rivals. The same could probably be said about individual-level theories and bureaucratic politics. Similarly, some of these individual-level theories might be good for making sense of something totally unexpected and seemingly irrational (such as why a weak country would attack a stronger one). Some of these individual-level theories might actually need rational-actor, system-level theories as the first step in their analysis; the individual-level theories then fill in some of the blanks on why policy looked the way it did. Often individual-level theorists are engaging in this sort of analysis implicitly; they require other information to work—but what sort of other information? That is something to remember when we apply theories from this level in the cases in Part III.

Notes

1. Alexander George, "The 'Operational Code': A Neglected Approach to the Study of Political Leaders and Decision-Making," *International Studies Quarterly* 13 (June 1969): 190-222; and "The Causal Nexus between Cognitive Beliefs and Decision-Making Behavior: The 'Operational Code' Belief System," *Psychological Models in International Politics*, ed. by Lawrence S. Falkowski (Boulder, CO: Westview Press, 1979) 95-124.

2. George, "The 'Operational Code' and 'The Causal Nexus.'"

3. For more on Dulles, see Ronald W. Preussen, *John Foster Dulles: The Road to Power* (New York, NY: Free Press, 1982).

4. Michael Brecher's list includes a high threat to something valued and a time constraint, but also the probability that the situation will end in some sort of military exchange before it is resolved. See Michael Brecher, "State Behavior in International Crisis," *Journal of Conflict Resolution* 23,3 (September 1979): 446-80, as well as Brecher's works with Jonathon Wilkenfeld. Also see Glenn Snyder and Paul Diesing, *Conflict Among Nations* (Princeton, NJ: Princeton University Press, 1977) 7. This specific list is from Richard Ned Lebow, *Between Peace and War* (Baltimore, MD: Johns Hopkins, 1981).

5. A prime example is Alan Bullock, *Hitler: A Study in Tyranny* (New York, NY: Harper and Row, 1964).

6. This problem appears in several arguments constructed inductively.

7. Alexander L. George and Juliette L. George, *Woodrow Wilson and Colonel House* (New York, NY: John Day, 1956). Then see Edwin A. Weinstein, James William Anderson, and Arthur S. Link, "Woodrow Wilson's Political Personality: A Reappraisal," *Political Science Quarterly* 93 (Winter 1978): 585-98; and Alexander L. George and Juliette L. George, "Woodrow Wilson and Colonel House: A Reply to Weinstein, Anderson, and Link," *Political Science Quarterly* 96 (Winter 1981-82): 641-65.

8. John Stoessinger counts Wilson as the first of his "crusaders" in American foreign policy. See John Stoessinger, *Crusaders and Pragmatists* (New York, NY: W.W. Norton, 1979).

9. For a view of Soviet generations, see the discussion in Richard Ned Lebow, "Generational Learning and Conflict Management," *International Journal* 40,4 (Autumn 1985): 555-85.

10. Michael Roskin, "From Pearl Harbor to Vietnam: Shifting Generational Paradigms," *Political Science Quarterly* 89,3 (Fall 1974): 563-88.

11. Blema Steinberg's *Shame and Humiliation* (Montreal, QC: McGill-Queens University Press, 1996) is an example of the correct way to compare cases. By illustrating Eisenhower's ability to assess his own skills objectively, she can compare his personality with those of the other presidents who were less objective in evaluating their own abilities. These self-images shaped how the different presidents dealt with advice.

Additional References

Brecher, Michael. *Decisions in Crises*. Berkeley, CA: University of California Press, 1980.

George, Alexander. "The Causal Nexus between Cognitive Beliefs and Decision-Making Behavior: The 'Operational Code' Belief System." *Psychological Models in International Politics*. Ed. Lawrence S. Falkowski. Boulder, CO: Westview Press, 1979. 95-124.

—. "Ideology and International Relations: A Conceptual Analysis." *Jerusalem Journal of International Relations* 9,1 (March 1987): 1-21.

Levy, Jack. "An Introduction to Prospect Theory." *Political Psychology* 13,2 (June 1992): 171-86.

CHAPTER 6
Ideas as Causal Factors

Increasingly, scholars in international relations have become fascinated with the way ideas shape the behaviour of states. Policy selection appears to be powerfully influenced by the popularity of particular conceptual frameworks. For instance, liberal policies have been highly favoured since the end of the Cold War. Scholars have noted that, historically, people have preferred different solutions to similar problems. It isn't always clear that one set of policies solves the problems better than others do; the popularity of the ideas may provide a better explanation for why one policy is employed, compared to a serious rational selection process. The popularity of liberal policies in IPE after 1990 may be easily understood by the failure of the Soviet bloc, but it is also worth remembering that liberal policies cannot solve every problem, nor can they help people achieve all the goals they may desire.

To understand the importance of ideas, Judith Goldstein and Robert Keohane describe the three most obvious ways in which ideas can influence policy. According to Goldstein and Keohane, "ideas influence policy when the principled or causal beliefs they embody provide road maps that increase actors' clarity about goals or ends-means relationships, when they affect outcomes of strategic situations in which there is no unique equilibrium, and when they become embedded in political institutions."[1] These roles may be more obvious in IPE than in other parts of international relations, because policy options are often dictated by our understanding of how the economy works. Economists change their models, and new economic models stress different economic and political variables. When a new variable is added, or old variables dropped, alternative policy options are instantly created or old policy options are immediately eliminated. Ideas clearly play a role in how policies are selected.

An Example of the Power of Ideas: Keynesianism and the Great Depression

The potential influence of ideas may be most evident in the wake of an economic crisis. In the early 1930s high unemployment and falling economic output wracked each of the industrialized countries. Things were not working as expected; predictions were not coming true; policies intended to rectify the situation were not delivering desirable results. Existing economic models offered little in the way of policy recommendations that were reliable or effective. A dramatic economic crisis such as this encourages economists and policy-makers to challenge existing models and propose alternatives.

Specifically, in the early 1930s the dominant view among theorists was that the economy would eventually right itself. Governments needed to sit patiently on the sidelines while the market resolved its own problems. Yet, as governments stood aside, economic problems worsened. Eventually, politicians ignored the economists and began trying any policies that might offer relief. Some of these policies, such as reintroducing protectionist tariffs, merely made matters worse. Through trial and error, decision-makers discovered that some of their old theories simply no longer held true. Old economic models failed to provide meaningful information concerning macroeconomic management. For example, policy-makers had believed that their most important rule in domestic monetary affairs was to focus their efforts on maintenance of the stability of the value of money. They achieved this goal by fixing the value of currencies in terms of gold. The gold standard sacrificed domestic monetary goals (and autonomy in monetary policy) to an external goal: convincing foreigners that the money was worth retaining. The domestic repercussions to these practices were generally positive, since the money supply was held stable and inflation was avoided. (Sometimes deflation occurred, however.) Yet the French experience of the 1920s, when that country had unwittingly undervalued its currency, proved that following a different monetary policy could deliver unanticipated benefits. The lower value of the franc boosted French exports. Britain, on the other hand, had stuck with orthodox thinking, inadvertently setting its money at too high a value in gold—and therefore too high a value versus other currencies backed by gold. In fact, Britain had set the value of the pound at the level at which it had stood for nearly a century before World War I began, but the situation was very different after the war. The new factors shaping the British economy and the pound should have been considered, rather than assuming the value was unchanged. This overvaluation made it very hard to sell British goods abroad. The unintended undervaluation of French currency helped stimulate that country's exports, which in turn raised employment higher than it otherwise would have been. In Britain, the overvaluation of the currency worsened the economic problems of the period.

Once the gold standard came apart in 1931, countries drew on these experiences. One of the lessons they thought they had learned was that they could manipulate their money supplies to undervalue their currencies, thereby promoting exports. Yet, since many countries tried to do the same thing at the same time, each ended up trying to undervalue their currency relative to others and failing. Their efforts merely cancelled each other out, and the sum of their efforts was to create financial problems alongside all the other economic problems of the era. The point here, though, is that old ideas no longer held sway, given the crisis. By abandoning the old thinking, many new policies were possible.

Of course, some economists had already been thinking about dropping the old gold standard / *laissez-faire* conceptions and were pondering ways in which government could play a more positive role in the economy. They soon developed models incorporating these ideas and describing new policy instruments. By introducing variables to represent government options, particularly noting how government could use fiscal policy as well as monetary policy in a discretionary manner to stimulate economic activity, John Maynard Keynes made sense out of these new policies. His models presented these new variables as possible levers governments could use to manage the economy. His vision of the economy changed the way government officials approached economic policy—including foreign economic policy—after the Great Depression.

Ideas, Theories, and Models as Constraints on Decision-Making

More than anyone else, social scientists should realize the power that a social science model can exercise on the way decisions are made. Again, international political economy is an area where we can appreciate this point, perhaps due to the technical nature of economic matters. The hard sciences often exhibit similar characteristics. A single framework or paradigm becomes dominant, and this paradigm (just like the examples from international relations described in Chapter 1) provides practitioners in the field with a way to understand the world, and operate in it.

Peter Hall speaks of *policy paradigms*. This is how he describes the impact of ideas:

> In technically complex fields of policy, such as macroeconomic policy-making, decision-makers are often guided by an overarching set of ideas that specify how the problems facing them are to be perceived, which goals might be attained through policy and what sorts of techniques can be used to reach those goals. Ideas about each of these matters interlock to form a relatively coherent whole that might be described as a *policy paradigm*. Like a gestalt, it structures the very way in which policy-makers see the world and their role in it.[2]

Hall's concept is quite useful as a way of identifying sets of ideas that shape the way decisions get made.

Goldstein and Keohane discuss three different types of beliefs, which can be thought of as the causal pathways in which ideas affect policy.[3] The first is a *world view*. This is a very broad concept, which covers everything from an actor's self-image to the beliefs an actor has of what is and is not possible. World views are provided by religion or ideology. These are perhaps the most important, for they are the deepest ideas—they shape identities and goals. The second category, labelled *principled beliefs*, denotes normative convictions concerning what is right (just) from what is wrong (unjust). While these principled beliefs tend to be grounded in a world view, most world views are broad enough to capture competing principled beliefs. (Goldstein and Keohane point to the example of slavery. Christianity was used first to justify slavery, then to condemn it.) The last type of idea they identify is *causal beliefs*. These are convictions about cause and effect. Such beliefs are grounded in consensus among an elite or across a community of experts. Causal beliefs are important, for they identify which policies or strategies are considered most effective.

Tracking the Influence of Ideas

Again, in IPE we can see certain ideas come to prominence and spread among the nations of the world. The tracking of economic models illustrates this point quite nicely. Whole economic frameworks come and go. As mentioned above, prior to 1920, the gold standard dominated thinking on foreign economic policies. It gave participating governments little discretion when enacting monetary policy, since government and central bank policies were aimed at meeting external objectives: maintaining currency stability. It was widely believed that markets would stabilize themselves if only governments would allow them to operate without interference. Thus, the gold standard was a set of obligations meant to deny governments' discretionary policy in the economic sphere.

When things went awry in the late 1920s and early 1930s, the ideas inherent in the gold standard were challenged. John Maynard Keynes created a model to capture the degree of government intervention in the economy then beginning to develop. From this model, Keynes was able to illustrate how governments could take action in the domestic economy in order to stimulate production and employment at the time of their choosing. *Keynesianism*, as these policies of intervention were soon labelled, involved demand management through the government's fiscal and monetary policies. Government expenditures were no longer viewed simply as what the government had to pay in receipt for minimal obligations of service, but rather fiscal policy was now a tool for provoking economic activity. Keynesianism was adopted in most countries in the West, though there were many experiments with socialism and fascism, as well. It seemed to provide a good understanding of how economies worked and offered policy solutions to most problems in a way that was easy to understand.

Figure 6.1: The Phillips Curve

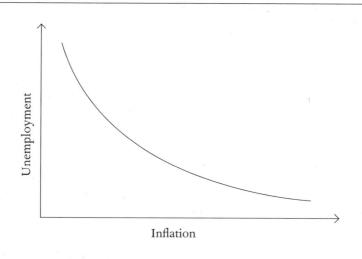

Politicians and decision-makers would use the Keynesian approach for several decades before new vexing problems arose. In the 1960s, but even more so in the 1970s, predictions based on Keynesian models seemed to be breaking down. Relationships between variables were coming apart, especially the relationship between unemployment and inflation. In the 1930s, when unemployment was high, discretionary use of fiscal and monetary policy had used inflation to stimulate the economy. This led one economist, A.W. Phillips, to posit a relationship between inflation and unemployment. When one rose, the other fell. This did not hold true completely, for as the rate of unemployment approached zero, no amount of stimulation could rid the unemployment problem completely. (Unemployment would drop to what economists refer to as the natural rate of unemployment; there would always be some people in between jobs, simply because they had moved from one city to another, or desired a career change, and so on, creating a "natural" or "normal" level of unemployment.) The relationship between the two variables was a curve, which came to be known as the *Phillips Curve*.

Policy-makers were supposed to decide where on this curve they wanted to place the country's economy and then select the appropriate mix of policies to shift the country along the curve. At one point in the 1970s, however, odd things began to happen. The relationship changed; Keynesian models didn't anticipate what was occurring. In the case of the Phillips Curve, inflation went up, but unemployment didn't fall. A whole new economic term was coined to capture the sense that we now had an economy with stagnant rates of growth but high inflation too: *stagflation*. Clearly this outcome did not make people very happy, and policy recommendations didn't seem to help. Stimulating the economy to increase employment only made inflation worse, but seemed to have little effect on jobs; tightening the money supply to reduce inflation only raised unemployment, with little effect on prices. As economic policies failed to ameliorate the situation, policy-makers and economists began searching for alternative ideas.

Among the alternatives available, there was one similar to the old gold standard. Popular among some academics, this approach said that the gold standard had worked well since it provided individuals with predictability. What governments needed to do was provide a stable economic environment for people—especially in the monetary realm, since the big problem in the 1970s was inflation. Economists argued that people's expectations of inflation had been raised by the government's constant use of policy to stimulate economic growth. These expectations needed to be broken. Otherwise, people would make their own plans based on the belief inflation would still be around; they would ask for higher returns for their own goods and services, thus ensuring that inflation would grow in the future (because a rational individual, expecting prices to rise, will charge higher prices for his or her own services and output; if everyone acts rationally in the expectation of inflation, prices will surely be increased). The economists knew it made little sense to argue that the money supply should be fixed by a country's gold reserves; history had proven why this was problematic.[4] Instead, they argued that the government should simply limit the growth of the money supply. By publicly announcing low targets for growth of the money supply, and sticking to these targets, government policy could become credible. People's expectation of future inflation would then be reduced. When they stopped planning on inflation, inflationary pressures would in fact lessen. Economists urging this line of thinking became known as *monetarists*, because their models identified changes in the money supply as the key policy variable. While monetarists' ideas drove much of the policy decisions in the 1980s, the debates between Keynesians and monetarists continue to be played out.

Which Matters More: Ideas, Individuals, or Institutions?

One of the difficult aspects of using ideas as a causal variable is our inability to separate their impact from the influence of other variables. Historically, we often associate specific ideas with the individuals who promote them. France signed a trade agreement opening up its economy to British goods in 1860, for instance (see Chapter 11); the treaty was proposed by Michel Chevalier, at the behest of Emperor Napoleon III. We know from his writings that Chevalier was a strong proponent of classical liberalism. What this case illustrates is the difficulty in separating out the impact of the idea of liberalism from the impact of the individual—would a different person promoting the treaty have pushed for a different result? We have no way of knowing, since both variables are present in this case. In the case of monetary policy described above, we associate the shift to monetarist policies not merely with the spread of the ideas, but also with the higher number of monetarists holding positions in government.

Other efforts to illustrate the power of ideas stress other types of actors as the carriers of the ideas. One popular approach examines the role of *epistemic communities*—a group of experts whose consensus on what constitutes knowledge creates a shared view of an issue.[5] As Albert Yee has noted, the emphasis on epistemic communities as a reference point conflates the role of experts with the role of ideas. Epistemic communities may have power independent of ideas, or the ideas prevalent at one point in time may help explain the existence of the epistemic community in the first place. The real difficulty is in identifying the characteristics making one idea more persuasive than another.[6] "Youth" isn't enough, for some ideas circulate for many years before becoming dominant.[7] One possible angle could be to explore the connections between crises and ideas.[8] By definition, a widespread crisis provides the necessary conditions for a collapse in the credibility of an idea or policy paradigm. It is not clear how a new policy paradigm gets selected, however.

The same sort of problem can occur with other potential causal factors. For instance, Goldstein and others have tried to show how institutions and ideas both have an impact. Institutions are created with specific attributes as a reflection of their duties or role—and those obligations or roles often reflect certain ideas. In fact, on closer examination, one sees the impact of ideas, institutions, and crises together, since institutions typically only change when they experience a crisis. As Goldstein and Keohane put it, "ideas embedded in institutions specify policy in the absence of innovation."[9] In this view, institutions mediate between ideas and policy. They are formed at a point in time and embody the causal and principled beliefs prevalent at that moment.

Yee is critical of how Goldstein tries to show the independent impact of ideas, because it is difficult to separate the impact of institutions from the influence of ideas.[10] Thus, for Yee, Goldstein's evidence is not simply illustrating the power of ideas in U.S. foreign policy; rather, the evidence indicates the strength of both institutions and ideas in that area.[11] Ideas cannot have a separate impact from institutions, in his thinking. Since the institutions embody the ideas, it may simply be impossible to find cases illustrating the impact of one of these factors without the other.

One way around this problem is to pose the role of ideas in a slightly different light. Geoffrey Garrett and Barry Weingast talk about ideas as focal points for joint action.[12] In other words, shared beliefs affect how actors come together for interaction. They point out that most problems of arranging effective coordination or cooperation can be solved in a number of ways. How do we understand which solution is likely to emerge? They emphasize the importance of shared beliefs in their explanation for the emergence of strategies for solving coordination problems.[13] Their work stresses the relevance of shared culture, history, or prior institutions, among other things. By backing up and considering strategies for actors' interaction, they offer an explanation for why some institutions are created in the first place. This, in turn, provides more insight into why and when institutional change takes place.

There are still those who doubt the importance of ideas in answering our most fundamental questions. Some theorists have tried to depict the debate about the role of ideas as idea-based theories versus interest-based theories.[14] This may be an overstatement, however, since most theorists using ideas as causal factors have aimed only at explaining a limited range of outcomes and often rely on a mix of variables, where ideas are one component of the cause-effect equation. Often, an outsider looking in on these debates notices how the two sides are merely engaged in a dispute over which came first, "the chicken or the egg?" Ideas may matter, especially when they limit the range of policy choices given serious consideration, yet material interests may be the source for innovation in ideas. We need a greater understanding of innovation in ideas, in institutional change, and the evolution of ideas before we can sort out this discussion and reach more solid conclusions.

Summary: Ideas are Important, But How Should We Study Them?

The impact of ideas on foreign policy has only recently been given serious study. Attempts to compare the strength of ideas versus rival causal factors have been undertaken only in a systematic fashion in a few instances.[15] As Goldstein and Keohane note, "reflectivist scholars have been slow to articulate or test hypotheses," though their edited volume is a step in this direction.[16] Works addressing the creation of particular bureaucracies, or the adoption of particular policies, has become increasingly widespread, though much of this research still struggles with the criticisms identified above.

Anyone who believes strongly that this is a variable whose strength is underestimated must pay careful attention to research design. On the one hand, it is easy to make a purely theoretical argument in favour of the power of ideas. Abstractly, the constructivists who have proposed such a point of view are very persuasive. Yet, it remains less obvious that their analyses of empirical results will answer those questions which other theories fail to answer. Where are the anomalies to structural realism or liberalism, and what sort of evidence could constructivists or the proponents of the power of ideas (or norms) bring to bear on those issues?[17]

Conclusions on the Levels of Analysis

As a way to group theories, the levels of analysis organize theories along one dimension: what assumption is made about the dominant actor? Is the key actor supposed to be a state or a group within a state? Is it an individual acting out a role, or is it an intangible force, such as an idea or norm? The range goes beyond the groupings identified here.[18] The key point to remember is that each specific theory can usually be placed within a paradigm (as discussed in the previous chapter) or a level of analysis. These are two separate ways of sorting out theories for comparison.

Paradigmatic debates tend to swirl around different questions than the debate over the utility of one level of analysis versus another. The levels of analysis debate has generally been about which types of theory best answer questions about the behaviour of a particular state in a particular circumstance. Why did the U.S. choose to break the link between gold reserves and the dollar in 1971? Paradigms more often compete in their ability to answer questions about broader changes in the international realm. Why did an international regime, such as the Bretton Woods monetary regime, fall apart? In some ways these may not be so different—when a state decides to act a particular way, it has consequences for the rest of the international system. In this case, the U.S. decision to break the link between gold and the U.S. dollar was the turning point in the story of the Bretton Woods regime. The cases we examine in Part III will all be examples of states making decisions which have proven to be turning points for the development of the international political economy. First, however, it is necessary to delve into the key issues dominating the research agenda of IPE.

Notes

1. Judith Goldstein and Robert Keohane, "Ideas and Foreign Policy: An Analytical Framework," *Ideas and Foreign Policy*, ed. Judith Goldstein and Robert Keohane (Ithaca, NY: Cornell University Press, 1993) 3.

2. Peter Hall, "The Movement from Keynesianism to Monetarism: Institutional Analysis and British Economic Policy in the 1970s," *Structuring Politics*, ed. Sven Steinmo, Kathleen Thelen, and Frank Longstreth (New York, NY: Cambridge University Press, 1992) 91-92.

3. Goldstein and Keohane 8-10.

4. Moreover, the two countries with the largest new supplies of gold were South Africa and the Soviet Union—and no one wanted to give either of these countries leverage over the international economy.

5. See the special volume of *International Organization* 46,1 (1992), especially the introduction by Peter M. Haas, "Epistemic Communities and International Policy Coordination" 1-36.

6. Albert S. Yee, "The Causal Effects of Ideas on Policies," *International Organization* 50,1 (Winter 1996): 86-87.

7. There is a lovely quote from Keynes's *The General Theory of Employment, Interest, and Money* (1936) to be found in the preface to John Odell's *U.S. International Monetary Policy* (Princeton, NJ: Princeton University Press, 1982).

8. The sort of work to emulate would be that of John Odell, especially his article "From London to Bretton Woods: Sources of Change in Bargaining Strategies And Outcomes," *Journal of Public Policy* 8,3/4 (1988): 287-315.

9. Goldstein and Keohane 13.

10. Yee 88-91.

11. Yee, speaking of Goldstein's book, *Ideas, Interests and American Trade Policy* (Ithaca, NY: Cornell University Press, 1993).

12. See Geoffrey Garrett and Barry Weingast, "Ideas, Interests, and Institutions: Constructing the European Community's Internal Market," *Ideas and Foreign Policy*, ed. Judith Goldstein and Robert Keohane (Ithaca: Cornell University Press, 1993) 176.

13. Garrett and Weingast 182.

14. Stephen Krasner's contribution to the Goldstein and Keohane volume comes close to this; see Stephen Krasner, "Westphalia and All That," *Ideas and Foreign Policy*, ed. Judith Goldstein and Robert Keohane (Ithaca, NY: Cornell University Press, 1993) 235-64.

15. One of the first was John Odell's *U.S. International Monetary Policy*, 1982.

16. Goldstein and Keohane 6.

17. This question is not meant to be negative; ongoing research aims to do exactly this sort of task. For instance, T.V. Paul is currently examining why some states have chosen not to develop nuclear weapons, even though they possess the requisite technology. His work suggests that international norms can have an effect on state policies, even in such crucial areas as security policy. His work is a direct challenge to realist thinking.

18. Some of the most popular texts identify as many as eight levels, though these often exhibit overlap. In *World Politics: The Menu for Choice*, 4th ed. (New York, NY: Freeman, 1992), Bruce Russett and Harvey Starr discuss the merits of six distinct levels of analysis.

Additional References

Goldstein, Judith. *Ideas, Interests and American Trade Policy*. Ithaca, NY: Cornell University Press, 1993.

Goldstein, Judith, and Robert Keohane (eds.). *Ideas and Foreign Policy: Beliefs, Institutions and Political Change*. Ithaca, NY: Cornell University Press, 1993.

Kapstein, Ethan. "Resolving the Regulator's Dilemma: International Coordination of Banking Regulations." *International Organization* 43,2 (Spring 1989): 323-47.

Yee, Albert S. "The Causal Effects of Ideas on Policies." *International Organization* 50,1 (Winter 1996): 69-108.

PART II
The Politicization of International Economic Issues

INTRODUCTION
The Interplay of Power and Wealth

We now turn to the substantive material in this book. International relations is often divided into two main subfields: security studies and international political economy. The examples examined in the rest of this book are drawn from international political economy. The cases were selected because they represent turning points in the evolution of the international political economy.

What exactly do we mean by the *international political economy*? The term "international" is fairly straightforward and should be a familiar concept to students. But what about "political economy"? Its methods and subject matter can be defined. For instance, according to Jeff Frieden, regardless of the paradigm one employs, modern political economy "studies how self-interested actors combine within or outside existing institutional settings to affect social outcomes." In terms of the methods typically employed, analysis is done through four steps: (1) defining actors and their goals, (2) specifying actors' policy preferences, (3) determining how actors will unite into groups for political action, and (4) following their interactions through and with social institutions.[1]

Frieden's definition is perhaps a bit broad; more narrowly defined, political economy is the analysis of the interaction of power and the processes of wealth creation. The subject matter could thus be described as the evolving distribution of wealth and power. Political economy combines techniques, subjects, and theories from a variety of fields. Obviously, it draws heavily from economics and political science, but it is not unusual to find much material from sociology, anthropology, and many of the other social sciences.

From political science, political economy borrows an emphasis on power. Power is the central concept in political science, which asks such questions as "where does power come from?," "how is power used?," and so on. As we saw in Chapter 1, the major drawback for political scientists is their inability to define power. We may know power when we see it, but can we identify power before it has been exercised?

Power and Wealth in International Political Economy

The difficulties in defining power are compounded when we turn from security issues and look more intensely at the politics associated with economic relations. How important is military power for understanding the development of free trade? As we shall see in the cases presented below, a realist would argue that it is very important. Most realists believe that certain types of power are fungible. That simply means these forms of power can be exercised across different issue-areas. A realist believes that military power can be used for defending one's territory, or it can be used to compel other countries into making trade concessions. Other forms of power might simply be issue-specific, rather than fungible. That means these other assets are useful only within a specific issue-area. Having a large supply of timber may give a country power only in negotiations concerning the international trade in wood products. Controlling stocks of timber does not translate however into power in very many other issue-areas.

Since specific questions in international political economy often come down to questions of policy within a single issue-area, the difficulties inherent in defining power and in dealing with concerns over the fungibility of power combine to make it difficult to apply many of our theories without generating some controversies. Whenever power is a key factor, these questions arise. Consider a dispute over fishing. Which countries should a realist focus on, when describing the distribution of power in this issue-area? Those with large fishing fleets, or those possessing large armed naval forces? (How does one measure the size of fishing fleets, anyway? By number of ships? Total tonnage? Ability to take fish out of the sea?) As noted in Chapter 1, these problems may hinder our ability to construct and refine theories.

Economists have had an easier time of it, for the central concept upon which most of their models are constructed is *wealth*. Economics is concerned with the creation and distribution of wealth. Unlike power, wealth in monetized market economies can be measured quite easily. All one has to do is discover the price of something—how much does it cost? A dollar figure can be established for just about everything, allowing us to consider the value of specific items. (Of course, for assessing the economic status of a society, economic indicators are not always that precise either.) As a result of this ability to specify their central concept, economists have developed their discipline into a more precise, scientific, and mathematical field. As such, political scientists often envy the progress economists have apparently achieved in the last few decades.

At the same time, a student of political economy should be wary of the ways in which both the terms power and wealth are used. Both concepts are considerably more "slippery" (or "woolly" as Susan Strange might put it!) in reality than they are in textbooks. The economists' definition of wealth often misses elements of the total concept they are trying to grasp. The more important idea behind their notion of wealth might be that wealth is anything that enhances "quality of life." Since markets do not exist for everything (examples range from a healthy ozone layer to national defence) economists can only estimate the market value of such things.

Political economy goes beyond either political science or economics by focusing on the relationship between power and wealth. At one time, these two concepts were considered so interrelated that it would have been nearly impossible to think of studying one without the other. Many of the great thinkers of the late eighteenth and early nineteenth century (such as Adam Smith or John Stuart Mill) were known as political economists for this very reason. The separation of political economy into two distinct disciplines only began about 100 years ago. Some universities maintained departments of political economy as recently as the 1960s. This split developed after liberal economists began to construct more abstract and mathematical theories. Because the liberals discounted a role for government in the economy, they left the role of politics (and power) outside their models. Since these abstract theories seemed to work powerfully without the role of power explicitly introduced, economics was able to develop apart from questions of the creation and intentional exercise of power.[2]

The liberal background of most economists of the period when this split between politics and economics began (about a century ago) meant that they viewed the use of power to resolve disputes between individuals or states as illegitimate or even unnatural. Political scientists tended to see power and its use or abuse as a fact, and something to be studied in its own right. This showed up in international relations in the debate between idealists and realists; the genesis of realism was the belief that one should set aside one's normative goals, choosing to study the world as it exists instead.

Despite their faith in the ability of markets to allocate resources efficiently and fairly, classical liberals discovered several situations where markets did not deliver the best outcomes for society as a whole. Modern liberals recognize these situations as examples where politics should play a role in the economy.[3] Public goods constitute the first and most significant of these situations. A *public good* has certain characteristics. First is non-excludibility—we cannot exclude someone from enjoying this good. An example of this might be clean air or, better yet, a lighthouse. A lighthouse provides a service by shining a light out to sea to tell passing ships where land is. But any ship can see the lighthouse—we can't shine the light on some ships and not on others. The second characteristic of a collective good is non-rivalry, which means that one person's consumption doesn't prevent someone else's consumption. Again, using the lighthouse example, when one ship sees the lighthouse, it doesn't absorb the light, preventing other ships from seeing the lighthouse, too.

What is the result of the combination of non-rivalness and nonexcludibility? Who would build a lighthouse? If we owned a ship, we might want one. But if we built a lighthouse for our own personal use, everybody else could use it. Could we ever charge the other users? Could we even tell if people were using it? Moreover, competitors would never wish to add to their costs, so they would do their best to force the cost of the lighthouse onto us. For these reasons, private lighthouses are rarely built. Instead, someone has to force all merchants to help pay for the lighthouse. Modern liberals see this as coercion—and the only actor allowed to exercise such coercion is the government.

We can model this as an example of market failure—that is, as a mechanism for delivering this sort of good, markets typically fail. (This situation can be illustrated by the prisoners' dilemma, discussed earlier, though we should note that public goods provision and the prisoners' dilemma are not necessarily synonymous.) This is an example where rational utility-maximizing individuals pursuing their own interests fail to achieve a situation where everyone is made better off. This is a paradox for classical liberals, since freely trading individuals making rational choices arrive at a suboptimal outcome; it illustrates a market failure, where even liberals now agree the government should step in.

A second major exception to liberalism's faith in markets comes from *externalities*. Externalities are situations where the market fails to cover the entire set of costs and benefits associated with a particular transaction. As by-products of a market transaction, externalities can be either positive or negative. Pollution is a good example of a negative externality.[4] A consumer orders something from a producer; the producer's factory makes the item in question, but in the process spews out smoke and soot that lands on the surrounding neighbourhoods. Everybody else in the neighbourhood is made worse off by the pollution. The damage to the neighbourhood exceeds the cost to the factory of placing air filters on its smokestacks. From the point of view of society as a whole, it would be worth it to put the air filters on. From the point of view of the factory operator, however, the injuries caused by the pollution are not his or her problem, whereas the cost of the filters would be—so the factory chooses not to put the filters on. The recourse for everyone else is to get the government to force the factory to make the smokestack improvements. Again, modern liberals identify here a role for government. Applying such thinking to the international system is difficult, however, since there is no legitimate authority above sovereign states. This is why modern liberals may see no easy solution to certain problems—good examples are acid rain or depletion of the ozone layer.

An economist, Ronald Coase, developed the *Coase Theorem* to describe possible situations where problems with externalities can be overcome in the absence of any government, thus shedding insight into typical situations we might find in international relations. The Coase Theorem states that if (1) there is a legal framework to establish liabilities, (2) there is perfect information (and also everyone understands their own preferences), and (3) there are zero negotiating costs (i.e., it doesn't cost anybody anything to sit down and engage in talks), externalities can be resolved through deal-making. Of course, in reality there are always some costs to negotiating, and again in the international economy there is no overarching government that can clearly establish liabilities in a firm way. With perfect information unattainable, we may think this theorem is interesting only as an abstract exercise. However, it poses some powerful insights into ways in which cooperation may be enhanced when we wish to reduce externalities.

Robert Keohane has employed the Coase Theorem in just this way. Keohane used Coase's insights to explain why international economic relations are governed by international regimes.[5] As noted earlier, international regimes are defined as principles, rules, norms of behaviour, and procedures around which actors' expectations converge.[6] This definition is designed to convey a complex idea. The easiest way to understand our thinking on regimes is to think of them as agreed-upon types or standards of behaviour. There are proper and improper ways to act. There may or may not be any penalties for acting improperly, but there are usually benefits for acting properly. Regimes exist to reduce negotiating costs, to provide stability, and to assess blame or responsibility—in short, they help to approximate the conditions Coase identified that would help resolve externalities in the absence of government. Regimes are the main way we conceptualize systems of interaction at the international level and are not the exclusive property of any one approach.

The third and final major exception found in classical liberalism lies in situations where the market is characterized by *monopoly* or *oligopoly*. Most of liberalism's conclusions on the benefits of markets arise only when there is perfect competition. Whenever there is oligopoly (where several large producers dominate the market) or monopoly (where one producer controls the market), the market may produce socially suboptimal outcomes. Monopolists and oligopolists are able to maximize their profits and hurt everyone else. They are able to make themselves better off at everyone else's expense. Since the market does not guarantee a beneficial outcome for everyone, modern liberals once again admit a role for government, in this instance, to regulate the economy.

So to summarize, classical liberals circumscribed the role for politics, because they believed rational, self-interested actors given freedom of choice and action would pursue their interests in ways benefiting all. Coercion was not only not needed, but harmful, since those being coerced were clearly not meeting their own interests. They failed to anticipate situations where everyone could not simultaneously make themselves better off through exchange. Modern political economists have discovered at least three examples where the market is unable to guarantee socially optimal results; these three examples are points of debate in political economics, since they are the most significant instances where modern liberals see a role for politics.[7] Liberalism (and neo-classical economics) still has a highly normative character to it: it prefers to rely on markets to allocate resources and wealth, and believe that in general politics just messes things up. Only in the cases where the market has failed is there a plausible excuse for government to get involved in the economy.

This normative tendency in economics has made it distinct from political science. The distinctions have become deeply ingrained in each of the fields. These differences may have been temporarily reduced in the 1930s and 1940s, but they resurfaced in the 1950s and 1960s. It was precisely in the post-World War II period that economic models became much more mathematical and sophisticated. These new models showed how well the economy could work when power was not playing a disruptive role.

In international affairs after World War II, the establishment of the international economy on liberal principles reinforced this division of studies. Because their models gave reasonably good answers to their most important questions, and their predictions were useful, the economists didn't need to consider what political scientists had to say about the role of power. Trade and economic development could be fostered in the absence of political interference. With the benefit of hindsight, we can recognize the importance of politics for the success of the neo-classical economists' models. Power played a vital role in the workings of the international economy, but this role was largely masked. The postwar liberal trading system worked well because the U.S. was willing to provide a particular set of political structures, and U.S. allies largely accepted this situation. As soon as disputes arose over how the liberal international economic system should be managed in the early 1970s, the links between politics and economics were unmasked. The political and economic turmoil of that decade illustrated very poignantly that political power could be used to manipulate markets, that markets would not necessarily function well in the absence of political order, and that market power could be translated into political ends. Scholars and policy-makers, realizing that the separation between international economics and international politics had been artificial, regained an interest in studying political economy in international relations.

At roughly the same time, political scientists had begun to emulate many of the analytical techniques employed by economists. In what has been referred to as the Behavioural Revolution, which swept through several of the social sciences in the 1960s, social scientists began to seek the objective bases of human behaviour. Behavioural models in political science were constructed on similar assumptions and theoretical formulations as models created in other social sciences. They began to look and sound much like the models used in economics as the logic employed in both disciplines became very similar. When the empirical problems of the early 1970s occurred, and people responded by returning their attention to the links between economics and political science, the participants in the two fields were in a better position to at least consult with each other. The similarities in analytical techniques allowed for political economy to re-emerge as a significant field of study in a very short time.

One of the political scientists destined to lead this reemergence of international political economy in the 1970s was Robert Gilpin, who identified the central subject of study in international political economy as the tension between the state and markets. He discusses states as territorial units, requiring loyalty, with exclusivity, and having a monopoly on the legitimate use of force. Markets, on the other hand, stress functional integration, contractual relationships, and expanding interdependence between buyers and sellers. On many separate points, states have desires and powers that create friction with the operation of markets. The tension Gilpin describes can only be addressed through political economic analysis. It results from the collision of the processes of wealth-creation and the exercise of power and highlights the cracks left by the separation of political science and economics.

The Substantive Issue-Areas Ahead:
Trade, Investment, and Monetary Relations

International political economy covers a wide range of topics.[8] These different issue-areas can be organized in many different fashions. Since this is an introductory text, we will use the broadest definitions and examine only three main areas: international trade, international investments, and international monetary relations. Trade is obviously very important—when one considers the politics associated with the international economy, trade disputes immediately come to mind. Trade qualifies as a topic in this field precisely because it is a method for creating and distributing wealth. Since states control levels of trade, and periods of relatively free trade have been quite rare, it is safe to assume that the interaction of states has shaped the characteristics of trade over time.

International investments also affect the levels of economic activity within countries. Jobs are created or lost and levels of industrial or agricultural output rise or fall as a result of decisions concerning where to locate production. It is worth noting that in recent years international capital flows have increased in value to the point that they involve much more wealth than trade flows.

Monetary relations are also an area where it should be quite clear that political decisions can have enormous repercussions on the ways in which wealth is created and distributed—both within and among countries. Changing a country's exchange rate will have immediate ramifications for trade by adjusting the relative prices of goods coming and going from the countries in question. Trade may be unnecessary if international investments mean products are produced locally rather than being produced overseas and shipped across borders. Shifts in exchange rates may make it profitable to invest capital in another country—or they could possibly wipe out any profits earned from those investments in a flash.

Thus, not only are these three issue-areas quite broad, what occurs in one will have consequences for activities in the other two. Taken together, they should give students the depth and the breadth of understanding necessary to engage in further study in international political economy.

Notes

1. Jeff Frieden, *Debt, Development, and Democracy: Modern Political Economy and Latin America, 1965-1985* (Princeton, NJ: Princeton University Press, 1991) 16. On the typical methods, this applies for those theoretical approaches which assume actors to behave rationally.

2. Alfred Marshall is a good example of someone who led this split. Marshall argued that the workings of the economy were based upon natural laws. He argued that these natural laws could be discerned through logic and observation, but, more importantly, they worked despite the intentions of individuals. Results came from the workings of the market. With this kind of approach, you could easily build models and theories which abstracted away from the acts of irrational human beings. This allowed economists to conceptualize the economy as a separate entity. There were no necessary roles for the government or power. Instead, the government becomes something exogenous, a force outside the economy, which merely steps in occasionally, usually upsetting the predictions of the nice models the economists constructed.

3. We should remember that classical liberals' assumptions drove them to expect that rational individuals could attain their interests through some sort of trading.

4. One can easily think of some sort of positive externality as well. For instance, when a new expensive building is constructed, it may change the way others regard neighbouring property. In this instance, the by-product has driven up the value of others' assets.

5. See Robert Keohane, "The Demand for International Regimes," *International Regimes*, ed. Stephen Krasner (Ithaca, NY: Cornell University Press, 1983) 141-71.

6. See Stephen Krasner (ed.), *International Regimes* (Ithaca, NY: Cornell University Press, 1983).

7. Most liberals have always seen a role for other services by the state: defining and enforcing property rights or providing for defence from outside aggression, for instance. The latter can be seen as a collective good, of course.

8. Some of the questions posed in the introduction of one textbook include: How do governments and domestic interests affect foreign economic policy? How do we understand the different ways political leaders and institutions are entangled in managing and conditioning market outcomes? What is the role of political power and international institutions in shaping the terms of trade flows and capital transfers? How does a nation's economic growth and technological prowess affect its international influence? See Thomas D. Lairson and David Skidmore, *International Political Economy: The Struggle for Power and Wealth* (New York, NY: Harcourt Brace, 1993) 9.

Additional References

Baldwin, David. "Power Analysis and World Politics: New Trends versus Old Tendencies." *World Politics* 31 (January 1979): 161-94.

Blau, Peter M. *Exchange and Power in Social Life.* New York, NY: John Wiley and Sons, 1964.

Dahl, Robert. "The Concept of Power." *Behavioral Science* 2,3 (July 1957): 201-15.

Jönssen, Christer. "Bargaining Power: Notes on an Elusive Concept." *Cooperation and Conflict* 16 (December 1981): 249-57.

Knorr, Klaus. *The Power of Nations: The Political Economy of International Relations.* New York, NY: Basic Books, 1975.

Lasswell, Harold, and Abraham Kaplan. *Power and Society.* New Haven, CT: Yale University Press, 1950.

March, James G. "An Introduction to the Theory and Measurement of Influence." *American Political Science Review* 49 (June 1955): 431-51.

Simon, Herbert A. "Notes on the Observation and Measurement of Political Power." *Journal of Politics* 15 (November 1953): 500-16.

CHAPTER 7
The Politics of Trade

The politics of trade are characterized by questions about distribution. Which countries benefit from trade? Does it matter whether one country benefits more than another? Who gains from trade within each country? Who is hurt by trade? By answering these questions concerning the consequences of trade, we can gain a better grasp of the related political issues. How do states determine their trade policies? Which matters more in trade policy decisions: domestic pressures, the international environment, or ideas? We shall begin with some fundamental questions. Perhaps the most basic is: why does trade take place?

The Reasons for Conducting Trade: Comparative Advantage

Economists use the concept of *comparative advantage* to explain why trade takes place, as well as to make the claim that free trade is mutually beneficial. This argument was initially described by Adam Smith in 1776. A short time later David Ricardo expanded upon the idea and developed a more elaborate mathematical and graphical interpretation.[1] Comparative advantage refers to an actor's ability to produce a good or service more efficiently than another actor's. Since we are interested in explaining international trade, the actors in this case are countries. If one country can manufacture paper more efficiently (that is, use fewer inputs such as capital and labour to produce a unit of paper, therefore producing paper more cheaply), it can shift all its resources into producing that good. If each country does the same, more of each good gets produced at a lower cost in terms of inputs consumed. There are more goods to go around (via trade), overall consumption increases, and everyone benefits. Thus trade, as explained by economists, involves *specialization* and a *division of labour*. The great advantages, according to economists, occur through improved efficiency and the production of a greater volume of goods and services. (Some people today are questioning whether greater production is necessarily beneficial, however.)

Why do peoples from different countries engage in international trade? Consider what would happen in its absence. A country's consumption would be restricted to those items that could be produced within its own borders. (This is a situation of *autarky*.) Take a simple mix of production, with only

Figure 7.1: The Production Possibility Frontier

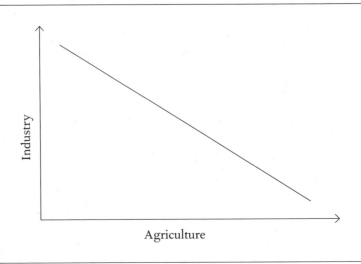

two goods: industrial and agricultural products. Cloth and wine were what Ricardo used in the first explanation of comparative advantage, reflecting two products involved in an ongoing trade dispute. The country could devote all its resources to the production of one good, to the production of the other, or to some mix of the two. Say country A produced only industrial goods up to 300 units. If it produced only agriculture, it could produce 150 units. Every unit of agriculture produced takes the same inputs as it takes for every two units of industrial goods. The country has a limit to how much it can produce in a limited time period, known as the *Production Possibility Frontier* (PPF). And these two points are the endpoints of the line representing this limit.

At some given rate, production can be shifted among these two products. This is referred to as the *rate of transformation*.[2] Following Ricardo's early example, we represent the PPF as a straight line. In reality, most PPFs are convex, since a point is typically reached where it becomes hard to combine inputs to increase the production of only one good. This same line also establishes the price for each good. It would take a reduction in output of agricultural goods of 30 units to get enough resources to produce 15 additional units of industrial goods. In essence, it costs two units of agricultural goods to buy one unit of industrial goods in this country.

Now consider a second country. If it devoted all of its resources to producing industrial goods, it would produce 80 units; if it threw everything into the production of agriculture, it could produce 240 units. The relative price here is three units of agricultural goods per one unit of industrial output. One country is very good at producing industrial goods, the other at producing agricultural goods. This can be seen in the price differences in the two countries—Country A can sell industrial output at a higher price per unit in Country B than at home (three agricultural units rather than two). From Country B's perspective, it is possible to purchase industrial goods at a cheaper price in Country A.

If each country then specializes, the result is the maximum of production possible out of any combination of production mixes. Country A specializes in industrial production (300 units) while Country B specializes in agricultural production (240 units). Trade takes place because of the relative prices of the goods in the two countries. The notion of comparative advantage captures this sense of different prices in different countries—comparative advantage exists when one country can produce an item at a lower cost in terms of opportunities foregone than can the other country. Absolute advantage, on the other hand, exists when a country can use fewer resources to produce a product than the other country. Absolute advantage does not replace comparative advantage, in that each country still has different prices for the products domestically.

It is important to recognize the assumptions at work in the theory of comparative advantage. For instance, the results hold when one assumes each economy is at full employment and that trade is balanced. These assumptions are rarely met in the real world. Moreover, the availability and price of inputs can be altered via policy (hence the sections to be discussed below on *strategic trade policy* and infant industries).[3] And, as we shall see below, there are several important observations about today's pattern of trade that cannot be easily understood using theories of trade based on comparative advantage. Despite these qualifications, theories of trade incorporating comparative advantage remain the most widely held. They provide the jumping-off point for most other theories concerning the political economy of trade.

The Consequences of Specialization

The theory of trade based on comparative advantage recommends that countries focus their production on those goods they can produce more efficiently compared to other countries. It calls on states to produce one set of goods and trade some of them for goods whose production was foregone. Countries are supposed to count on other states to buy and sell with them.

According to critics of neo-classical economics, the division of labour born from this trade structure may have serious political and economic repercussions. The Marxists who developed the idea of the Modern World-System point to the example of the Southern Baltic region in the 1600s. As trade first began to boom in early capitalism, the regions in Eastern Europe (today's eastern Germany, Poland, Belarus, and Ukraine) specialized in the production of grain, which they exported to the Netherlands, which was more urbanized and needed to import foodstuffs. In order to have wares to exchange for grain and other foods, the Netherlands specialized in manufacturing a variety of goods such as textiles. As time went on, the Netherlands became more industrialized and wealthier. Eastern Europe, on the other hand, continued to produce grain, failed to industrialize, and did not get substantially richer. Politically, the trade had enormous consequences as well. Within Eastern Europe, trade increased the wealth of those who held the most land: the aristocrats. Trade enabled these landholders to continue to wield both economic and political power for centuries in these regions, while in the Netherlands the aristocrats declined in power and wealth as the merchant class ascended. According to the Marxists, some states enter into the international division of labour and get frozen in place; they are unable to escape the economic role in which they are initially cast. Since trade does not necessarily benefit states in the Marxist analysis, and certainly does not benefit states equally, there are important repercussions to being in one role or another. Being at the top of the international division of labour is certainly much better than being at the bottom.

Another criticism comes from the realists. According to them, states are pursuing power, not wealth. States want relative gains, not absolute gains. Realists argue that states are concerned with becoming richer than their neighbours, not just richer than they have been in the past. Put another way, each state wants more money than its neighbour, not the most money it could possibly earn. If the realists are correct, the prisoners' dilemma applies to trade as well as security. States will want their neighbours to pursue free trade while they themselves will apply protectionist policies. This allows the state pursuing protectionist policies to control the distribution of gains from trade more directly than otherwise. As with the previous example of the security dilemma, in this game there is a dominant strategy. The end result depends upon the decision each actor makers; each actor finds itself better off, regardless of the decision of the other actor, by selecting protectionism. The end result is joint protectionism, even though this joint outcome is not as satisfying as the result where both pursue free trade. As with the example of the security dilemma version of this game, the important point it illustrates is that two self-interested actors, worried about relative gains, will make the outcome less than socially optimal through their interaction. Both would be better off with free trade, but, because both cheat, the outcome is rampant protectionism.[4]

The Domestic Impact of Trade

The idea of comparative advantage, first described mathematically by Ricardo, provided the basis for further developments in our understanding of trade. Two Swedish economists, Eli Heckscher and Bertil Ohlin, developed

Figure 7.2: The Prisoners' Dilemma Applied to Trade

A'S HIERARCHY OF PREFERENCES:

highest = to follow protectionism, but have B pursue free
trade (4)

next highest = both pursue free trade (3)

low = both pursue protection (2)

lowest = pursue free trade, while B follows protectionism
(1)

B'S HIERARCHY OF PREFERENCES:

highest = to follow protectionism, but have A pursue free
trade (4)

next highest = both pursue free trade (3)

low = both pursue protection (2)

lowest = pursue free trade, while A follows
protectionism (1)

		B	
		FREE TRADE	PROTECTIONISM
A	FREE TRADE	3 , 3	1 , 4
	PROTECTIONISM	4 , 1	2 , 2

a more sophisticated model to explain why a country should specialize in the production of one good or another. The *Heckscher-Ohlin (H-O) model* has since become the foundation for most modern economic analyses of trade. Heckscher and Ohlin argued that each country can be assessed in terms of its endowments of inputs, referred to as the *factors of production*. Starting with the simplest version, they described two countries with two factors of production (capital and labour). They argued that each country would export goods which intensively use the locally most abundant factor. Imports would then be composed of the goods whose production required intensive use of the locally scarce factor of production.

The great insight in this analysis is that the prices of factors of production vary from country to country, depending on their availability. Since the prices

Important Aspects of the Heckscher-Ohlin (H-O) Model

1. A country's endowments of the factors of production determine its exports and imports.
2. The results hold when the number of factors of production or the number of goods is increased.
3. The model is an elaboration on the theory of comparative advantage.

of goods and services reflect the costs of inputs, the comparative costs of inputs will allow us to compare the prices of final goods. In a country where labour is abundant compared to capital, labour will naturally be cheaper than capital. That country will be able to produce cheaply those goods that are labour-intensive. Goods that require intensive use of the locally scarce factor, capital, will be more expensive to produce. The cheaper, labour-intensive products will be easier to sell abroad; other countries, where capital is abundant and labour is scarce, will have cheaper capital-intensive goods to exchange for the labour-intensive exports. The sources of trade can thus be found in the different attributes of countries—these attributes allow them to produce different goods with greater or lesser costs.

Using the H-O model, Wolfgang Stolper and Paul Samuelson developed a theorem in 1941 to examine the distribution of gains and losses within a country once trade takes place. While expanded trade may lead to gains for the country as a whole, the H-O model does not tell us who within the country receives the gains. To test their ideas, Stolper and Samuelson applied their argument to a real case. They argued that the relatively scarce factor of production in the U.S., labour, will lose real earnings when trade levels rise. Trade gives consumers the opportunity to import goods made intensively with labour in places where it is relatively more abundant (and therefore cheaper to use as an input). Trade has the effect of substituting for flows of the actual factors of production. In a market where labour is relatively scarce compared to capital, labour-intensive imports will bid down the returns to labour. Since U.S. labour is relatively scarce compared to capital, U.S. workers enjoy relatively high wages. Since trade substitutes for flows of the factors themselves, the U.S. is likely to import labour-intensive goods that can be produced more cheaply abroad. Bringing in such goods has an effect similar to bringing in more labour. If labour is less scarce, it will earn a lower return. Labour in the U.S., therefore, will try to prevent trade liberalization through political action. Conversely, because capital is relatively abundant in the U.S., returns to capital-intensive

---

Important Aspects of the Stolper-Samuelson Theorem

1. The holders of the scarce factor of production will oppose trade liberalization; the holders of the abundant factor of production will gain from trade expansion.
2. Trade increases gains for the country as a whole (or is neutral), but the specialization entailed redistributes income within the country.

---

sectors within this market are lower than the returns these sectors can earn from exports. Capital-intensive sectors profit from trade liberalization.

Since the Stolper-Samuelson argument assumes that labour and capital can switch from employment in one sector to employment in the other with ease and without cost, one single market will exist for each factor. This one market sets one rate of return for each factor regardless of the sector it is employed in. Stolper and Samuelson illustrated that while trade produces gains for the country overall (when compared with the situation without trade), the distribution of the gains within the country are neither neutral nor unpredictable. By changing the relative prices of the two goods involved, trade engenders a redistribution of income. In the specific case Stolper and Samuelson analyzed in 1941—labour in the U.S.—they demonstrated that increases in trade would drive the real wage down and the real return to capital up. Applying such a model, we should thus expect trade politics to be dominated by a division between the factors of production.

Ronald Rogowski employed the Stolper-Samuelson theorem in a broad analysis of the formation of political coalitions.[5] Rogowski argues that changes in the level of trade sharpen the definition of economic interests, which in turn brings new political alliances into being. Some political coalitions form to influence trade policy, but if these coalitions are enduring, they shape other policies as well. Rogowski modifies the original Stolper-Samuelson model by considering three factors of production: capital, land, and labour. Following along the same lines of logic, the relatively abundant factors will form a coalition in favour of trade liberalization, while the relatively scarce factors will seek protection. Depending on which factors share relative abundance or scarcity, Rogowski expects two broad political patterns to emerge. In one, there is class conflict (because the interests of land and capital differ from that of labour), in the other an urban-rural split (because labour and capital are divided from land).[6]

One shortcoming of the Stolper-Samuelson approach is that observable political activity concerning trade policy rarely falls completely along factor-based lines (i.e., capital versus labour in the two-factor version), as would be expected. If the Stolper-Samuelson assumptions were always accurate (which we would not expect), then the domestic politics of trade could always be modelled as class-based. Landowners, capitalists, and labour would align based on the country's relative endowments of the factors of production. We can observe such splits at times. Yet, often trade policy creates sector-based splits, where the different factors of production within one industry unite to oppose an alliance of factors drawn from another industry.[7] Rather than see all workers side on a trade dispute against all capitalists, we often observe workers in one industry aligning with their employers to face off against the capitalists and labour in another sector. Such evidence suggests that it might be more useful for political analyses to assume that the factors of production are *sector-specific*, since these could better account for industry-based political alliances.

Once again it is important to recognize that these results depend upon the assumptions theorists have made. When Stolper and Samuelson wanted to study the domestic distribution of the gains from trade, they assumed there were no costs to factors of production shifting employment. In other words, they assumed that when specialization occurs, all workers, all machinery, and all land can quit producing one good and switch to the production of another with no difficulty—and no costs. This is clearly unrealistic, though perhaps true when we consider the long run, when adjustment costs can be amortized. If we introduce barriers to adjustment into the model, we can more easily explain sector-based interests in trade. While some scholars claim one set of assumptions about the mobility of factors of production across sectors is most useful, there are just as many using the opposite set.

The most important assumptions in the H-O model itself have to do with technology. For instance, if technology does not produce constant returns to scale or if some states possess much more advanced technology than others, it is not clear that the same results hold.[8] Constant returns to scale imply that an increase in inputs of a certain percentage causes output to change by the same percentage; when this is not present, the H-O model may not hold. Moreover, a host of other factors, such as preferences or marketing can also affect trade. Most of these have been integrated into ever more sophisticated models, yet most still use the basic H-O model as their point of departure. For this text, we will focus on the simple version of the theory, but simply note that more refined and complex theories, which may also be more difficult to apply, are available.

We also note that the H-O model assumes that trade is the primary economic interaction taking place between different countries. Other options exist—if capital and labour are receiving very different returns for the same activities in different countries, trade in goods and services is one option, but movements in the factors of production themselves are also possible. Capital has traditionally been more mobile than labour, so international investment will receive more in-depth treatment in a later chapter. Increasingly, however, labour mobility has improved. The movement of people over international borders has increased in recent decades and creates numerous political and economic issues. On the other hand, the terrorist acts of September 11, 2001, have triggered increased attention on border security. Security measures have focused on people crossing borders, not goods. Thus, while trade agreements ensure the ever greater flow of goods across borders, it may become harder and harder for large numbers of people to do the same. More research in this area may soon highlight the significance of international flows of the factors of production.

Current Anomalies in the Issue-Area of Trade

When one is considering current trade relations, a number of different anomalies arise. Based on the traditional theories of international trade, we should not expect to find that the greatest volume of trade exists between the most advanced countries, yet that is the case. After all, these countries have very similar economies (all industrialized), with similar endowments of the factors of production, all characterized by similar cost structures (i.e., relatively expensive labour and relatively cheap capital). Moreover, the goods traded between these very similar economies are mostly the same sort of products. Germany, Japan, France, Britain, Canada, and the U.S. all export automobiles—to each other. This intra-industry trade can be explained in a number of ways.

First, unlike the assumptions made in most trade models, perfectly competitive markets do not exist. Some markets may approach perfect competition, but these are rare and rarer still at the international level. In fact, much international trade is conducted by multinational corporations (MNCs). Trade generated by MNCs often does not reflect a market transaction. Instead, it is the shipment of components from one branch of an MNC to another branch (e.g., a car engine from Detroit to Montreal); the price of the good isn't set by competition in markets, it is a decision made within a single corporation. The corporate headquarters may value the goods in trade as part of a strategy to reduce taxes or maximize foreign exchange flows within the firm.

Second, these trade patterns may be driven by differences in taste. Economists have trouble incorporating variations in consumers' preferences into their models. If the hot car on the U.S. market is a brand from Germany, German exports to the U.S. will likely rise. It may have nothing to do with any underlying economic forces (such as endowments of the factors of production) but might instead reflect a slick advertising campaign. Preferences have a powerful influence in economics, but are very difficult to incorporate in models.

Third, in all the various theories of trade based on comparative advantage, trade results from differences in the cost of goods. Costs are shaped by a number of causes, not simply the relative distribution of the factors of production. Economists have turned to several other sources of cost differences to explain why trade patterns are inconsistent with H-O predictions. Examples of such forces influencing production costs include a number of concepts that may be familiar to students. Economies of scale (that is, when the volume of output increases, it is possible to employ technology in ways which allow for more efficient use of inputs and thus reduce the price of the output) and learning curves in production are but two. There are many others. These may explain why patterns in trade do not fit consistently with the expectations of the H-O model.

Another major anomaly is known as the *Leontief Paradox*. Wassily Leontief, a Harvard economist, was skeptical of the H-O results. He decided to conduct an empirical analysis to see if they held for the U.S. Taking data on U.S. imports and exports (beginning in 1947), Leontief's analysis showed that the U.S. exported and imported a wide variety of goods—the mix did not clearly fit the expectations of the H-O model. Later replications of Leontief's work, using data from later years, produced similar results. The intra-industry trade mentioned above seems to play a vital role. Also, the number of factors of production in the analysis can be expanded, as we subdivide capital, labour, land, and other inputs into more discrete categories. Perhaps with a more sophisticated understanding of the range of factors of production, the Leontief Paradox would disappear.

Despite these anomalies facing the H-O model, it remains the predominant theory economists use to understand the reasons trade takes place. While these anomalies have provided clues to the creation of possible alternative explanations of trade, the H-O model (and its derivatives) continues to provide the most comprehensive and convincing explanations for the content and patterns of trade. For political scientists interested in the politics of trade, the H-O model and Stolper-Samuelson Theorem are an excellent foundation.

Strategic Trade Policy

In recent years, some economists have argued that comparative advantage is not fixed by the country's characteristics. Important assets a country can have include a skilled workforce (human capital) and other factors that can be manipulated by government policy. Moreover, if trade is driven by cost differences, if all inputs are valued by domestic markets, and if government policy can intervene in these markets, then government policy can shape the prices of inputs in such a way that the country can export a different mix of goods. By choosing a *strategic trade policy*, states hope to change the benefits from trade, either by altering the position of particular firms or by changing the relative position of their economies in the international division of labour.[9]

A common, narrow definition of strategic trade policy places the concept within industrial policy. In Krugman's initial views on the subject, the international location of economic activity was driven by a host of factors such as historical accident, economies of scale, geographic location, etc., not simply comparative advantage as narrowly laid down in the H-O model.[10] This meant that government policy was just as important for determining where things were produced as any other factor, since policy could enhance or negate many of these factors. In the words of Gilpin: "...in a highly interdependent world economy composed of oligopolistic corporations and competitive states, it is possible, at least theoretically, for the latter to initiate policies that shift profits from foreign to national corporations."[11] In this view, strategic trade policy is primarily aimed at ensuring profitable firms in key sectors.

It is not such a far step to go from such thinking to the idea that a state could manipulate the position of its economy within the international division of labour.[12] Currently, many developing countries hope to emulate the economic development of the smaller states in East Asia. South Korea, Taiwan, and Hong Kong appear to have used government policies to shift their comparative advantage away from labour-intensive production to industrial manufacturing. These countries have successfully changed the content of their exports and used their trade strategy to support their economic development. This *export-oriented industrialization* (EOI) has made these countries economic success-stories. They have gone from exporting textiles and raw materials to exporting ships, automobiles, and computers.

The economics of such policies is of interest to us, primarily because of the political questions they provoke. (We can leave the economic issues aside, for an economics course or textbook.) How do states choose such a strategy? How can we explain such a dramatic change in trade policy? When do they decide to make such a move? We will try to answer these questions and more in the chapter covering South Korea's trade policy of the early 1960s. How do such policies shape a country's interaction with others? How do such policies fit in with international regimes?

It is important to remember that many factors shape the final results reaped from employing a strategic trade policy. Just deciding to pursue EOI or a strategic trade policy is no guarantee that exports will be expanded or the economy will shift into those sectors designated as targets. These policies have worked in some cases and not in others. In the last two decades, international competition has intensified. As more countries have adopted EOI, it has been more difficult for any of them to make profits. Since the level of competition varies from sector to sector, picking the right sector to target is extremely important. There are also a host of factors beyond a country's control that can influence whether its EOI strategy will succeed. Demand in the markets of the industrialized countries may unexpectedly sag or be blocked by trade barriers, leaving no other alternative consumers; the new regional trade deals often create market opportunities for some exporters, while others will find their goods displaced. In sum, deciding to pursue a strategic trade policy will not ensure its success. Many other decisions must be made, and the policy well executed, for the state's goals to be attained.

Barriers to Trade: What are the Possible Benefits of Protectionism?

More often, government policy is aimed at providing some form of protection against foreign competition. An economist would point out the costs to society of any sort of protectionism, yet such policies remain common. The answer lies in politics. The economist would say that protectionism results from a political failure: the state has adopted a policy which does not maximize the wealth of the society as a whole. The political scientist sees the same evidence very differently: protectionism reflects a political success by someone within the society. That person or group has been able to enrich itself at someone else's expense.

Different forms of protectionism have different economic and political consequences. *Tariffs* are a tax on goods as they cross a border. The tax raises the price of the good, discouraging consumers from purchasing the import. The additional cost to consumers is captured by the government, rather than being profit for the foreign producer of the goods. (Local producers can charge higher prices of course, yet still undercut the price of the imports.) When tariffs were extremely common (as in the nineteenth century), they provided governments with an important stream of revenue. Altering tariffs can still be difficult because of the fiscal strain such a step places on the government.

Quotas are another common type of barrier to trade. A quota limits the volume of goods coming into a country in a straightforward way—it establishes a specific quantity which may be imported. Compared to a tariff, a quota has very different economic results. The quota leaves some of the local market unsatisfied by imports, and therefore local producers will be guaranteed some sales. Because the imports are made scarcer by the quota, the price of each unit tends to rise. This time, however, the high cost to consumers is translated into higher per unit profits to the foreign producer. Therefore, foreign producers do not resist quotas as vigorously as they resist tariffs.[13]

The type of protectionism most common today is the *non-tariff barrier* (NTB). These barriers come in many forms and are difficult to identify because they are usually well hidden. Since tariffs are obvious, they are easy to eliminate with treaties, NTBs are different. Governments regulate activities in many areas, such as safety, environment, health, and so on. By skillfully crafting regulations in one of these areas, the government can effectively block foreign goods from entering the market. While such practices have been the target of international negotiations for a couple of decades now, they have proliferated.

What has been Predominant: Free Trade or Protection?

Given that economists have tried to explain how beneficial trade can be for both countries involved in an exchange, one might expect that free trade has been the norm. This intuition is enhanced by the current situation, because today trade flows relatively freely among many countries. Historically, periods where free trade has reigned have been quite rare. The major economic powers pursued policies of free trade for several decades in the mid-eighteenth century, but then some began defecting from the free trade regime. World War I totally disrupted trade flows, but in the immediate years after the war a free trade regime was again established. This reconstructed trade regime was short-lived. Another free trade regime was erected after World War II, based on the General Agreement on Tariffs and Trade (GATT).[14] This regime has evolved into a new institutional arrangement—the World Trade Organization, (WTO)—and appears to have a long future. Yet, as trade has become increasingly important, it has caught the attention of more and more people. The WTO has therefore become a lightning rod for attention. In recent years, its meetings have become the focal point for protestors concerned with government policies affecting employment, the environment, and other issues. Since trade can have an influence on all, governments are being pressured to consider what policies they adopt.

What explains this coming and going of free trade? Why do some states adhere to a free trade regime while others default? These have been some of the major questions prompting analyses of past cases. The answers provide the insights guiding the design of regimes; with that information, regimes may last longer and encourage more comprehensive adherence to the rules. To reach an understanding of some of these issues, examples of each of these problems have been included among the cases in Part III. We will investigate several examples of states deciding to liberalize their trade in some dramatic fashion (Britain in 1846, France in 1861, Canada in 1985), as well as three classic examples of states defecting from an existing free trade regime (Canada in 1878, Germany in 1902, the U.S. in 1930).

The rise and fall of free trade regimes suggests several points. First, despite the strength of liberal ideology, the world has been slow to learn what economists try to teach us. People seem to forget that free trade is mutually beneficial. Second, politics is always part of the story. As we have already seen, realists argue that politics is really the determining factor in the rise and fall of free trade. In their view, free trade occurs only when there is a single powerful state that wants free trade to exist. Modern liberals (i.e., those who accept that market failures exist and that markets are not naturally self-correcting) see a role for powerful states to set up and enforce the rules necessary for a regime to operate smoothly.

The arguments used by both realists and liberals to explain the existence of free trade actually overlap in a curious way. Realists argue that free trade regimes (or in fact any regimes) are most stable and strongest when the system has a hegemonic distribution of power.[15] That single most powerful state can create a strong regime; it will choose to establish free trade because it will feed into its own strength. The resulting theory has become known as *hegemonic stability theory*, because the presence of a hegemonic power is arguably necessary for the regime to be stable.[16] True to realism, the hegemonic state pursues a policy to maximize its strength relative to other states.

Liberals see the need for a hegemonic power, but in a different way. Modern liberals realize that markets often need some sort of management; they are not always self-correcting and sometimes need to be stabilized. Only a very powerful economic actor can actually stabilize an international market. Moreover, only a large actor would have the interests to stabilize a market—that actor would have to benefit enough from the market's stable operation that it would be willing to accept the costs of stabilization.[17] True to liberalism, what the hegemonic state is doing is maximizing its own wealth—the hegemonic state is unconcerned with the relative distribution of the gains from trade in this view.

Both these arguments were developed initially to explain periods when free trade seemed to be waning rather than on the rise. Liberals such as Charles Kindleberger created this sort of argument to explain the collapse of free trade in the early 1930s. Kindleberger argued that the U.S. would have been acting in its own interest if it took measures to stabilize international markets in the early stages of the Great Depression.[18] He was thinking of the regime as a public good. If we reconsider the example of merchants in need of a lighthouse, Kindleberger was posing the regime as the object merchants needed. Only now he was arguing that if one merchant owned enough ships, it made sense for that merchant alone to pay for the lighthouse—by saving the cost of ships lost, a merchant with many ships at stake would save money by building the lighthouse. The logic was then applied to the policy issues contemporary to Kindleberger's writing: was the U.S. willing to make such sacrifices to keep

international markets stable in the 1970s? At that time, realists were just beginning to argue that in fact the trade regime was breaking down because the U.S.
was no longer enforcing the rules. Without enforcement, other states would
try to maximize their power by defecting from the regime. Both theories then
were extended backwards; if it takes a powerful state to maintain the regime,
does it take a powerful state to establish the regime in the first place?

As will be seen in several of the cases, it isn't clear which of these two
versions of hegemonic stability theory is more persuasive—liberal or realist.
In some of the historical applications, theorists often blend the two arguments
together in a somewhat inconsistent manner.[19] Marxists will always mix
together the economic and political arguments to form theories about the
growth of the modern world-system; for Marxists the economic and political
sides are always inseparable. Institutionalists and constructivists will offer
totally different arguments for the development and evolution of trade
regimes.

Summary: Questions to be Explored in the Cases

For our purposes, two important questions remain. For rival paradigms we
ask, "What causes the trade regime to change?" The answers we find will help
us understand the pressures working to support or to undermine the current
trade regime. For theories drawn from the different levels of analysis, we ask,
"Why do states rapidly shift their trade policy in one direction or another?"
The answers to this question will prove helpful for anticipating the behaviour
of states that are currently members of the WTO or even those states that
have elected to stand outside the regime. Together, the answers to these two
questions should provide insight into the future of trade relations in the coming decades.

Notes

1. Adam Smith, *The Wealth of Nations* (1776; Oxford: Clarendon Press, 1976;
David Ricardo, *Principles of Political Economy and Taxation* (1817; London: Dent,
1965).

2. This is merely the slope of the PPF curve.

3. Stephen D. Cohen, Joel R. Paul, and Robert A. Blecker, *Fundamentals of U.S.
Foreign Trade Policy* (Boulder, CO: Westview, 1996) 59-60.

4. Robert Axelrod has developed an argument explaining how this type of outcome
can be broken. See Robert Axelrod, *The Evolution of Cooperation* (New York, NY:
Basic Books, 1984).

5. Ronald Rogowski, *Commerce and Coalitions* (Princeton, NJ: Princeton University
Press, 1989).

6. Rogowski 4-16.

7. See the research of Stephen Magee, "Three Simple Tests of the Stolper-Samuelson Theorem," *Issues in International Economics*, ed. P. Oppenheimer (London: Oriel Press, 1978) 138-53; and Stephen Magee, "The Political Economy of Protectionism: Comment," *Import Competition and Response*, ed. J.N. Bhagwati (Chicago, IL: University of Chicago Press, 1982).

8. Cohen, Paul, and Blecker 61.

9. For a brief discussion of such policies, see Richard G. Harris "The New Protectionism Revisited," *Canadian Journal of Economics* 22,4 (November 1989): 751-78. For more in depth information, see Paul R. Krugman (ed.), *Strategic Trade Policy and the New International Economics* (Cambridge, MA: MIT Press, 1986). Also, for a review of the literature on the subject, see J. David Richardson, "The Political Economy of Strategic Trade Policy," *International Organization* 44,1 (Winter 1990): 107-35.

10. Krugman.

11. Robert Gilpin, *The Political Economy of International Relations* (Princeton, NJ: Princeton University Press, 1987).

12. As this statement makes clear, I see a close relationship between strategic trade policy and more general theories elaborating how states can develop policies to use trade for economic ends.

13. See Richard G. Harris, "Why Voluntary Export Restraints are 'Voluntary,'" *Canadian Journal of Economics* 18,4 (November 1985): 799-809; and Kent Jones, "The Political Economy of VER Agreements," *Kyklos* 37,1 (1984): 82-101.

14. For an overview of GATT's existence, see Jock A. Finlayson and Mark W. Zacher, "The GATT and the Regulation of Trade Barriers: Regime Dynamics and Functions," *International Organization* 35,4 (Autumn 1981): 561-602.

15. Stephen D. Krasner, "State Power and the Structure of International Trade," *World Politics* 28,3 (April 1976): 317-47; Robert Gilpin, *U.S. Power and the Multinational Corporation* (New York, NY: Basic Books, 1975).

16. This phrase was actually coined by Robert Keohane, in "The Theory of Hegemonic Stability and Changes in International Economic Regimes, 1967-1977," *Changes in the International System*, ed. Ole R. Holsti, R.M. Siverson, and Alexander L. George (Boulder, CO: Westview Press, 1980) 131-62.

17. Charles P. Kindleberger, *The World in Depression, 1929-1939* (Berkeley, CA: University of California Press, 1973).

18. These stabilizing functions are: (1) to act as a market for exports which otherwise will not find a market, (2) exchange rate management, (3) to engage in counter-cyclical lending, (4) coordination of macroeconomic policies, and (5) to assume the responsibility of international lender of last resort. See Charles Kindelberger, "The Functioning of Financial Centers: Britain in the Nineteenth Century, the United States since 1945," *Princeton Essays in International Finance* 157 (September 1985): 7-18.

19. Kindleberger's later writings illustrate some of the aspects of the overlap between the two paradigms, and his attempts to separate out such thinking. See Charles Kindelberger, "International Public Goods without International Government," *American Economic Review* 76,1 (March 1986): 1-13; and Charles Kindelberger, "Dominance and Leadership in the International Economy," *International Studies Quarterly* 25,2 (June 1981): 242-54.

Additional References

McKeown, Timothy J. "Firms and Tariff Regime Change: Explaining the Demand for Protection." *World Politics* 36,2 (January 1984): 215-33.

Milner, Helen. "Trading Place: Industries for Free Trade." *World Politics* 40,3 (April 1988): 350-76.

Pincus, Jonathon J. "Pressure Groups and the Pattern of Tariffs." *Journal of Political Economy* 83,4 (August 1975): 757-78.

Rogowski, Ronald. *Commerce and Coalitions*. Princeton, NJ: Princeton University Press, 1989.

CHAPTER 8

The Politics of International Monetary Relations

International monetary issues have traditionally been considered secondary to trade issues. Trade has long been treated as the most important form of economic intercourse, though this may have changed in recent years. As a consequence, political scientists have shown greater attention to monetary issues in the last decade. Moreover, some of the best examples of the ways in which regimes constrain states and influence how states conduct economic intercourse come in the issue-area of monetary relations.

The Characteristics of Monetary Orders

Money performs three essential functions. It serves as a measure (or unit of value), as a medium of exchange (useful for intermediation), and as a store of value (or credit). Money is critical for the successful functioning of any complex market, for it facilitates transactions. Without money, trade could take place only via barter. This would require the complicated process of matching up buyers and sellers who each hold what the other wants—what economists refer to as establishing the "double coincidence of wants."[1]

If international markets are to work via market exchange, then some form of international money is needed. In this sense, the supply of money shares some of the features of a collective good. Exclusion may well be possible, but would always be difficult. Non-rival consumption is clearly an essential characteristic of money; the more widely a money is used, the more effective it usually is.[2] Similar to so many other public goods, we typically find the government provides and manages the supply of money in the domestic economy.[3] Since the international political economy lacks an overarching political authority, the international political economy also lacks a true international currency.

In studying international monetary regimes, we use three main characteristics to describe and compare them: *exchange rates*, the nature of *reserves*, and the *convertibility* of capital (the nature of the links between capital markets).[4] The first characteristic refers to the rules governing how national currencies are traded. Exchange rates themselves are only the prices of one currency in terms of other currencies. The central question in terms of regime characteristics is whether exchange rates are fixed, freely floating, or somewhere in between. On one end of the spectrum, exchange rates can be fixed; that is, political authorities set the rates at which currencies are exchanged. On a day-to-day basis, the rates are supposed to remain unchanged. In a regime with floating exchange rates, on the other hand, markets are left to determine the rates at which currencies are traded. Changes in the supply of and demand for the currency cause the rates to change. Obviously, in such a situation governments can still use policy to shift supply and/or demand for currencies, so in a way political authorities may still be able to set exchange rates.

Reserves can vary widely in nature yet still serve their primary purpose. Historically, there have been two main types of monetary reserves. First is a commodity. Most often in the past this commodity has been a precious metal such as gold or silver, which can serve as a monetary reserve because they have some high intrinsic value recognized internationally. In short, these goods are extremely desirable in their own right. The second likely form of reserve asset is a national currency. A national currency can become internationally attractive because it is believed to have value and is widely accepted. This normally requires that foreign holders of this currency have access to the issuing country's domestic market (i.e., the issuing country should practise relatively free trade). A third possible form of reserves is a money created by an international agency, though moneys issued by international organizations have historically played only minor reserve roles.

The third monetary regime characteristic on our list involves the nature of controls on financial connections and/or capital flows. This characteristic refers to how open or closed the international financial system is. It also indicates how well national financial markets are integrated. This has significant ramifications not only for the amount of international investment that can take place (see the next chapter), but also for the financing of trade and other economic activities.

According to W.M. Scammell, a successful international monetary system must have four integrated parts. These parallel the discussion above. Scammell identifies the need for a medium of international exchange, adequate ties between nations' financial institutions (in order to utilize the medium of exchange), and some method (or methods) of managing balance of payments adjustments (i.e., some agreed-upon technique for paying for goods and services traded internationally). He added a fourth requirement to this list, which captures some of the issues involved with hegemonic stability theory: there must be management of the international monetary system.[5] Scammell was applying some of the modern liberal views on solutions to collective action problems: there is a clear role for a political authority to play.

Exchange Rates: Fixed versus Floating

Exchange rates are easy to understand if you think about them in terms of supply and demand. They are simply the price of one currency in terms of another. In decades past, the exchange rate between the deutschmark (DM) and the U.S. dollar was 2 DM to $1. In other words, it took two DM to buy one U.S. dollar—or to put it another way, 50 cents would buy one DM. By the 1990s, however, the exchange rate between these two currencies was around 1.5 DM to $1. Changes in the exchange rate affect the prices of goods and services in each country. If a currency rises in value against another, the same amount of the first currency will buy more of the second than before. Assuming domestic prices in each country do not change, people from the first country can take their money, purchase a greater volume of the second currency than before, and therefore purchase more goods in the second country than they could prior to the shift in the exchange rate.

To understand why the value of a currency changes over time, think of the price of a currency in its own terms. The price for money is established in interest rates, for interest is the price incurred when borrowing money. When we want to switch money from one currency to another, we must pay a price for the money we're buying. The price will be determined by the interaction of supply and demand. If there is a lot of the currency available, the price will fall; if the currency is scarce, the price will rise. The same logic applies to domestic monetary policy and interest rates; the less money available, the higher the price (i.e., the interest rate goes up).

The supply and demand for a country's currency can be driven by numerous factors. The size and nature of a country's economy shapes the supply of a currency. A country such as the U.S. has a large economy and therefore large amounts of currency in circulation when compared to almost any other economy, but especially when compared to one with a lower level of economic development. Also, the demand for a country's currency depends on the type of demands there are for making payments to that country to purchase its goods and services. Transactions for goods and services or involving international investments therefore influence the exchange rate.

Exchange rates are also the target of government activities. Monetary policy refers to how government institutions manipulate the supply of a currency to make the interest rate rise or fall, thus making it easier or more difficult to borrow money. The government hopes to influence economic activity in this way. Different governments have different institutional arrangements, which give them different policy instruments for adjusting the money supply. Along the same principles, the government can try to stimulate exports or imports by changing the relative price of its currency. Again, it does so by shifting supply.

In addition, it can shift supply by selling more of its currency at cheap prices, thus driving the price down on exchange markets. Or it can force the rate up by purchasing much of its own currency using foreign currencies, thus bidding the price higher and reducing the supply. These are known as exchange rate interventions. Such a policy is often disguised as a floating exchange rate, and hence is referred to as a *dirty float*. As we shall see in some of the cases, the effectiveness of such policies has varied enormously in the past.[6]

The exchange rate affects exports and imports in a simple and direct fashion—when the price of the currency is changed, the prices of the goods within the economy are changed. This can make products or services appear cheaper or more expensive, thereby changing the competitiveness of goods in trade. A higher value on the currency makes all the goods in the country look relatively more expensive, thus making it harder to export and more difficult to compete against imports. Conversely, a lower valuation of the currency has the effect of making all goods within the country look cheaper, thus making it easier to export and easier to compete against imports. Monetary policy can interact with or substitute for trade policy. One of the tricks to understanding foreign economic policies is grasping how trade balances, monetary policy, and exchange rate actions intertwine.[7]

When governments choose an exchange rate policy, they must consider the full implications of the policy. As Robert Mundell and Marcus Fleming described, policies on exchange rates, openness of the capital market, and domestic monetary policy autonomy are intertwined. If a country desires true autonomy in setting domestic monetary policy, it must insulate itself from the international market. Otherwise, whenever it changes domestic interest rates, it will also affect the relative value of its money *vis-à-vis* other currencies. The *Mundell-Fleming conditions*, as they are known, describe how policy makers' preferences on two dimensions of monetary policy necessarily dictate the decision in the third; decisions on exchange rates, international capital flows and domestic policy autonomy simply cannot be separated. In the current era, most countries want access to international capital markets, but if they also want a stable exchange rate, domestic policy must then support that valuation of the currency, and cannot be set to hit other targets (such as full employment). The Mundell-Fleming conditions are therefore a useful way to discuss the acceptance of globalizing economic pressures and opportunities in monetary affairs.

The Balance of Payments

The *balance of payments* simply refers to a nation's accounting records. It is important to understand what goes into the different accounts in order to appreciate what these terms mean. Often there is confusion over the relationships between different terms. Like any balance sheet in accounting, there are credits and debits, which give a balance (positive or negative). In this case, the effort is to establish how much wealth is coming into the country or going out.

The flows of goods, services, and funds are broken down into various sub-categories. On the broadest level, these are divided between the *current account* and the *capital account*. Net changes in a country's claims on foreigners are handled in the current account, while the capital account largely records the borrowing, selling, or purchasing of assets. Within the current account, one category counts merchandise exports and imports (the tangible goods shipped into and out of the country); another is made up of exports and imports of services (intangible economic exchanges, such as insurance, banking, consulting, and so on). These two categories are added together to find a gain or loss, and this is known as the balance of trade. While the balance of trade seems to measure all international intercourse both in goods and services, it in fact does not include many other economic transactions. The balance of trade is therefore only a part of the balance of payments.

Other components of the balance of payments can be sizable. Separate categories take investment income and payments into account by tracking the monies sent to other countries to pay off debts or which the country has earned by lending abroad. Another category covers government exports and imports, plus any changes of funds caused by foreign aid flows. Joining these two accounts with the balance of trade produces the balance of the current account. Note that a country with a negative balance in trade could still have a positive balance on its current account if it is earning income from foreign investments or through the government's international transactions. And since we are usually more interested in overall payments—how much money is coming in or going out—we are not always interested in the balance of trade alone.

The balance on the current account still does not cover all international economic transactions. While it captures income generated by international investments, that income only represents the payments of interest on loans or dividends on stock—it is the earnings from international investments, but does not include the investment itself. Thus another account, the capital account, tracks the actual transfers of capital when an investment is placed in another country or received from another country. This account often breaks investments down into other subcategories, such as long term or short term. Beware the accounting principles used in the capital account. Exports of capital count as a debit and imports as a credit. This is confusing, since any investment placed in another country is actually an asset which will produce earnings, while any investment entering from abroad might have to be repaid.

Figure 8.1: The Balance of Payments

CURRENT ACCOUNT:

  net merchandise (or visible) trade
+ net services (or invisible trade)
_____
= *balance of trade*

  balance of trade
+ net factor payments
_____
= *balance on current account*

CAPITAL ACCOUNT:

  net direct investment
+ net portfolio investments
_____
= *balance on long-term capital*

  balance on long-term capital
+ net short-term capital
_____
= *balance on capital account*

  balance on current account
+ balance on capital account
+ statistical discrepancy
+ changes in official reserves
_____
= *total balance*

This category, however, is intended to keep track of capital flowing in or out of the country. The balance on capital account is clearly important for understanding how states view the international investment regime.

The next category within the capital account is the measure of official reserves. This account has been more important in some eras than in others, as we will see in some of the historical cases. It is important to remember that changes in the official reserves represent attempts to pay for things purchased from abroad or deposits made with money earned from international dealings. When funds are transferred from one currency to another, the central bank has to accommodate these changes and thus alter its own holdings of currency. Today there isn't much concern with this measure, though it can be an important factor for countries that have chosen to fix their currencies to others in some fashion. For such countries, reserves are necessary for intervening in international currency markets.

The last category on the balance of payments is an error term, representing statistical discrepancies. This ensures a real balance at the bottom of the sheet, since it is a common accounting practice to have all transactions sum to zero. Perhaps the most important point to remember is that the balance of trade is not the only measure of success in international economic transactions. As we shall see, some countries have been able to run balance of trade deficits for long periods of time, yet have succeeded economically because they are earning money on their international investments. The political ramifications of these actions are extremely interesting, as we shall see, especially in the area of international monetary relations.

Balance of Payments Adjustment

People are usually interested in the balance of payments because they want to know how much their country is earning from or owes to its trading partners. It is important to remember that most economists now agree that the balance of payments is shaped by an array of economic forces, ranging from trade policy to domestic savings rates; international forces are only part of the picture. *Balance of payments adjustment* refers to the way in which states settle their bills. The methods for making such payments have varied from one monetary regime to the next. When a country has a balance of payments deficit, it is in effect taking in more in value than it is exporting. The extra value in imports has to be paid for in one way or another. One method is for the deficit country to make up the difference it owes by paying out monetary reserves. Another is to allow the deficit country time to increase its exports (or decrease its imports) in such a way that it can pay off its deficit. This can be helped along by rules or norms found in international regimes or can be done completely through domestic policy adjustments.

When a country pays out monetary reserves to adjust its balance of payments, there are numerous economic ramifications. First, no country has an infinite supply of reserves, and in fact most have very limited resources. Therefore, something else has to be done to restrain imports and enhance exports if reserves are not to be completely drained. But changes in reserves can actually catalyze the necessary economic policy changes. Under a set of rules where there is a fixed ratio between reserves and money in circulation, whenever reserves drop, the money supply should shrink. When the money supply contracts, prices drop, because there will be less money chasing the same amount of goods. This price drop makes the country's exports look cheaper, and therefore the country should sell more; imports will look relatively more expensive, and therefore the country will buy less of them. If the country has a balance of payments surplus rather than a deficit, and adjustment occurs through reserve changes, then the same process is invoked, but in the opposite direction. Reserves expand, which increases the money supply. Inflation results, because now more money is chasing the same amount of goods. Inflation makes imports look cheaper, and exports look more expensive. Whether in surplus or deficit, the change in monetary reserves will naturally stimulate the adjustment process.

Balance of payments adjustment that occurs through changes in monetary reserves has numerous economic effects. For example, adjustment through deflation usually means an economic downturn, including higher unemployment. To avoid such effects, other systems of adjustment have been tried. Under the Bretton Woods monetary regime, adjustment from a balance of payments deficit was supposed to be eased. Members of the regime deposited funds with an agency, the International Monetary Fund (IMF). The IMF, in turn, loaned funds to countries which developed a deficit, so that these countries could make their payments in the short run while using other policies to alter the flow of imports and exports. Whether this regime has functioned well depends on one's perspective. Ultimately, trade flows have to be changed to achieve balance of payments adjustment. The ease with which such changes occur depends on a variety of actors and the other characteristics of the monetary regime.

The Distribution of Gains from Undertaking the Key Currency Role

A national currency that carries out the function of an international money is often referred to as a *key currency*.[8] Establishing an international money provides a valuable service to other members of the international economy, but it will also allow the leading state itself to garner specific advantages.[9] Because of the currency's dominance in finance, the state's control over the currency becomes a potential bargaining weapon *vis-à-vis* other states. Invisible earnings may be increased, because others utilize the nation's services more than they would otherwise; financial actors with a base in the leading country have an edge in that they have greater access to the source of the international currency. Finally, practice has shown that the state whose currency is accepted as an international money has the option of allowing a deficit in its balance of payments, since working balances of its currency may accumulate abroad without any negative ramifications in the short run.[10]

Disadvantages to this specific form of leadership may emerge as well, making an overhang very possible.[11] An overhang occurs when foreign holdings of a currency on a fixed exchange rate expand beyond the value of reserves backing that currency (i.e., there are more claims on the reserves than there should be). If the national currency is the numeraire of the system (i.e., the standard of value for other national currencies), devaluation is not an option for resolving a balance of payments deficit. Other macroeconomic policies may then be slanted towards external targets rather than towards domestic goals. Finally, policies designed to maintain a country's money in the key currency role may support certain sectors and foster international investment, but conflict with balance of payments policies and policies benefiting the competitiveness of other sectors.[12]

The Needs of the International Economy: Balancing Confidence and Liquidity

The reason Scammell argued that the international monetary system required some sort of management came from observations of domestic monetary systems. In the domestic economy, governments have established agencies, usually a central bank, to manage money supplies. The difficult task confronting such authorities is the balancing of the twin targets of *confidence* and *liquidity*. The three primary functions of money create conflicting pressures, for each suggests that a different amount of money should be introduced into circulation. The less money in circulation, the better it can serve as a store of value. If too much money is introduced into the economy, inflation results; inflation erodes the value of the currency. When money is relatively scarce, people have confidence that the money will maintain its value. To serve as a medium of exchange, there has to be enough of the currency in circulation that it supports many transactions. The more money in circulation (or liquidity), the better it can serve as a medium of exchange.

In the domestic economy, central banks have developed a number of policy instruments enabling them to manage this balancing act. These instruments, however, are predicated on certain powers a government can exercise in the domestic realm. For instance, in most countries the domestic currency is legal tender. This means that merchants must accept the currency as payment—they cannot refuse it. Obviously, the same sort of mechanisms cannot be utilized in the international political economy, for there is no ultimate political authority. In the management of an international currency, domestic policies must be managed in such a way that, in combination with international policies, foreigners can get enough of the money to undertake transactions but also have some assurance that their money will continue to retain its value over time.

For countries which decide to develop their currencies into the role of an international money, or which simply find that their currencies fall into this role, monetary authorities inevitably confront more complicated choices. The political agencies managing the national currency face two possibly competing sets of targets—a certain level of confidence and liquidity might be correct for the international economy but inappropriate for the national economy, and vice-versa. How do national authorities handle such situations? How do national monetary policies affect other economic policies? Those questions will be addressed in two of our cases, where a national currency enjoyed the key currency role.

Hegemonic Stability Theory and Monetary Regimes

The idea that some countries might desire to manage the international economy returns us to the mixture of liberal and realist debates on hegemonic stability theory. Hegemonic stability theory argues that, in the absence of an overarching international political authority, the collective goods which support liberal international economic relations will exist only when a state with the requisite capabilities decides to provide them. The establishment of an international money therefore is one of the classic issues hegemonic stability theory was intended to explain. If the hegemonic leader is trying to create and maintain an open economic subsystem, then it is necessary to establish a monetary regime where a stable international money is accepted throughout that subsystem. The more widely the international money is accepted, the more widely markets are integrated. In the absence of a single widely accepted currency, transaction costs rise and can become a formidable barrier to economic intercourse.[13]

Proponents of realism argue that monetary regimes require some sort of management by a hegemonic power but also that the regime's characteristics and management will reflect the power and interests of the hegemonic country. Examples of ways in which the management of the regime is directed towards the hegemonic state's interest may be easier to identify. According to realists, the regime's rules should reflect the interests of the hegemonic state as well. If the hegemonic state wishes to see one set of exchange rate rules, or one type of balance of payments adjustment, then the regime will have those very rules.

Liberals will examine the regime's characteristics from a different perspective, which underscores the links between liberals and institutionalists. Liberals are primarily concerned with how well the regime supports individuals' abilities to conduct economic transactions across international boundaries. It is the performance of the regime that most interests them—this emphasis on the regime's functions typifies an institutionalist analysis. Marxists and dependency theorists look at these same issues from a different angle. They argue that monetary regimes are likely to be dominated by a single powerful state (or perhaps a small group of states), but that the monetary regime serves to reinforce the international division of labour. As such, the monetary regime enhances the concentration of capital in the hands of fewer and fewer people within the most economically advanced and politically powerful states. The monetary regime serves to integrate markets and is part of a comprehensive picture that includes international investment and trade patterns.

Four Characteristics of the Classical Gold Standard (1871-1914)

1. The exchange rate of each currency was fixed in terms of gold, hence all were fixed against each other.
2. Gold served as the only reserve.
3. Gold was allowed to flow freely from one participating member of the gold standard to another, both as the form of balance of payments adjustment but also as capital flows.
4. Some have argued that Britain's Bank of England, as the monetary authority of the world's major trading power and international investor, was able to manage the gold standard.

Comparing Monetary Regimes

If we consider the four characteristics of monetary regimes together, we get a quick and simple synopsis of any historical example that we can then use to make comparisons. For instance, the main traits of the classical gold standard are summarized in the box above. The workings of the gold standard, the sterling overhang which developed, and the British policy response are explored in Chapter 16. After World War II, a new monetary regime was developed to mimic some aspects of the gold standard, but with modifications to enhance balance of payments adjustment and exchange rate management. The creation of this regime is discussed in Chapter 18; its downfall is then discussed in Chapter 20.

If we were to list the characteristics for the current monetary situation, the differences compared to the gold standard would be glaring. For the most part exchange rates are not fixed, though there are some attempts to fix exchange rates in some regional groupings. Dirty floating is the norm. Reserves are a mixture of foreign reserves and precious metals, though reserves have less meaning when exchange rates are not fixed. Capital controls in the major economic powers exist in only limited form these days, though capital controls are more extensive in other places. The U.S. dollar serves as the international money, though use of other currencies (especially the Japanese yen and the German deutschmark) has risen in recent years. Whether the U.S. manages the international monetary order in any way is doubtful—certainly when compared to the ways in which the U.S. could manage affairs in the 1950s and 1960s, when the Bretton Woods monetary regime was in place. Today's international monetary regime is based much more on coordination of policies among the major financial powers, as will be seen in Chapters 23 and 24.

Summary: Monetary Policies, Politics, and International Relations

The main questions concerning monetary regimes and international monetary policy reflect our efforts to untangle a variety of issues. On the one hand, national authorities must manage monetary policy in a way that meets domestic and international goals. If a country's currency is playing the role of an international money, the balancing of monetary goals becomes quite complicated. Policy decisions are also complicated because of the ways in which monetary policy can substitute for trade policy. Since monetary policy can manipulate the price of exports and imports, it can substitute for protectionist policies. At the same time, since monetary policy can also affect all goods and services available for trade, it is politically difficult to manipulate monetary policy without inviting opposition. Policy decisions may reflect national competition, the pursuit of power, the constraints of international regimes, the struggle between various domestic interests, or bureaucratic politics. Only an investigation of cases will persuade us that one point of view is superior to others.

Notes

1. See, for instance the discussion in Paul de Grauwe, *International Money: Postwar Trends and Theories* (Oxford: Clarendon Press, 1989) 1.

2. Non-rival consumption refers to the fact that one person's use of the money does not prevent another from using it. In this case, the more a money is used, the more effectively it serves as a medium of exchange. For a deeper discussion of the characteristics of money, and their relevance for international exchange, see de Grauwe 1-4.

3. This was not the case in the past, and there remain many proponents of the "free banking" approach. If the free banking proponents are correct, then there should be little or no problems with a floating exchange rate system internationally.

4. Richard N. Cooper, "Prolegomena to the Choice of an International Monetary System," *International Organization* 29,1 (1975) 63-97.

5. W.M. Scammell, *The Stability of the International Monetary System* (Totowa, N.J.: Rowman and Littlefield, 1987) 9.

6. This of course shapes degrees of satisfaction with floating exchange rates. See Robert M. Dunn Jr., "The Many Disappointments of Flexible Exchange Rates," *Princeton Essays in International Finance* 154 (December 1983).

7. For a broader discussion, see Jeffry Frieden, "Invested Interests: the Politics of National Economic Policies in a World of Global Finance," *International Organization* 45,4 (Autumn 1991): 425-51.

8. Susan Strange, "The Politics of International Currencies," *World Politics* 23,2 (January 1971): 215-31.

9. For a similar discussion, see C. Fred Bergsten, *The Dilemmas of the Dollar* (New York, NY: New York University Press, 1975) 101-12.

10. Scammell 55.

11. According to C. Fred Bergsten, such internationally used currencies typically develop overhangs; see Bergsten 129-30.

12. Scammell 55.

13. Of course, today, with extensive information and the ability to process it rapidly, such transaction costs can be greatly reduced. This was not true of most of the time periods considered in the cases.

Additional References

Cooper, Richard. *The International Monetary System: Essays in World Economics*. Cambridge, MA: MIT Press, 1987.

de Grauwe, Paul. *International Money: Postwar Trends and Theories*. Oxford: Clarendon Press, 1989.

Milner, Chris (ed.). *Political Economy and International Money, Selected Essays of John Williamson*. New York, NY: New York University Press, 1987.

Scammell, W.M. *The Stability of the International Monetary System*. Totowa, NJ: Rowman and Littlefield, 1987.

Strange, Susan. "The Politics of International Currencies." *World Politics* 23,2 (January 1971): 215-31.

CHAPTER 9
The Politics of International Investment

International investments have become one of the fastest growing areas of concern in public debates concerning international political economic relations, especially in the U.S. For many years, U.S. investors have purchased foreign businesses, established firms in foreign countries, or made loans abroad. U.S. policy was primarily focused on creditors' rights and privileges; citizens of other countries were more interested in establishing debtors' rights. The U.S. has become a focal point for international investments in the last 20 years, causing Americans to reconsider the politics of international investments.

Reasons Why International Investment Occurs

The reason international investment takes place is obvious. Someone wants to make a profit by taking capital from one country to another. As our discussion from the chapter on trade revealed, the factors of production are distributed unevenly. Because capital is relatively scarce in some areas and relatively abundant in others, capital earns different rates of return depending on which economy it is in. One response to these different rates of return is to engage in trade. Another response for the holders of capital where it is abundant (and therefore not earning as much as capital elsewhere), is to organize their capital into a mobile form and move it to someplace where capital is relatively scarce. Still another reason investment takes over borders arises from the very fact that borders exist. Each country exercises its own laws, creating different economic practices and, ultimately, different profit rates from investments.

Less obviously, trade itself can drive firms' decisions regarding the location of investment. Several theories in economics consider the ways in which firms compete, and the way they seek markets, to be important factors driving investment abroad. Microeconomics tells us that firms do not always seek profits over other goals. In some situations, firms may well have to decide between maximizing today's profits or pursuing other goals that could enhance profits over the longer run. Thus, firms may turn down immediate profits in favour of greater market-share or attaining economies of scale in production. As part of their strategies aimed at achieving these other goals, firms often incorporate a plan to invest abroad. Individuals also invest internationally, but these investments depend on the international financial mechanisms available.

Politically, there are several contentious aspects to international investment. Are states willing to see money leave their own country and be spent on the economic development of another country? Realists will certainly have something to say about the wisdom of such a policy, though they must also be able to explain why so much international investment takes place. Liberals will have no trouble answering this last question by relying on the arguments of economists. Yet, when they address questions about why the forms and the volume of international investment have fluctuated over time, liberals will have some of the same problems that appeared in their theories about the evolution of trade. The challenge for liberals is to provide arguments that are consistent over time.

Of course, the countries hosting the international investment may also question its value. The host country receives money to help the country develop, but at what cost? Is it beneficial to receive funds if the price is handing over critical decisions determining the country's economy to foreigners? Liberals, realists, Marxists, and others will naturally disagree about the answers to such questions. We can only discuss how political scientists analyze decisions made about international investment by first recognizing some of the different forms in which international investment takes place. Each form has different consequences for the home country, the host country, investors themselves, and the borrowers. Different forms have also been popular at different points in time.

The Different Forms of Investment

Different forms of investment reflect a combination of contemporary business practices (which are constantly changing), but they also reflect reactions to the problems of particular historical periods. In international business, some problems have been constant: How can risks be reduced? How can geographically dispersed operations be coordinated? How can profits be amassed and reinvested? These questions have been more perplexing in some periods than others, but in each case the answers are profoundly shaped by political factors.

The initial form of international investment in the modern period centred on the family. In order to overcome the risks involved with international operations in a period when communications were underdeveloped and legal controls were likewise primitive, operations were kept within the family. In the 1600s, for instance, if a Dutch businessman wanted to purchase grain in the Baltic region, ship it to the Netherlands, convert that grain into gin or some other type of liquor, and then sell that liquor in Britain, he faced a challenge.

How could he establish a business in these other countries? If he simply handed over capital to someone in the Baltic or England, or hired a foreigner to handle the local operations, he bore the risks concerning the foreigner's honesty. Given that it would take some time to get information about any problems, if the foreigner simply took the capital, the investor would be in trouble. The host government was unlikely to care about the foreign investor's dilemma.

The common solution to such problems confronting international investors in the 1600s was to dispatch a son to run the foreign branch. In the example above, one son would live in a Baltic coast town and run that end of the business. Another son (or son-in-law) would set up a business in London to handle affairs there. In this situation, risk was lowered because family ties kept the managers of the disparate units loyal to the overall firm. While that reduced some of the economic risks associated with international investment, the political risks remained. Monarchs claiming absolute political power could always try to seize their citizens' property—foreigners' investments were an even easier target for such rulers.

Other major obstacles remained during this time period. Communications were undeveloped, so that coordination of operations was difficult. More importantly, many countries were practising mercantilism. *Mercantilism* prevented individuals from taking capital out of their home country. However, the citizens of those countries which did allow capital exports (such as the Dutch Republic) confronted a second problem. Once capital was placed in another country that practised mercantilism, one would probably be prevented from removing any profits. Those countries pursuing mercantilist policies pushed investments into large trading companies, which invested in the home country's colonies rather than in the economies of other major powers. They often exercised a monopoly over the trade from a particular colony or region, or perhaps over the trade in a specific item, and thus they made huge profits. Under mercantilism, investment patterns and trade flows were closely linked.

Some of these trading companies were the first to issue shares, which allowed them to operate as limited liability companies. Previously, firms were either individually owned or were partnerships. Partnerships could raise money only to the extent that they could bring people together; moreover, partnerships (or firms owned by a single individual) did not have a separate identity. If such a firm had debts, the owner or owners were personally responsible. In a limited liability operation, control was exercised through stock ownership; the firm was an entity unto itself. If the firm went bankrupt, the stockholders lost money in the value of their stock, but they were not personally liable for the firm's debts. This innovation obviously encouraged investment by people with small amounts of capital and allowed for many small amounts of capital to be pooled together into larger amounts.

Another important distinction has to do with the management of limited liability firms. In most instances of partnerships, the partners ran the day-to-day operations themselves. In limited liability firms, the ownership was divided among numerous stockholders, each with only a small stake in the firm; none would likely be in a position to claim the right to run the firm. Instead, professional management was brought in to handle the company's operations. This division between ownership and management is important for understanding how portfolio investments work, as well as for appreciating the differences in the political consequences of portfolio investment compared to other forms of international investment.

Portfolio Investments

A *portfolio investment* is an indirect investment, one where ownership or invest-ment does not entail direct management of the economic activity resulting from investment. The most common portfolio investments are stocks, bonds, or simple bank loans. The term portfolio refers to the nature in which investors handle these investments.

Portfolio investments have occurred since the development of the modern international political economy. For instance, in the seventeenth century sev-eral governments (the Dutch especially) became adept at floating bonds for their publics to purchase. Dutch citizens became accustomed to earning steady returns on such items. These portfolio investments became international and occurred on a large scale once Britain's Parliament assumed political dominance in the Glorious Revolution of 1688. William III, who as Prince of Orange was already the most important political figure in the Netherlands, was invited to become King of England; England and the Netherlands became steadfast allies. To the Dutch public, investing in English parliamentary bonds was sensible because they trusted Parliament to repay its debts, English and Dutch political interests were interwoven (and with William III involved in both governments, policies were loosely coordinated), and the investment could even be seen as patriotic. Since the Dutch were not practising mercantil-ism, Dutch investors became the first to invest heavily in the form of inter-national portfolio investments.

When we consider the political questions circling international investment, the particular characteristics of portfolio investments are critical to keep in mind. Portfolio investments link together capitalists from different countries. No matter what the specific type of investment (bank loan, bond, or what-ever), capitalists in one country are lending money in one form or another to capitalists (economic agents, public or private) of another country. The capi-talists therefore share an interest in seeing that the investments earn a return;

portfolio investments are an economic bond between capitalists. If the deal is entered into voluntarily, why should such lending ever lead to economic friction between the home and host?

Look at the basic economic cause of the investment in the first place. Capitalists in a country with relatively abundant capital will wish to earn higher returns on their investments by placing that capital in a country where this resource is relatively scarcer. In the end, however, portfolio investments always mean that more capital is supposed to leave the host country than went in—more capital will flow back to where capital was already relatively abundant. Why? Because with portfolio investments, such as a simple loan, the debtor always has to pay back the principal—the amount borrowed—*plus* interest. The trick is for the borrower to spend the money wisely, making enough to pay back the principal and interest, and still have some left over.

In the nineteenth century, the country with the most capital to invest at home or abroad was Britain. For a variety of reasons, Britain's investments primarily took the form of portfolio investments. At first, these reinforced British trade. Portfolio loans in the form of stocks or bonds were floated on the London markets, often by foreign national or municipal governments. The foreign governments used the money to invest in their own public infrastructure, spending the funds they had borrowed on new canals, bridges, port improvements, and, above all, railroads. Construction of train lines meant these same actors would have to purchase iron rails, steam engines, and railroad cars. Britain, as the first country to experience the Industrial Revolution, held a huge technological lead in producing these items efficiently. By loaning money to foreigners, British investors stimulated the demand for British industrial exports.

That was true for the first half of the nineteenth century, though perhaps not for the second half. As other countries began to industrialize, their exports began to compete with Britain's. British loans could be spent purchasing goods produced elsewhere. The situation changed even more dramatically by the end of the 1800s. British investments were increasingly fuelling the creation of economic rivals. Foreign borrowers created mills and factories to compete with British exporters.

Such patterns had an impact on Britain's policy stance on trade. The investments hurt Britain's trade in goods, although, interestingly, the country had already been running a deficit in the trade of visible goods. Britain remained committed to a policy of free trade despite its changing fortunes. Some argue this was because of the income generated through international investments, but there may have been other reasons. The free trade regime remained important to Britain, because foreign borrowers had to be able to sell their goods in order to repay their debts.[1] As the prime source of capital for the financing of trade, insurance, transportation, etc., Britain also did very well whenever any two countries traded. Still, when trade policy rose to the top of the political agenda, it was possible for broad groups in society to voice their opinions on trade in elections. Given how many more people were employed in industry, as opposed to finance and shipping, the political campaigns could well have turned out differently. We examine these elections, and different ways of explaining Britain's commitment to free trade up to World War I, in Chapter 14.

The Multinational Corporation

After World War I, international financial leadership was increasingly shared between London and New York. The U.S. had amassed vast amounts of capital to invest prior to 1914. World War I accelerated these economic trends. Britain was forced to sell off some of its international investments in order to finance its war effort and had even been forced into debt by borrowing from private banks in New York. These war loans were typical of the initial U.S. investments abroad, which were, at first, primarily composed of portfolio investments.

World War II accelerated this pattern of change. Britain once more had to sell off international holdings to purchase war material from abroad. The British government and other allies borrowed mostly from the U.S. government rather than from private banks. As we saw in the previous chapter, monetary policy practices had changed just prior to World War II, so governments everywhere were much more willing to run very large budget deficits.

But most of U.S. private investments after World War II took a form different from British investments in the nineteenth century. Instead of exercising indirect control—loaning money out but not managing how it was invested—U.S. capitalists tended to practise direct investment. This reflected the form of capitalism dominant in the U.S. in the twentieth century: the corporation. Most often in the post-1945 era, U.S. corporations invested abroad by purchasing an existing business within a foreign country. The foreign firm would then be integrated into the parent company's corporate structure. Sometimes the U.S. corporation moved into the foreign market by establishing an entirely new enterprise, but either way, the U.S. firm ended up with a subsidiary it operated directly.

The political consequences associated with *foreign direct investment* (or FDI) are not at all like those associated with portfolio investment. With FDI, foreign capitalists are entering into direct competition against local entrepreneurs. Whereas portfolio investment builds links between capitalists from the investing country and the host country, so that they share an interest in seeing the investment make a profit, FDI turns the investing capitalists into competitors vying within the host country.

The Reasons Firms Choose to Go Multinational

There are several reasons firms choose to establish multinational operations. First, the firm might be seeking either vertical or horizontal integration to exercise market power. Second, oligopolistic practices and pressures may push a firm to pursue market shares. Third, firms may try to protect and exploit their intangible assets. All of these factors seem to be in play in the decision of so many large U.S. firms investing abroad in the post-World War II era.

Vertical integration refers to the uniting of the various stages of production. A firm producing aluminum cans has to worry about securing sources of its key input—namely, aluminum. Aluminum is produced from bauxite ore, the processing of which requires a large amount of energy. To secure a steady supply of cheap aluminum, a firm producing cans would try to control some source of bauxite plus cheap sources of energy. Bauxite isn't found in that many places, so the firm might well have to move into foreign operations to control this input.

Vertical integration was often a response to the threat that someone else might take control of the world's supply of a particular input. To continue with the previous example, a firm might wish to establish a monopoly over the world's supply of bauxite and therefore be in a position to charge a monopoly price for that input. That would be an example of *horizontal integration*—expanding a firm so as to establish a monopoly over a single step in the production process. Horizontal integration can therefore also be a reason for firms to go multinational. If foreign competitors exist, then one way to eliminate or control that competition is to take over the foreign suppliers. Strategies of market control, and counter-strategies, were often reasons for the very first multinational investments.

The Product Cycle

One of the most popular explanations for international investment, developed by Raymond Vernon, is known as the *product cycle*.[2] He focused on a particular set of firms producing specific sorts of products. Consumer electronics are a perfect example. These products go through a characteristic life-cycle, and it is this life-cycle that determines when and where production will be internationalized. The first stage is product innovation. Here a firm in an economically advanced country develops a new product that is expensive to make, for the home market is composed of wealthy consumers. The firm may initially have a monopolistic edge over competitors because of its innovation.

The second phase comes as the home market is saturated with the good, and the product is exported to other markets. Because of economies of scale or learning curves in production, production costs tend to fall over time. As the price falls, the product can be sold in other markets where the population has less disposable income. The firm responds to this opportunity by exporting the good to these other countries.

The next phase is the product maturation phase. This is when FDI first occurs. Exports of the product serve to disseminate the technology necessary to produce the good. If the product goes to consumers, a number of firms will arise to service these goods. Through understanding how the technology works comes understanding how to produce similar goods. Since there is the risk that foreign firms may try to produce similar goods, the home producer establishes foreign branches to pre-empt any rivals. Once foreign competition does emerge, the innovating firm's margin of profitability is cut. The original firm must lower its prices, making it sensitive to any factors that might increase the cost of the good, such as transportation, marketing, and labour. Differences in these costs between what the innovating firm is paying versus what its foreign rival pays could make all the difference in whether the firm turns a profit. The firm can respond by locating production as closely as possible to the new markets, thereby reducing transportation costs—yet another reason to pursue FDI.

The final phase is product standardization, which occurs when production has become so mechanical and so routine that production goes to the country where labour costs are lowest. Firms shift all their production to the labour-abundant, less economically developed countries in an effort to control production costs. Ironically, the firm can only supply the original home market by exporting these goods from its foreign operations.

This is exactly the pattern of trade and investment we have seen in several products, but perhaps the most striking examples have occurred in consumer electronics. Colour television was originally developed, and at one time only produced, in the U.S. Eventually, the production spread to other economically advanced countries, and then to the less economically advanced ones, until finally all production shifted to the less developed countries. For some time, colour TVs were no longer produced in the U.S. at all.

Other Economic Explanations for FDI

One of the most powerful new explanations for the rise and spread of MNCs looks at the incentives firms face, in the same way as Vernon's product-cycle explanation does. Instead of focusing on technology as the driving force, or treating integration of production as the key factor influencing the decision to invest abroad, this explanation looks at the control of transaction costs. In several sorts of transactions, it is difficult for firms to know what price to charge. This holds true for tangible goods, such as technology, but is even more true for intangible assets, such as brand names or marketing information.

By tapping into the importance of marketing, this explanation highlights a critical factor in the success or failure of many firms. Brand names are very valuable to corporations, which spend millions to develop and protect the images of their products. Successfully developing an image in one country often has a natural spillover in other nearby markets. To licence a foreign firm to produce and market the same type of good involves a calculated risk. The original firm may earn high payments in the short run, but if the foreign firm operating under licence produces goods of poor quality, the product's image can be severely damaged in other markets. Given the high risks involved in the licencing of production and use of brand names, firms may be uncertain of the proper fees to charge in such deals. It is very difficult to develop a licencing scheme that adequately covers the original producer's risks and still leaves the new foreign producer a reasonable profit.

As Richard Caves explains, firms that do not know what price to charge for such intangibles may simply internalize the transaction by refusing to sell the asset at stake (technology, information, trade-mark, or whatever).[3] Instead of selling rights to the asset to a foreign firm, the corporation may create a foreign subsidiary. In this way, the corporation can retain the profits derived from its asset. Such arguments fit nicely into other theories of oligopolistic competition (i.e., situations where a few large firms dominate the market), because whenever FDI has been spurred by uncertainty over transaction costs, it generates other consequences which may benefit an oligopolistic firm. By moving abroad, the firm can limit the development of foreign rivals. Rather than allow a foreign firm to develop competitive goods in a foreign country, the firm may seize that opening, enabling it to squeeze potential competitors out of the market. Since the oligopolistic firm can use technology (or trade-marks, or any other intangible asset, or combination of assets) already developed, this strategy builds on sunk costs and entails few new risks.

Another reason for firms to go international is to capture economies of scale. They may simply produce for foreign markets and achieve the economies of scale necessary by relying on exports. But they may also be drawn into foreign countries to pursue the linkages in production needed to support economies of scale. This is another argument that builds on the obvious fact that most firms involved in multinational production are oligopolies. Caves, having noted that there are several types of oligopolies, has used these firms' characteristics to provide several possible explanations for MNCs' investment activities.

Caves identifies three sorts of MNCs: horizontally integrated, vertically integrated, and diversified firms. Horizontal and vertical integration have already been discussed. Diversified firms are involved in the production of similar sorts of goods as well as totally dissimilar ones. This can only be explained as either a combination of the above patterns or as risk avoidance. Firms may expand in areas alien to it (i.e., not only foreign but also technologically different) in order to learn more about another country or about another area of production. For instance, a Japanese firm might buy a U.S. firm in a completely unrelated field, not because it wants to merge the two but because the Japanese company wants to learn more about the U.S. market. This information will help the Japanese firm decide if it should expand its operations in the U.S. In just such a transaction, General Motors (GM) bought another multinational, Hughes Aircraft, in the hopes that GM could learn more about high-tech production techniques. While there was the possibility that GM could generate some aerospace spin-offs to use in their automobiles, its real reason for wanting Hughes Aircraft was to see how Hughes managed its automated production. So this is another possible explanation for the existence of diversified MNCs.

The Returns Earned by FDI

Unlike portfolio investments, foreign direct investment does not automatically mean that capital should ever flow out of the host country at a higher rate than it is coming in. A foreign firm that invests in a country may decide to leave its investments there, plowing its profits back into the international investment—or it may not. This creates a strong contrast with portfolio investments. As mentioned above, when the transactions made in the form of portfolio investments work according to plan, more capital leaves the host country than entered; the borrower must pay back the principal plus interest.

With FDI, this too may be the case. An MNC may decide to end its investment by selling off the operation. It would clearly prefer to make a profit, thus taking more money out than it initially invested. But if an MNC opens up a factory in a foreign country which services the local market, and the factory is successful, the MNC will presumably continue the operation. Profits might be taken out, but the original investment would remain (as an asset held by foreigners, of course).

Interestingly, the political reaction to each form of investment is often very different. In either case, more money is being pumped into the host economy. That translates into more jobs; higher wages, as workers' pay is bid up; greater demand for other local inputs; and a stimulation of the economy. None of this stimulation necessary penetrates very deeply into the economy, however; it often creates economic distortions with unwanted side-effects. Yet portfolio investments usually do not generate political opposition, whereas FDI does. This obviously is due to two factors: first, with portfolio investments, key decisions on day-to-day matters remain in the hands of locals. Second, in portfolio investments, local capitalists have a role to play, whereas FDI means competition against local capitalists. Capitalists from the host country therefore prefer portfolio investment to FDI, and thus the politics associated with FDI have been much more nationalistic compared to the politics associated with portfolio investments.

The State versus the MNC? The Issue of Regulation

Discussions about the politics of foreign investment span a wide spectrum. At one point, some people believed that firms, organized around economic ends, were not only becoming more powerful than nation-states, but would soon replace political units in degree of importance. As one proponent of this viewpoint argued "the nation-state is just about through as an economic unit."[4] While this comment was made in the 1960s, and was echoed by many others at the time, it perhaps reflects an extreme view. Nonetheless, MNCs can be seen as having a commanding role in the international economy. Statistics for the late 1980s show that U.S.-based MNCs accounted for nearly two-thirds of merchandise exports, so clearly MNCs play a major role in international trade.[5] Of course, on the other extreme, we have the realist viewpoint, which has always assumed that states are the most important actors in international affairs.

The classic realist response to the extreme liberal viewpoint of someone like Kindleberger (or George Ball) came from Sam Huntington, who stated in 1973 that

> Predictions of the death of the nation-state are premature. They overlook the ability of human beings and human institutions to respond to challenges and to adapt themselves to changed environments. They seem to be based on a zero-sum assumption about power and sovereignty: that a growth in the power of transnational organizations must be accompanied by a decrease in the power of nation-states. This, however, need not be the case.[6]

Another realist counterpoint from Waltz was perhaps less prophetic. In commenting on Kindleberger's views, he posed the question:

> Who is likely to be around 100 years from now—the United
> States, the Soviet Union, France, Egypt, Thailand, and Uganda?
> Or Ford, IBM, Shell, Unilever, and Massey-Ferguson? I would
> bet on the states, perhaps even Uganda.[7]

Of course, there are several good reasons why governments are wary of FDI, since MNCs do indeed pose a challenge to them. MNCs can use their mobility to evade and even overturn governments' policies. In some ways that is one of the very reasons firms undertake multinational operations: to link markets or production centres that are politically kept separate.

The challenge MNCs pose to governments must be noted for other significant reasons. MNCs do have home bases, where they often have political links. They can protect their interests by calling on one government to oppose the actions of another.[8] This often pits an economically advanced country of the North against an economically developing country of the South, but it also may pit northern countries against each other, as when the U.S. and Canada argue over the treatment of U.S. corporations in Canada. Now we can add in South-South tensions as more MNCs of southern origin arise, as when a Korean MNC begins operations in the Philippines.

Part of the North's response to the inability to control MNCs or regulate their activity has led to an increase in attempts to exert *extraterritoriality*, the extension of national jurisdiction beyond a nation's own borders. Thus, a country such as the U.S. tries to implement its own anti-trust laws to keep a U.S.-based corporation from buying up its competitors even outside the U.S. The U.S. government also tries to keep MNCs from engaging in international sales of equipment or technology deemed strategically significant. For example, in the 1980s the U.S. enacted sanctions against Toshiba's operations in the U.S. to show its displeasure with Toshiba-Japan selling high-tech engineering equipment to the Soviets. Although this deal violated an agreement between the U.S. and Japan, it is not clear why this dispute should not have been an intergovernmental problem, resolved between the Japanese government and Toshiba, nor why the subsidiary in the U.S. should have been punished.

In a similar vein, taxation schemes based on the notion of extraterritoriality are becoming more and more common. Rather than taxing an MNC on its operations within a particular government's jurisdiction, some governments are now assessing each MNC on the basis of its global operations. The state of California, for instance, wishes to tax corporations on their total global returns, not just their operations within California, or even within the U.S. The state's right to do this is not clearly established in international law or by any precedents; the real problem probably remains with enforcement anyway. If an MNC doesn't comply with the state's regulations, the state can deny the corporation the licences necessary for conducting business in the state. If the state in question is California, enforcement means cutting the MNC off from a lucrative market, and therefore such regulations must be taken seriously. This particular example involving California's tax code was not upheld by the U.S. Supreme Court, though the issue has continued to resurface.

Because many less economically advanced states do not have large markets or other benefits they can deny MNCs, they have a harder time exerting controls over MNCs operating within their own jurisdictions, let alone enforcing extraterritoriality. At the same time, we should note that at the basic theoretical level, the issue facing both the economically advanced countries and the economically less developed states is the same: how should the state go about regulating the MNC's activities? There is considerable overlap in all states' goals in implementing regulation, since all states would like a greater success rate in meeting their policy objectives and in raising taxes. This shared interest in regulation should prove a fertile ground for some sort of international agreement to regulate the practices of MNCs, yet little progress has ever been made in this issue-area.

This problem over regulation is a classic example of failed collective action. If it is possible for all states to agree on an issue that would make them all better off, such as raising taxes on MNCs, why don't they all do it? The problem is getting all to act together, collectively. (This is another example of the prisoners' dilemma.) If all raise their taxes up to the same level at the same time, MNCs could not easily evade the tax hike. But if one state fails to raise its taxes, that would leave an opening for the MNCs to exploit (e.g., Panama with shipping regulations). Since the governments are interested in total taxes collected rather than rates per se, the greater volume generated by being a tax haven could easily mean more tax revenues. So there is going to be a defection problem with any collective action on regulation of MNCs. This same sort of collective action problem hampered the regulation of corporations in the U.S. at the turn of the century, when regulation of business activity was in the hands of the individual states—firms could play one state off another. Eventually the federal government had to take over business regulation. At the international level, there is no higher body to turn to; states must come together and agree on minimum regulations. Resolution of the collective action problem is an inherently political activity.

Nonetheless, it would be wrong to argue that states cannot exercise their sovereignty when they wish. On September 11, 2001, as U.S. officials struggled to figure out what was going on, they ordered the country's borders shut. As part of this action, they also closed U.S. airspace to all traffic, in the process diverting hundreds of flights to Canada. Though this was a costly measure, it proved that even one of the most open societies on the planet could seal its borders when necessary.

The Resurgence of Portfolio Investments

While MNC operations were the norm in the 1950s and 1960s, portfolio investments never disappeared. They increased once again in the 1960s and 1970s and have continued to mushroom. As a potential threat to sovereignty, governments in many developing countries increasingly opposed FDI. The creation of large pools of cheap and available capital means that these countries could turn away from MNC investments and replace them with borrowing from foreign sources. The most prominent source of portfolio investments were European banks which had U.S. dollars to lend.

This *Eurodollar market*,[9] as it was called, was created as a way of avoiding certain government regulations concerning financial markets. U.S. dollars were the most attractive currency to hold in the post-World War II years. It was the currency used in most international transactions, and the currency used to price goods sold on international markets. When the Soviet Union exported diamonds or natural gas, the prices were set in dollars. Payment was normally made in dollars as well. Yet, for a wide variety of goods, the U.S. dollar was only accepted as payment in the U.S. itself. Banks were interested only in handling local money, so if someone earned a foreign currency they would traditionally exchange that for their own currency or take that currency back to its country of origin to deposit there. When the Soviet Union earned dollars from the sale of resources, it didn't want to exchange them into Russian money (what was the point?), instead desiring to spend those dollars on international markets. The money was very useful—but where should the Soviets put it? Under conventional practice, they were supposed to deposit those dollars in a bank in the U.S.

The Soviet government was worried about this option, however. If it held large amounts of money in U.S. banks, it left itself open to some sort of retaliation or pressure by the U.S. government, which could order the freezing of these assets. To avoid such problems, the Soviet government convinced a British bank to hold the Soviet's dollar deposits. With that, the Eurodollar market was born—U.S. dollars held by banks outside the U.S. government's jurisdiction. This opened up a whole new range of economic activity, because these accounts were largely left unregulated.

Banks earn profits by lending out depositors' funds. As other countries and firms began to make deposits in U.S. dollars, the banks found they had a large amount of U.S. funds to lend. Moreover, these accounts were largely unregulated—that is, national laws were unclear on how such accounts were to be managed. In most countries, commercial banks receive deposit insurance from the central bank in exchange for accepting the central bank's regulation. The central bank oversees that each bank does not engage in excessive lending; this is the way the banks avoid their own collective action problems associated with competition. The central bank usually asserts control by issuing regulations that order the bank to maintain a certain percentage of deposits on hand at all times, so as to meet depositors' potential demands. Banks may decide to hold even more. In return, the central bank promises that if the commercial banks make sensible transactions, but find that for an unexpected reason they lack enough funds to meet demands from depositors, the central bank will loan the commercial bank the necessary funds. When the Eurodollar market developed, such rules and promises only applied to deposits in national currency. Without any rules forcing the commercial banks to maintain a certain percentage in reserve, the banks became less and less prudent. They began to keep ever smaller amounts of money on hand and loaned out more and more; they also charged less and less interest over time. Competition forced them to play an increasingly risky game.

These tendencies were exacerbated by new U.S. dollar funds accumulating in these off-shore accounts. Other depositors wanted their dollar holdings kept outside the legal boundaries of the U.S. When the Arab states organized the OPEC oil embargo in the early 1970s, they forced the price of oil much higher. This translated into increased earnings of U.S. dollars, but there was a fear that the U.S. government would retaliate by freezing the OPEC countries' assets. The massive amounts of money earned could not be spent right away, so the OPEC countries deposited these petrodollars (as they were known) in the Eurodollar market. Competition between the banks to place loans simply intensified.

On the positive side, the international system could handle the huge jump in the price of oil thanks to petrodollar recycling. The profits made by OPEC were deposited in European banks, which loaned the money out to developing countries that often spent those dollars on purchases of oil. The dollars could be recycled because the market mechanisms were in place. With so much money available to be lent out, countries could refuse to accept FDI or place stringent terms on new FDI by replacing the lost investment capital with money borrowed on the Eurodollar market. International bank lending in 1975 accounted for perhaps $40 billion; by 1990 that figure had risen to $300 billion. Bond lending, too, had increased from less than $20 billion in the mid-1970s to more than $170 billion in 1990.[10] The side effect was that countries amassed large debts owed to the private commercial banks, which would eventually have to be paid back—plus interest.

The Changes in the Investment Regime over the Centuries

These descriptions of recent patterns of investment underscore the fact that the international investment regime continually changes. One of the most critical questions about this concerns the rise and fall of international investment levels over time. Realists provide possible answers to some of these key questions. Low levels of international investment occurred prior to the nineteenth century, but when Britain began to pursue portfolio investments, the level rose steadily. Investments increased in the twentieth century, but with some periods of reduction, especially in the 1930s.

Liberals follow the economists' arguments and therefore expect to see fairly consistent patterns of international investment. How well can they explain these fluctuations? Realists, on the other hand, offer hegemonic stability theory. Investments rise and fall, according to them, because investors must make political calculations as well as economic calculations. The economic incentives to invest are constant, but investors do not always have the guarantees that their property rights will be protected or that capital will be allowed to flow freely over borders, allowing them to move their profits wherever they wish. Realists argue that states still remain the most important actors—if governments don't want investments, they can exercise sovereignty and block them or even block investors from taking their capital out of the home country. How realistic is such a view today? With governments everywhere in debt, international lenders can often exert immense pressure on them.

Marxists make analyses similar to the realists, since they argue that the powerful states are able to impose their investments on weaker states. Moreover, Marxist analyses cause us to consider several related questions. Marxists usually believe that international investments are one more mode of integrating nation-states into the international division of labour. Investments therefore serve the interests of the home country (and their capitalists) and are not mutually beneficial. As such, international investments make the host countries dependent on the home countries.

There are other important questions about the international investment regime. Why does one form of investment dominate at one point in time? Is it merely a reflection of capitalist practices, or does the form of international investment reflect the practices of the hegemonic country? How are investors' rights protected? Are they protected at the expense of states' ability to exercise sovereignty?

Today, international investments are powerfully influenced by technology. Capital markets are large, fast, and interconnected. Capital can flow across borders with electronic transfers; billions of dollars are traded across borders each day. MNCs have extensive holdings; a single MNC may operate in dozens of countries. The largest MNCs, such as GM or IBM, operate with budgets larger than the gross national produce (GNP) of many countries. The value of international investments and capital flows has come to overwhelm the value of trade itself.[11] Our ability to answer these questions about the international investment regime is more important than ever.

The Opportunities and Problems that International Investment Entails

MNCs' activities are characterized by their ability to operate internationally across several political jurisdictions. This mobility means MNCs can upset or offset government policies. Clearly, MNC operations can counteract government attempts to rectify balance of payments problems. They are large holders of currencies, with wide-ranging knowledge, and great flexibility to respond to market incentives. When governments try to shift their exchange rates, MNCs can respond quickly and massively to opportunities, thereby garnering huge profits. This often makes the government's job of stabilizing or hitting an exchange target that much more difficult. Remittance of profits, internal pricing, and other MNC activities profoundly affect the exchange rate too, by determining which currencies are actually exchanged. As major actors in international trade, MNCs' corporate strategies can also affect trade policy.

In the area of government revenues, MNCs often locate as much of their activities as possible in the areas where taxation is the lowest. Competition between countries for MNC operations follows, with the country which asks for the least in taxes often winning—meaning that all countries are able to ask for less in taxes. This same mobility in terms of locating production allows MNCs to play a major role in broader macroeconomic policies, such as employment levels and overall performance of the economy.

MNCs are also a possible resource. They are not only the purveyors of jobs or the source of taxes. These are things they obviously provide, because these are the very things that may cause them to move elsewhere. But they also possess technology. They do not merely physically control the technology, they also control it legally. Because they hold patents on technology, they have the ability to monopolize its use. MNCs also control information and communication networks, which, since they often employ the latest in technology, are quite advanced. Several MNCs have the capability to garner and assess economic information on a global basis.

MNCs also are often the masters of expertise. Large corporations are knowledgeable about their own activities and products, and often have impressive amounts of knowledge about other markets and political economic factors. In order to develop marketing strategies, MNCs form profiles of consumer types and their locations. This information is quite detailed and often much better than government census material. MNCs know how to do certain things better than many governments because often they are more experienced than those governments. When a Third World country decides to build its first chemical plant, for instance, it has no first-hand expertise in this subject, whereas several large European or North American construction firms have built dozens of such plants. This expertise is important for doing jobs correctly and most cost efficiently.

In this sense, MNCs not only pose problems for governments, but they also represent opportunities. Whether the MNCs are viewed as an opportunity or a threat depends on the balance of power between the government and the MNC. These relationships between MNCs and governments are true for both economically advanced countries and those countries just beginning to industrialize and develop their economic potential. The less economically advanced states, however, are more vulnerable to the actions of the MNCs. It isn't so much that the MNCs' power varies, but rather that the governments of the North are better able to regulate the MNCs' activities than the countries of the South.

One of the obvious differences here, though, is that the economically less developed countries have goals different than the economically advanced countries. While both are concerned about taxes and employment levels, the less economically developed countries are also concerned with economic development issues and political issues surrounding the issue of nation-building, as well as being more sensitive to foreign ownership. As we will see in Chapters 12 and 15, Canadians too have worried about such issues.

Summary: Questions to be Explored in the Cases

The question we might pose about the international investment regime parallels the one we asked about the evolution of the trade and monetary regimes. Why does the regime change when it does? Moreover, we will examine how the investment regime influences decisions in monetary affairs, especially when a country responds to a currency overhang (as explored in Chapters 14, 16, and 20). We will also look at the debtors' views as well. Why would a state allow itself to become so indebted? How does a state respond to situations where it is deeply in debt? These questions are raised in Chapter 21, when Brazil's actions in the debt crisis are explored. Part III begins, however, with cases concerning the creation of a free trade regime in the nineteenth century.

Notes

1. Jeffry Frieden, "Capital Politics: Creditors and the International Political Economy," *Journal of Public Policy* 8,3/4 (July-December 1988): 265-86.

2. Raymond Vernon, "International Investment and International Trade in the Product Cycle," *Quarterly Journal of Economics* 80,2 (1966): 190-207.

3. Richard Caves, *Multinational Enterprise and Economic Growth* (New York, NY: Cambridge University Press, 1982).

4. Charles P. Kindleberger, as quoted in Andrew Walter, *World Power and World Money* (Hertfordshire: Harvester Wheatsheaf, 1991) 12.

5. Ethan Kapstein, *Governing the Global Economy* (Cambridge, MA: Harvard University Press, 1994) 3-4.

6. Samuel Huntington, "Transnational Organizations in World Politics," *World Politics* 25 (April 1973): 363, as quoted in Kapstein 11-12.

7. Kenneth Waltz, *Theory of International Politics* (Reading, MA: Addison-Wesley, 1979) 95.

8. See Jeffry Frieden, "The Economics of Intervention: American Overseas Investments and Relations with Underdeveloped Areas, 1890-1950," *Comparative Studies in Society and History* 31,1 (1989): 55-80.

9. A euromarket has been defined by Benjamin Cohen as "an organized market for foreign currency deposits." See B.J. Cohen, *In Whose Interest?* (New Haven, CT: Yale University Press, 1986)19. See the general discussion in Kapstein 32.

10. Kapstein 4.

11. Jeffry Frieden, "Invested Interests: the Politics of National Economic Policies in a World of Global Finance," *International Organization* 45,4 (Autumn 1991): 425-51.

Additional References

Caves, Richard, Harold Crookell, and J. P. Killing. "The Imperfect Market for Technology Licenses." *The Oxford Bulletin of Economics and Statistics* (August 1983): 249-67.

Cohen, Benjamin J. *In Whose Interest?* New Haven, CT: Yale University Press, 1986.

Dunning, John H. *Explaining International Production.* London: Unwin Hyman, 1988.

Frieden, Jeffry. "Capital Politics: Creditors and the International Political Economy." *Journal of Public Policy* 8,3/4 (July-December 1988): 265-86.

Gilpin, Robert. *U.S. Power and the Multinational Corporation.* New York, NY: Basic Books, 1975.

Helleiner, Eric. *States and the Reemergence of Global Finance.* Ithaca, NY: Cornell University Press, 1994.

Kapstein, Ethan. *Governing the Global Economy.* Cambridge, MA: Harvard University Press, 1994.

Krasner, Stephen D. *Defending the National Interest.* Princeton, NJ: Princeton University Press, 1978.

Lipson, Charles. *Standing Guard: Protecting Foreign Capital in the Nineteenth and Twentieth Centuries.* Berkeley, CA: University of California Press, 1985.

Vernon, Raymond. *Sovereignty at Bay.* New York, NY: Basic Books, 1971.

PART III
Turning Points in Foreign Economic Policy Behaviour

CHAPTER 10
Britain's Repeal of the Corn Laws

Britain's Mercantilist Past and the Industrial Revolution

Mercantilism was the dominant form of foreign economic policy followed throughout Europe after the advent of capitalism. It was based on the assumption that wealth and power were synonymous.[1] Wealth could easily be turned into power, since armies were largely composed of mercenaries, and power could easily be translated into wealth through conquest—especially of rich native peoples in North America, Africa, or Asia. Wealth was defined only in terms of precious metals such as gold and silver. Since there is a finite amount of these precious metals, people treated the pursuit of wealth as a zero-sum game—if one country got more gold, that left less for all the others. Since wealth and power were one and the same, foreign economic policies were geared to maintaining a positive balance of payments (i.e., an inflow of gold). Mercantilism entailed a set of policies designed to maintain an inward flow of money, but these policies were barriers to trade and international investment. In trying to prevent their neighbours from earning any money internationally, mercantilist countries were hurting themselves.

Britain moved away from mercantilism in the 1780s, only to return to such policies during the wars with Napoleonic France. By the 1830s, though, the old pressures for trade liberalization resurfaced in a more sophisticated form, as the gains from trade were now better understood in economic models. Specifically, the works of David Ricardo illustrated in good liberal fashion how international trade and specialization in national comparative advantages could lead to a more efficient use of international resources. With greater overall production, someone had to be made better off through trade, since there was more to consume.

Britain's comparative advantage in the 1830s and 1840s lay in the production of manufactured goods. The development of domestic markets, the transition to full-blown capitalism, and the impetus of war production propelled it into the Industrial Revolution. Because it was the first to experience this shift, Britain in 1840 was far ahead of other countries in utilizing non-organic resources in energy and capital embodied in machinery. Technologically, it stood on top. And, following the then-recent liberal ideas, British manufacturers began to trade manufactured goods for the import of raw materials. This was the lesson they learned from Ricardo's theories on international trade. The domestic market was being developed, but, clearly, profits could also be made in foreign trade, because their technical edge meant they could best other producers. Profits could be increased if other countries would accept British exports.

Several significant domestic barriers remained, though. Britain's own mercantilist policies had limited all kinds of imports. In Britain as elsewhere, mercantilism protected inefficient sectors, agriculture being one very important and well-protected such area. During the Napoleonic Wars, when France attempted to block European exports to Britain, mercantilist legislation had been reasserted in order to make the British economy self-sufficient, especially in food production. A set of regulations, known as the Corn Laws, established a floor price for grain; that is, the laws made sure that the price of grain did not fall below a certain level. Any time grain imports threatened to push prices down, tariffs were automatically applied to keep the price high enough that farmers weren't hurt. This guaranteed British grain farmers a profit and kept them producing grain.

After the Napoleonic Wars ended, debates over Britain's proper foreign economic policies resumed. While some elements of the mercantilist barriers were dismantled, new barriers were actually erected.[2] Meanwhile the Industrial Revolution, stimulated by the war effort, continued to alter the economy and society. Because Britain's political institutions had not been changed in some time, pressure was growing for some sort of political adaptations to bring Parliament in line with the economic changes. Where there had been only fields a century before, industrial cities had sprung up. Tens of thousands had left the countryside for the towns and cities, yet parliamentary districts failed to reflect these changes. A coalition of groups allied with one party, the Whigs, were finally able to push through the Reform Act of 1832. This act redrew district boundaries, redistributing political power away from the conservative agricultural areas (dominated by the Conservatives or Tories as they were called), to the new industrial classes. It is important to recognize that only a small portion of males could vote for Parliament at this time. The working class would not participate fully until universal male suffrage was adopted in 1918. The redistribution of political power, therefore, was merely between the capitalists in the agricultural sectors—largely aristocrats—and the new industrial capitalists.

The Tories received most of their political support from aristocrats and rural areas; their leader was Sir Robert Peel. Despite the Reform Act, they remained the single most powerful party in Parliament. Peel and others were concerned, however, that further pressures might build for greater democratic reforms. They also stood to lose economically if protectionist barriers were lowered and foreign grain was allowed to compete against their own production. Yet, as prime minister, Peel enacted the repeal of the Corn Laws, dividing his party and being forced out of office in the process.

The Repeal of the Corn Laws, completed on June 26, 1846, is seen as the final, conscious step in Britain's abandonment of mercantilism. Within a few years, the last remaining pieces of protectionist legislation were also removed.[3] Britain embraced foreign competition, trusting its economic future to the international market. British agriculture survived, somewhat battered, by shifting into more specialized production. Thus, the Repeal of the Corn Laws represents the first time a major economic power adopted free trade.

System-Level Theory: The Rise of a New Hegemonic Power?

From a realist perspective, Britain's adoption of freer trade merely reflected the new distribution of political and economic power in the international system. Emerging victorious from the Napoleonic Wars, Britain held the necessary ingredients for dominating the international political economy. Although its army was not very large, it commanded the world's most powerful navy, which, from a system of bases strung around the globe, maintained fleets wherever necessary. And, economically, Britain alone was industrialized.[4]

According to this perspective, Britain was pursuing power by liberalizing international trade.[5] As Krasner put it, "a hegemonic distribution of potential economic power is likely to result in an open trading structure."[6] Moreover, hegemonic power will create and maintain an open international economic order. Krasner was careful to elaborate his view of hegemony in largely economic terms. As indicators of the distribution of economic power, he used per capita income, aggregate size of the economy, share of world trade, and share of world investment. In each of these categories (except for size of the economy), Britain led the world in the mid-1800s. According to realists, this structural position provided both the interest and the capability to shape the international political economy. Thus, Britain should be seen to follow foreign economic policies that would ensure that it stayed ahead of other countries in terms of economic and political power. Since Britain stood to gain from free trade because it was in a unique position in the world economy, its own trade liberalization was an effort to maintain this dominance.[7]

Several questions arise with this interpretation of events, however. First, the timing seems questionable. After all, Britain stood militarily victorious in 1815, yet the economic policy associated with its new structural position was not enacted until the 1840s.[8] Second, Britain's military power waned over this time; that is, its naval dominance fell between 1815 and 1846, only to be reasserted later. Third, Britain's trade liberalization was unilateral—it did not send out ambassadors to negotiate new trade treaties at first, although it was using force to open up trade with weaker powers outside of Europe.

Was Britain acting as a hegemonic leader when it unilaterally lowered its tariffs? What sort of leadership was this, if no international negotiations were undertaken?[9] Peel's own writings, however, do not mention any concern with foreign responses to Britain's actions.[10] Since these sorts of details are missing in the support of the systemic arguments, numerous counter-arguments from other levels of analysis have been constructed.

Domestic Politics: Economic Interests, Parliamentary Reforms, and the Anti-Corn Law League

The alternative interpretation most often proposed is found at the level of domestic politics. Timothy McKeown, for instance, argues that the most parsimonious explanation for the Repeal of the Corn Laws can be found without examining the structure of the international system.[11] Instead, he and others have argued that the Repeal of the Corn Laws can be understood purely in domestic political terms, though one must first consider the economic consequences of trade liberalization to understand the motivations for each of the political groups within the country.

Workers wanted to repeal the Corn Laws because after trade liberalization, cheaper grain could enter the country. They would be able to spend less on food and more on other goods. The industrial capitalists wanted to eliminate the Corn Laws for two reasons. First, they wanted cheaper food prices, because cheaper food prices meant they could reduce the wages they paid to labour, thus pushing down their own costs. Moreover, since food was a major expense for most workers, falling food prices might placate labour unrest for some time. Second, an end to the Corn Laws would promote the industrialists' international interests. Foodstuffs could be more efficiently grown on the American or Canadian prairies or on the plains of Eastern Europe. Britain could import this food, and these imports would be paid for by the greater export of manufactured goods.

Meanwhile, the aristocrats who owned much of the land remained in favour of maintaining the Corn Laws, which supported the price of their output and thus maintained their incomes. This illustrates how specialization in trade reflects the endowments of the factors of production, as in the H-O model, while, using the Stolper-Samuelson theorem, we can also see a redistribution of domestic wealth through international trade.

Britain was endowed with several factors of production that gave it an edge in the area of industrial manufacturing. It held the premier position in terms of capital per worker, which was manifested in low interest rates, extensive use of machinery, and higher technology. Britain's capital-intensive service sectors also did a booming business, especially banking, insurance, and the financing of trade. These economic sectors did well in international competition by utilizing the cheap capital available to them, just as the H-O model predicts. Moreover, freer trade increased the profits going to these sectors and reduced those flowing to agriculture, as the Stolper-Samuelson theorem predicts.[12]

Understanding the interests of the various groups is not enough to explain political outcomes. At least two other steps have to be undertaken. First, how easily can each group organize its members for political action? Second, once organized, how do they interact with political institutions to affect policy? In this case, the aristocrats held the upper hand. Only aristocratic landholders sat in the House of Lords, which, in those times, still played an important role in the passage of legislation. Also, aristocrats used their local influence and patronage to control voting for the House of Commons.

One argument holds that the Repeal of the Corn Laws was possible only because the political power of the old landed aristocracy was lessened through a revision of political institutions. Specifically, the aristocrats' power in Parliament declined after the Reform Act of 1832. Since the Reform Act altered the pattern of representation in the House of Commons and redistributed political power to the new industrial capitalists, some have suggested that this enabled the industrial sector to drive policy to its advantage. It was only after this political shift that we see the effective pressure for an alteration in Britain's foreign economic policy.

There are several problems with this account. It was a Tory administration that carried out the Repeal—so the Tories appear to have been on the wrong side in the dispute. Why would they vote for the changes? Two competing explanations have recently been put forth which attempt to provide a deeper understanding of the situation. The first, developed by Cheryl Schonhardt-Bailey, argues that the economic divisions so easily identified in theory were blurred in reality.[13] Schonhardt-Bailey executed extensive field research to develop economic profiles of particular voting districts. Her insight was that aristocrats played a double role—they earned an income from their land, but at the time they were also the major holders of investment capital in Britain. They were the investors backing many of the new industrial enterprises. They would, therefore, have mixed motives in any questions concerning trade liberalization.

In the other new rendering of these political events, Michael Lusztig places the Repeal of the Corn Laws within the broader context of domestic politics.[14] The critical player in the domestic political game was the prime minister, Robert Peel. Trade was merely one issue among several on Peel's mind, including pressures for political reform and crop failure in Ireland. For

Lusztig, Peel was primarily motivated by a wish to defend Britain's existing political institutional structure from new pressures for further reform. The Reform Act of 1832 had changed some of the rules respecting parliamentary elections, but by and large the revisions had not altered the power of groups represented within Parliament.

Interests in favour of trade liberalization were organized and vocal. The Anti-Corn Law League was formed to attack the series of laws protecting agriculture from foreign competition. By itself, the League was not powerful enough to overturn the institutional structure, yet Peel worried that it might have the ability to increase its power by mobilizing other groups interested in reform. A number of such disgruntled groups existed: the urban working class was not yet allowed to vote, many of the workers in the cities had been forced off rural land and thus were dissatisfied, and several groups were displeased with the political power exercised by the House of Lords.

Much of Lusztig's interpretation relies on a close analysis of Peel's bargaining and political tactics. In discussions over how to respond to the crop failure in Ireland, Peel suggested it was time to repeal the Corn Laws. His Tory Party was split. Whig leader Lord John Russell placed his party squarely behind the notion of repeal. Without the Tories in both the House of Commons and the House of Lords in full support, no one believed Peel could get the repeal passed. Peel then pulled off a risky political ploy. He resigned, thus throwing the ball into Lord Russell's court. Yet Peel knew full well that Russell did not have the support in the House of Lords to get the repeal accepted. After Russell was unable to gather enough support to be an effective prime minister, Peel then resumed the reins of government, having illustrated that he was the only person likely to cobble together the coalition required to achieve repeal.

For Peel to get the repeal through the House of Lords, he had to use his close connections with the key conservative leader in the Lords, the Duke of Wellington. He did so by underlining the likelihood of some sort of retribution against the House of Lords if it stood in the way of such a publicly popular bill. Thus, Peel used the Whigs' support, however many of the Tories he could bring along, and the members of the Anti-Corn Law League in the House of Commons, plus the Tories led by the Duke of Wellington in the House of Lords to repeal the Corn Laws. But such tactics had a price—within days Peel's government fell to attacks from Tory backbenchers. The Tories were split over the wisdom of his manoeuvres, and many viewed the Repeal of the Corn Laws as too great a sacrifice no matter the alternatives.

Lusztig's account differs from Schonhardt-Bailey's in that he emphasizes the role of political parties and the "nesting" of the tariff issue within a broader political game. He also suggests that a key piece of the explanation rests with

Peel himself and his attitudes towards change (see below, under individual level).

Bureaucratic Politics: Tariffs as Revenue

Another factor is the role of tariffs in generating revenues for the government. Britain had been at war against France for some 20 years by 1815. To conduct its war effort, the government incurred extensive debts. In the years between 1815 and 1846, this debt was reconsolidated, but it remained large. Since the government's primary source of revenue was the tariff, any reduction in the tariff would have tremendous consequences for its ability to pay down this debt. In fact, Britain, like most European governments of the time, raised the bulk of its funds through high tariffs on a small range of goods (such as tea, coffee, sugar, and tobacco); dumping tariffs on those few goods was especially risky, since that might destroy the government's major source of funds.

Reducing tariffs, therefore, involved not only those interested in trade policy but also the Treasury. The government was only willing to drop tariffs because it planned to reinstitute the income tax. This was somewhat unpopular, however, since the income tax had never been used in peacetime before then, and people associated it with emergencies.[15] Without this ability to substitute a new revenue stream, Britain would have had a hard time altering the tariff.

The budget of 1842 included several new measures, including the standardization, simplification, and a minor reduction of tariffs. These changes caused the Treasury to anticipate a fall in the government's annual revenues of £3,780,000. The reintroduction of the income tax was supposed to counter the shortfall. The actual revenues lost that year turned out to be around £3,979,000, due to an error in the timing of the collection of taxes. Once this error was corrected, the next year's budget moved into surplus to the tune of £4,165,000.[16] This set the stage for tariff reform. To a certain extent, the fiscal changes prevented an impending bureaucratic struggle, for the Treasury would otherwise have blocked tariff reform. As a result, the bureaucratic politics aspect of the tariff reform is largely missing.

Individual Level: Peel the Conservative Reformer?

Lusztig comments that Peel was concerned with the likelihood of grievances among the lower classes leading to some sort of radical, if not even revolutionary, change in Britain. The aristocratic class still enjoyed incredible privileges. The experiences on the Continent—especially in France, where Revolution had occurred in 1789, followed by a second serious uprising in 1830—sent a message which Peel thought should have been clear to Britain's elite: they had a duty to respond to the problems of society's aggrieved. If they did not, they risked the consequences.

Lusztig argues that Peel feared further democratic changes in Britain. The Reform Act of 1832 was potentially the beginning of a series of such reforms. To head them off, Peel thought it was important for the elite to make some economic sacrifices which might improve the average person's lot in life. By dropping protection of aristocratic estates' agricultural production, food prices could be lowered. Such logic was expressed in Peel's speeches to Parliament, but they were not unanimously held. Peel's vision was hardly popular among the Tories, which is why the Repeal of the Corn Laws cost him his office. Lusztig suggests that a different Tory leader may have made different calculations and conclusions. Certainly, the political manoeuvring which Lusztig details would have been undertaken in a somewhat different fashion.

The Consequences of the Repeal of the Corn Laws

The Repeal of the Corn Laws was just about the last step in making Britain's trade "free"—in 1849 the last of the Navigation Acts were repealed. In 1840 the number of items which had duties placed on them was 1,146. By 1860 that number had fallen to 48, and of these only 36 were meant to protect British producers from foreign competition, with the other 12 being luxury goods on which the government levied customs to raise a significant amount of money.[17]

Peel's domestic political strategy seems to have worked. When liberal revolutionary challenges swept the governments of Europe in 1848, similar disruptions failed to materialize in Britain. According to Richard Cobden, Peel noted that Britain's government had already responded to popular pressures, even if those pressures hadn't been expressed through direct political or electoral channels.

One of the first reactions to Britain's unilateral moves was an implicit deal with the U.S. concerning the repeal of the Corn Laws. The U.S. watched to see what the British were doing in 1846; when the Corn Laws were repealed, the U.S. moved to lower tariffs on manufactures, because it now believed it could successfully export grain to Britain. This new lower U.S. tariff was the Walker Tariff. Russian grain exports to Britain surged after 1846 as well.

Britain's unilateral actions, then, can be seen as one possible way of encouraging others to lower their tariffs: Britain offered its domestic market to other countries unilaterally and hoped these other countries would realize the comparative advantage that would come through free trade. The only countries that readily moved in this direction, though, were those that already specialized in agricultural production. The U.S. (where the South produced cotton for the British textile mills and the West produced grain to feed British cities) and Denmark (which produced ham, cheese, and butter for export to Britain) altered their production and lowered their tariffs. It would take more direct negotiations to spark a widespread opening of the European markets. These began when Britain and France implemented the Cobden-Chevalier Treaty in 1860, as discussed in the next chapter.

Notes

1. For the best discussion of the characteristics of mercantilism, see Jacob Viner, "Power versus Plenty as Objectives of Foreign Policy in the Seventeenth and Eighteenth Centuries," *World Politics* 1,1 (October 1948): 1-29; and Eli Heckscher, *Mercantilism Vol. I-II* (London: George Allen and Unwin, 1934).

2. For example, the Reciprocity of Duties Act was enacted in 1823.

3. Most notably, the last of the Navigation Acts controlling the use of shipping were taken down in 1849.

4. Robert Gilpin, *U.S. Power and the Multinational Corporation* (New York, NY: Basic Books, 1975) 81-82. Also see Stephen Krasner, "State Power and the Structure of International Trade," *World Politics* 28,3 (April 1976): 317-47.

5. We should note how the modern world-system perspective largely parallels the arguments of the realists, with only a few differences. The major differences involve the motivations for Britain's actions. From the modern world-system perspective, Britain was acting at the behest of its most important capitalists—the new industrialists. It chose free trade as the best policy to implement in order to restructure trading relations so that its capitalists would benefit. Otherwise this perspective also emphasizes Britain's military and strategic power.

6. Krasner.

7. It is worth noting that one contemporary observer, Friedrich List, agreed with this assessment. List proposed that German states continue with mercantilism to counter Britain's attempt to dominate the international political economy. See Friedrich List, *The National System of Political Economy* (New York, NY: Augustus M. Kelley, 1966), originally written between 1841-44.

8. This and other questions are raised by Timothy McKeown, "Hegemonic Stability Theory and Nineteenth-Century Tariff Levels in Europe," *International Organization* 37,1 (Winter 1983): 73-92.

9. This is simply restating the question driving the article by Scott James and David Lake, "The Second Face of Hegemony: Britain's Repeal of the Corn Laws and the American Walker Tariff of 1846," *International Organization* 43,1 (Winter 1989): 3.

10. See Michael Lusztig, "Solving Peel's Puzzle: Repeal of the Corn Laws and Institutional Preservation," *Comparative Politics* 27,4 (July 1995): 393-408.

11. McKeown.

12. For more details, see Mark R. Brawley, *Liberal Leadership: Great Powers and Their Challengers in Peace and War* (Ithaca, NY: Cornell University Press, 1993) Chapter 4.

13. Cheryl Schonhardt-Bailey, "Specific Factors, Capital Markets, Portfolio Diversification and Free Trade: Domestic Determinants of the Repeal of the Corn Laws," *World Politics* 43 (1991): 345-69.

14. Lusztig.

15. Arthur A. Stein, "The Hegemon's Dilemma: Great Britain, the United States, and Economic Order," *International Organization* 38,2 (Spring 1984): 355-86.

16. J.F. Rees, *A Short Fiscal and Financial History of England* (London: Methuen, 1921): 90-92.

17. See Trevor May, *An Economic and Social History of Britain, 1760-1970* (New York, NY: Longman, 1987) 184-85. This view is contested by several recent accounts, which argue that protectionist measures remained effective. See John Vincent Nye, "The Myth of Free-Trade Britain and Fortress France: Tariffs and Trade in the Nineteenth Century," *Journal of Economic History* 51,1 (March 1991): 23-46; and Patrick K. O'Brien and Geoffrey Pigman, "Free Trade, British Hegemony, and the International Economic Order in the Nineteenth Century," *Review of International Studies* 18 (April 1992): 89-113.

Additional References

Anderson, Gary, and Robert Tollison. "Ideology, Interest Groups and the Repeal of the Corn Laws." *The Political Economy of Rent-Seeking.* Ed. Charles Rowley, Robert Tollison, and Gordon Tullock. (Boston, MA: Kluwer Academic, 1988). 199-216.

Eastwood, David. "Peel and the Tory Party Reconsidered." *History Today* 42 (March 1992): 27-33.

Howe, A.C. "Free Trade and the City of London, c. 1820-1870." *History* 77, 251 (October 1992): 391-410.

Irwin, Douglas. "The Welfare Effects of British Free Trade: Debate and Evidence from the 1840s." *Journal of Political Economy* 96,6 (December 1988): 1142-64.

Lusztig, Michael. "Solving Peel's Puzzle: Repeal of the Corn Laws and Institutional Preservation." *Comparative Politics* 27,4 (July 1995): 393-408.

McKeown, Timothy. "Hegemonic Stability Theory and Nineteenth-Century Tariff Levels in Europe." *International Organization* 37,1 (Winter 1983): 73-92.

—. "The Politics of Corn Law Repeal and Theories of Commercial Policy." *British Journal of Political Science* 19 (July 1989): 353-80.

Nye, John Vincent. "The Myth of Free-Trade Britain and Fortress France: Tariffs and Trade in the Nineteenth Century." *Journal of Economic History* 51,1 (March 1991): 23-46.

Schonhardt-Bailey, Cheryl. "Specific Factors, Capital Markets, Portfolio Diversification and Free Trade: Domestic Determinants of the Repeal of the Corn Laws." *World Politics* 43 (1991): 345-69.

James, Scott, and David Lake. "The Second Face of Hegemony: Britain's Repeal of the Corn Laws and the American Walker Tariff of 1846." *International Organization* 43,1 (Winter 1989): 1-29.

Spall, Richard Francis Jr. "Free Trade, Foreign Relations, and the Anti-Corn Law League." *International History Review* 10,3 (August 1988): 405-32.

Williamson, Jeffrey. "The Impact of the Corn Laws Just Prior to Repeal." *Explorations in Economic Literature* 27 (1990): 123-56.

CHAPTER 11
The Cobden-Chevalier Treaty

In the previous chapter, we saw how Britain changed its own foreign economic policy in favour of free trade and how some other states responded. Yet overall, the impact of the Repeal of the Corn Laws was limited to changes in the content and pattern of trade flows. Other states adjusted their exports and imports as Britain specialized in industrial production, but most were reluctant to abandon mercantilism. Thus, it is impossible to characterize the international trade regime of the time as free. Other countries needed more encouragement and prodding to open up their trade and to lower their tariffs.

One of the first specific missions sent by Britain to negotiate lower tariffs after the Repeal of the Corn Laws occurred when Richard Cobden visited France in 1860. Behind the scenes, contacts had been made many years before, so that the setting was ripe for a trade deal between the two countries. Napoleon III had recently been proclaimed the Emperor of France, though his actions were still constrained by Parliament. He was interested in establishing closer commercial ties with Britain, though his motivations remain the subject of much debate. The French government agreed to lower its tariffs on British goods, even though this was not very popular in France. Napoleon III had in fact been unable to pass the tariff through his own Parliament until he had signed the deal with Britain. Moreover, the agreement had some very specific strategic ramifications, which provide the seeds for several different theoretical interpretations of the event.

System-Level Theory: The Lure of British Power

Realists naturally focus on the role of Britain in these negotiations.[1] They expect to see Britain taking the initiative in attempting to construct a free trade regime. Repeal of the Corn Laws had been a unilateral act, but now, with Cobden's mission to France, Britain took direct action. Moreover, realists point to the role of British power in achieving the results desired. Rather than seeing this power purely in coercive terms, they suggest that it may have made Britain an attractive ally. France, in short, wanted Britain as a political ally and was willing to make trade concessions in order to develop a closer relationship.

In return for France's lower tariffs on British manufactures, Napoleon III negotiated Britain's acquiescence to French imperial ambitions. He let Britain get the economic deal it desired, as long as Britain promised to accept his military adventures.[2] He ordered his army to invade Northern Italy to attack the Austro-Hungarian Empire's Italian provinces; Britain remained neutral. It is worth noting that Napoleon III tried to achieve glory in Italy, but in the end military affairs were his undoing. France's defeat in the Franco-Prussian War in 1870 ended his rule.

Napoleon III had important reasons to seek Britain's favour. Austria had been defeated at the battle of Solferino in the previous months, and peace negotiations were underway in Zurich when the possibility of a commercial treaty was raised. Britain was largely in favour of Italy becoming a unified state; it therefore viewed Napoleon III's moves towards the annexation of Savoy with great suspicion and disapproval.[3] When one Englishman asked Michel Chevalier if the 1860 commercial treaty had been signed simply to reconcile Britain to Napoleon's moves in Italy, Chevalier responded "Utterly false." His position was that the treaty could not have been a ploy on the part of Napoleon III because Chevalier himself had initiated the talks through communications with Cobden in Britain and with members of Napoleon's cabinet. (That evidence is presented below.) Chevalier realized, however, that Napoleon III may well have thrown his support behind the treaty in order to improve relations with Britain.[4]

This is one example of how Britain could use military power in a positive sense to support those who were willing to make economic deals. This was done explicitly in the case of the Cobden-Chevalier Treaty, but was done implicitly as well. When France overran Spain during the Napoleonic Wars, some of Spain's American colonies rebelled, gaining their independence. The U.S. enunciated the Monroe Doctrine, which proclaimed that the North American hemisphere should be kept separate politically from the conflicts and problems of Europe, but there really wasn't much the U.S. could do to back that up. Instead, it was Britain that prevented outside interference in the new South American states, thanks to the strength of the Royal Navy. Because these South American countries exported raw materials and imported manufactures, it was in Britain's economic interest to keep them independent and outside of any other country's closed mercantilist system.

Britain, of course, could and did use military power in the more obvious coercive sense—forcing countries to adopt free trade. Those same South American countries could be bullied by the Royal Navy to loosen up their trade barriers. Among the more egregious examples of Britain's coercive use of power were the Opium Wars against China. Opium was produced in the British colony of India and sent to China, where it was being consumed in ever larger proportions. This was a great money-earner, but one that clearly was costly to the Chinese economy and society. The Chinese government decided this was unacceptable and barred the importation of opium. British ships and troops attacked China and forced Chinese ports to accept opium shipments. The Opium War was perhaps one of the crudest exercises of power, but there are other examples of British policy which weren't quite so brutal or involved trade that was much less morally troublesome and more even.

Therefore, realists tend not to worry about the domestic changes in Britain, instead focusing on the importance of the Napoleonic Wars, which ended in 1815 with Britain emerging as the dominant power in the system. It was said in those days that "the sun never sets on the British Empire," which circled the globe. The Royal Navy was the strongest in the world and could project British power virtually anywhere. Realists argue that this political position enabled Britain to make the rules of the international economy and get everyone else to agree to those rules.

Realists go on to argue that Britain's unique position meant that it would establish a particular set of international rules. Since states aim to maximize their power, Britain would set up a system with rules that benefit Britain and enhance its power. Having gone through the Industrial Revolution ahead of all others, Britain had a technological lead and, with this head start, was quick to desire free and open international economic competition, knowing that it would dominate.

The Domestic Level: The Interplay of Sector-Based Interests and Political Institutions

Since it includes both the domestic and system levels, the modern world-system interpretation for this case actually spans the most important aspects of the realist and the more sophisticated liberal viewpoints. Modern world-system theorists look first at British domestic politics: the rise of the capitalist class economically and politically and how it controlled British foreign economic policies to further its material aims. This approach should also sound similar to the realists' arguments, since in its explanation of systemic changes it too emphasizes Britain's international role. Of course, not all the bourgeoisie in Britain gained from free trade, and, given Schonhardt-Bailey's arguments noted in the previous chapter that the aristocracy and the bourgeoisie were intermixed, it is difficult to see a class acting here. Instead, one part of the British bourgeoisie got its way despite the wishes of other sections of the same class. The liberal view, therefore, has some advantages over a class-based analysis.

The typical domestic politics explanation of trade liberalization begins with the Stolper-Samuelson theorem. Having identified which groups benefit from free trade and which lose, we then consider how each group organized and interacted with domestic political institutions to set policy. This argument does not work well for explaining French policy in this case. While there were sector-based interests who stood to gain from free trade, they were on the whole much less well-organized and much weaker than those interests that feared the impact of liberalization.

There was in France a long prior tradition of public support for protectionist policies.[5] Agricultural groups were politically the most important. French agriculture was dominated by small landholders, since the Revolution had eliminated many of the large ones. As one contemporary, Auguste Arnauné, put it in 1848:

> Our land is in the hands of a peasant democracy. The duties on the products of agriculture and on livestock seem to be imposed, not in the interest of a few great landowners, but for the benefit of a whole nation of farmers, both large and small.[6]

The big negotiating point for France was the British wine tariff (see the previous chapter). While Britain had unilaterally reduced or eliminated most tariffs, some, especially on wine and alcoholic spirits, had been retained for revenue purposes. These were obviously important export items for France, so convincing Britain to reduce those tariffs became an important issue in the negotiations.[7] In the end, Britain kept some small tariffs on wine and spirits in exchange for French reductions on many of its tariffs.[8] On the other hand, French officials were also interested in placating consumer demands. In order to bring the emergent industrial sector on board, it was important to get cheap access to British coal. Thus, the French asked for Britain to agree to prohibit any limits on coal exports in the future and to prohibit any export duties on coal.[9]

The French negotiators were very interested in garnering some benefits in the deal with which they could construct a pro-free trade coalition. They knew building such a coalition would be difficult, since the government had already failed in earlier efforts to lower French tariffs unilaterally. The opposition in Parliament from the agricultural sectors (which needed some benefits in terms of new markets), artisans (the hand-manufacturing sectors), and the newly emerging industrial sectors (which were afraid of British competition) had previously blocked the government's attempts to reduce tariffs.

As a result, Napoleon III ordered his government to execute the negotiations with Britain in secret. Precautions were taken to prevent public discussion of the treaty within France until after it had been completed. He feared that if the public became aware of the talks, protests would erupt, the Chamber of Deputies would become a battlefield for the protectionists to air their views, and in all likelihood the treaty would never come to pass.[10] The negotiations took only about three months, but then the deal had to be sold to both governments and their publics. The domestic ratification process in the two countries took nearly a year.[11]

Once the deal was put together it was made public. In France, opponents demanded and received a public inquiry in the Chamber of Deputies, which stretched on until the protectionists had their say. They were forced into publicly declaring their inability to compete—a step few were willing to take. Moreover, the treaty did include aspects meant to weaken some of the opposition, and these measures may have had some impact. Ultimately, as well, the opposition would have had a tough time overturning the treaty anyway.

The institutional structure of the French political system had introduced an avenue for Napoleon's government to circumvent most parliamentary powers. In the quote above, Arnauné bemoaned the fact that peasants dominated the democratic political institutions in 1848. Institutional arrangements had changed within a short time. In December 1852 the Second Empire was proclaimed. Napoleon III was given the title of Prince-President which brought with it special powers (all through popular measures). Parliament was willing to hand over discretionary powers in several areas including important responsibilities in foreign affairs. Already, with the Constitution adopted on January 14, 1852, the then Prince-President had been given the power to sign treaties. The role of the Chamber of Deputies and Senate had not been made clear—would they retain the right to ratify deals that the Prince-President signed? Once Napoleon III was made Emperor, the Senate (by 64 to 7) gave the Emperor power to sign commercial treaties without the assent of Parliament.[12]

This suggests the possibility that the Cobden-Chevalier Treaty resulted from a domestic strategy employed by the government of Napoleon III. If the government was convinced that free trade was the best policy for France, yet public opposition was too fierce to get the policy approved in Parliament, unilateral free trade was not a possibility. The government thus turned to the area where it had autonomy from Parliament—foreign affairs. Free trade was enacted by treaty, rather than through domestic legislation. This interpretation raises an interesting question: How do we explain the government's preference for free trade if it wasn't a reflection of domestic interests? To answer that question, we need to consider bureaucratic politics, individual personalities within the French government, and the force of ideas.

The Budget and the Evidence of Bureaucratic Politics

In Britain, the biggest potential bureaucratic fight over the Repeal of the Corn Laws had revolved around the budget. Most of tariffs were removed and replaced by income tax. When the Cobden-Chevalier Treaty eliminated some of the last tariffs, those that had specifically been left to generate revenues, the income tax had to be increased. Enough people in Britain stood to gain from the increased trade that this was acceptable. Napoleon III's problem was different, for he had to sell the tariff deal to the public.

Once again, the budgetary situation had to be favourable for the government to be willing to reduce its own revenues. As long as budget allocations to different departments were not upset, few internal battles arose. The fights within the cabinet reflected personal beliefs, not bureaucratic interests (and as such are mentioned below); thus, the bureaucratic politics battle was avoided. Yet, the French government had to go even further in its budgetary changes than the British had been forced to in 1846. The treaty was sold to the French public by packaging it with various measures aimed at assisting the adjustments associated with specialization for trade. The package included money for reforestation in agricultural areas, assistance for the improvement of drainage to increase agricultural production, funds for the construction of canals and railroads, and government loans to industry.[13]

Interestingly, the shortness of the war with Austria suggested the possibilities of such assistance to Napoleon III's administration. The government had borrowed for the war in 1859. Its loan had been oversubscribed (that is, there were more people willing to lend more money than the government required), so when the war in Italy went well, it did not need to spend all that it had borrowed for this purpose. With these extra funds on hand, the government could compensate those who might be hurt by the trade liberalization. Most importantly, it could make cheap loans to industry, the one sector most likely to feel the pressure of competition from Britain.[14] While this evidence helps clarify how the government enacted its policy, it still does not provide insight into why it preferred free trade in the first place.

Individual Level: The Ideology of Cobden and Chevalier

Individual level analysis emphasizes the role of knowledge, in particular the spread of the perception that free trade was mutually beneficial. Naturally, the analysis turns to the particular individuals involved in arranging the negotiations.

Richard Cobden, the chief British negotiator, had been a powerful proponent of liberal ideology for several decades[15] and had played a critical role in the passage of the Repeal of the Corn Laws. His French counterpart, Michel Chevalier, was a professor at the Collège de France. From his academic post he spoke constantly about the benefits of free trade. He had already enjoyed a brief career as a politician: he was elected to the Chamber of Deputies for the Department of Aveyron in 1845, but his passionate support of free trade led to his defeat in the next election by a candidate running on a protectionist platform.[16]

What gives particular authority to the individual level of analysis in this specific case is the close connection between the two negotiators. Cobden and Chevalier met in 1846, when Cobden was conducting an international tour in the wake of the passage of the Repeal of the Corn Laws. He was basking in the glory of his political success, and other liberals, like Chevalier, listened intently to his advice. The two men exchanged letters. In short, they knew each other quite well, not simply from reputation.

In Chevalier's letters in 1856, we see him as the true initiator of discussions, detailing specific ideas on a treaty between the two countries.[17] However, because he did not hold an official post, he had little but a behind-the-scenes role in the negotiations once they began.[18] The most important French negotiator was undoubtedly Napoleon III himself. Without his support the treaty would never have been signed. Yet it is unclear if Napoleon III believed in the mutual benefits of free trade or merely saw the treaty as part of a broader international strategy involving his imperial ambitions (as discussed above).

Another sign of the important roles individuals can play is found in the intrigues within the French cabinet. Walewski, the Foreign Minister, opposed Napoleon III's goals in Italy. He was not only leery of any deals with the British, but was also apparently a believer in protectionism. He had to be excluded from the negotiations completely. Baroche, the Minister of Commerce, was in favour of some liberalization, and supported both Napoleon III's policy toward Italy and the commercial treaty with Britain. Within two weeks of Walewski's discovery of the secret negotiations with Britain, Baroche was brought in to replace him as Minister of Foreign Affairs[19] to ensure that the right individuals were in control of the key positions within the cabinet. In this case, idiosyncratic personalities mattered more than official roles.

An Early Constructivist Interpretation: The Power of Liberalism as an Ideology

One of the most well-known interpretations of the Cobden-Chevalier Treaty and its consequences comes from Charles Kindleberger.[20] Kindleberger examines the roles of sector-based pressures, British power, and individuals in the French decision to engage in these negotiations and finds evidence that all were involved. He is also interested in explaining why other states chose to pursue free trade in the same period.

In order to explain not only the French decision, but also the British decision to repeal the Corn Laws and the decisions of the German states and the

Netherlands to pursue free trade a short time later, Kindleberger reaches for a broader causal factor. The politics within each country differed, both in terms of the arrangement of proponents and opponents of trade liberalization and in terms of political institutional arrangements. For Kindleberger, the fact that all turned to the same policy at roughly the same time can best be explained by a single force sweeping through Europe: the power of liberalism as an ideology. Liberal practices were new and appealing, since they seemed to be working so well for Britain.

The problems with this explanation, unfortunately, are difficult to resolve. On the one hand, it is difficult to falsify. People must have believed in the efficacy of liberal policies if they chose to pursue them; thus, their beliefs in these ideas had to matter somewhat. Did they follow these beliefs against their own economic interests? That is hard to show, since liberalism argues that all benefit from free trade in the long run. Second, this explanation only works with the change occurring in one direction—the rise of free trade. If free trade spread because of the power of liberal ideas, why didn't states stick with liberalism? What explains the defection of states from the free trade regime? After all, the first serious protectionist barriers were re-erected at the end of the 1870s—less than a quarter of a century after free trade swept across Europe. Two of those examples will be discussed in the next two chapters.

The Consequences of the Cobden-Chevalier Treaty

The Cobden-Chevalier Treaty is the one event that signals the shift of the international system towards freer trade. Thus, it is worth explaining how it sparked wider changes within Europe. Britain and France negotiated and agreed to lower tariffs on a number of items and wrote the treaty in such a way that it could be extended easily to third parties.[21] In so doing, the changes were transmitted into other international relationships through the *most-favoured-nation clauses* in existing trade treaties.

A most-favoured-nation clause (MFN) designates the rights and obligations specified in trade treaties between countries. If one country extends MFN status to another, the first country guarantees it will impose the most favourable tariffs it offers to any other state. MFN status traditionally comes in two forms—conditional and unconditional. Conditional MFN says that concessions given to one country are extended to others only if they take steps to earn the concessions. For example, assume that France and Belgium have a trade treaty that grants Belgium conditional MFN status on French tariffs on coal. Britain and France later negotiate the Cobden-Chevalier Treaty, and, as part of that, Britain wants to export more coal to France. Britain negotiates a lower French tariff on coal, in return for lower British tariffs on French wines.

Belgium then has the right to the lower French tariff on coal, as long as it also takes the lower tariff on wine imports. This is how conditional MFN clauses can spread the results of bilateral negotiations to third parties.

Unconditional MFN works much more simply. Assume Belgium has unconditional MFN status with France. As soon as Britain and France agree to lower the French tariff on coal, Belgium can use the new low tariff also. With unconditional MFN, Belgium can use the tariffs at the same rate as "the most-favoured-nation's" tariff, without making any concessions.

In 1860, many European countries were linked in trade treaties with MFN clauses, but since tariffs were only going up, the MFN clauses had no positive impact. When the Cobden-Chevalier Treaty was signed, the MFN clauses served to spread the impact of liberalization. Because Britain and France signed a treaty lowering tariffs on an extensive range of important goods, and because they were already linked to third parties through these MFN clauses, changes occurred throughout these relationships. Tariffs governing trade among many European countries were reduced as a result of a chain reaction. Within a short time, most of the major European governments were practising free trade—the international trade regime had been transformed. Yet, as noted in the previous section, this free trade regime did not last long. The reasons for some of these defections are addressed in the next chapter.

Notes

1. See Charles P. Kindleberger, "The Rise of Free Trade in Western Europe," *Journal of Economic History* 35,1 (March 1975): 20-55.
2. The logic may have worked in the opposite direction as well. Despite the strength of the Royal Navy, Britain had reason to fear France. Several war scares wracked Britain in 1858-59. The presence of another Napoleonic Empire across the English Channel was enough ammunition for the popular press to conjure up images of a possible invasion. Such ideas not only gripped the public imagination, they also influenced politicians. Britain suddenly began to invest not only in the Royal Navy, but also in military fortifications on the British Isles. To avoid any conflict, or simply to avoid the greater expenditures associated with these defences, Britain's political leadership was interested in improving political relations with France. See Arthur Lewis Dunham, *The Anglo-French Treaty of Commerce of 1860* (Ann Arbor, MI: University of Michigan Press, 1930) 50-52.
3. Dunham 61-62.
4. Dunham 61; also see Dunham 77 (fn 23). Dunham, one of the historians who has looked closely at the Commercial Treaty of 1860, argues that its primary impact was economic. There may well have been other goals for Napoleon III and the French, but these diplomatic aims were short-lived. Britain and France did not enter into close enough relations to form a true alliance.
5. Dunham Chapter 1.
6. As quoted in Dunham 17.

7. Dunham 88-92, 99-100. Interestingly, O'Brien and Pigman have argued that these tariffs were left on in Britain as a protectionist measure for agriculture, not for revenue purposes. See Patrick K. O'Brien and Geoffrey Pigman, "Free Trade, British Hegemony, and the International Economic Order in the Nineteenth Century," *Review of International Studies* 18 (April 1992): 89-113.

8. In order to keep the budget in order, the income tax had to raised again. The number of articles covered by a tariff fell from 419 to 48, and the revenues thereby lost totalled £2,000,000. See Dunham 110.

9. Dunham 99-100.

10. Dunham Chapter IV.

11. Dunham 102.

12. Dunham 38.

13. Dunham 124.

14. Dunham Chapter VIII.

15. Peter Cain, "Capitalism, War and Internationalism in the Thought of Richard Cobden," *British Journal of International Studies* 5,3 (October 1979): 229-47.

16. Dunham 34.

17. Dunham 44.

18. Dunham 59.

19. Dunham 62.

20 Kindleberger.

21. Dunham 102.

Additional References

Cain, Peter. "Capitalism, War and Internationalism in the Thought of Richard Cobden." *British Journal of International Studies* 5,3 (October 1979): 229-47.

Kindleberger, Charles P. "The Rise of Free Trade in Western Europe." *Journal of Economic History* 35,1 (March 1975): 20-55.

Ratcliffe, Barrie M. "Napoleon and the Anglo-French Commercial Treaty of 1860: A Reconsideration." *Journal of European Economic History* 2,3 (Winter 1973): 582-613.

Reybaud, Louis. *Economistes modernes*. Paris: M. Levy Frères, 1862.

Waleh, Jean. *Michel Chevalier économiste Saint-Simonien 1806-1879*. Paris: J. Vrin, 1975.

CHAPTER 12

Sir John A. Macdonald and the Introduction of Canada's National Policy

In many respects, the 1870s represent a watershed in the international political economy. Freer trade had spread out internationally in the wake of the Cobden-Chevalier Treaty, so that most major economies had adopted liberal trade policies. Yet this greater openness to trade was soon unpopular in many countries, as increased productive capacity, coupled with major breakthroughs in transportation (such as the spread of railroad networks and improvements in steamship operations), flooded many markets with commodities. As markets were inundated, prices dropped, and countries suddenly faced painful trade adjustments.

Canada was no exception. In the election of 1878, the Tories won on a platform featuring protectionism. As their leader, Sir John A. Macdonald, pronounced to an audience of businessmen in Ontario during the campaign, "Tell us how much protection you want, gentlemen, and we'll give you what you need." The electorate, already frustrated with the failure to negotiate a better trade deal with the U.S. in the previous few years, doubted the Liberals would be able to open up trade as they intended.[1] The Tories, therefore, were in a position to promise protection to those sectors that were asking for it, without being too severely punished by voters who might have held other preferences. The Liberals stuck with their traditional support for free trade. As one Liberal, David Mills, charged during the campaign, "We are not simply traveling upon divergent roads: we are seeking to persuade you to take opposite directions."[2] The Tories' platform emphasizing protection proved more popular, since they went from 60 seats behind the Liberals to hold a majority of more than 60.[3]

U.S. interest in trade liberalization had declined with the severe economic downturn of the 1870s. Hard times hit Canadians too. Canada's industrial sectors wanted protection from foreign competition, and protectionism appealed strongly to both labour and capital in heavy industry. The Tories needed to draw votes away from other segments of the economy, of course. In this economic downturn, however, groups with less clear-cut interests on trade surely worried about the security of their employment.[4] Protectionism could be fashioned to appeal to these groups by expanding the tariff to cover other products.

But there were also those who would not benefit from higher barriers to trade. For groups unambiguously hurt by protection, such as grain growers, the Tories offered compensation. Tariffs were pitched as one part of a set of reforms—though agricultural tariffs helped farmers little, since they did not fear foreign competition. The National Policy therefore packaged two other policies, meant to assist farmers in particular, with the tariff increases. Support for the Canadian Pacific Railway's (CPR) transcontinental rail line was as central to the National Policy as the tariff. New railway construction would make it easier and cheaper for farmers to ship goods to markets. Thus, the National Policy supported expansion of the rail network through direct subsidies of money and land, tax breaks on railroad assets (as well as on construction materials), and the granting of a 20-year monopoly on traffic to and from western Canada to the CPR.[5]

The second policy covered immigration and settlement of the western regions. Previous governments had taken several steps in this direction. The Dominion Lands Act, passed in 1872, encouraged homesteading, and the North West Mounted Police were established in 1874 to provide order to the territories where settlers were headed.[6] Support for Western interests was essential to the National Policy. If tariffs helped eastern industries, these sectors would need a domestic market. Farmers would constitute that market, but only if their numbers increased and only if the regions of Canada were integrated via the transportation network. The three elements of the National Policy— tariffs, railroad construction, and immigration and settlement—would work best in conjunction with each other.[7] Politically, it was also important for the Tories to package these policies together, though the tariffs enacted included raising rates on goods whose producers hadn't asked for protection.

The Tories relied on the National Policy as the centrepiece of their government for nearly 20 years. They not only used trade policy to create a majority, but this majority held together for quite some time. In their attempts to knock the Tories out of government, the Liberals focused on the tariff in several elections fought between 1878 and 1896, so politicians clearly thought majorities could be built around either protection or free trade. Why did Macdonald adopt the National Policy? Why was it so enduring?

The System Level: What Choices did Canada Have?

As mentioned above, the systemic setting did create the incentive to pursue protectionism in 1878. The economic downturn of the 1870s had severely affected many countries, and most would implement some form of protectionism around the same time as Canada. Just as today, the U.S. represented Canada's principal trading partner, and U.S. decisions shaped Canadian options then, as now. Alexander Mackenzie's Liberal government, in office leading up to the 1878 election, had negotiated a trade deal with the U.S., only to have it rejected by the U.S. Senate.[8] Realistically, Canada had only two choices: remain open while others closed their markets to Canadian exports or retaliate.

Also important, of course, was the nature of the international arrangements governing trade. In the wake of the Cobden-Chevalier Treaty, free trade had spread via clauses in bilateral trade agreements. There were no widespread treaty conventions, no broad rules spelling out obligations or norms of behaviour. The free trade regime rose in an ad hoc fashion and deteriorated in the same way. As one country defected on the liberal norms, so did others, again in a ripple fashion. Without a regime with explicit rules on behaviour, states could act as they chose. Moreover, with no prior historical experience to fall back on, states believed that they could defect first, reaping the benefits of having their markets protected from foreign competition while still holding access to foreign markets. Such beliefs were short-lived, however, as retaliations occurred, and trade wars enveloped numerous countries in the 1880s.

Still, there were those countries that chose not to adopt protective tariffs in the wake of the depression. Britain is the best example, but there were others, such as Belgium. Moreover, the National Policy tariffs did not serve well as retaliatory devices, for they were never used to leverage a better deal from the U.S. That may have been by choice on the part of the Tories, however, since they were accused by the Liberals of not pursuing opportunities to do so. That raises the other question pertinent here: Would the systemic environment also explain why the National Policy lasted so long?

Along the same lines, the systemic environment may provide some sense of why the National Policy included domestic policies. The logic of developing a transnational railroad was clearly linked to economic independence from the U.S. Lacking a high-speed transcontinental link, the western provinces could only trade with the east via U.S. railroads or overland along long, winding roads. The railroad was vital for successfully standing back from the economic ties with the neighbour to the South.

The idea of increasing settlement in the west was also critical for the National Policy's success. Adopting protectionist tariffs was a common response to the economic downturn of the era, because markets were shrinking—producers wanted to maintain their volume of business by eliminating competition. But when other states retaliate, export markets are lost; the home market must then grow. Moreover, to continue economic growth, the country must have balanced resources. In Canada's case, industrial producers were losing the U.S. market. The domestic market needed to grow, and that was why the immigration policy was so important. Combined with the railroad link, the new settlers would be suppliers of agricultural products to urban areas and a market for industrial goods. Self-sufficiency, at least *vis-à-vis* the U.S., was a clear goal.

Domestic Politics: Cleavages on Trade

Not all Canadians agreed. The Tories won a substantial majority in 1878, and they used this majority to enact the package of policies meant to appeal to all sectors. Yet it is also easy to see why these policies lost their attractiveness over time. We can start by looking at the tariffs, but we also need to consider the two other major aspects of the National Policy.

If we consider the relative endowments of factors of production, it should come as no surprise who supported the National Policy tariffs and who did not. In the late nineteenth century, Canada was relatively well-endowed with only one major factor compared to other countries: land. Capital was relatively scarce, as was labour. Using the Stolper-Samuelson theorem, we would expect landowners (farmers) to prefer free trade, while industrial interests wanted protection. This is largely what we observe in this era, though farmers were often divided on the issue as well. In the early years, the western votes which we associate with agricultural interests (and particularly land-intensive grain production) were overwhelmed by votes from Ontario, Quebec, and the provinces further east.

Other dimensions of the National Policy were problematic, as well. Construction of the transcontinental line of the CPR took longer than expected and cost more than planned. As a result, the CPR was allowed to charge high rates for transporting goods along its main line. This caused resentment among the farmers and shopkeepers in the west who had little choice but to use it. The Liberals charged that what the country needed was greater competition in transportation and supported the construction of a rival rail line across the country.

The immigration policy also did not work as planned. Although the Tories had argued that the domestic economy could be increased by settling more people in the west, creating a domestic market for eastern manufacturers, they did little to support immigrants. In fact, whenever the Canadian economy did less well than its neighbour to the South, people moved. Although Canada was attracting immigrants, it was also losing population to the U.S.—often more people were leaving than entering! Thus, it may be fair to charge that the National Policy failed to deliver on all three parts of the strategy. Without a rapidly expanding economy, including a booming west easily accessible as a market for eastern producers, the Tories had a weaker justification for the tariff.

The electorate was also divided along other lines. In Quebec, nationalism soon stirred the interests of the voters. This affected trade policy issues, because foreign economic policy was tied to Canada's role in the British Empire. There were other important regional differences, sometimes linked to the importance of immigrant populations, sometimes because of the variation in terms of the strength of local ties to the U.S. economy, sometimes because of the differences with which goods made within the region were treated under the tariffs. In short, while the appeal of the National Policy helped build the Tories a majority, there were plenty of reasons why it might not have endured as long as it did.

Bureaucratic Politics: The Tariff and Taxes

As with other examples of trade policy decisions in the late nineteenth century, decisions to alter the tariff were intimately related to the health of government revenues. When the global economy entered a recession in 1873, the Liberals then in power in Canada faced tough decisions. As trade declined, revenues from the tariff dried up. The government had to choose between cutting expenditures during hard times or raising the rates charged on the remaining goods in trade. After trying to reduce government outlays, they had to raise the tariff upwards.[9]

The National Policy raised these rates higher. In fact, later election contests often pitted the Tories, lauding the National Policy in all its dimensions, against the Liberals, arguing instead for a tariff "for revenue only." Thus, the Liberals were not about to engage in completely free trade, at least not in this era. The Tories preferred a higher tariff, one that would offer protection to certain sectors. The two parties were both interested in having tariffs, but they held different ideas in terms of their shape and size.

The desire to raise revenues with the National Policy can be seen in how the rates were set. Previously, Canada had charged an *ad valorem* rate; that is, the duty paid was a percentage of the declared value of the imported item. Yet the critical driving force of the 1870s downturn was the flooding of goods on markets, causing prices to crash. With an ad valorem tariff, as prices dropped, so too did the revenue collected. Thus, when the Tories altered the tariff, they also changed the type of charges to specific rates (i.e., a set charge per item) or at least established minimum rates below which ad valorem rates could not fall.[10]

That the economic downturn of the 1870s led to a protectionist tariff is not particularly surprising—it fits with the actions of many other states. What is more curious is the length of time Canada held on to the National Policy tariff. The Liberals argued in favour of tariff reductions but did not regain office until 1896. Even then, they only tinkered with the tariff, but made few substantial reductions.

Individuals and Ideas: Liberalism Loses its Appeal

Most of the credit for engineering the National Policy goes to Sir John A. Macdonald. He was a shrewd politician, who clearly had a vision for his country. He had the skills to get the support for these policies and the nerve to argue for protectionism when the dominant ideas of the era were surely more akin to classical liberalism. Evidence, including his political career prior to 1878, suggests he was comfortable with a range of foreign economic policies and swung to protectionism as the situation dictated.

Like so many others, his thinking was changed by the experience of the 1870s. Liberalism had promised that with the opening of trade between countries and of market relationships domestically, all could be made better off. Initially, this appeared to be the case, as the world enjoyed an economic boom in the 1860s. But when economies collapsed in the 1870s, liberal ideas were no longer successful. As often happens when a severe crisis occurs, old thinking is challenged. Liberal notions—not just about free trade, but about the importance of domestic competition, the role of government in the economy, and so forth—were all brought into question. In some places, socialism became much more popular. In many, individual firms dealt with their difficulties by negotiating arrangements to limit their competition with their rivals. In Europe, cartels developed; pools, monopolies, and later trusts arose in the U.S. Some states, such as Germany, began experimenting with social welfare legislation in order to prevent economic crises from inspiring political unrest. It is no surprise, then, that Canada, like so many countries, turned its back on liberal international policies. Macdonald merely changed his thinking to adapt to his changing environment.

Macdonald's skill as a politician may tell us more about why the National Policy lasted as long as it did. If we associate the enactment of tariffs with an economic slow-down, why didn't the return of good times lead to another liberalization of trade? This should be especially true when we consider how limited the other two dimensions of the National Policy turned out, as described above. The railroad was built, but it remained fairly expensive to ship goods across the country. Settlement of the prairies was slow, and Canada actually had a declining population at times, despite immigrants coming in. Still, the Tories remained in office for 20 years. Macdonald, a fierce campaigner, held together the interests of the eastern urban centres (who continued to prefer the tariff), called on patriotism when needed (urging further national development independent of the Americans), and relied on patronage. When he died in 1891, he was still in office, and the National Policy remained in force.

The Liberals Adopt the National Policy

The Liberals finally defeated the Tories in the election of 1896. The Manitoba schools question brought out the most vitriolic debates, but economic issues accounted for Liberal gains in Quebec and the Maritimes.[11] Agrarian discontent with the National Policy had long been present in the west, and that counted for some of their support as well. The Liberals made it known they preferred freer trade, but only in the right conditions. This helped them appeal to small farmers out west, but it also drew support from some workers and businessmen in central Canada.

Yet, when it came to the tariff, those who expected immediate changes were disappointed. The Liberals did not move to lower the tariff, instead seeking benefits from doing so. The Tories immediately charged the Liberals with hypocrisy. As O.J. McDiarmid describes so aptly, "Vociferous though the Liberals were in criticism of high tariffs and in extolling the theoretical principles of free trade, they failed to tear down the protective walls when they came into power."[12]

Frustration in their attempts to deal with the U.S. held the Liberals back. In Laurier's famous phrase after one such failure, "there will be no more pilgrimages to Washington." Even a sympathetic writer such as L. Ethan Ellis noted that "when Laurier and the Liberals came to power in 1896 it was easy to forget the low tariff and pro-reciprocity planks which had largely aided their election, and to slip into a relationship with the protected interests not unlike that of their Conservative predecessors."[13] The Liberals' first changes to the tariff merely echoed those the Tories had executed several years before—a lowering of some rates to reduce prices of farmers' inputs—but in general rates were kept high.[14] Only when the U.S. proved accommodating did Laurier and the Liberals offer freer trade to the voters. They had to wait until 1911 to do so.

Although they did not alter the tariff significantly, the Liberals substantially altered the other aspects of the National Policy. To focus solely on the tariff obscures the way the trade policy interacted with other policies economically and politically. The Liberals handled the railways differently and pursued much more active and positive policies on immigration and land settlement. In 1897 they negotiated the Crow's Nest Pass agreement with the CPR, lowering shipping rates for the prairie provinces. This made it less expensive for farmers to export their grain, but also made it cheaper for settlers to bring along their necessary stores.[15] By encouraging the development of rival rail companies, the Liberals challenged the CPR's monopoly on east-west traffic, thereby reducing transportation costs for farmers and small businesses.[16]

Average annual government expenditures on immigration (if we ignore expenditure on quarantine facilities) rose dramatically. In the early years of the National Policy (1878 to 1886), Tory governments spent $228,000 per year; between 1886 and 1896 the annual average fell to $196,000. Under the Liberals it shot up to $748,000 (1897 to 1913).[17] The results were just as obvious. Despite the National Policy, net immigration had gone from −1.5 per cent in 1871-81 to −3.4 per cent in 1881-91, and then slowed a bit to −2.7 per cent in 1891-1901. As the Liberals' policies took hold, however, net immigration swung sharply into the positive: +15.1 per cent in 1901-11.[18]

Immigration policies were also reoriented to focus on attracting farmers. Money was spent on advertising the potential of the western provinces to foreigners. Of the 2.5 million immigrants who came to Canada between 1896 and 1914, 1 million settled on the prairies.[19] These immigrants could settle these areas successfully because the Liberals also changed the policies covering land and homesteading. Land grants to railroads were ended, and unused grant land was opened up simply by implementing the Dominion Lands Act as originally written. Simplifications in filing homestead claims helped as well.[20] The rise in wheat prices also encouraged settlement. A bushel of wheat commanded only 84 cents in 1896, but as much as $1.13 in 1913. Improvements in technology, including advances in developing strands of wheat that grew in short harsh climates, made it possible for more farmers to be successful.[21] Homestead entries went from 88,863 in the 25 years leading up to 1900 to 111,115 in 1900-05.[22]

The economic payoff was in additional agricultural exports and overall growth in the national economy. Up to 1900, Canada provided only a meagre 4 per cent of the international market for wheat. At that level it was comparable to other exporters such as India and provided much less than Australia or the U.S. Liberal policies on land and immigration helped Canada's wheat exports grow so fast that by 1915, Canada held 16 per cent of the international market.[23] The additional exports, plus the extra economic activity generated by the settlers and continued railroad construction, stimulated the national economy.

While the Liberals pursued these other elements of the National Policy for new results, they did not alter the tariff significantly. Average rates dropped only slightly. In 1891, the average duty had been 32 per cent, and this had been lowered to 30 per cent by 1896 under the Tories. After seven years of Liberal government, the average rate still stood at 27 per cent.[24] The Liberals were certainly more sensitive to complaints linking the tariff to the rise of monopolies and combinations. Their first tariff included a clause specifically addressing this issue. If it was shown that the tariff led to a monopoly in Canada, the protective rate could be removed.[25] The Liberals revisited the issue of combinations in the restraint of trade in the Combines Investigation Act of 1910. This was a response to complaints posed by farmers and small businesses about the negative indirect effects of the tariff.[26] The law did not produce any dramatic court cases, but it did shine the public spotlight on the behaviour of industry. It highlights the different bases of support each party rested on, as well as how the National Policy was converted into something the Liberals could call their own.

Conclusions: Building a National Economy

The Tories relied on the National Policy as a cornerstone for nearly 20 consecutive years in office. Macdonald is credited, rightfully, with having cemented the Canadian provinces together into a single country after Confederation, with the National Policy being a pivotal instrument in that success. The National Policy clearly shaped Canadian economic development and strongly influenced the outlines of Canadian infrastructural development, its degree of integration with the U.S., and the subsequent freedom of action Canada would have in its dealings with its large, powerful neighbour.

Notes

1. W.L. Morton, *The Kingdom of Canada*, 2nd ed. (Toronto, ON: McClelland and Stewart, 1969) 356; Roger Riendeau, *A Brief History of Canada* (Markham, ON: Fitzhenry and Whiteside, 2000) 155.

2. O.J. McDiarmid, *Commercial Policy in the Canadian Economy* (Cambridge, MA: Harvard University Press, 1946) 156.

3. Oscar Skelton, *The Canadian Dominion* (New Haven, CT: Yale University Press, 1919) 169-70.

4. McDiarmid 156.

5. Even with these advantages, the CPR would be asking for further assistance by 1885. For a short description of this dimension of the National Policy, see Riendeau 156-57.

6. Riendeau 158.

7. Donald Creighton, *A History of Canada* (Cambridge, MA: Houghton-Mifflin, 1958) 346; Diane Eaton and Garfield Newman, *Canada A Nation Unfolding* (Toronto, ON: McGraw-Hill Ryerson, 1994) 119-20.

8. John S. Moir and D.M.L. Farr, *The Canadian Experience* (Toronto, ON: McGraw Hill Ryerson, 1969) 280.

9. Moir and Farr 278, 281.

10. McDiarmid 161.

11. McDiarmid 202; Joseph Schull, *Laurier: The First Canadian* (Toronto, ON: Macmillan, 1965) 322; Morton 390-91.

12. McDiarmid 202.

13. L. Ethan Ellis, *Reciprocity 1911: A Study in Canadian-American Relations* (New Haven, CT: Yale University Press, 1939) 5. Also see Skelton 240; John W. Dafoe, *Clifford Sifton in Relation to His Times* (Toronto: Macmillan, 1931) 120; Creighton 389-90; Moir and Farr 319.

14. Schull 343-44; John T. Saywell, "The 1890s," *The Canadians 1867-1967, Part I*, ed. J.M.S. Careless and Roger Craig Brown (Toronto, ON: Macmillan, 1968) 128.

15. Kenneth Norrie and Douglas Owram, *A History of the Canadian Economy*, 2nd ed. (Toronto, ON: Harcourt Brace, 1996) 235; Robert Brown and Ramsay Cook, *Canada 1896-1921: A Nation Transformed* (Toronto, ON: McClelland and Stewart, 1974) 147-48.

16. David J. Hall, *Clifford Sifton*, Vol. 2 (Vancouver, BC: University of British Columbia Press, 1985) 97.

17. William Marr and Donald Paterson, *Canada: An Economic History* (Toronto, ON: Macmillan, 1980) 350.

18. Norrie and Owram 218-19.

19. Riendeau 174.

20. Brown and Cook 55; Hall 61-62.

21. Brown and Cook 51-53.

22. Hall 57.

23. Norrie and Owram 235.

24. Norrie and Owram 249.

25. Saywell 129-30.

26. Henry Ferns and Bernard Ostry, *The Age of Mackenzie King* (Toronto, ON: James Lorimer, 1976) 100; Brown and Cook 93.

Additional References

McDiarmid, Orville, J. *Commercial Policy in the Canadian Economy*. Cambridge, MA: Harvard University Press, 1946.

Neill, Robin. *A History of Canadian Economic Thought*. New York, NY: Routledge, 1991.

CHAPTER 13

The Failure of Caprivi's New Course: Imperial Germany Defects from the Free Trade Regime

Germany was one of the first states to defect from the free trade regime. The country had been unified under the leadership of Prussia when the numerous German states that fought alongside each other in the Franco-Prussian War came together. Prussia's Otto von Bismarck led this diplomatic manoeuvring and then took up the most important executive post (after the monarch) in the new German government. The political structure of the new German Empire was dominated by Prussia—and Prussian interests. The new state first adopted free trade because it was in the interest of Prussia's aristocrats, the Junkers, who owned large tracts of land and grew grain. Since Germany was endowed with much land and was not yet industrialized, the country exported those goods made intensively with its locally abundant factors of production. The international economy was rapidly changing, however. In the 1870s, improved technology expanded the number of countries and volume of commodities involved in international trade. These changes altered the competitiveness of various sectors in the German economy, as will be explained below.[1]

Bismarck now had a different domestic political task on his hands. He wanted to protect the economic, political, and social status of the Junkers. He had to protect their income from grain production by establishing a protectionist tariff. He gathered together a coalition uniting the conservative agriculturalists and the new industrial capitalists, a coalition referred to as the "Coalition of Iron and Rye." The tariff was Bismarck's single most important tool—the Junkers did not want to face the agricultural competition from the developing countries, while the industrialists did not want to face exports from Britain.[2] Most analyses of Germany's trade policies between 1870 and 1914 focus on Bismarck's machinations and leave us with the impression that the Coalition of Iron and Rye held sway right up until World War I.

What we examine in this chapter, however, is something a little different. Germany's policies did not run in a smooth consistent pattern from 1879 until

1914. Bismarck's protectionist coalition came unglued, and a free trade coalition held power for a brief period. Given what economists tell us about the pay-offs from trade liberalization, the free traders should have been in a position to compensate the protectionists (or at least some of them) and therefore solidify their hold on power. Why didn't this occur? Peter Gourevitch notes that the free trade coalition should have been able to hold onto power since it was "perhaps even a majority of the electorate."[3] It was given the opportunity to consolidate its preferences after the election of 1890, when Leo von Caprivi took over the office of chancellor. As Gourevitch asks, "Why did this coalition lose over the long run?"[4] Is it simply a domestic-level story—as suggested by our discussion so far—or were there other factors at work as well?

Background: Bismarck's "Coalition of Iron and Rye"

Prior to Germany's unification in 1872, the Junkers were politically dominant in Prussia. This political dominance was maintained within the federal government of the new united Germany, due to institutional arrangements. As large-scale producers of grain, the Junkers had long been successful exporters. They had naturally supported free trade.[5] This makes perfect sense when we use the H-O model (and the Stolper-Samuelson theorem) to assess Germany's position *vis-à-vis* the country's main trading partners within Europe; Germany's abundant factor of production was land. Manufacturing interests, primarily in the western regions of Germany, were more interested in protection from British goods, reflecting Germany's lower ratio of capital to labour compared to Britain. In formulating Germany's original tariff policies just after the country unified, industry argued in favour of protection while agriculture pressed for free trade.[6] The Junkers' dominant political position meant Germany adopted low tariffs.

By the end of the decade, however, the European economy soured. Prices dropped as new trade competitors emerged. Cheap grain flowed into Europe from the plains of the U.S., Canada, Russia, and Argentina. These agricultural regions were suddenly able to export bulk commodities such as grain due to the extension of the railroads into the interior of continents, which lowered transport costs substantially.[7] Since one assesses a country's factor endowments relative to its trading partners, and Germany's trading partners were essentially different now, Germany could no longer be considered relatively abundant in land. The Junkers could not produce grain at competitive prices. Naturally, they reversed their stance on trade.[8] Since industry still desired protection from British competition (and this was intensified due to an economic downturn which meant lower demand), Bismarck offered a protective tariff to industry. The tariff united heavy industry and the Junkers. Bismarck reorganized the conservatives into a new political party, developing the party's program around economic policies designed to appeal to agrarian interests.[9]

The pattern of change, however, was not straightforward. Between the Coalition of Iron and Rye in 1879 and the outbreak of World War I, Germany's tariffs briefly moved back towards freer trade, only to reverse direction again. In the early 1890s, the government of von Caprivi temporarily lowered Germany's tariffs. These efforts were short-lived, and when Caprivi's government fell, trade policy swung back to protectionism.

The System Level: Retaliations—Or the Lack Thereof?

If the German tariff of 1879 signalled Germany's defection from the free trade regime, how did other countries react? One of the obvious things to remember, when we consider the systemic factors at work in the late 1800s, was that the free trade regime in place was completely informal. There may have been international norms created by Britain's Repeal of the Corn Laws and the Cobden-Chevalier Treaty, but there were no explicit obligations to the regime. The regime had taken some time to establish itself and had been created in an ad hoc fashion. Now it fell apart slowly, also in an ad hoc fashion. The erosion of the regime is often blamed on Germany (along with some other states).

The only restraints placed on Germany's policies by the regime, therefore, were the implicit threats of retaliation from those wishing to continue to pursue free trade. These retaliations had not been very strong in 1879; demand had fallen already, so what were these other states denying Germany? Since their purchases of German exports were already low, retaliation would not have achieved much. Perhaps this explains the reaction of Britain; as stated earlier, Britain earned substantial sums from the services associated with international trade. It could afford to have a balance of trade deficit, because it made so much more from international investments and services that it still came out ahead in the overall balance of payments. If Britain had retaliated against the protectionist policies of Germany or other countries, it would have hurt itself. So, in response to the erosion of the free trade regime in the 1870s-80s, Britain did nothing.

What were the rewards, then, for Caprivi's government to liberalize Germany's tariffs in the early 1890s? For one thing, Germany had begun to export an assortment of goods and was ready to compete internationally in industrial production. The German economy's characteristics were changing. It was much more industrialized, and the country itself more urbanized. Its leading economic sectors (e.g., chemicals, electrical goods, steel, etc.) were at the forefront of technological development. These groups, while competitive, nonetheless benefited from protection since the tariffs allowed them to charge higher prices within Germany. In order to continue to grow, however, these businesses needed export markets. The Coalition of Iron and Rye was headed to a divorce, since the agricultural sectors were declining in competitiveness and required protectionism more than ever, while the industrial sectors could afford to abandon protectionism.

Specifically, the exporters were concerned about the series of trade negotiations nearing completion in the 1890s. The most important market at stake was the U.S. Unlike Britain, the U.S. had no large earnings from international services yet. In fact, it had had its own form of protectionism in place for some time. German industrialists wanted to gain entry into the U.S. market, but Germany's high grain tariffs were clearly an obstacle for reaching any positive agreement. The U.S. exported vast amounts of grain, and U.S. farmers wanted access to the German market. Since the U.S. was not going to let German industrial goods in without first being able to export its own agricultural goods, and the U.S. market was critical for heavy industry's exports, Germany's industrial sectors began to speak out against high agricultural tariffs. The chemical industry led the change in direction when it formed a new lobbying organization (the Bund der Industriellen, or BdI) early in 1891.[10] The BdI was a powerful voice in favour of trade liberalization, but it needed allies.

There was additional systemic pressure to reverse some of the protectionist tariffs. Germany's military and political strategies had to be supported by foreign economic policies. While many scholars have stressed how agricultural self-sufficiency was a goal pursued for military purposes, the truth is a bit more mixed. By 1890, German politicians were concerned about encirclement and about being isolated by an opposing coalition. The alliance between France and Russia put tremendous pressure on German decision-makers. Securing stable allies became a top priority. One way of attracting and solidifying alliances was to offer economic concessions. Some concessions on agricultural tariffs were made to the Scandinavian countries, making it easier to import pork products into Germany. Tariff negotiations with Austria-Hungary were ongoing at that time as well—and that country would almost certainly be seeking to export agricultural goods to Germany.[11] Germany needed Austria-Hungary as an ally, and therefore some sort of trade concession would be extremely useful.

By the summer of 1891, agricultural prices seemed to be headed in an upward spiral, thrust to higher levels by the tariff. Germany's agricultural production was not increasing in response to the higher prices; exporters felt that their interests were certainly threatened. The opposition to protectionism—previously only voiced by the heavy industrial sectors—now started to gel. Because grain prices continued to rise in 1891, Caprivi was forced to take action.[12]

When he took office in 1890, Caprivi had two choices. If protectionism continued or even increased, there would be trade wars on several fronts. If, on the other hand, he changed Germany's policies, it would be possible to negotiate the opening of several important markets. It was with this second path in mind that Caprivi undertook talks with the Austro-Hungarian Empire, Italy, Switzerland, and several other countries. Germany would pursue trade policy in a new direction until Caprivi's administration fell in October 1894.[13] So while the systemic factors have largely been downplayed in most accounts of Germany's tariff decisions in the 1890s, they do in fact play an important role.

The Domestic Level: Economic Changes and Interests

According to the Stolper-Samuelson theorem, as the German economy changed, the distribution of benefits from trade should have been redistributed. After 1870 the German economy was characterized by rapid capital accumulation, which manifested itself in a spurt of industrialization, the application of more machinery in production, and higher rates of savings and investments. These changes in the endowments of the factors of production should have led to a realignment of the political supporters of free trade and protection. Those interested in free trade should have gained strength over time, as key components of the protectionist Coalition of Iron and Rye lost interest in maintaining barriers against imports.

In the 1870s, two-thirds of Germany's population lived on the land; by 1914, two-thirds lived in the cities. Industrialization was clearly the motor behind such a change.[14] Among the fastest growing elements of this industrializing economy were iron and steel production, along with those businesses that transformed iron or steel into other products. Production of machinery and instruments grew rapidly. Trade and banking grew apace.[15] The railroad network in Germany increased in scope and scale. In 1878, there were 5,000 kilometres of tracks established. By 1890 the length of track laid had risen to 25,000 kilometres, but that wasn't the end of the construction boom. By 1910, the amount had risen to 37,000 kilometres.[16]

As noted earlier, Bismarck had cemented the Coalition of Iron and Rye by raising the tariff but also by forming a new conservative party, which focused attention on the interests of the Junkers. At first, it had included heavy industry, but in the 1890s, elements of heavy industry were ready to re-enter an alliance with small businesses, which had long backed the various Liberal parties.

There were other important political parties, reflecting other interests. Labour was represented by the Social Democratic Party, Catholics by the Centre Party. As the economic characteristics of the country changed, the capital-intensive sectors became more and more interested in expanding exports and less and less fearful of foreign competition. The land-intensive sectors (i.e., agriculture), on the other hand, were increasingly less competitive compared to international rivals and therefore became more and more interested in protection. Labour was divided—it wanted freer trade as a way to reduce the price of food, but it too feared that foreign competition would lead to lower wages.[17] Thus, we have the ingredients for applying a sector-based model of trade politics, as opposed to the Stolper-Samuelson theorem.

Of course, to follow through on the domestic politics model, we next need to see how the different economic interests organized themselves for political action and then interacted with the various political institutions. In the 1890s, organized interest group activities began to matter much more than they had in the past, primarily because the cost of elections rose. Political parties had to raise more and more money to compete. Trade policy remained where Bismarck had placed it—at the top of the political agenda; it proved to be one of the strongest forces provoking groups to organize and to donate funds to political parties.[18]

One of the groups most interested in challenging the existing policies of protectionism was the working class. In many sectors, workers were already organized in unions. The labour movement was divided, however, between the socialists and the Catholics, with each set of unions having a relationship with a specific party. The rising price of bread ate into the real earnings of workers, and as a result working-class agitation rose. The number of strikes in 1889 was a sharp increase from preceding years. The workers' greatest weakness, however, was their inability to win power in state elections. The single most powerful state in the German federation was Prussia, and in Prussian state elections the workers were completely underrepresented. Since voting rights were linked to taxes and wealth, the poor could be effectively excluded. And Prussia's policies were determined by the Junkers.

The various state governments sent their representatives to Germany's upper legislature, the Bundesrat. Prussia held enough power there to veto most policies; since the Junkers controlled Prussia, they could indirectly dominate the German government. If the workers were ever to play a significant role, their unions and political parties would have to join forces with others. There were potential allies, since there was a second group interested in overturning the protectionist policies: exporters. In the closing years of the 1880s, German exports had been relatively stagnant. Exporters were beginning to blame protectionism for the closure of other markets to German goods. Exporters believed their interests were not being taken into account. They formed several organizations to raise money and promote the liberalization of trade; the two most important were the BdI and the Hansa-Bund.

Caprivi used trade liberalization to get support not only from the Liberals, but also from the Social Democrats and the Centre Party. A coalition between capital in the industries producing for export and the working class was not very stable. While Caprivi tried to forge some of these links once he came to power in 1890, the disagreements between the workers and employers were just too deep to overcome. Certainly trade policy alone could not bridge their differences; other policies, such as tax reform, voting reform, and expanded social benefits would have to be enacted to keep such a coalition together. Caprivi was never able to satisfy so many different groups with different demands at once.

Caprivi latched onto some aspects of the idea of trade liberalization and attempted to use it to sever the relationship central to the conservative protectionist coalition: the tariff binding heavy industry and agriculture. Heavy industry was in fact interested in liberalization and at first seemed to throw its support behind Caprivi's "New Course." Heavy industry was easy to organize—there were few actors, since these sectors were dominated by monopolies and cartels. Heavy industry had formed the Centralverband der Industriellen (CdI) during the 1870s to promote protectionism, and this group still played a very important role. It was the primary channel of support for the National Liberal party, which was a critical ally for the Conservatives outside of Prussia. The fact that these industries were largely monopolized or cartelized might also explain their tendency to support protection—the monopolies were able to charge higher than market prices and therefore needed tariffs to keep foreign competitors out. Caprivi could bring some firms over to his side, but on the whole, the CdI stuck with protection.

Caprivi tried hard to connect trade issues to an issue dearer to the hearts of the agrarians—emigration. Caprivi argued that Germany would have to export either goods or people. Without an expanding economy based on exports of manufactured goods (which were necessary to pay for imports of raw materials, including foodstuffs), Germany could not maintain employment at levels conducive to social order.[19] Thus, Caprivi was playing on the Junkers' two greatest fears: political unrest at home and the loss of the rural workforce. The Junkers were unswayed.

Instead, the Junkers responded by copying the tactics of the promoters of free trade. Since the proponents of lower tariffs had formed mass organizations to build support and raise money; the Junkers would do the same thing, via the Bund der Landwirte (BdL). The financial clout of the BdL came from Prussia, but the organization created links between the Junkers in the east and small farmers in the west and south of Germany. It soon became extremely powerful.[20] The BdL blamed falling grain prices and the general hardship in the agricultural sectors on Caprivi's policies. The CdI and the BdL working together helped engineer the downfall of Caprivi's administration. The succeeding regimes would have to wait until his trade treaties expired, but once they did, Germany's tariffs would be brought back up to high levels.

Consensus among the Experts and the Minor Role of Ideas

If we try to locate the role of ideas among the shifts from protectionism to free trade, we run into some difficulties. Trade policy rarely occurred in a vacuum. The economic experts might have agreed on one policy, but the Junkers saw the tariff largely in terms of the support it gave to their own incomes, which in turn was the foundation for the continuation of their own social standing. End the tariff, the Junkers argued, and not just the economy but the entire society would change. Others viewed the tariff in strategic terms, arguing that Germany needed to stay focused on agricultural production if it was to have the basic materials and the manpower needed for a large army. (This was obviously foolish, since industry provided the real sources of military strength.)

Perhaps unsurprisingly, the economists of the day were largely opposed to protectionism—though this statement must be qualified. The opponents to protectionism could call upon a number of the most famous economists in Germany (Gustav Schmoller, Lujo Brentano, etc.) for support, although these economists were not die-hard liberals. Orthodox liberalism had been decisively discredited when the European economy collapsed in the 1870s and had not been able to right itself. No one proposed that markets could stabilize themselves. Government intervention in the economy was not opposed on principle; it was the manner of the intervention that garnered debate. Therefore, the economists had to use their skills to illustrate and underscore political points. Instead of engaging in theoretical debates on principles, they had to argue about the degree to which one group or another benefited from the policies at issue.

The economists who favoured freer trade were naturally located at universities in regions where the local interests were in favour of free trade. Schmoller, for instance, was at the University of Leipzig in Saxony. The most important firms in Saxony were textiles and other producers of finished goods. Heavy industry was located far to the west, and the Junkers to the east. Saxony elected representatives from Liberal parties who naturally argued for lower tariffs. It is a good example of the links then developing between the political forces and those agents needed to promote particular ideas.

In this particular case, it is difficult to distinguish an independent role for ideas. There was no clear division in terms of ideas, and no clear principles that strongly divided the experts. Nor was there any clear consensus on one specific policy. Since the experts agreed that some sort of government intervention was

THIRTEEN | *The Failure of Caprivi's New Course* [237]

probably necessary, but couldn't agree on what that intervention should entail, it is not clear that ideas had a powerful role to play in these debates.

The Reactions to Caprivi's Policies

Caprivi's term ended much the same as it had begun, full of sharp disagreements over trade policy. The BdL very actively opposed any further treaties that might reduce protectionism, and the agrarians were especially against any deal with Russia. As a result of the BdL's ability to block a treaty, a tariff war between the two countries erupted in August 1893. Industrial exporters perceived significant losses as a result, since they had trouble entering the Russian market. The McKinley Tariff in the U.S. was already hurting them.[21]

Caprivi's successor, Fürst zu Hohenlohe, was in office from October 29, 1894 until October 1900. In trade policy, Hohenlohe tried to work around the margins; that is, he did not attempt to undo the treaties Caprivi had negotiated, though he did move in minor ways to provide some additional protection for the agricultural sectors. He raised export duties on some products not previously taxed and placed customs on products outside the agreements signed by Caprivi's government.[22] This, however, left the protectionist forces unsatisfied.

The next government, led by Fürst Bülow, was in power from October 1900 until 1909. This administration worked much more actively to return Germany's trade policy to protectionism. Bülow too had a choice to make, similar to that which Caprivi had faced. Caprivi had chosen to pursue freer trade, in the hopes of making Germany a "trading state" and of building a stable dominant coalition to support his government. He had failed. Bülow now tried the opposite strategy: to support agricultural interests against the interests of industry, even if this sparked retaliations abroad.[23]

The tariff passed in 1902 was intended to strengthen the agricultural sectors (although it didn't come into force until March 1906). The tariff rates on grain were raised, as were the rates on other agricultural products, such as horses, cows, and various animal products.[24] As expected, other countries retaliated by charging higher tariffs on Germany's industrial exports. Also as expected, the higher grain tariffs helped the agrarians, not least by putting upward pressure on their income and land prices. The big owners—the real supporters of the BdL—came out ahead.[25]

Industry was wary about the return to protectionism. There were three reasons for this anxiety. First, by 1900, fewer elements of big business needed protection from foreign competition because they now held technological advantages. Second, some industrial sectors had important concerns about exports, and their experiences in the previous decades showed that a higher agricultural tariff resulted in losses in these markets due to retaliation. Third, many of these same firms had seen strong growth in the 1890s as a result of Caprivi's policies and were deeply suspicious of the policies Bülow was pursuing.[26] The conservatives therefore exerted immense energies to solidify the capitalists in one coalition—they did so by painting the socialists as the enemy. This Sammlungspolitik, as it was called, was intended to bind together the capitalists and unite them in struggle against the Social Democratic Party.

The Consequences of Protectionism: Economic Competition, Rivalry, and World War I

The failure of Caprivi's "New Course" had a number of significant consequences. Germany's return to protectionism has been linked on the international level to increased friction between Germany and other major powers, especially Britain and Russia. The differences over economic policies certainly did nothing to build goodwill between the countries and in that sense may have played a role in the rising international tensions prior to 1914.

The economic conflicts within Germany itself also had repercussions. The instability of the German regime is often cited as a reason for Germany's role in initiating war in 1914. The regime was built on the coalition of politically conservative groups—namely, the Junkers and heavy industry. The impact of trade continually threatened to push these two groups apart, however, by redistributing wealth in the country. In order to keep them together, and keep the working class and liberals apart, policies were packaged in ways that created problematic side-effects. Some argue that Germany's foreign policy was manipulated, in order to achieve these ends.[27] The conservatives could agree on nationalistic programs, so these became the centrepieces of foreign policy, which then enveloped foreign economic policy. This had the advantage of downplaying class divisions within society.

The other view, put forth recently by Jack Snyder, was that protectionism was one facet in the logroll which kept Germany's conservative coalition together.[28] Logrolling is a legislative tactic, where a coalition is kept together by essentially promising every group whatever it is they want. In this case, protectionism and imperialism were used as blanket policies which the government could use to promise benefits to its varied bases of support. When the government tried to deliver on these promises, it got Germany involved in international crises, entangling alliances, and arms races; these things, in turn, played a critical role in the outbreak of World War I.

World War I reshaped the map of Europe, and altered the distribution of economic and financial power around the world. It sparked economic development in the U.S. and Japan, boosting them to the fore as economic

THIRTEEN | *The Failure of Caprivi's New Course* [239]

powers and turning New York into a powerful financial centre. Germany was initially weakened by defeat; Russia dropped out of the conflict before it was over, thanks to the Revolution. Yet it took some time—and many economic conflicts—for contemporaries to recognize these changes. Among the most important, yet largely unappreciated, effects of the war was the relative decline of Britain. Britain emerged victorious in 1918, yet with a very different economic, financial, and military position. The great difficulty of adjusting Britain's policies to fit its new stature takes us to the next chapter.

Notes

1. For a broader application of this type of argument, see Ronald Rogowski, *Commerce and Coalitions* (Princeton, NJ: Princeton University Press, 1989).

2. Peter Gourevitch, "International Trade, Domestic Coalitions, and Liberty: Comparative Responses to the Crisis of 1873-1896," *Journal of Interdisciplinary History* 7 (1977) 281-313.

3. Gourevitch 288.

4. Gourevitch 289.

5. Hans-Ulrich Wehler, *The German Empire 1871-1918*, trans. Kim Traynor (Dover, NH: Berg, 1985) 11-12.

6. Ivo Lambi, *Free Trade and Protection in Germany 1868-1879* (Weisbaden: Franz Steiner Verlag, 1963) 59.

7. Lambi 132; and Gourevitch.

8. Wehler 36.

9. Hajo Holborn, *A History of Modern Germany 1840-1945* (Princeton, NJ: Princeton University Press, 1982) 266.

10. Rolf Weitowitz, *Deutsche Politik und Handelspolitik unter Reichskanzler Leo von Caprivi 1890-1894* (Düsseldorf: Droste Verlag, 1978) 22-23.

11. Weitowitz 19.

12. Weitowitz 25, 34.

13. Jürgen Schneider, "Die Auswirkungen von Zöllen und Handelsvertrgen sowie Handelshemmnissen auf Staat, Wirtschaft und Gesellschaft zwischen 1890 und 1914," *Die Auswirkungen von Zöllen und anderen Handelshemmnissen auf Wirtschaft und Gesellschaft von Mittelalter bis zur Gegenwart*, ed. Hans Pohl (Stuttgart: Franz Steiner Verlag, 1987), (Viertaljahrschrift für Sozial- und Wirtschaftsgeschichte, Beiheft 80) 294.

14. John C.G. Röhl, "Beamtenpolitik im Wilhelminischen Deutschland," *Das kaiserliche Deutschland, Politik und Gesellschaft 1870-1918*, ed. Michael Stürmer (Düsseldorf: Droste Verlag, 1970) 288-289; Hans-Jürgen Puhle, "Parlament, Parteien und Interessenverbaende 1890-1914," *Das kaiserliche Deutschland, Politik und Gesellschaft 1870-1918*, ed. Michael Stürmer (Düsseldorf: Droste Verlag, 1970) 342.

15. Siegfried Mielke, *Der Hansa-Bund für Gewerbe, Handel und Industrie 1909-1914, Der gescheiterte Versuch einer antifeudalen Sammlungspolitik*, Kritische Studien zur Geschichtswissenschaft, Band 17 (Göttingen: Vandenhoek and Ruprecht, 1976) 14-15.

16. Röhl 288-89.

17. This argument is laid out in more detail in Mark R. Brawley, "Factoral or Sectoral Conflict? Partially Mobile Factors and the Politics of Trade in Imperial Germany," *International Studies Quarterly* 41,4 (December 1997): 633-53.

18. Thomas Nipperdey, "Interessenverbände und Parteien in Deutschland vor dem Ersten Weltkrieg," *Moderne deutsche Sozialgeschichte*, ed. H.-U. Wehler (Berlin: Kiepenheuer and Witsch 1966) 378; Thomas Nipperdey, *Deutsche Geschichte 1866-1918, Zweiter Band, Machtstaat vor der Demokratie.* (München: Verlag C. H. Beck, 1992) 577; Hans Jaeger, *Unternehmer in der deutschen Politik, 1890-1918* (Bonn: Ludwig Röhrscheid Verlag, 1967) 149.

19. Weitowitz 6-7, 14. Also see Friedrich-Wilhelm Henning, "Vom Agrarliberalismus zum Agrarprotektionismus," *Die Auswirkungen von Zöllen und anderen Handelshemmnissen auf Wirtschaft und Gesellschaft von Mittelalter bis zur Gegenwart*, ed. Hans Pohl (Stuttgart: Franz Steiner Verlag 1987) (Viertaljahrschrift für Sozial- und Wirtschaftsgeschichte, Beiheft 80)254. Caprivi is quoted as saying: "Wir müssen exportieren: entweder wir exportieren Waren, oder wir exportieren Menschen." See Hans-Peter Ullmann, *Der Bund der Industriellen* (Göttingen: Vandenhoek and Ruprecht, 1976) (Kritische Studien zur Geschichtswissenschaft, Band 21) 22.

20. Schneider 310; and Ullmann 23-25.

21. Ullmann 23-25.

22. Schneider, 295-96.

23. Schneider 296.

24. Schneider 296-97.

25. Schneider 311.

26. Schneider 304.

27. Eckhart Kehr, *Economic Interest, Militarism and Foreign Policy*, ed. Gordon Craig (Los Angeles, CA: University of California Press, 1977).

28. Jack Snyder, *Myths of Empire* (Ithaca, NY: Cornell University Press, 1991).

Additional References

Brawley, Mark R. "Factoral or Sectoral Conflict? Partially Mobile Factors and the Politics of Trade in Imperial Germany." *International Studies Quarterly* 41,4 (December 1997): 633-53.

Gourevitch, Peter. "International Trade, Domestic Coalitions, and Liberty: Comparative Responses to the Crisis of 1873-1896." *Journal of Interdisciplinary History* 7 (1977): 281-313.

Kehr, Eckart. *Economic Interest, Militarism and Foreign Policy.* Ed. Gordon Craig. Los Angeles, CA: University of California Press, 1977.

Rogowski, Ronald. *Commerce and Coalitions.* Princeton, NJ: Princeton University Press, 1989.

Snyder, Jack. *Myths of Empire.* Ithaca, NY: Cornell University Press, 1991.

CHAPTER 14
Britain's Refusal to Retaliate on Tariffs, 1906-1911

As other countries moved away from the liberal trade regime in the late nineteenth century, Britain steadfastly maintained policies of relatively free trade, refusing to retaliate when others adopted ever higher tariffs. Such tariff increases were a distinct possibility, and the subject of intense political debate in Britain. Yet when the issue was placed on the top of the political agenda in two elections in the decade prior to World War I, the protectionist platform was soundly rejected. Why did Britain not retaliate?

The System-Level View: Erosion of the Free Trade Regime

The typical argument from the system level stresses Britain's hegemonic position in the international system. As an established hegemonic power, Britain's pound was widely used to finance trade; British ships carried a vast amount of world trade; British firms dominated the international insurance industry. Indeed, it is easy to look at Britain's overall economic position to discover that, whereas it had been an industrial powerhouse in the first part of the nineteenth century, by the beginning of the twentieth century its industries were no longer the most competitive in the world. Yet Britain was the dominant financial centre in the international system, and this guided Britain's foreign policy more than concerns about trade.[1]

This can be best observed in Britain's balance of payments. Trade in these invisibles earned Britain much more money than did trade in tangible goods. In fact, Britain had been running a trade deficit in tangible goods, but making a great surplus in invisibles, especially in terms of interest earned on overseas investments. (See Table 14.1.) Therefore, the argument typically made here is that Britain continued to pursue free trade, even in the wake of defections from free trade by other major economic powers, because its economic welfare rested with its continuation. Retaliations by Britain might have sparked tariff wars, with others retaliating in kind, and the whole system closing down, thus destroying the competitive services and investments British supremacy rested on.

Table 14.1: British Foreign Earned Income (millions of pounds)

	Balance on Goods	Balance on Services	Combined Balance	Net Interest	Current Account
1851–1855	−27	23	−4	12	8
1856–1860	−34	43	9	16	26
1861–1865	−57	57	0	22	22
1866–1870	−58	68	10	31	40
1871–1875	−62	87	25	50	75
1876–1880	−125	94	−31	56	25
1881–1885	−104	101	−3	65	62
1886–1890	−91	94	3	84	88
1891–1895	−130	88	−42	94	52
1896–1900	−161	100	−50	100	40
1901–1905	−175	111	−64	113	49
1906–1910	−142	136	−6	151	146
1911–1913	−134	152	18	188	206

Source: Adapted from Michael Brown, *After Imperialism*, London: Heinemann, 1973.

Marxists, such as Immanuel Wallerstein, who apply core-periphery models, note that hegemonic countries often go through such transformations.[2] By dominating industrial production and trade, they accumulate capital and earn ever greater incomes from investments, including international investments. Eventually, policies geared toward maintaining international investments dominate those supporting trade. This sort of policy dispute came to a head in the years after World War I. Before that war, the evidence should show, in this scenario, that tariff retaliation was rejected because of the strong position of financial interests as opposed to industrial interests.

As will be seen below, however, such arguments lead us to expect particular disputes within the dominant group of decision-makers—and evidence of such domestic disputes is weak. Tariff reform became politically salient in the years after 1903, becoming the most important issue in two elections (1906 and 1910), in which industrial interests voted strongly for free trade, not for protectionism. There was some support for protection among industrialists, but this was limited to particular industries employing skilled labour, which faced fierce international competition.[3] The other dominant source of protectionist votes was land-intensive agriculture, which had long been the loser in Britain's free trade policies. This pattern is much more consistent with domestic explanations as opposed to system-level theories.

One other system-level factor is worth noting: British security policies. While the chief architect of tariff reform, Joseph Chamberlain, was motivated by economic concerns, he wrapped the issue up in nationalism. In order to justify renewed protection for agriculture, he argued that Britain needed more domestic food suppliers in case of war. He also tried to develop a moderate tariff that would recreate the mercantilistic relationships Britain had had with its colonies in previous centuries. Under such a plan, Britain would establish a multi-tier tariff, giving preferences to its present and former colonies. It would raise agricultural tariffs, but allow in goods from its empire—especially agricultural goods—at a lower duty. Such a policy meant that Britain could still import foods from abroad, but also bind itself economically to its empire for strategic benefits. The fact that tariff reform was soundly rejected at the polls, however, means such arguments did not play well with the public.

Domestic Politics: Voices For and Against Free Trade

Ultimately, a policy such as this would have to be affirmed domestically. The argument above rests on the idea that the British government knew about these security and economic interests and, therefore, chose rationally to ignore the preferences of protectionists. Having adopted the policy yielding the most economic benefits for the country, the government could then retain and redistribute some of these gains so that all benefited. The only problem with this idea is that the government had to justify its policies to the electorate. Little of this thinking matches the political debates on trade policy in those years. Instead, redistributive policies were on everyone's mind precisely because the working class was clamouring for greater political participation. Britain had not adopted universal manhood suffrage yet, so many working-class men still did not have the vote. Yet it was clear that in coming reforms, the workers would eventually win the right to vote. Thus the two major parties, the Liberals and the Conservatives (the Tories), were positioning themselves to woo the working class.

Tory leaders knew this would be a challenge for them, because their conservative social policies did not appeal strongly to the lower classes. The Liberals, too, had challenges, since their main support was from urban middle classes—and classical liberalism had denied a role for the state in supporting the welfare of the lower classes. So leaders from both parties faced difficult questions as they entered the twentieth century. Unemployment assistance, relief for the poor, help in finding new employment, creating new jobs—these were on the minds of politicians of every stripe. They also had to think of how to pay for such policies.

When Joseph Chamberlain urged tariff reform, he did so in the context of appealing to the working class. He argued that the tariff would defend jobs otherwise lost as Britain imported more industrial goods and that the money earned from the tariff could be used to pay for greater social welfare schemes benefiting workers; further, he claimed that the tariff reforms could be integrated with imperial preferences to benefit Britain strategically. If capital and workers in industry preferred protection, while financial interests in London preferred free trade, surely Chamberlain's followers would win seats in these elections in industrial regions, but lose them in London. This is not what happened—indeed, the Tories were badly beaten in the 1906 election, then lost again (winning just as few seats in industrial areas) in 1910.

Therefore, we should turn to one of our models of the domestic interests concerning trade. Most arguments here emphasize the ideas that Britain's financial sectors looked strong internationally; that large parts of British agriculture were no longer competitive; and that, using an approach such as the Stolper-Samuelson theorem, Britain was relatively abundant in capital and labour compared to other countries. It was relatively poor in land; thus, we would expect tariff increases to appeal to those who held land, producing goods made intensively with land. We would expect those who owned primarily labour or capital—those in urban areas—to support free trade. Thus, those employing the Stolper-Samuelson perspective describe the domestic split arising over tariff reform as pitting urban areas against rural ones.[4]

However, this argument works only partially. What evidence we have in voting patterns confirms that the working class voted fairly solidly for free trade. There were only a few pockets where urban working-class districts elected protectionists. Of 153 seats in England (not counting Ireland, Wales, or Scotland) in working-class neighbourhoods in 1906, 138 (or 90 per cent) elected Liberals—Chamberlain himself and four of his followers in Birmingham were among the few Tories able to win seats in industrial areas that year. Birmingham's industries employed skilled workers, who were presumably in shorter supply in Britain; certainly, these particular industrial sectors faced fierce competition from foreign firms.

The 1906 election ended in a landslide for the Liberals because they did well not only in the urban areas but also in rural districts. They did better in certain rural areas where land ownership was widely dispersed among small farmers. Again, to consider the distribution of seats, this time in the English counties, the Liberals won a majority of the seats in counties where landholdings averaged above 50 acres, but won a very high 85 per cent of seats in counties with farms averaging below 50 acres. If we were to add in seats in Wales or Ireland where farms were also small, this percentage rises even higher. This suggests a strong sector-based split in agriculture, inconsistent with the Stolper-Samuelson theorem.

Meanwhile, in the upper-class urban areas (with as many seats as working-class voters commanded, given the restricted suffrage of those days), the tariff reform message seems to have found a stronger following. This may be best understood in terms of the tax issue. Tariff reform would place duties—taxes really—on basic items, taxes which many people would then pay when they purchased them. If these revenues were not forthcoming, then any government would have to find new money through some other devices. The alternatives were naturally less appealing to some of the upper class, since they would either tax income or property and undoubtedly do so in a progressive fashion (i.e., those who made more would pay a higher tax rate).

Thus, the pattern expected by the Stolper-Samuelson theorem can only partly be found in the electoral results. The working class voted strongly in favour of free trade, as most would expect. Skilled workers, in short supply in Britain in this era, voted more strongly for protection, but they were too few in number and too dispersed to have their votes translate into more than a handful of seats. Rural areas where small farmers dominated voted for free trade, while large landowners (and their workers) voted for protection, illustrating evidence of sector-based splits in agriculture. Thus, neither the extreme conditions elaborated by the Stolper-Samuelson theorem or by the assumptions of sector specificity seem to apply fully.

The Bureaucratic Level: Tariffs as Taxes, Once Again

At the bureaucratic level, we can once again consider the connection between tariffs and taxes. Only here the situation is more interesting, because the British government's financial requirements were steadily rising and expected to go higher. They had been under pressure in the 1890s, during the arms race with Germany. Moreover, politicians from both the left and the right anticipated spending more on social services in the future. There had been several extensions of the suffrage over the years, though prior to World War I, out of a population of over 40 million in the United Kingdom, less than 6 million men cast ballots in the 1906 election (a turnout of 82.6 per cent of eligible voters). Nonetheless, further incorporation of the working class into politics was going to happen. Therefore, politicians expected greater demands on government services in the near future.

The situation became more critical during the Boer War, which took much greater efforts than the Tory government then in power had expected. It lasted longer, required more troops, and cost much more money than originally planned. The Tory government therefore faced a serious shortfall in 1901, which was met by the reintroduction of a registration duty on grain. The duty was put back in place at the level it had been in the 1860s, but with the much lower price of grain four decades later, the duty (as a percentage of the good's value) worked out to a much higher level.[5] Still, the Chancellor of the Exchequer responsible for this decision, Sir Michael Hicks-Beach, considered the measure a temporary expediency.

Nonetheless, the situation opened up the possibility of protection for a wider variety of goods, under the pressing need to raise government revenues. Joseph Chamberlain, a leading Tory, called for tariff reform in a speech in May 1903. The speech was a challenge not only to the public and the opposition Liberals, but, more importantly, Chamberlain directed his arguments to his own cabinet colleagues.[6] He argued that the Tories needed to take the lead in offering certain services to the working class. To pay for things such as unemployment assistance, relief for the poor, and so forth, the government needed new revenues, which Chamberlain linked to tariff reform.

Chamberlain's position grabbed the public's imagination. It became the major item of debate between the two largest parties in the subsequent elections in 1906 and 1910. Without the opening provided by the shortfall in the budget, tariff reform might never have been raised as a major issue. Nonetheless, the budget problems could be resolved through a variety of alternatives. Lower spending was out of the question, since there was pressure to spend on both social policies and armaments. However, there were other possibilities for raising taxes. In the election campaigns, the Liberals argued in favour of tax increases focused on landowners and those making large incomes, and these policies were enacted in the wake of each Liberal victory. Liberal Prime Minister Herbert Asquith described his second budget (submitted in April 1907) as proof that social reform and free trade were compatible. Estate taxes were raised, but the income tax reduced—a relief to the working class. Workmen's Compensation was expanded considerably in these years as well.[7]

The Individual Level: Political Leaders as Champions of Competing Ideologies

We must look more closely at the leaders of the two parties who competed in the elections. Chamberlain was not leader of the Tories yet—the former prime minister, Arthur Balfour, was not convinced that tariff reform was a wise idea. Balfour knew he would have to argue in favour of some sort of tax increase; the question was which one would be the most successful in terms of popularity. He worried, as did many other Tory leaders, that Chamberlain's tariff reform would appeal only to the Tories' existing core supporters:

large landowners. Small farmers might not like it, nor would the working class. Thus, in Balfour's view, the policy would secure some Tory support, but cost it elsewhere. Therefore, he was unwilling to completely endorse the idea. Instead, he took deliberately vague and ambiguous positions whenever addressing the issue publicly.

The rifts within the Tory party over the issue became sharp, with intense infighting. Some 15 sitting Members of Parliament (MPs) switched to the Liberal party, because they refused to accept the tariff ideas. These included some well-known individuals, including Winston Churchill. Churchill was convinced that the Tories were destroying their electoral chances by driving the working class away by toying with the idea of tariff reform. As Chamberlain and his followers put increasing pressure on party MPs to join them, many of the older members chose to retire. We have no good records on how many party activists switched to the Liberals on the issue of trade, though we know many did.[8]

In the election of 1906, the Liberals won a great majority. Not only did they win more votes than the Tories (even without counting the votes for the young Labour party, aligned with the Liberals), but they dominated in terms of seats. The Tories won only 157 out of 670 seats available across the United Kingdom. The next election, in January 1910, was again fought over tariff reform. The Tory message was more focused on trade issues than before, but the results were much the same: they won only 273 seats, well below the mark needed for a majority.

On the competing side, the Liberals were considerably more unified around their idea of free trade. The true alternative was formulated by a rising new star in the party, David Lloyd George. Lloyd George was Welsh and understood well the issues of rural Britain. His argument was that tariff reform would not help small farmers—small farmers did not fear foreign competition. Instead, they needed greater support in the form of education and infrastructural improvement (roads, schools, etc.). Lloyd George's political stature rose out of his promotion of the counter policies to tariff reform.

Conclusions: Britain Stays with Free Trade

As a result of the overwhelming rejection of protection, Britain carried on with relatively open trade relations up to 1914. World War I drove the country to close off its markets with tariffs and presented it with problems of adjustment it would struggle with in the interwar era. As the beginning of this chapter laid out, the question here was why something *didn't* happen. The consequences of Britain failing to retaliate against others' tariffs, such as those raised by the Germans in 1903, may have been to dampen the rate at which countries were closing themselves off in trade.

By far the most important consequences, however, were on the domestic scene. Lloyd George's reforms were embedded in the budgets he submitted, beginning in 1909. His tax policies were naturally supported in the House of Commons by his fellow Liberals. Yet in 1910, the House of Lords still held veto power over Commons legislation, including the budget; filled with large landowners allied to the Tories, the Lords rejected Lloyd George's budget.[9] This caused a constitutional crisis and a second election in 1910. When this second election confirmed the Liberal government, the King intervened to settle the constitutional rift. The House of Lords lost its power over the budget and has declined in political importance ever since.

More directly, the economic policies the Liberals brought in helped British agriculture continue to adjust towards the sort of production economically rational for a country with abundant labour and capital but relatively scarce resources of land. Small farms, employing capital and labour intensely, could specialize in items such as pork, poultry, and dairy items, and succeed in the face of foreign competition. Grain production was unlikely to be as successful as long as trade was liberalized. By supporting not just free trade, but also improvements in infrastructure in rural areas, in housing for small farmers, access to government services, reallocation of land to small farmers, and so forth, the country's production patterns were changed. Britain remained the ideal example of a country following liberal trade policies, if only for a few more years.

Notes

1. For an historian's account see Paul Kennedy, *Strategy and Diplomacy, 1870-1945* (Aylesbury: Fontana Paperbacks, 1983). On Britain's hegemonic position and the importance of finance, see Stephen D. Krasner, "State Power and the Structure of International Trade," *World Politics* 28,3 (1976): 317-47.

2. Immanuel Wallerstein, *The Modern World-System II* (New York: Academic Press, 1980).

3. Douglas Irwin, "The Political Economy of Free Trade: Voting in the British General Election of 1906," *Journal of Law and Economics* 37 (1994): 75-108.

4. See, for example, Michael Hiscox, *International Trade and Political Conflict: Commerce, Coalitions and Mobility* (Princeton, NJ: Princeton University Press, 2002).

5. B. Mallet, *British Budgets 1887-88 to 1912-13* (London: Macmillan, 1913) 190.

6. Neal Blewett, *The Peers, the Parties and the People, The General Elections of 1910* (London: Macmillan, 1972) 29-30.

7. H.V. Emy, *Liberals, Radicals, and Social Politics 1892-1914* (Cambridge: Cambridge University Press, 1973) 148.

8. Neal Blewett, "Free Fooders, Balfourites, Whole Hoggers. Factionalism within the Unionist Party, 1906-1910," *The Historical Journal* 11,1 (1968): 95-124.

9. Blewett, *The Peers, the Parties and the People* 68-71.

Additional References

Blewett, Neal. "Free Fooders, Balfourites, Whole Hoggers. Factionalism within the Unionist Party, 1906-1910." *The Historical Journal* 11,1 (1968): 95-124.

—. *The Peers, the Parties and the People, The General Elections of 1910*. London: Macmillan, 1972.

Coats, A.W. "Political Economy and the Tariff Reform Campaign of 1903." *Journal of Law and Economics* 11 (April 1968): 181-229.

Irwin, Douglas. "The Political Economy of Free Trade: Voting in the British General Election of 1906." *Journal of Law and Economics* 37 (1994): 75-108.

Marrison, A.J. "Businessmen, Industries, and Tariff Reform in Great Britain, 1903-30." *Business History* 25 (July 1983): 148-78.

CHAPTER 15
The Reciprocity Election in Canada, 1911

The election of 1911 in Canada presents an intriguing puzzle. Sir Wilfrid Laurier, an experienced and successful politician, leading a party that had been in power for more than a decade, offered Canadian voters a chance to liberalize trade with the U.S. Both major parties, the Tories and the Liberals, expected this deal to be quite popular. When the agreement was announced in the Canadian Parliament, the Tories sat in stunned silence, while the Liberals prepared to celebrate. Yet in the election centred on this issue, the confident Liberals were soundly defeated. What happened?

As we saw earlier (in Chapter 12), the Tories first introduced the National Policy in 1878 and then held onto this policy—and office—for almost two decades. The Liberals were elected in 1896, but they themselves stuck with the National Policy, only choosing to emphasize different elements of it. They appeared to accept its strategic principles: greater national integration via tariffs and support for infrastructure, plus immigration. Indeed, the Liberals were much more successful in achieving the stated goals of the National Policy than the Tories had been. Yet Laurier and the Liberals had campaigned on the idea that they preferred freer trade ideologically, arguing that circumstances would not allow them to adopt such policies—until the deal with the U.S. was struck.

System-Level Factors: The Opportunity to Liberalize Trade

When we turn to the system level, three factors are prominent. First, trends in tariffs were mixed. Second, Canada's neighbour to the south and major market, the U.S., seemed ready to negotiate liberalized trade. Third, Canada was redefining its links to Britain, just as Britain was questioning its own commitment to free trade. As we have just seen, Britain chose to maintain free trade, rejecting Chamberlain's ideas about imperial preference.

Tariffs were moving upward in most countries from the late 1870s through the end of the nineteenth century. When economies dipped into another serious economic downturn in the early 1890s, many adopted even higher tariffs, including France, Italy, and, most importantly, the U.S. Often these tariffs were not only higher but more complex than before, targeting ever more specific goods, and including a greater range of items. By the early 1900s, another important change was occurring. Countries were developing various schedules, or levels, of tariffs. In this manner, a country could give favourable treatment to the goods of those who would likewise give their exports favourable treatment. Reciprocity was a tool to help countries ensure that they could negotiate lower tariffs. Thus, while high tariffs remained on the books, successful negotiations between some trade partners were reversing some of these trends.

Economically, the situation seemed to be right for further liberalization of trade when Laurier negotiated the deal with the U.S. After the severe economic downturn of the 1890s, economic situations were stabilizing. For Canada, the economy seemed to be poised for good times in 1910 and looked quite healthy when negotiations with the U.S. began. In fact, the economic cycle peaked in 1910 only to drop right through to the election a year later.[1] As economic activity declined, the appeal of freer trade waned, opening the door for the Tory counterattack.

These growing complexities in tariff rates and levels presented Canadians with some difficult choices concerning opportunities in the international economy. Up to 1910, Canada could emphasize its economic links to either the U.S. or Britain, both of which were not only its two largest trading partners, but also two of the largest economies in the world. If Chamberlain's tariff reforms held sway in Britain, Canada's raw materials and agricultural goods would be offered preferential access to Britain's markets. The defeat of tariff reform, however, made this preferential treatment less likely; perversely, Britain's continuation of very liberal trade policies (equally open to goods coming from an array of countries), undoubtedly pushed Laurier to consider closer ties with the U.S. Nonetheless, the first theme Laurier's opponents seized on was that the deal would inevitably bring Canada under the sway of the U.S., breaking historic ties to Britain.

For its part, the U.S. had moved its tariffs both higher and lower in the previous decades, with Republicans generally favouring higher tariffs, Democrats preferring reductions. The McKinley Tariff of 1890 raised U.S. tariffs on numerous items, killing off earlier Canadian hopes of gaining better access to U.S. markets. When the Democrats lowered U.S. duties in the later 1890s and Laurier first entered office, he had sought some sort of trade deal. Yet frustrations and failures led him to declare in 1897: "There will be no more pilgrimages to Washington. We are turning our hopes to the old motherland."[2] Thus, Laurier, though initially elected on a platform of tariff reductions, found himself turning his back on tariff reductions with the U.S.

Relations with the U.S. improved in the early 1900s, as the two countries successfully negotiated issues concerning the border and fishing grounds.

When the U.S. proposed trade negotiations early in 1910, Laurier was interested in maintaining positive relations and agreed to hold talks. These began in November, and much to the Canadians' surprise, the U.S. was willing to liberalize much more than had been expected. Thus, the treaty negotiated by the beginning of 1911 was surprisingly broad, and one that could be considered a coup by those desiring freer trade. The successful negotiations were announced on January 26, 1911, to a Parliament that listened intently as the details of the deal were described by William S. Fielding, the Liberals' Finance Minister. At the end of Fielding's speech, Liberals cheered, while Tories were aghast. The Liberals could claim, rightly, that they had pulled off a deal both parties had hoped for in the preceding administrations.

Thus, the systemic environment had created not only an opportunity for trade liberalization, but the U.S. moves had handed Laurier a gift. System-level factors were permissive at least in that sense, and it seemed as if Canada would be liberalizing its trade and finally moving away from the National Policy. But then the Tories responded, making trade policy the chief election issue. Despite the system-level factors, the decision to liberalize trade still rested with the Canadian public.

Domestic-Level Arguments: Shifting Support for Protection

Both parties understood the important advantages or disadvantages of undoing the National Policy and the merits of the deal. Timing proved complicated, however, because Laurier was slated to visit London that year for an Imperial Conference and the Coronation of King George V. He preferred to call an immediate election, but his cabinet and advisors convinced him to wait until after he had returned from Britain. Already the tables were slowly beginning to turn in the Tories' favour.

Trade interests naturally defined the possibilities for coalitions in this election. The Liberals' campaign slogan was "Laurier and larger markets."[3] Following the Stolper-Samuelson theorem, Canada's endowments of land, labour, and capital made agricultural interests the natural base for trade liberalization. Agricultural discontent hit new heights in 1910-11 because several factors had hurt crop yields in 1910. That additional pain, the probability of a coming election, plus the hint of reciprocity negotiations in the air, combined to enthuse farmers.[4] They had already formed organizations within several provinces to voice their complaints under the old National Policy. In 1909, these provincial organizations formed a national body, the Canadian Council of Agriculture.[5] Supporters of reciprocity were better organized than ever before.

Farmers' interests varied from region to region, however. Those in Ontario and Quebec had different needs and interests than their counterparts on the prairies. Farmers out west grew mostly grains, whereas those in the central provinces had shifted their production away from grain and into more capital-intensive dairy products. Initially, technology made it possible to sell dairy solids (such as cheese and butter) to the U.S. and even British markets. But as refrigeration improved in the early 1900s, it became possible to ship fluids as well, though only for much shorter distances. Given the choice of selling cheese or butter to U.S. cities, or milk to Canadian ones, farmers realized they could make more money doing the latter.[6] Thus, their interests in exports were falling by 1911. While the Stolper-Samuelson theorem suggests that owners of the relatively abundant asset, land, should be the strongest supporters of freer trade, landowners were in fact divided along sector-based lines.

Agriculture was declining as a percentage of the gross domestic product (GDP). This decline was not matched by a rise in industrial output, however, but rather by a rise in the services sector.[7] In the prairies themselves, it is probably incorrect to focus only on grain production. The majority of land was wrapped up in grain production, but by 1911, 35 per cent of the population in these provinces lived in cities. Winnipeg was the third largest urban area in the country.[8] Manufacturing was still concentrated in Ontario and Quebec, but changes had occurred there too. Whereas the western provinces accounted for very little manufacturing when the National Policy was first implemented in 1878, perhaps as much as 13 per cent could be found in the western provinces by 1911.[9]

The manufacturing based in the west was mainly in processing raw materials. In particular, businesses were concerned with milling grains and canning meat and vegetables. These industries were likely to face stiff competition from U.S. firms, if trade in their products were to be opened up. (Of course, some U.S. firms already owned subsidiaries operating in these markets.) More advanced industrial production was concentrated in Ontario and Quebec, though Quebec's industry tended to be smaller scale and more labour-intensive than Ontario's. More skilled labour was in Ontario and Quebec as well.[10] The Canadian Manufacturers' Association (CMA) was already making the case—well before the final deal on reciprocity was announced—that moderate protection met Canada's needs the best, even for westerners. The CMA argued that the National Policy was critical for Canada's continued industrial development and therefore should be left alone.

Oddly, too, the appeal of free trade in a democracy with the economic characteristics of a country such as Canada in the late nineteenth century could easily prove unpopular. If labour is relatively scarce, then it may prefer protectionism—Stolper and Samuelson's original finding. Moreover, in a country relatively abundant only in land, the idea that free trade will raise agricultural prices by allowing for greater exports may convince the working class that their interests as consumers will not be met.

In short, there were groups with straightforward concerns. Grain growers and many other farmers stood to gain from the deal; though most were not directly affected by tariff reductions, workers and industrialists in eastern cities feared competition from the U.S. Support for freer trade was questioned by more and more people as the economy performed poorly in 1911. Labour-intensive manufacturing sectors or capital-intensive farmers, such as dairy producers, had been more focused on the domestic market in recent years. Their interests were less clear. Even today, we debate their interests, since they do not fit easily under the assumptions of the Stolper-Samuelson or sector-specific models of trade. Such groups had been the traditional base of support for the Liberals in the past. Laurier not only hoped to maintain their support but also to get small farmers and less skilled workers (as consumers) behind his government. If successful, the Tories would have support only from capital and labour in the industrial sectors.

Yet, as the debates dragged on over the summer while Laurier was in Britain, not only did the economy enter a slump, but newspapers began to pick up the Tories' theme. They questioned the decision to bind the economy to the U.S. and asked whether this would not open up the Canadian economy to U.S. monopolies and trusts. The Liberals had already seen fractures appear, as their supporters in Montreal and Toronto quickly rebelled against Laurier's leadership. Key defections identify the other groups that switched sides. Perhaps most critical was Clifford Sifton's decision to side with the Tories. Sifton was a dedicated Liberal from the west, well-known for his prior experience in cabinet. In opposing reciprocity he stressed that, while heavy industry deserved some protection, industrial interests in the west did not necessarily want trade liberalization. He cited millers in the western cities as an example. A tariff could help such producers survive against U.S. competition.[11] In fact, millers, meat-packers, and other sectors formed delegations to protest the deal struck with the U.S.[12]

Another important defection occurred in Quebec. Henri Bourassa successfully mobilized support for the Quebec Nationalistes against the Liberals. Initially, Bourassa and the Nationalistes had argued in favour of a deal with the U.S. as a way to prevent stronger ties to Britain. Now that the deal was done, these groups had second thoughts, undoubtedly based on the opposition voiced not only in the business community in Montreal, but also among small farmers in the province. Bourassa also opposed Laurier's support for construction of a Canadian navy, which, he argued, would only be of value to Britain in its imperial wars. Helping the Tories to victory would not change this situation, of course, so Bourassa's cooperation with the Tories is harder to explain. Indeed, in Ontario Laurier and the Liberals were attacked for not supporting Britain enough! Still, the Tories and the Nationalistes made explicit arrangements on where each would run candidates in Quebec so as to maximize their chances of winning.[13] To better understand the Nationalistes' strategy, we need to consider the economic calculations in Quebec.

Bourassa consistently supported reforms slowing down the trend to ever larger firms. His proposal on public control of utilities stressed this same point: defend the interests of small, labour-intensive businesses. This corresponds to his vision of the ideal social order in Quebec.[14] Big business often meant domination by English Canadians, making it a popular target for reform in Quebec. These stands on economic policies, and the more immediate issue concerning the naval contingent, had been staked out well before 1911.[15] With Quebec agriculture shifting towards dairy production, it is not surprising that Bourassa and the Tories made gains there.

Was capital divided on sector-based lines? Liberal support in the more capital-intensive manufacturing sectors, located in Ontario and Quebec, certainly defected. The railroads and heavy industry always preferred protection. More damaging was the shift of other business interests, so that the Liberals were severely hurt in Ontario. Sir George Ross, a Liberal senator and former premier of Ontario, was among the first to question why tariffs should be changed at all.[16] Prominent Liberal businessmen in Toronto publicly voiced their disapproval shortly after the deal was made public.[17]

Was labour divided along sector-based lines? William Lyon Mackenzie King was Laurier's Minister of Labour in 1911. In the campaign, he stressed that he and the Liberals had supported labour's interests before and that reciprocity would help lower the cost of living to labour's advantage.[18] Liberal claims may have been poorly received, since the government had failed to defend labour's interests in the Grand Trunk Railway strike the previous year. Mackenzie King also did his best to counter the Tories' emphasis on patriotism, but in the end his efforts were not very successful.

Altogether, there was a decent chance Laurier might have gained broad support for reciprocity if an election had been held shortly after the negotiations were concluded. But over the summer of 1911, the interests of certain groups sharpened, the Tories built up their local organizations, the press began arguing against the deal, and the Nationalistes cut a deal with the Tories in Quebec. As the economy slumped, more groups questioned their economic interests, and the balance of votes slipped to the opposition.

Beyond the Electorate: Bureaucratic Politics, Individual Leaders, and Ideas

There is little evidence to warrant an argument in favour of bureaucratic politics, save for one critical issue. As we have seen in so many other cases, the issue of government revenues in Canada was wrapped up intimately with the tariff in the period before World War I. A reduction in the tariff could only be contemplated because the budget was in a healthy state. In fact, the budget surplus for 1912 was the largest produced up to that point.[19] In that sense, there were no strong bureaucratic opponents to free trade, so to Laurier conditions appeared ripe for a change in policy.

One of the most interesting aspects of the question has been why Laurier, a very experienced politician, miscalculated. Economists argue that the groups left out of the trade deal, such as pork farmers in Quebec, were ignored by Laurier, costing the Liberals pivotal support. Yet the political process one would tie to the economists' arguments is a bit sketchy: why didn't the Liberals hear the demands from the interests involved?

On the other hand, we do have the testimony of Liberals such as Sifton, who had a better sense of how interests were likely to shake down. Interestingly, Sifton and Laurier were both strong believers in liberal ideas. A close inspection of Sifton's arguments show that, while he supported the idea of free trade, he also feared that U.S. businesses—controlled in many sectors by trusts or monopolies—would be able to sell their goods at unfairly low prices in Canada. This was not the route to benefits for all. Markets bring benefits only when they near perfect competition. Thus, he had good liberal grounds for opposing the deal.

The Tories appealed to nationalism once again, and brash U.S. talk helped them out. This may have tipped the scales in the Tories' favour, though the ambiguity of the economic models works both ways. The economic models suggest who was lured to the protectionist coalition on economic grounds, but some groups that might have benefited from freer trade voted for the Tories for patriotic reasons. At the same time, the patriotism issue was rather complicated. Patriotism in those days focused on Canada's ties to Britain. The Liberals' policies won them little praise from voters demanding stronger ties to Britain, who voted for the Tories, while at the same time they earned strong criticism in Quebec for bowing to London's wishes. Indeed, some described the alliance forged between the Quebec Nationalistes and the Tories as "an unholy alliance," since it bound together parties with opposing principles.

Ideological factors matter, especially given how close the election was in the popular vote. Yet, given how long the National Policy had been in place, building up groups unsure of their support for liberal trade in practice, and given the divisions within the leadership of the Liberal Party itself, it may come as no surprise that we have trouble deciphering exactly why the Liberals lost an election in September that everyone expected them to win only months before.

Conclusions: The Election Results

When the votes were tallied, the Liberals received 623,554 to the Tories' 666,074—it was a close race in that sense. In seats, however, these numbers translated into a Tory landslide: 134 to the Liberals' 87 (with Quebec Nationalistes accounting for 27). In Ontario, the Liberals won only 13 seats to the Tories' 73, leading Laurier to claim this was where the election turned.[20] Later analyses have suggested that the defection of Liberal businessmen and the resulting collapse of the Liberal campaign machine in Ontario may in fact be the key to the catastrophe for Laurier. The Liberals won majorities in Alberta, Saskatchewan, and the Maritimes and held the lead in seats in Quebec by a slim margin. They won only two seats out of 10 in Manitoba, and none at all in British Columbia.[21] Politically, it was decisive defeat.

Economic interests clearly shaped the results in 1911. Laurier was not reckless or foolish in pursuing reciprocity, nor can we conclude that voters were duped into throwing away their material interests by the Tories' nationalistic rhetoric. Instead, the groups with definitive interests in trade, such as small farmers or capital and labour in heavy industry, supported their respective sides in the campaign. Yet some groups swung from their expected position, and our models cannot settle all these issues so easily.

The Tories, now in office, kept one of their campaign promises on trade. They established a commission to consider a "scientific tariff." This commission recommended only minor reforms, which were then blocked by Liberals in the Senate. As a result, the tariff was essentially unchanged, despite having been the key issue in the election.

Having rejected freer trade with the U.S. in an era when the U.S. was receptive (it would institute a lower tariff for everyone in 1913), Canada passed on an opportunity that would not come again for some time. In the interwar period, efforts to open up trade ultimately failed. The election of 1911 set Canada's policies on a tilt towards protection for not just the coming years, but in fact for many decades. It would be some 70 years before another Canadian politician would seek dramatic trade liberalization with the U.S.

Notes

1. See G. Rich, *The Cross of Gold* (Ottawa, ON: Carleton University Press, 1988) 38.

2. O.J. McDiarmid, *Commercial Policy in the Canadian Economy* (Cambridge, MA: Harvard University Press, 1946) 228.

3. Diane Eaton and Garfield Newman, *Canada A Nation Unfolding* (Toronto, ON: McGraw-Hill Ryerson, 1994) 124.

4. O.J. McDiarmid, *Commercial Policy in the Canadian Economy* (Cambridge, MA: Harvard University Press, 1946) 227.

5. Donald Creighton, *A History of Canada* (Cambridge, MA: Houghton Mifflin, 1958) 430; W.L. Morton, *The Kingdom of Canada* (Toronto, ON: McClelland and Stewart, 1969) 411.

6. William Marr and Donald Paterson, *Canada: An Economic History* (Toronto, ON: Macmillan, 1980) 109-15.

7. Kenneth Norrie and Douglas Owram, *A History of the Canadian Economy* (Toronto: Harcourt Brace, 1996) 221-22.

8. Norrie and Owram 238.

9. Nowrie and Owram 264-65.

10. Norrie and Owram 264-65; Robert Brown and Ramsay Cook, *Canada 1896-1921: A Nation Transformed* (Toronto, ON: McClelland and Stewart, 1974) 85-86; Brown and Cook 128.

11. John W. Dafoe, *Clifford Sifton in Relation to His Times* (Toronto: Macmillan, 1931) 357, 363-64.

12. Joseph Schull, *Laurier: The First Canadian* (Toronto: Macmillan, 1965) 524.

13. Oscar Skelton, *The Canadian Dominion* (New Haven, CT: Yale University Press, 1919) 247.

14. Joseph Levitt, *Henri Bourassa and the Golden Calf* (Ottawa, ON: Les Editions de l'Université d'Ottawa, 1972) ix, 35.

15. Examine for instance the Nationaliste's program from 1903. See Levitt 151-54

16. L. Ethan Ellis, *Reciprocity 1911: A Study in Canadian-American Relations* (New Haven, CT: Yale University Press, 1939) 74.

17. Brown and Cook 181.

18. Henry Ferns and Bernard Ostry, *The Age of Mackenzie King* (Toronto, ON: James Lorimer and Co., 1976) 142.

19. Brown and Cook 198.

20. Brown and Cook 185; Schull 533.

21. Skelton 251; John S. Moir and D.M.L. Farr, *The Canadian Experience* (Toronto, ON: McGraw Hill Ryerson, 1969) 352; Morton 413; Eaton and Newman 124.

Additional References

Beaulieu, Eugene, and J.C.H. Emery. "Pork Packers, Reciprocity and Laurier's Defeat in the 1911 General Election." *Journal of Economic History* 62,4 (December 2001): 1083-1101.

Hiscox, Michael. *International Trade ad Political Conflict*. Princeton, NJ: Princeton University Press, 2002. Chapter 8.

Johnston, Richard, and Michael Percy. "Reciprocity, Imperial Sentiment, and Party Politics in the 1911 Election." *Canadian Journal of Political Science* 13,4 (1980): 710-29.

Percy, Michael, Ken Norrie, and Richard Johnston. "Reciprocity and the General Election of 1911." *Explorations in Economic History* 19 (1982): 409-34.

CHAPTER 16

Britain's Return to the Gold Standard After World War I

How the Gold Standard Supposedly Worked

With the spread of free trade in the middle of the 1800s, and the increasing levels of international trade after that, ever larger international payments had to be made. The shift away from mercantilist policies created pressures to change international monetary relations to facilitate trade, including paying off international debts. This required some kind of international currency, some means of payment accepted almost universally. The nineteenth-century solution to this problem stressed the ideological links to free trade. The gold standard was in effect a market solution to the international payments problem, one that integrated some national markets together quite well.

The gold standard solved the international payments problem because all participating currencies were convertible into gold. Every currency could be cashed in at its central bank for a specified amount of gold, and every currency had the same fixed rate of exchange for gold. Ultimately, gold was the medium of international exchange. If a German wanted to do business in France, he or she exchanged German marks for gold at the German central bank, took this gold to France, and bought French francs at the central bank there.

This is a complete reversal of official policy under mercantilism. Under mercantilism, all international flows of gold were supposed to be strictly managed or blocked; gold was hoarded within countries, and national policies were designed to achieve that end. At the height of the British Empire and free trade, gold was supposed to flow freely between countries, and national policies were redirected towards this.[1] Liberals argued that, in the long run, the market would automatically drive countries towards a perfect balance in the value of imports and exports and that free trade, over time and under ideal conditions, would lead each country to balance its exports and imports automatically—an equilibrium. If this were the case, there would be no problem with international payments; it was a perfect Liberal solution: purely a matter of the market without the exercise of power. Those participating in the international market would eventually find their correct equilibrium point. This fit with the Liberals' notions that the international market was a natural, neutral forum for solving international payments problems.

The gold standard system was intended to be part of this natural and neutral system. Gold was seen as the one "special" good that would make up any marginal differences in the balance of trade. Imports and exports of gold would be linked to the volume of currency, and therefore the flows of gold would influence prices. It was this connection between flows of gold and prices that caused many to describe the gold standard as a "corrective mechanism," since the changes in prices would affect competitiveness.

How was this supposed to work? Let us begin with the example of a country in a balance of payments deficit: it is importing more goods than it is exporting. In order to pay for the greater value of imports coming in, gold has to flow out. Being on the gold standard means that the amount of currency in circulation is tied directly to the amount of gold the country holds. In other words, the money supply is determined by the amount of gold people bring in to the bank and exchange for currency. If they have to make payments overseas, people bring currencies in and take gold out of the bank to give to foreigners, or the foreigners paid in the country's currency convert that currency to gold before transporting it home where they exchange it for their own currency. If gold leaves the country, then the amount of currency in circulation is also affected—an outflow of gold automatically constricts the money supply. A reduction in the money supply, in turn, affects prices. When the money supply drops, there is less currency chasing the same amount of goods (i.e., deflation), which means prices fall.

This pushes the country towards an international payments balance because, when the prices of goods are falling, goods look cheaper to consumers than international goods. So within the country there is a change brought about by this deflation which makes imports less competitive. Internationally, the same thing happens: cheaper prices for things really means that goods can be exported at cheaper prices, so that exports are more competitive on international markets than previously. This same set of links works as a corrective for a balance of payments surplus. If a country successfully exports more than it imports, other countries pay off debts in the form of gold—so the first country's gold supply increases.

Because of the direct link between gold supply and the amount of currency in circulation, this increase in the supply of gold increases the money supply. More money chasing the same amount of goods is inflationary, so prices rise. This rise in prices affects the country's appetite for imports; the price of goods has risen, so imports are cheaper compared to goods. At the same time exports begin to look expensive to everyone else. The country is driven out of this balance of payments surplus, back towards an equilibrium. Because the system drives countries back towards equilibrium whenever they deviate from it, the system is described as corrective or self-correcting. If a country gets in a balance of payments deficit, the gold standard drives it back towards surplus; if it starts with a surplus, the gold standard drives it back towards deficit.

The Benefits of the Gold Standard

Liberal theorists still see real beauty in this system in that it works through the market and contains no role for power or government intervention. The system is self-regulating and self-equilibrating. Theoretically, a government could join the gold standard, establish the links between the currency and gold, and forget about balancing trade—the market would do that. While it wasn't that simple, it may have seemed so to contemporaries. After the major powers joined the gold standard in the late 1800s, international monetary affairs took on a whole new set of characteristics. First, the system of exchange rates had to be stable if this were to work. Given that gold is the same everywhere, if all currencies were fixed to a set amount of gold, it is easy to figure out how much one currency would buy of any other currency also on the gold standard. Since these currencies were fixed in terms of gold (and weren't supposed to be changeable) and indeed remained fixed for long periods of time, merchants and investors knew what exchange rates were going to be for the foreseeable future.

That stability of exchange rates allowed for economic predictability. Economic actors could figure out future returns on international deals without having to risk fluctuations in currency exchange rates. As long as another country was on the gold standard, its currency could be accepted and exchanged for gold which could then be transferred into one's own currency. Holding this foreign currency for a while would not be very risky in terms of the value changing *vis-à-vis* one's own currency. This predictability also affected how actors would get involved in another country's economy. They could more easily make long-range plans, even though communication systems were underdeveloped.

The extensive use of the gold standard radically altered the policies prohibiting or limiting international investment. Gold can be moved internationally. If someone decided to invest in another country, he or she could take gold there. Most importantly, in contrast to mercantilism, states would not prohibit individuals from removing gold from their own country. Moreover, if they wanted to invest in another country, they would be able to use their own currency to pay for things in other places, because their currency was convertible first into gold and then into other currencies—their currency should be as good as gold! Since foreigners could take their currency into their central bank and get gold in return just as easily as locals could do, they might accept foreign currency as something equivalent to gold. That was another way this system of payments stimulated international investment and trade.

We can now turn to how the gold standard solved the international confidence and liquidity problem. Confidence in gold was very high, and when a country fixed its currency in terms of gold, the currency took on that same confidence. Gold was accepted in international deals, but so were currencies backed by gold, so national currencies on the gold standard enjoyed international confidence: people had confidence in their value. The system was specifically designed to solve the problem of confidence. But remember the tension between confidence and liquidity? Confidence meant people were willing to accept something because they valued it. High confidence is then associated with high value—if people tend to hold onto, or hoard, things they value, there may not be enough of these things to go around. In this case, if gold was accepted everywhere, and everyone wanted to use it internationally, was there enough to go around? Was there a liquidity problem internationally? Moreover, there was a close connection between free trade, the rising levels of trade, and the gold standard. More trade was taking place, which required more gold or currencies to be used to facilitate trade. High confidence and increased demand in general leads us to expect a liquidity problem to arise.

Where did liquidity come from under the gold standard? As the model of the payments disequilibrium showed, all money supplies were supposed to be determined by the supply of gold in each country, and international liquidity depended on the global supply of gold. Control over the supply was removed from government policy-making, which in effect should have also removed international liquidity from the realm of government policy manipulation.

The supply of gold depended upon the discovery of new sources of gold. Purely by accident, new such sources were discovered at the most opportune time. The gold rush in California in 1849 and the subsequent development of gold mines there provided an initial spurt. In the later 1800s, there were periods when the liquidity problem re-emerged, but there were more gold strikes in Alaska, the Yukon, and of course in South Africa, and new mines were developed. Each helped relieve the liquidity squeeze on the international system as the volume of payments and investments grew. Because of these fortuitous discoveries, the liquidity problem didn't appear to matter at the international level. At the national level, though, there were problems, because some countries were growing at a faster rate than their money supply. Being on the gold standard, these governments effectively tied their hands when it came to monetary policies. Some countries got stuck in deflationary trends they had trouble escaping.

A second source of liquidity also existed: British pounds. Since Britain had honoured the gold standard rules for so many years, foreigners had confidence in the future value of sterling. Since London was the source of so much finance and investment, and so many other goods could be found there, it was easier for foreigners to hold on to their pounds outside of London. Balances soon built up, and these plus credits from London provided additional international liquidity.

This discussion so far has been about how the system was supposed to work. The design of the gold standard fits very closely to the way liberals wanted things to work; in particular, note how the system was supposed to be neutral and natural. The markets were self-equilibrating, and there was no reason for governments to intervene in international exchange markets.

The Sterling Overhang and the Impact of World War I

The gold standard worked well for the decades prior to 1914 in terms of how well international payments and investments were eased by the monetary regime. However, flaws were developing. Most obviously, the amount of British pounds in circulation was well beyond the amount backed by gold in the vaults of the Bank of England. An overhang occurs when, in a system of fixed exchange rates, there is so much of a currency in circulation that the supply overwhelms the reserves set aside to back it. Despite the supposedly rigid rules of the gold standard, several countries were holding extensive amounts of currencies as reserves alongside gold and/or silver. Sterling remained the most important single foreign currency in other countries' reserves. By 1913, sterling holdings clearly outstripped the combined gold reserves of the Bank of England and all other private banks in Britain by a ratio of at least 2.5 to 1.[2] This weakness was not a problem as long as there were no other attractive alternative currencies.

The gold standard was suspended by the outbreak of World War I, but just as in trade, there were attempts to reconstruct it. The attempts failed. To a great extent the developments in monetary relations paralleled those in trade, so one story is linked to the other. As part of the war effort, countries blocked any exports of essential materials, including gold—and this meant they had to abandon the gold standard. Moreover, going off the gold standard allowed governments to manipulate their money supplies to conduct policies supporting their war efforts. By going off gold they could follow deficit spending programs by pumping more cash into the economy. This naturally created inflationary pressures, but these inflation rates varied across countries.

Having very independent, unconnected inflation rates undermined the old system of fixed exchange rates. Inflation was very high in Germany during the war, moderate in Britain and France, and very little in the U.S., which continued to adhere to most of the gold standard rules. The exchange rates should have been adjusted to take into account the different rates of inflation (i.e., the new real values of the currencies) and, in the early 1920s, the currencies were allowed to float, in order to find their true value *vis-à-vis* each other.

The real problem emerged when countries tried to fix their exchange rates again and to honour the rules of the gold standard. Germany returned to the gold standard in 1924, Britain in 1925, and France in 1927. The pound had fallen in its real value versus the dollar, and the attempt to bring it back onto the gold standard at its pre-war value proved disastrous for British industry. The overvalued exchange rate made British prices relatively non-competitive internationally. Britain's policy hurt trade competitiveness, but of course the opposite was also true. France, for instance, maintained an undervalued rate for the French franc at this same time. This made French prices very competitive internationally, making French exports rise. The French were able to improve their balance of payments without resorting to high tariffs, because this low valuation of the currency helped all sectors. The earnings of foreign currency allowed the French central bank to collect gold from other central banks, so France went from a minor holder of gold in the early 1920s to the second largest in the early 1930s.

British Monetary Policy Immediately After World War I

While there was some pretenses to returning to the gold standard immediately after the war, the British government decided to break the links between the pound and gold in 1919. The decision was reached by the cabinet, which was not the traditional authority in charge of exchange rate policies. That duty lay with the Bank of England. The government did not want to defend Britain's gold reserves under the gold standard rules, since that would drive up unemployment. The government also wished to stimulate trade, particularly in goods transiting the country. The two bureaucracies responsible for monetary policy, the Treasury and the Bank of England, had other concerns. The Treasury feared that the government's debts were already so high that taxes would have to be kept extremely high for the foreseeable future. If the government failed to repay its debts, business would lack the capital necessary for new investments. Additional government debt was out of the question, since that would push interest rates higher, thus making the existing debt even more expensive to carry.[3]

The Bank of England, on the other hand, considered its primary goal to be the restoration of the pre-war financial system, with London as the key financial centre. The Bank wanted government debt to be paid down quickly, a new funding of other short-term debt as soon as possible, and a policy to restore confidence in the pound.[4] Despite concerns about official debts, the Treasury would accept an upward valuation of sterling; as one Treasury official put it in 1920, "the community as a whole stands to gain enormously from the improved standing of British credit."[5] Interest payments on government debt had been only a minor concern before, but after the war they accounted for about 30 per cent of government expenditures. The initial split between the Bank of England and the Treasury after the war was not over the ultimate goal of monetary policy, since they both agreed the value of sterling needed to be raised, but rather over the means to pursue that end. The Bank wanted to reassert its control over financial markets, pushing interests rates up. The Treasury was concerned that this would make it difficult to sell new Treasury bills and other forms of short-term government debt. Yet, since both feared inflation, their agreement that the first priority should be restoring confidence in the pound formed the basis of the Cunliffe Commission's findings. This Commission, officially known as the Committee on Currency and Foreign Exchange, guided official decision-making.[6] Its report assumed that the goal of British monetary authorities was to return to the gold standard as soon as possible. The Committee on Financial Facilities, which was made up of representatives from industry and commerce, reported at this same time and also assumed the same goals for monetary policy. The recommendations from both committees were in agreement. The government should stop borrowing money as soon as possible; "Bank rate" (the interest rate the Bank of England charged others) should be used to stop any drain of gold reserves, as well as deflect inflationary pressures at home; and national gold reserves should be concentrated in the hands of the Bank of England.[7]

Yet the monetary authorities were slow to realize how the setting for action had changed. The success of the government's own war financing effort had changed the mix of assets in the London market. This naturally affected the relative utility of different policy tools. Treasury bills were much more important than before, since they now made up around half of the market for monetary devices. Before the war, monetary policy had relied on the use of Bank rate to maintain exchange markets. Bank rate would not be as effective as it once had been, since it would have to drive up the rates offered on Treasury bills to draw in money from outside Britain. Investors did not necessarily find Treasury bills attractive enough to transfer money from other countries to London.[8] If the Bank of England were to rely on Bank rate alone to draw in foreign funds, or block the expansion of trade credit, it would now have to change Bank rate more dramatically. This was especially true now that New York was a rival source of credit and an alternative destination for deposits. These new factors were not considered in the Cunliffe Committee's analysis.

The overhang created the desire to tighten credit, while a return to a peace-time economy created the desire for economic growth. The British economy boomed briefly when the government, fearful of unemployment, initially loosened wartime controls. This was followed by a slump in 1920-22, but the economy largely recovered by 1924. Problems remained with the export-oriented sectors, however; exports in 1924 were still only about three-fourths those of 1913.[9] The government was very interested in policies that promised to assist in the recovery of these sectors.

Recovery could not be allowed to stimulate inflation, however. If inflation sparked a devaluation of sterling, this would undermine the real value of Britain's income from overseas investments that were denominated in sterling and set at fixed amounts. Without examination, it was assumed that inflation hurt the internationally oriented service sectors, too. In fact, inflation might not have hurt the service sectors as feared, since services tended to charge commissions. Commissions are often percentages of transactions, and therefore these would have risen with inflation.[10] As long as the Bank and the Treasury feared inflation the most, policy emphasized the bolstering of sterling's international value.[11] A fall in confidence in the currency would cause foreigners to unload their holdings of pounds and shift into stronger currencies.

Monetary policy decisions may have been influenced by a variety of forces. On the one hand, there were system-level factors, especially the rise of an attractive rival currency (the U.S. dollar). There were the ingredients necessary for a decision to be shaped by bureaucratic politics, since the Treasury and the Bank of England had overlapping responsibilities, and over time their goals diverged. Sector-based interests also may have played a role, since the impact of monetary policy was felt differently in different sectors. Each of these theories offers insight into the decision actually taken: to place the pound back on the gold standard in 1925 at the pre-war exchange rate.

System-Level Theory: Britain's Hegemonic Afterglow

The typical system-level argument for Britain's difficult policy choices in this period draws on the changing distribution of capabilities in the international system. World War I heralded the relative decline of British economic and financial power and the rise of the U.S. Britain was no longer the single most important source of credit or trade—it had to share that role with the U.S. The U.S. had its own uncertainties about the role it was to play in the international political economy. Whereas Britain struggled to retain the premier position, the U.S. avoided many of the responsibilities it perhaps should have undertaken.[12] In short, there was no clear hegemonic power during this period of transition.[13]

If Britain was no longer clearly dominant, why then did it persist in the pursuit of hegemonic policies? This example of hegemonic "afterglow" can only be described by adding other causal variables from other levels of analysis. For instance, when Stephen Krasner sought to explain why Britain retained hegemonic policies into the 1920s, he argued that it was because these policies were supported by arrangements constructed during hegemonic ascendance. In Krasner's words, "the British state was unable to free itself from the structures that its earlier policy decisions had created."[14] Susan Strange made essentially the same point to explain British international monetary policy at a later time: "...it has been the misfortune of British policy since the Second World War to have inherited from this distant imperial hey-day, associated ideas which no longer apply to Britain's changed situation, but have nevertheless proved remarkably hard to shed or modify."[15]

These scholars were noting that Britain's international monetary policy after World War I (and even much later) was not rational from the perspective of the nation as a whole. Industry's competitiveness in particular was hurt by the monetary policies of the 1920s. Most researchers also link these policy outcomes to an institution created much earlier—the Bank of England. As an essentially system-level argument, hegemonic stability theory has been ill-equipped to deal with such questions. Krasner's immediate intention in suggesting a role for institutions was to explain the time lags he observed between the onset of hegemonic decline in structural terms and the end of leadership in terms of policy. By introducing factors, his explanation for the afterglow was an addendum to an otherwise structural theory. It suggests that hegemonic stability theory could not explain everything on its own. A similar problem arises, as will be seen in the next chapter, when we consider what the U.S. was doing at this time.

The Domestic Level: Industry versus the City of London

The basic alternative arguments, drawn from the level of politics, support this assessment. The proponents of these arguments question why system-level factors should be considered at all. Instead they suggest that the policy decisions can be best understood by looking at the winners and losers involved. On one side stood the set of financial actors (banks, insurance firms, etc.) loosely termed "the City" and on the other was British industry. At first glance, one might think the two sets of actors would have many links, but in fact the City had always been involved more heavily in investing abroad and in financing international trade rather than investing in home industry.[16]

The City was concerned with dealing with the overhang in such a way that international confidence in sterling remained high. As Peter Katzenstein put it, the British definition of policy objectives reflects a "banker's" rather than a "business" view of the world. The former view has found its most ardent proponents in London's City, whose economic survival, it was thought until the mid 1960s, depended on defending the position of sterling as a reserve currency.[17]

In short, the City wanted interest rates to continue to be high in order to draw in pounds from abroad, as well as to encourage people to hold their sterling in savings rather than spend it. It feared that if foreigners lost confidence in the pound, they would switch their transactions to U.S. dollars; as a result, transactions would go through New York rather than London, and the City's income would fall. The financial actors considered their own competitiveness to be aided by a strong pound.

However, a strong pound would make industry's products look relatively expensive on international markets. Industry's international competitiveness had already been on the wane for some time. British industry had been at the forefront of manufacturing technology in the first half of the nineteenth century, but as new technologies were created that position slipped. British industry, unable to easily adopt the new technologies, was uncompetitive and needed lower interest rates so it could finance retooling. Yet that went directly against the interests of the City. And, as noted earlier, Britain earned more from international services and international investments than it did from trade in goods. The City was in a better position to argue its point of view.

Yet at first, this split was not all that apparent. Representatives of the Federation of British Industry, the central organization for industry, argued in favour of a return to the gold standard. Before one government advisory committee in 1924, industry representatives said that resuming the gold standard was "in the interests both of the financial position of this country and also for its advantages and benefits to the industry and business of this country." The same representatives also noted, however, that "a British initiative in restoring the gold standard at an early date ... would be premature and inadvisable" because it would lessen their ability to sell exports and therefore likely increase unemployment.[18] The committee listened to this information, yet recommended a return to gold with the exchange rate set at the pre-war level ($4.86 = £1). This was done in 1925, and industry soon faced serious difficulties.

The exchange rate certainly placed too high a value on sterling, but debate remains as to how much this accounts for British industry's difficulties. The overvaluation of sterling cannot be separated from broader economic problems. The high pound did not cause all of the broader adjustment problems that industry faced, but it surely eliminated some policy options. The underlying difficulties were, therefore, that much more difficult to deal with.[19] After 1928, there was wider recognition that industry's most pressing problem seemed to be the combination of deflation at home and the overvaluation of sterling.[20] The higher value of sterling caused demand to fall off, made it more difficult to invest in new machinery, hurt overseas sales, and forced industry to begin laying off workers. The workers responded with a nation-wide strike in 1928. Because of the way in which the gold standard had supposedly worked in the past, goals (such as employment levels) were being sacrificed for international targets.

This was a dangerous game for politicians to play in the 1920s.[21] As part of the government's attempts to stimulate the war effort, Britain had finally extended the vote to the working class in 1918. For the first time, the workers in Britain had their own powerful voice in Parliament: the Labour Party. The politics associated with monetary policy would be played out differently from that time on, since the workers were more interested in priorities.

Bureaucratic Politics: The Treasury and the Bank of England

A rival explanation for Britain's monetary policy decision in 1925 can be found in bureaucratic politics, though it is difficult to untangle this argument from the politics laid out above. The different parts of the economy had close ties with particular parts of government. The City naturally had many links with the Bank of England, which interacted with financial actors quite regularly. Moreover, the Bank's responsibilities had always been laid out in terms of defending the pound's international value. The Treasury, on the other hand, had the government's budget as its primary responsibility. Moreover, the Treasury had obligations to the cabinet and therefore to the electorate.

In the early 1920s, the Treasury and the Bank of England largely agreed on policy, perhaps because the government's annual budgets were still in surplus. Both institutions agreed on a return to the gold standard as the best way to improve trade and increase employment. At the same time, leaders of both institutions failed to consider all the consequences associated with moving Britain from its existing position to the one they wanted. Rather than understanding the gold standard and the exchange rate as means to an end, the return to the gold standard became an end in itself. In the early 1920s, policy-makers from each institution shared a common goal—the wish to retain London's role as the premier international financial centre—which they understood also meant keeping sterling in its international role.[22] Sector-based influences do not seem to have had an impact on the institutions' policy positions up to this time, except to the extent that both were influenced by the financial sector. The only serious disagreement between the two bureaucracies came over the policies to be used.[23] The Bank wished to employ higher interest rates to strengthen the pound, while the Treasury felt this would lead to higher interest charges; debt service had accounted for a mere 11 per cent of government expenditures in 1913, but had risen to 24 per cent in 1920. It climbed to more than 40 per cent by 1930, and this drove the two institutions apart.

If anything, the bureaucratic politics argument suggests that a common set of sector-based interests emanating from the City may have dominated both institutions, but bureaucratic politics led to a division. The public airing of this division in institutional views opened the way for others to enter the debate over monetary policy, and this in turn created the opportunity for the institutions to mobilize groups for political action in ways that were never possible in the pre-World War I era.[24] In short, this view argues that the bureaucratic politics explanation is reinforced by political struggles.[25]

The Bank considered its primary obligation to be the maintenance of the international exchange value of sterling.[26] Though the Bank and the Treasury were not acting completely independently of each other, coordination between the two could have been much better. The Bank did not inform the Treasury of its complete resources or of its actions. The Treasury eventually took action through Parliament. The *Currency and Bank Notes Act* of 1928 gave the Treasury access to more information on the Bank's foreign exchange reserves held by the Issue Department. Still, the Treasury could not find out about all of the Bank's foreign currency holdings, which the Bank was starting to use to intervene in exchange markets.[27]

The Bank was searching for alternative policies which would allow it to avoid relying on the government. When the question of going back on the gold standard arose in the early 1920s, Bank Governor Montagu Norman worked in close coordination with the New York Federal Reserve Bank (the Fed), often with little guidance from the government. Norman successfully coordinated some aspects of British and American monetary policies. While the Fed relaxed interest rates in New York, the Bank of England raised interest rates in London, thereby adjusting the exchange relations between the two markets. International borrowing focused on New York, making it easier for Britain to keep sterling's value high and hence resume participation on the gold standard.[28]

The Treasury's vulnerability to broader societal pressures played a role in the battles between the two institutions after 1925, though these concerns were hardly linked to the lobbying activities of any specific sectors. By 1928, the Treasury would deter greater deflation, because it feared that rising unemployment would be politically and fiscally unacceptable. One of the major expenditures, and certainly one that worried the Treasury most, was the unemployment insurance fund. The Treasury prevented a higher Bank rate, taking away the Bank's most important short-term policy instrument. The Bank was forced to turn to international cooperation more often.[29]

Once Britain returned to the gold standard at a high valuation of sterling, it was all too clear that some sectors were hurt by the Bank's use of interest rates. As the *Westminister Bank Review* stated in 1929, finance and industry no longer had similar interests.[30] It remains somewhat debatable whether the Bank was ready to allow industry to be continually run down in order to stay on the gold standard at the high valuation. In negotiations with the Bank of France in May 1927, Norman threatened to take Britain off the gold standard lest there be further damage to the competitiveness of British industry. When defending the high exchange rate in the later months of 1928, the Bank chose not to use Bank rate to avoid further harm to British industry. Instead Norman relied more on direct intervention in the exchange markets.[31]

Publicly Norman continued to argue that industry and finance had the same interests. When testifying before the Macmillan Committee in March 1930, he was asked whether "the advantages of maintaining the international position outweigh in the public interest the internal disadvantages which may accrue from the use of means at your disposal." Norman replied that:

> the disadvantages of the internal position are relatively small compared with the advantages to the external position ... we are still to a large extent international bankers. We have great international trade and commerce out of which I believe considerable profit accrues to the country; we do maintain huge international markets ... and the confidence and credit which go with them, are in the long run greatly to the interest of finance and commerce.[32]

The Macmillan Committee's report mirrored the Bank's position. Its conclusions rebuffed calls for a devaluation on the grounds that such an act would undermine faith in sterling. Even though this committee assessed a wider spectrum of views than most of the earlier inquiries precisely because they were responding to industry's frustrations, its report stated that Britain's "international trade, commerce and finance are based on confidence."[33] Despite the Committee's recommendations, Britain would have to devalue sterling in a few years.

Ideas: The Faith in Liberal Ideology

Perhaps a more powerful explanation can be found in the realm of ideas. Liberal ideology was so strong that it drove many of the policy decisions in the years immediately after 1918. Britain had been so successful economically in the years before the war that policy-makers and the public may have failed to consider why this had been and how the world had changed. The greatest evidence in favour of this type of explanation comes in the form of the questions that were not asked.

For example, in the debates concerning the return to the gold standard in 1924, policy-makers focused intently on the rate at which the currency would be fixed. Little thought was given to the timing of the revaluation itself.[34] Moreover, few policy-makers challenged the assumption that the gold standard was the best international monetary regime for Britain. Winston Churchill, who had been made head of the Treasury, never questioned the wisdom of returning to the gold standard at the old parity. He only wanted a monetary policy that would complement free trade.[35]

The goal of returning to the gold standard at the old rate (of $4.86 = £1) was persuasive because nearly a century of experience had shown that the standard and Britain's adjustment mechanisms had worked smoothly and swiftly. Sterling's value had effectively been fixed since 1821, and the other major currencies had not changed in value much in the 30 years prior to 1914. These experiences and beliefs meant that other possible options were not adequately explored, even when officials accepted that the transition to such a high exchange rate would be difficult.[36] These beliefs could very well have muted any sectoral opposition to a return to gold as the solution to the overhang.

Consequences: The Short-Lived Reconstructed Gold Standard

The difficulty in this case comes in measuring the impact of ideology separately from institutional factors.[37] System-level theories also contribute something, if only to provide insight into how the problem of the overhang came about. Since all the arguments point to similar outcomes, the only way to test them is to compare more details in the evidence. It is also possible to specify our questions in different ways. For instance, we could compare how each type of theory explains the specific timing of the return to the gold standard or in what order the different types of actors organized and acted. The bureaucratic politics argument may give us more insight here, simply because of the nature of the issue. It is hard for groups to ask for monetary policy changes without some sort of disagreement among the monetary institutions.

After Britain struggled to get back on the gold standard, and even sacrificed industry's interests, defending the overvalued exchange rate was still difficult. The problems eventually came to a head in 1931 when financial crises in other countries caused many banks to hoard gold. Pounds were brought back to Britain and cashed in for gold; on Wednesday September 16th, £5 million were exchanged for gold. On Thursday, the figure rose to £10 million and on Friday to £18 million. The Bank of England had only another £130 million worth of gold left, so over the weekend, they decided to suspend convertibility into gold, lest the reserves be drained completely. France had contributed to this problem, since the French central bank had been converting pounds into gold all summer. After Britain suspended convertibility, the French central bank was left holding £62 million.

Others followed Britain's move. The U.S. went off the gold standard in 1933; France held out until 1936, which was much too late. By staying on gold for so long, the French policy-makers constrained their own choices, which prevented economic recovery before World War II. By going off gold, other countries were able to replicate some of the policies they had pursued to their advantage during the war. They were free to manipulate the money supply. They all first tried to devalue quite quickly—what is also known as a *competitive* or *predatory devaluation*, since devaluing has the effect of lowering prices relative to everyone else. The aim was to expand exports, which should stimulate production and pull the economy out of its downward spiral. There is a great incentive to be the first to devalue, since whomever goes first gets the most gain. Of course, within a relatively short time, many of the major economies had done exactly the same thing, so none gained any special advantage.[38]

Countries began to exert greater control over international transactions and international exchange, with repercussions in other issue-areas. The Germans, in order to prevent money from leaving the country, had already set up barriers preventing capital exports in August and September 1931. Other countries soon adopted similar policies. As a result, new international investments fell off, and it became harder to pay debts from existing international investments. Meanwhile, countries had already been doing some of the very same things in the area of trade. Britain set up a monetary bloc, based on use of the pound, around the colonies and Commonwealth. The Japanese set up a yen bloc in Asia. The U.S. had a de facto dollar bloc in Latin America. These blocs made trade flow along preferential lines, since payments were easier within the blocs. Trade had started to close down soon after the economic downturn following the stock market crash of 1929. The U.S. response had been to implement the trade policy equivalent of predatory devaluations. The reasons for that, and the consequences, are examined in the next chapter.

Notes

1. There were significant departures from this ideal operation of the standard in practice. In fact, many large countries had so little of their economies involved in trade that the flows of gold were too small to force through the adjustments described here; Britain developed practices which manipulated the flows of capital in and out of London, so that it could avoid adjustments if desired; not all countries could maintain the gold standard rules because they lacked the institutions necessary. The system

could hardly be considered natural and neutral. See Marcello de Cecco, *Money and Empire* (Totowa, NJ: Rowman and Littlefield, 1975); Donald N. McCloskey and Richard J. Zecher, "How the Gold Standard Worked, 1880-1913," *The Monetary Approach to the Balance of Payments*, ed. Jacob A. Frenkel and Harry G. Johnson (London: Allen and Unwin, 1976).

2. See Peter Lindert, "Key Currencies and Gold, 1900-1913," *Princeton Studies in International Finance* 24 (August 1969).

3. Susan Howson, *Domestic Monetary Management in Britain 1919-1938* (New York, NY: Cambridge University Press, 1975) 11-13.

4. Howson 14.

5. Howson 25.

6. Howson 28.

7. John Guiseppi, *The Bank of England* (Chicago, IL: Henry Regnery Co., 1966) 147.

8. D.E. Moggridge, *The Return to Gold, 1925: The Formulation of Economic Policy and its Critics* (London: Cambridge University Press, 1969) 23; and Alec Cairncross and Barry Eichengreen, *Sterling in Decline* (Oxford: Basil Blackwell, 1983) 50-51.

9. Moggridge, *British Monetary Policy 1924-1931* (New York, NY: Cambridge University Press, 1972) 28-29; Howson 24.

10. Moggridge, *The Return to Gold, 1925* 21.

11. Howson 1.

12. M.E. Falkus, "U.S. Economic Policy and the 'Dollar Gap' of the 1920s," *Economic History Review* (Second Series) 24,4 (November 1971): 599-623.

13. This is well laid out in David Lake, "International Economic Structures and American Foreign Economic Policy, 1887-1934," *World Politics* 35,4 (July 1983): 517-43.

14. Stephen Krasner, "State Power and the Structure of International Trade," *World Politics* 28,3 (April 1976): 342. This argument is also consistent with that put forward by Judith Goldstein in *Ideas, Interests, and American Trade Policy* (Ithaca, NY: Cornell University Press, 1993). As she puts it (xii), "the creation of rules and procedures to enforce a particular economic strategy at one point acts as a constraint not only on current behavior but also on the range of options available to future entrepreneurs." This also fits in with broader theories about institutions and path-dependency. As Geoffrey Garrett and Peter Lange point out in their assessment of historical structural arguments on the role of institutions in "Internationalization, Institutions and Political Change," *International Organization* 49,4 (Autumn 1995): 628, "institutions invariably outlive the constellations of interests that created them, and hence provide barriers to market-driven policy change."

15. Susan Strange, *Sterling and British Policy: A Political Study of an International Currency in Decline* (New York, NY: Oxford University Press, 1971) 47.

16. Michael Edelstein, "Rigidity and Bias in the British Capital Market, 1870-1913," *Essays on a Mature Economy: Britain after 1840*, ed. Donald N. McCloskey (Princeton, NJ: Princeton University Press, 1971) 83-105.

17. Peter Katzenstein, "Conclusion: Structures and Strategies of Foreign Economic Policy," *Between Power and Plenty*, ed. Peter Katzenstein (Madison, WI: University of Wisconsin Press, 1978) 309.

18. Moggridge, *British Monetary Policy 1924-1931* 46.

19. Bernard Elbaum and William Lazonick, "The Decline of the British Economy: An Institutional Perspective," *Journal of Economic History* 44,2 (June 1984) 581.

20. Moggridge, *British Monetary Policy 1924-1931* 236-37.

21. For a more in-depth discussion, see Beth Simmons, *Who Adjusts?* (Princeton, NJ: Princeton University Press, 1994).

22. Moggridge, *British Monetary Policy 1924-1931* 99-100.

23. Howson 36, 141.

24. Cairncross and Eichengreen 41.

25. Mark R. Brawley, *Afterglow or Adjustment?* (New York, NY: Columbia University Press, 1999) 73-75.

26. Moggridge, *British Monetary Policy 1924-1931* 145.

27. Moggridge, *British Monetary Policy 1924-1931* 160-61.

28. Strange 50; Howson 56.

29. Moggridge, *British Monetary Policy 1924-1931* 237; Howson 9.

30. As cited in Cairncross and Eichengreen 38.

31. Cairncross and Eichengreen 46-47.

32. As quoted in Cairncross and Eichengreen 54.

33. Cairncross and Eichengreen 60-61; and M. June Flanders, *International Monetary Economics, Between the Classical and the New Classical* (New York, NY: Cambridge University Press, 1989) 87-88, and 100.

34. Moggridge, *British Monetary Policy 1924-1931* 86-87.

35. Moggridge, *British Monetary Policy 1924-1931* 57-58.

36. Moggridge, *British Monetary Policy 1924-1931* 3-4, and also his *The Return to Gold, 1925* 65; also see Cairncross and Eichengreen 29.

37. It is easier to treat these as two separate but reinforcing forces; see Goldstein.

38. The depreciations may have helped stimulate some recovery nonetheless; see Barry Eichengreen and Jeffrey Sachs, "Exchange Rates and Economic Recovery in the 1930s," *Journal of Economic History* 45,4 (December 1985): 925-46.

Additional References

Blank, Stephen. "Britain." *Between Power and Plenty*. Ed. Peter Katzenstein. Madison, WI: University of Wisconsin Press, 1978. 89-137.

Bordo, Michael K., and Anna J. Schwartz (eds.). *A Retrospective on the Classical Gold Standard, 1821-1931*. Chicago, IL: University of Chicago Press, 1984.

Eichengreen, Barry. *Golden Fetters: The Gold Standard and the Great Depression*. Oxford: Oxford University Press, 1992.

Frieden, Jeffry. *Banking on the World*. New York, NY: Harper and Row, 1987.

Keynes, John Maynard. *The Economic Consequences of Mr. Churchill*. London: Hogarth Press, 1925.

Kunz, Diane. *The Battle for Britain's Gold Standard in 1931*. London: Croom Helm, 1987.

CHAPTER 17

The Passage of the
Smoot-Hawley Tariff

The Trade Regime after World War I

Just as monetary relations were upset by World War I, so too were trade patterns. During the war, each country tried to manipulate its international economic relations to aid its own war effort. European governments acted to direct trade and international payments towards political goals. Even Britain finally moved away from free trade. Two significant measures were taken by Britain to protect domestic industry and reduce imports, since it wanted to spend precious foreign currency on war material only, not on foreign goods which could be produced at home. The first step away from free trade occurred with the enactment of the McKenna Duties, which were put in place in 1916. After the war, in 1921, they were reinforced and rationalized by the postwar *Safeguarding of Industries Act*. These represent the first time since 1846 that Britain raised tariffs.

Other countries raised tariffs during the war. The U.S. had been moving towards free trade before the war broke out, with the Underwood Tariff passed in 1913. The Underwood Tariff was the lowest tariff the U.S. had adopted up to that time. But since the war was seen as disrupting existing trade patterns, the U.S. decided to insulate its own economy by passing new, higher tariffs. These incentives were especially strong since all the major combatants had raised tariffs on industrial goods during the war, but most had been eager to import food. The U.S. managed to increase its agricultural exports during the war; however, once the war ended, European countries tended to keep their industrial tariffs in place, and likewise began to protect agriculture, in order to shift back to more normal production mixes. In some regions, the war had altered political settlements, such as Eastern and Central Europe where several old empires were dissolved. These new countries had political and economic goals which made it more likely they would employ tariffs. They each wanted to develop their own industrial base, which meant they all adopted high tariffs to discriminate against exports of finished goods.

The U.S. became concerned with the role of tariffs in the postwar adjustment process, as countries returned to peacetime production. In 1921 the U.S.

passed the Emergency Tariff, which raised duties on a few selected items. The Emergency Tariff signalled a change in behaviour, however, and heralded some of the tariff competition to follow. In 1922, the U.S. raised tariffs across the board and for the first time raised agricultural tariffs, in order to protect the domestic producers who had recently lost access to European markets.

These early tariff wrangles were symptomatic of the deeper problem faced in the 1920s—how could all these countries end their wartime production and return their economies to peacetime practices? This problem took on different dimensions in different places. The problem in the U.S. was that it had done well in industry, services, and agriculture during the war because foreign competition had more or less disappeared. Once the war ended, the competition returned, and agriculture in particular had problems. The same sort of thing was happening in Latin America and the Pacific, where local industrialization had picked up or regional trade had increased in new and different ways. As international competition returned, it threatened to undo the recent changes and to push trade back to historical patterns. This was being pursued by those who wanted their old markets back, but was resisted by those who now considered these markets their own.

The critical sector turned out to be agricultural. In the 1920s, all the major trading countries raised their tariffs on agricultural goods. Overproduction would have occurred anyway, but the tariffs made the problem worse. Agricultural goods flooded the international markets, and prices fell to lower and lower levels, until they were only at about 20 per cent of pre-war price levels. This obviously drove many farmers out of business. The U.S., for instance, began to import agricultural goods in 1927 for the first time ever, because international prices fell so low. The political response was not surprising—farmers went to the government and demanded protection.

The stock market crashed in 1929, financial crisis spread everywhere, and demand was falling off in the U.S. and elsewhere. When the farmers asked for protection this time, they had potential allies. Other sectors were interested in protection too, so the deal that was struck was broad and its impact forceful. Everyone else was willing to support the farmers' demands, as long as they too received protective tariffs. This is an example of a legislative technique called "logrolling." In order to get one group's legislation through, many other groups' narrow conditions must be met; the various demands are wrapped up in one package and passed. The result, the Smoot-Hawley Tariff of 1930, moved U.S. tariffs from among some of the lowest to among some of the highest. Whereas the U.S. had appeared to be one of the strongest proponents of trade liberalization in 1913, it now led the closure of the trade regime in the 1930s.

System-Level Theory: A Failed Hegemonic Transition?

For realists, this episode creates a number of serious questions. If hegemonic stability theory is correct, the U.S. policy is difficult to understand. Since the U.S. emerged from World War I as the economic and financial centre of the international political economy, was its interest not in recreating and then maintaining an open trading system? By leading the closure of the trade regime, the U.S. was certainly not stabilizing it. Why wasn't the U.S. acting more like a hegemonic power? More importantly for realists, could these questions be answered while remaining focused on systemic variables?

One possible answer comes from David Lake.[1] Lake's argument hinges on how one identifies a hegemonic power. In short, he tries to make his own definition of hegemony more specific, while also identifying roles for other countries in the system. He argues that only a state with significant involvement in the international economy and also high productivity relative to other states will have the interests and capabilities to act as liberalizing hegemonic leaders. Productivity is used to gauge a country's economic competitiveness. States heavily involved in trade but with low productivity are more likely to act as "spoilers"; that is, they would participate in the trade regime, yet resist opening up their own economies to foreign competition. States with a medium-level of involvement in international trade and high relative productivity, on the other hand, have an interest in seeing the trade regime liberalized, but may not have the capabilities to act as a leader; thus, Lake termed such states "supporters."

The central question becomes where one draws the lines between medium and heavy involvement in the international economy, since that divides hegemonic powers from supporters.[2] Lake used the level of 15 per cent of world trade to mark where a state holds hegemonic status. Britain's share of world trade had slumped below this level prior to World War I, yet the U.S. share would not rise above that line until after 1918. In this interpretation, there were two "supporters" in the interwar years. It was a time of transition from one hegemonic leader to another, but one that was incomplete. While it was possible for these two countries to cooperate to provide stability and leadership, this cooperation was difficult to attain.

Rather than cooperation, a different sort of game took place. Each knew the other was interested in maintaining freer trade in the international political economy—they were in head-to-head competition in several sectors and in many different regions of the world. Thus, each knew the other might take up some of the costs associated with providing leadership. They engaged in a game of competitive irresponsibility, which we can model in game theory as "Chicken."[3] By acting irresponsibly, one state could hope to force the other to carry more of the burden. This seems to capture the U.S. attitude in particular, since it was doing its best to avoid any costly foreign policy activities. As the international economy became more unstable, and concessions from the two supporters were less forthcoming, export markets were at risk. Without export markets, each of the two supporters had less and less to gain from leadership, until one—the U.S.—moved to defect from the regime first.

Domestic Level: The Logrolling of Sector-Based Interests

While the system-level arguments of the realists provide a superficial fit with the evidence, questions remain. Why was the U.S. unwilling to carry more of the burdens of leadership? To answer that question, one must turn to the domestic level and consider politics within the country. Moreover, domestic-level theories may offer greater insight into the timing of the event. They may be able to tell us why the tariff was passed in 1930, as well as why the tariff took the shape that it did.

The Smoot-Hawley Tariff has long been the subject of political research. In some of the earliest analyses, the role of "pork barrel politics" in the formation of the tariff took centrestage.[4] Pork barrel politics refers to the traditional U.S. practice where members of Congress worry about the impact of legislation only in terms of their own constituency. The institutional structure of the U.S. government encourages this pattern, leaving the president to worry about the impact on the country as a whole. The logroll of the tariff thus served many narrow interests, but, taken overall, its impact was negative for the country. In this analysis, the tariff is understood as the product of congressional practices.

Later analyses still rely on this sort of thinking to establish the conditions for such a logroll to take place, but argue that the conditions existed long before the Smoot-Hawley Tariff was passed. The same institutional setting had produced the Underwood Tariff, which had been extremely low. What nudged Congress in the protectionist direction? According to Robert Pastor, the answer can be found in party politics.[5] The Republicans had been in favour of protectionism for some time, while the Democrats had not. In the elections of 1928, the Republicans won a majority. A Republican, Herbert Hoover, was elected president. Pastor argued that the Republicans placed faith in protectionism as an effective policy for remedying certain economic problems, so that when groups came and asked for help, they were more than willing to oblige with a tariff. Then the logroll took place, and the tariff grew in size and scope.

One of the strongest insights to be raised more recently about the importance of domestic-level factors in the passage of the Smoot-Hawley Tariff comes from Barry Eichengreen. Eichengreen largely agrees with the earlier analyses of Schattschneider, in that interest groups pursuing pork-barrel politics brought about the "logroll." As Eichengreen points out, if interest groups were to blame, along with congressmen worried about narrow interests, then we would expect the vote to be a landslide. After all, the pressures would be the same for all congressmen. Instead, the vote fell along party lines.[6] At first blush this seems to support Pastor's argument. In fact, Eichengreen disputes this and points out that both parties had supported protectionism (albeit at lower levels) at points in the recent past. Neither side in the debate could expect to support free trade by standing on principle. It would not have been a credible position—and in fact the opponents of the tariff did not use ideological arguments as their centrepiece.

Eichengreen returns to the arguments about interest groups, but examines how their political power changed in the 1920s. Participation in World War I had profoundly altered the relationship between government and interest groups in two important ways. First, government had encouraged the organization of interests in order to promote economic activity as part of the war effort. It encouraged both industry and agriculture to organize into large bodies in order to simplify the bureaucratic tasks of placing large contracts for goods and services. So, as a result, in the 1920s interest groups were more numerous than before, had more members, and were attuned to dealing with government. This increase in organized interest groups was reflected in the number of groups which presented arguments in the debates surrounding the passage of the Smoot-Hawley Tariff.

That leads us to Eichengreen's other observation about the changes in the relationship between the government and interest groups. The interest groups had more extensive links to government than ever before. Prior to World War I, interest groups stood apart from government; by the late 1920s, the same groups were now right in the midst of political activities, via numerous access points.[7] They were deeply involved in the legislative process and, naturally, could be found on both sides of the debates. The strength of each coalition was therefore very important for the tariff's passage. Prominent among the pro-protectionist groups were northern farmers (who grew grain) and labour-intensive industries. Labour organizations such as the American Federation of Labor (AFL) also turned protectionist. Farmers in particular were overrepresented, according to Eichengreen.

The main opponents to protectionism came from sectors which used a lot of capital in their production of goods and services. Heavy industry, but also banking, fall into this category. Southern farmers (who grew cotton and other competitive crops) tended to support freer trade. These groups could not rally the same support as the protectionist forces, however. If we were to return to our economic models of the distribution of the benefits of trade liberalization from the Stolper-Samuelson theorem, we find that these alignments fit our expectations. The U.S. was moving from a relatively labour- and land-abundant economy to one where capital and land were relatively abundant. Yet these groups were unable to prevent the passage of a new higher tariff, because they lacked the political power within Congress.

In a similar analysis, Jeffry Frieden lays out the two opposing coalitions. His argument is that the coalition of the domestically oriented sectors and the coalition of the internationally oriented sectors were about the same strength.[8] Each side controlled elements of the U.S. political system, so that a stalemate resulted. Policy therefore was driven first in one direction, then the other; on closer inspection, it is easy to see how U.S. foreign economic policy in this period often contained contradictions. By moving to a broader picture (i.e., not simply looking at trade and tariffs), we can see how trade policy and monetary relations were not always headed in the same direction.

Bureaucratic Politics: The Fed's
Attempts at International Leadership

Such arguments blend together domestic politics arguments with those from bureaucratic politics. They are less useful for explaining the passage of the Smoot-Hawley Tariff, but shed light on how the U.S. was pursuing a mix of policies. The nationally oriented economic actors had strong organizations which gave them power in Congress (hence the tariff was protectionist), but the anti-protectionist forces had their allies within the government, too. The banking community, for instance, had extensive connections with the Federal Reserve Banks. The banking community therefore tried to influence outcomes through the policy of the Federal Reserve Bank of New York (the Fed). While this did not do them much good in trade policy, it did mean that in the 1920s the U.S. had exhibited some facets of leadership in the area of monetary policy. However, these efforts were not sanctioned by the president or Congress.

The governor of the Fed, Benjamin Strong, urged the U.S. to hold an international conference to resolve the issue of debts after the war ended. Private firms in the U.S. had lent billions to allied governments before the U.S. officially entered the war. The allies didn't want to repay the debts, arguing that they had made more substantial sacrifices for the war in terms of their human losses. Strong proposed that all payments should be suspended for up to five years, or even longer if possible, and that they be reduced as much as possible, with the U.S. government extending credit to countries in difficulty.[9] Strong's views reflected those of the internationally oriented financial firms based in New York, which saw gains from the U.S. leading the reopening of the liberal international economic system. Instead, official policy set by the executive branch refused to take on any burdensome obligations. The U.S. funding commission set up in 1922 to renegotiate debt repayments refused any reduction of the amounts outstanding. This prompted the U.S. to refuse to send an official participant to the Geneva Conference held in 1922, thus leaving it without representation in crucial international monetary negotiations.[10]

Another example comes from 1927, when there was a surge of gold flowing out of Europe and into the U.S. Other central bankers appealed to the Fed to ease its policies and reduce the amount of gold the U.S. was drawing in. Strong complied, so the Fed ran a counter-cyclical policy. This was only the second time such a policy had been attempted; the first had been in 1924, when the goal had been to return to the international gold standard. The aim was to establish an interest rate differential between New York and London which would divert international funds to Britain; rather than manage policy towards purely domestic goals, the Fed was trying to stabilize international flows.[11] Strong hoped that this would not only stabilize the two currencies, but also help New York attract some of London's traditional business.[12]

These actions ended the strong flow of gold and stabilized the international financial system, but Strong's opponents pointed out how domestic economic goals had been subordinated to international needs. Worse still, because bank holdings were high, when extra reserves were released by the low interest rates in New York, the banks engaged in risky loans which in turn merely fuelled stock market speculation prior to the Crash of October 1929.[13] Herbert Hoover, who served as Coolidge's Secretary of Commerce prior to becoming president, clearly linked the Fed's international interests to its easy money policy and to the stock market speculation and crash. Others have argued, however, that while Fed policy was slanted towards international goals in 1927, it followed a policy guided by domestic concerns when sterling was under pressure in 1928-29.[14] Since different federal reserve banks were doing different things, both interpretations have an element of truth.

Policies outside of trade, therefore, looked somewhat different from trade policy. But the banking community did not have the connections to change trade policy itself. Instead, different facets of foreign policy ran in competition with each other. The result was failed leadership. This evidence supports the arguments made in the earlier section; it also points out how in foreign economic policy-making, bureaucracies have fairly clearly defined constituencies to which they respond. It makes it more difficult to use a bureaucratic politics analysis in the absence of a domestic politics argument.

Ideas and the Failure of Experts

One of the most poignant aspects of the debate leading up to the passage of the Smoot-Hawley Tariff was the numerous presentations made by the academic community. Professional economists seemed nearly unanimous in their opposition to the tariff. Many correctly predicted the disastrous results which would unfold if the tariff was passed and other countries retaliated. These predictions came true. The Smoot-Hawley Tariff did not help American businesses, but rather did them great harm.

This poses several questions for those who argue that ideas, by themselves, are powerful factors shaping foreign economic policy. Here the ideas were strongly supported by the relevant community of experts. Moreover, this consensus among the experts had existed for some time. Their belief in the correctness of free trade had been held for decades and there was no surge of new ideologies or theoretical arguments to challenge them. Rival ideas, such as socialism or even the pre-theories surrounding the utility of government intervention in the economy, could not command much support in the U.S. political system yet. As Eichengreen pointed out, the ideological aspect of the debates were played out at the margins, not at the forefront.[15]

Those who would have us see ideas as independently powerful factors need to elaborate the conditions under which they can play an important role and the conditions under which an epistemic community has power. Some analyses of U.S. trade policy suggested that within a few years, liberalism would become entrenched in institutions.[16] Why were the ideas supporting a policy of free trade so weak in 1929-30, yet so strong such a short time later? The interactions of ideas with other causal forces needs to be further elaborated.

The Consequences of the Smoot-Hawley Tariff

When the American market was effectively closed off, it started a chain re-action, though it might be better to compare the reactions with a race. The producers of goods previously exported to the U.S. suddenly had to find new international markets; since Britain was the next most open economy for international trade, all the producers tried to shift their sales to Britain. Britain suffered a crisis as a flood of cheaply priced goods entered the market, so that British producers needed protection. The government felt compelled to close itself off as well. Other countries felt the same sorts of pressures, so they too raised tariffs.

These tariff strategies are referred to as "beggar thy neighbour" policies because whoever moves first gains in the short run, but makes the impact worse for everyone else. (It fits the prisoners' dilemma game quite well.) So after 1930 and until 1933, tariffs on all sorts of goods were rising in all the major countries. Britain, which had resisted the temptation to close off the empire and dominions from international competition during its relative economic decline, reversed its stance. In 1931 Britain enacted the Imperial Preference System, which focused trade and international investment almost totally on the empire. For example, in 1913, Britain sent 22 per cent of its exports to the empire; by 1938 that had changed to 47 per cent. In 1913, 20 per cent of Britain's imports had come from the empire, but by 1938 that figure had risen to 39 per cent. While this supported some of Britain's previous international economic interactions, Britain had lost the U.S. market, as well as many others.

Trade collapsed. Since the Great Depression was just beginning, these tariffs wrecked whatever possibly positive role trade could have played in lifting countries out of their economic downturns. As exports fell, exporting sectors also began to lay off workers, so that the downward spiral of the economy accelerated. As more workers got laid off, they were unable to afford goods; demand fell lower, so that firms cut back production, and the cycle built on itself. Worse, the economic downturn and the collapse of trade encouraged several countries to create regional trade blocs aimed at economic self-sufficiency; if countries needed resources which they could not get through trade, they used other policies to attain their needs. In places where unemployment was extremely high, fascist regimes took power. These countries saw conquest as the best way to do without trade. Soon Nazi Germany and Imperial Japan would use warfare as an element of their foreign economic policies. The collapse of trade, sparked by the Smoot-Hawley Tariff, helped lead to World War II.

Notes

1. David A. Lake, "International Economic Structures and American Foreign Economic Policy, 1887-1934," *World Politics* 35,4 (July 1983): 517-43.

2. As for relative productivity, a country is either above average or below.

3. See Chapter 5 in Mark R. Brawley, *Liberal Leadership* (Ithaca, NY: Cornell University Press, 1993).

4. E.E. Schattschneider, *Politics, Pressures and the Tariff* (New York, NY: Prentice Hall, 1935).

5. Robert Pastor, *Congress and the Politics of U.S. Foreign Economic Policy, 1929-1976* (Berkeley. CA: University of California Press, 1980).

6. Barry Eichengreen, "The Political Economy of the Smoot-Hawley Tariff," *Research in Economic History* 12 (1989): 1-43.

7. Eichengreen.

8. Jeffry Frieden, "Sectoral Conflict and U.S. Foreign Economic Policy, 1914-1940," *The State and American Foreign Economic Policy*, ed. John Ikenberry, David A. Lake, and Michael Mastanduno (Ithaca, NY: Cornell University Press, 1988) 59-90.

9. Lester V. Chandler, *Benjamin Strong, Central Banker* (Washington, DC: Brookings Institution, 1958) 143-45, 294-95; Stephen V.O. Clarke, "The Reconstruction of the International Monetary System: The Attempts of 1922 and 1933," *Princeton Studies in International Finance* 33 (November 1973): 15.

10. Clarke, "The Reconstruction of the International Monetary System 7-8.

11. Elmus Wicker, *Federal Reserve Monetary Policy 1917-1933* (New York, NY: Random House, 1966) 106, 114-15; Stephen V.O. Clarke, *Central Bank Cooperation 1924-1931* (New York, NY: Federal Reserve Bank of New York, 1967) 125.

12. Clarke, *Central Bank Cooperation* 72-73.

13. Donald F. Kettl, *Leadership at the Fed* (New Haven, CT: Yale University Press, 1986) 33-34; William Grieder, *Secrets of the Temple* (New York, NY: Simon and Schuster, 1987) 301-03; Albert Fishlow, "Lessons from the Past: Capital Markets during the Nineteenth Century and the Interwar Period," *International Organization* 39,3 (Summer 1985): 80-81.

14. Clarke, *Central Bank Cooperation* 42-43.

15. Eichengreen.

16. Judith Goldstein, *Ideas, Interests, and American Trade Policy* (Ithaca, NY: Cornell University Press, 1993).

Additional References

Callahan, Colleen M., Judith A. McDonald, and Anthony Patrick O'Brien. "Who Voted for Smoot-Hawley?" *Journal of Economic History* 54,3 (September 1994): 683-90.

Conybeare, John. "Trade Wars: A Comparative Study of Anglo-Hanse, Franco-Italian and Hawley-Smoot Conflicts." *World Politics* 38,1 (October 1985): 147-72.

Eichengreen, Barry. "The Political Economy of the Smoot-Hawley Tariff." *Research in Economic History* 12 (1989): 1-43.

Frieden, Jeffry. "Sectoral Conflict and U.S. Foreign Economic Policy, 1914-1940." *The State and American Foreign Economic Policy.* Ed. John Ikenberry, David A. Lake, and Michael Mastanduno. (Ithaca, NY: Cornell University Press, 1988). 59-90.

Hayford, Marc, and Carl Pasurka. "The Political Economy of the Fordney-McCumber and Smoot-Hawley Tariff Acts." *Explorations in Economic History* 29,1 (January 1992): 30-50.

Lake, David. "International Economic Structures and American Foreign Economic Policy, 1887-1934." *World Politics* 35,4 (July 1983): 517-43.

Pastor, Robert. *Congress and the Politics of U.S. Foreign Economic Policy, 1929-1976.* Berkeley, CA: University of California Press, 1980.

Schattschneider, E.E. *Politics, Pressures and the Tariff.* New York, NY: Prentice Hall, 1935.

CHAPTER 18

The Creation of the Bretton Woods Monetary Regime

While trade and monetary regimes were already largely closed off before World War II, the war itself naturally disrupted the relations that had been maintained. The war had another effect—it once again stimulated the economic growth of the U.S. thanks to the massive orders for war material. Having come out of the high unemployment period of the Great Depression, U.S. policy-makers were especially concerned with avoiding postwar economic problems this time around.

Both the U.S. and Britain wanted to reestablish international economic regimes around liberal principles. Their leaders held several meetings during the war to design these regimes.[1] Participation by other nations in some of these meetings was considered essential if these arrangements were to succeed, since other states would have to participate.

One of the most important of these wartime discussions was held in Bretton Woods, New Hampshire, in 1944. Some 44 allied nations sent representatives to these talks, which had the explicit aim of constructing the postwar monetary system. The results, however, were largely dominated by the need to construct a consensus among the most important financial powers.[2] The discussions culminated in the creation of the International Monetary Fund (IMF) and the International Bank for Reconstruction and Development (IBRD, better known as the World Bank). The IMF was created to assist countries with short-term balance of payments problems, while the World Bank was to aid in recovery from the war and future economic development.[3]

These two institutions signalled a new approach to the construction of economic regimes. First, they embodied institutional support for liberal practices. They were, in that sense, a reflection of the new attitudes about the need for government action to stabilize or manage markets. There were three goals in the Bretton Woods system, as it came to be called: (1) to establish free capital flows, (2) to make currencies convertible into gold and/or other currencies, and (3) to create stable exchange rates. These goals reflect the desire to regain the benefits associated with the gold standard, but were also shaped by the needs of the trade and investment regimes which were being established. If international payments on trade were to be made, there must be some form of convertible payments. The investment regime, if based on liberal economic principles, would require free capital flows.

Within these three characteristics, though, many different arrangements were possible. For instance, the gold standard achieved similar ends by fixing all currencies in terms of gold. Because of the troubles adjusting currencies to each other, this regime had been difficult to recreate after World War I. Gold had also been poorly distributed for return to such a system after 1918; in 1945, gold reserves were concentrated in U.S. vaults; therefore, it would have been impossible to base numerous countries' reserves entirely on gold. The gold exchange standard set up briefly after World War I was intended to achieve the same three goals, but the fixed exchange rate regime established under the Bretton Woods agreement did so through different mechanisms and rules.

These new mechanisms and rules drew on lessons learned from the experiences of the 1930s. The most important lesson learned was that market forces created problems—governments needed to manage the international system, especially since all governments wished to pursue Keynesian programs domestically. Although this lesson was universal, that did not guarantee any agreement on how to establish an international regime congruent with new domestic practices. In fact, new problems with an international monetary regime based on purely liberal principles were anticipated, since all governments were no longer following laissez-faire economics domestically. There was no consensus on the best way to resolve the tensions created.

In the U.S., the greatest fear was that there would be another recession after World War II. Production in the U.S. had risen dramatically in the war, and some leaders feared overproduction in many areas after Europe got back on its feet economically. Therefore, the economic nationalists in the U.S. wanted to make sure the U.S. could use Keynesian interventions in the economy to prop up demand if necessary. This group, led by Henry Morgenthau, the Secretary of the Treasury, and Harry Dexter White, the Assistant Secretary of the Treasury, wanted to make sure that any international agreement on monetary affairs would not bind the U.S. government's ability to act at home. Remember how the gold standard had forced inflation or deflation on governments? Morgenthau and White wanted to ensure that any future arrangements would allow the U.S. government to pursue inflationary policies whenever necessary.

Morgenthau and White pushed to break the link between domestic inflationary policies and the impact of the balance of trade. There were domestic opponents to this perspective, especially among the representatives of the international business community. These groups had their own representatives in the U.S. government, led first by Cordell Hull, the Secretary of State, and then by his successor, Dean Acheson. While this side of the debate obviously agreed that the U.S. should do all that it could to avoid any postwar recession, they also thought the U.S. could do this without having to give up the possible restraints imposed by a fixed exchange rate system.

At first, the economic nationalists won. They convinced President Franklin Roosevelt of the correctness of their views, so he appointed some of them to draw up plans for the postwar monetary system. White, who had the greatest input into the design of the system, was assigned the post of chief U.S. negotiator in the international bargaining.

The White Plan versus the Keynes Plan

White's plan envisioned an IMF with strong powers to advise governments on domestic macroeconomic policies. He wanted to give the IMF power to force or at least strongly encourage governments to pursue Keynesian full-employment policies. More importantly, he wanted the IMF to get countries to pursue such policies together. Everything would work well if all the countries stimulated their economies at the same time, and none engaged in competitive devaluation or protectionism. As White put it, when there was no economic cooperation between countries, relations would "inevitably result in economic warfare that will be but the prelude and instigator of military warfare on an even vaster scale."[4]

In accordance with this plan, the IMF would have veto powers over any country's decisions to change its exchange rate. This would give the IMF the power to prevent one problem from the 1930s: competitive devaluations. At the time of the negotiations (1944), the U.S. had to convince Britain to go along with this rule, in which Britain wasn't very interested. There were some 44 other countries represented at these talks, but they were all so weak in financial and economic terms that their views only mattered to the extent that they coincided with either the U.S. or British perspectives. The British representative was John Maynard Keynes himself. He opposed White's position; although he, too, was concerned with full employment, he felt that the problems confronting Britain differed significantly from those the U.S. faced.

In order to finance World War II, Britain was forced to sell off most of the remainder of its foreign investment and so lost the ability to live off the returns on earlier foreign investments. This meant British imports in the future would have to be paid for by British exports—Britain would have to learn to produce competitive exports again. Keynes knew this would take time to arrange (he had no idea just how long!). What he wanted was an IMF that would serve British needs—an IMF that would give out credits and loans so that Britain could rebuild her economy.

Also important to Keynes was that any international monetary system constructed be outside of the sole control of the U.S. This, of course, was the opposite of White's view. Since Keynes didn't want Britain at the mercy of the U.S., he proposed an alternative institution to monitor and coordinate international monetary relations: the International Clearing Union (ICU). As its name indicates, this would be a clearing house for national currencies; currencies would not have to be convertible into other assets or each other, at least not in any public market. Countries could eliminate their outstanding balances with each other via transactions entirely within the ICU. Moreover, as Keynes envisioned it, the ICU would have the ability to make loans to deficit countries. While this sounds like White's IMF, the financing of these loans was to be quite different. Deficit countries, such as Britain, would be loaned money on easy terms, while the ICU would tax those countries with a surplus, though there would be only one surplus country in the near future, the U.S.

The agreement reached at Bretton Woods set forth the IMF charter, and it, as we might guess, reflected U.S. arguments rather than British.[5] What were the specific rules set up? First, the system was designed to operate in a stable international environment; but the rules recognized the probability of problems with adjustments in the years immediately after the war; therefore, countries were allowed to exempt themselves from the rules for the first five years, while they recovered. Second, members pledged to maintain fixed exchange rates. In other words, they declared an exchange rate (a parity), and they pledged to keep their exchange rates within plus or minus 1 per cent of this parity by intervening in exchange markets, that is, by buying or selling on the exchange markets. It was hoped that by intervening in exchange markets to deal with pressures on exchange rates, domestic policies could be separated from exchange rate policy. Money required for intervention in exchange could be loaned to governments by the IMF. Finally, the policy-makers didn't want to be stuck defending a parity indefinitely. They therefore created a loophole. If a country was in a condition of "fundamental disequilibrium," an official change of the exchange rate would be allowed; changes greater than 10 per cent would still have to be approved by the IMF first. "Fundamental disequilibrium" was left undefined.

As part of the set-up, each nation was assigned a quota, based on the size of the country's economic and financial resources, to contribute to the IMF's funds. This assessment had to be paid one-quarter in gold and three-quarters in national currency. More importantly, voting within the IMF was directly proportional to the quotas—the U.S. had the largest quota, which made up more than one-third of the total. Not too surprisingly, the rules stated that important decisions within the IMF required a two-thirds majority—in effect, the U.S. got veto power over critical decisions. And, since any exchange rate changes of more than 10 per cent had to be approved by the IMF, the U.S. could exercise a veto over those judgements as well.

Borrowing from the IMF was to be done in multiples of a country's quota, or tranche, as these are also called. But with each tranche, the restrictions the IMF could place on the borrowing country went up. These conditions spelled out the adjustment policies a country would need to implement if it was to correct its balance of payments deficit. In effect this placed the entire burden of adjustment on countries in deficit. The rules of the regime basically punished countries with serious balance of payments deficits, but did nothing to countries running large surpluses. (Compare this to the workings of the gold standard, which in theory forced both surplus and deficit countries to adjust.) This presumably reflected the interests of the U.S. in the late 1940s, as the single largest country running a surplus, and also reflects the desires of economic nationalists.[6] The U.S. did not want the international monetary regime to drive them out of a surplus and force them to raise unemployment levels. It is clear that White's desires were largely met, rather than those of Keynes, at least in the way the rules were laid out.

The Bretton Woods Regime in Operation

The Bretton Woods system as it was designed in the late 1940s was a victory for the U.S. economic nationalists, led by Harry Dexter White. But as soon as the system was put into practice, the U.S. international business sector once again fought a battle over the roles of the IMF and the World Bank. The rules allowed the participating countries to follow Keynesian full-employment policies and broke the link between fixed exchange rates and balance of payments adjustment as a means of disciplining the domestic economy. It was with this point that the international sectors, bankers especially, were uncomfortable. The internationalists were concerned that the World Bank and IMF rules would make borrowing too easy and therefore would stimulate not just growth but inflation—in other words, they feared the international system would have too much liquidity. (Bankers always oppose inflation since it devalues savings.)

What happened in practice turned out to be a compromise, because the IMF and World Bank had to be very conservative with their funds. There are two ways of looking at this outcome. First, Roosevelt died, and the new president, Truman, did not particularly like White and Morgenthau; he followed the advice of Acheson instead. A second explanation focuses on the pressures existing on the IMF and World Bank. For the latter to work, for instance, it had to raise money. Donations to it were small, and therefore it had to raise capital the only other way open to it—it floated bonds, but it had to gain the confidence of the banking community in order to sell them. The result was that the IMF and World Bank both began to follow much more conservative policies. The change in practice reflects the needs of the institutions to appease the bankers.

In practice, then, things did not work as White had intended. Borrowing from the IMF could be done only with some serious strings attached. Of course, another factor was that the devastation caused by the war was more than anyone had expected. Europe was in very bad shape, and the initial European harvests after the war were very low, partly because of very severe winters, which worsened conditions. Some of the initial policy responses the Europeans considered hinted at protectionism, so there was a threat that the open trading and monetary systems would never have a chance to operate. In fact, there are those who would argue that the IMF and World Bank had already been made too conservative by the late 1940s to do the job White had hoped it would do!

Since the institutions were unable to carry out their obligations, and most countries weren't prepared to adhere to the rules anyway, the U.S. took action unilaterally. It stepped forward to manage two parts of the international monetary system by itself: (1) providing liquidity and (2) aiding in the adjustment of exchange rates. The way the system had been designed, gold was supposed to be the reserve asset, the backing for national currencies. But there were several problems with this plan. First, there was not enough gold in the international system, and what there was, was in the U.S., which held 49.8 per cent of total world monetary reserves in 1950. The U.S. was also the only country consistently running a surplus in balance of payments, so no gold was leaving the country.

Just as important at this time was the fact that holding dollars was preferred to holding gold. It was clear that dollars could be turned in and exchanged for gold, but most actors would rather have the dollars, because dollars could be deposited at a bank where they would earn interest—dollars were better than gold. But this still left the problem of a liquidity shortage—the U.S. had a payments surplus, meaning it was exporting goods and drawing in not only gold but other currencies, too. So there was in practice not so much a gold shortage as a dollar shortage. U.S. policy-makers determined that this dollar shortage was an obstacle both to further economic growth and, especially, to the expansion of trade. The difficulty was in infusing the right amount of dollars into the international system so as to stimulate growth but not to create inflation, as well as how to achieve this when the U.S. economy had such an edge over all its economic competitors. These difficulties continued even after the rules of the Bretton Woods regime came into full effect, creating some of the very pressures which would undermine the regime, as will be discussed in Chapter 20. The point to consider now, however, has to do with understanding how we should explain the design of the Bretton Woods monetary regime.

The Liberals' Explanation: The Liberal Principles at the Heart of Bretton Woods

From the liberal viewpoint, the regime's most important aspects were the ways in which it supported liberal trading and financial practices. It promised to tie national markets together and reduce the risks of undertaking international economic exchange. It aimed to remove barriers to international transactions, thereby allowing individuals and firms to pursue their economic interests. This was done in ways which reinstalled liberal practices in international economic relations.

Exchange rates would be fixed to provide economic predictability reminiscent of the gold standard. The fixed exchange rates were meant to be somewhat flexible, however. The IMF was supposed to approve of exchange rate changes when needed in order to provide both stability and flexibility. Financial markets would be open to private individuals and firms. This would be necessary for capital to flow over borders, as international investments took place. The monetary relations would be consistent with liberal economic regimes in other issue-areas.

Of course, there were some tensions here, especially from the liberal perspective. For instance, private actors buying and selling currencies on exchange markets should mean that currencies would fluctuate in value as supply and demand changed. Yet, under the regime, governments promised to intervene in these markets so that the outcome was always the same. This could be done with little effort if exchange markets were small; what the regime's designers failed to anticipate was the massive growth of international investments and capital flows. Nowadays, speculative capital flows are worth much more than the money that crosses borders to finance trade.

John G. Ruggie notes that when the liberal perspective in general is put into practice, it tries very hard to "disembed" the economic system. In their models, liberals treat the economic system as something separate from other aspects of society. They remove other factors so that they can study the market as an abstraction. When liberals give policy prescriptions, they argue that the market should be separated from other forces.[7] That can never be done in its entirety; more often, the policy as proposed founders on social forces which were unaccounted for.

Karl Polanyi has shown how the 1930s were a period when the market broke down in most industrialized countries. Certainly, there was widespread agreement that the international market and the international financial system failed to function properly. As Polanyi stresses, in most countries the politics of the 1930s are characterized by the efforts of social forces to control the market once again.[8] Nowhere was this clearer than in the domestic struggles over monetary policy in the 1930s. The discussion in Chapter 16 on Britain's resumption of the gold standard illustrates one example of this conflict, but the struggle was played out along similar lines elsewhere.

In the Bretton Woods regime, the liberal practices at the international level had to be reconciled in some manner with interventionist policies within the domestic economy. Institutions to facilitate coordination were required, giving credence to some aspects of the institutionalist perspective; because the particular way of balancing these domestic and international practices was largely consistent with White's views, realists argue that the liberals confuse their description of the regime with an explanation. The regime may have been based on liberal principles, but that may have been because liberal practices were in the interest of the strongest state which participated in the regime.

A Realist Explanation: A Regime to Protect American Interests

From the realist perspective, what is important is the way in which the rules of the Bretton Woods regime reflected U.S. interests. U.S. views dominated the decision-making at the Bretton Woods conference. Thus, for realists, the regime is the product of the distribution of power. The U.S. emerged from World War II with the most powerful economy and the greatest financial resources, as well as the most military power among the Western democracies. The U.S. exercised these resources in such a way that the monetary regime created after the war operated to its own benefit.

Evidence supporting the realist perspective comes in several forms. In the new institutions created, the U.S. wielded extensive power. Among all the post-World War II international organizations, these were the only ones to have such proportional voting, except, of course for the U.N.'s Security Council, where voting was not proportional but where the U.S. exercises a veto. The U.S. ensured, even in the face of Britain's opposition, that it would have a dominant role to play within these institutions.

Moreover, the ways in which the IMF supported the fixed exchange rates reflected U.S. interests. As the only country running a balance of payments surplus, and the only one likely to run a surplus in the near future, U.S. negotiators wanted to ensure that surplus countries would not be punished. The set of rules proposed by Keynes, for instance, would have the surplus countries bearing some of the brunt of adjustment, since surplus countries would be taxed. Deficit countries would draw on these taxes to finance their adjustments. Instead, the U.S.-backed rules placed the entire burden of adjustment on deficit countries.

The U.S. dollar became the true international currency, though that would have happened by default. The U.S. had to take several steps in the 1950s to boost international liquidity. Payments for goods at U.S. military bases, tax laws, and other policies were used to stimulate a flow of dollars out of the U.S. and into the international political economy. This wasn't in the original plans for the Bretton Woods regime, which expected that gold would be the primary reserve asset for participating countries. This did not come to pass, and the U.S. stepped up to provide its own currency as a reserve. The U.S. stabilized the regime, but also benefited from placing its currency in this role. Realists certainly argue that the ways in which the regime evolved in practice those first few years showed how U.S. leadership mattered, both for the regime's functioning and for garnering benefits for the U.S. The U.S. had to take direct, unilateral action in order to help countries with their balance of payments adjustments.

The Constructivists' Criticisms

Constructivists are critical of realist arguments. On the surface, the realists have a powerful interpretation, especially if we were to examine how the regime operated over time. But if we stay focused on the rules of the Bretton Woods monetary regime as originally designed, the constructivists point out that the realists fail to explain its overarching thrust. As Ruggie put it, the regime's "social purpose" cannot be deduced from the distribution of power alone. It can only be understood by looking at previous monetary regimes and the problems of the interwar period.[9]

Ruggie argues that the Bretton Woods monetary regime represents a compromise between the goal of having a monetary regime based on liberal economic principles (i.e., one that supports the free flow of goods, services, and capital internationally) and domestic policy autonomy. While this served U.S. interests, those interests were largely domestic aims, not international goals. According to Ruggie, the rules of the regime hardly represent those the U.S. could have installed if it was truly interested in the pursuit of international power. The realist approach is therefore useful, but limited, in Ruggie's point of view.[10] In short, the distribution of power tells us about which countries to focus on, but we cannot deduce those countries' interests merely from their position in the international structure.[11]

Also important in the constructivists' view is the way in which the realist argument is supposed to work—it assumes that a hegemonic state will rationally create the system which maximizes its power. That implies that the hegemonic state can choose any set of rules it desires—it will construct the regime with the set of rules which benefits itself relatively the most. That is impossible, argue the constructivists. The rules always are embedded in some broader social setting, which cannot be evaded. In this particular instance, the choices were constrained by the experiences of the 1920s and 1930s. The regime's rules, constructivists argue, were designed to deal with the problems of the past, not with maximizing U.S. power.

One of Ruggie's important contributions, using this constructivist framework, is to point out that power and social purpose do not always change simultaneously, nor do they have to push change in the same direction. In terms of theory, the results expected from a realist type of analysis may clash with the results from an analysis based on an examination of social purposes. For political scientists, it may not always be clear which of these forces takes precedence, nor is it always clear how the clash of these forces is reconciled.

Another Rival View: Rationalist Institutionalism

Rationalist institutionalists also challenge the realists' interpretation of the creation of Bretton Woods. For them, the most important point is the role of all the participating countries; that is, the regime was not simply the product of U.S. designs. Representatives from 44 other states took part in the Bretton Woods Conference, and ultimately the principles and rules adopted were a compromise between the main creditor country, the U.S., and the numerous debtors represented by Britain, which was still a financial power, but thanks to World War II was in debt to the U.S.

Rationalist institutionalists argue that, if power was the key determinant to who participated in the negotiations, the U.S. should have had its way completely. Why did Keynes even produce an alternative plan? Why was this alternative plan debated? Britain did play a role in these negotiations, and this becomes clear when we look at the trade regime created at the same time. Parallel to the Bretton Woods monetary regime with its international institutions, the World War II allies wanted to construct a trade regime based on liberal principles and led by a multilateral institution. The planned institution to govern trade, the International Trade Organization (ITO), was never actually established, however, due to difficulties in the negotiations. In these talks, held in Havana in 1948, the Soviet Union and Third World countries successfully included their own perspectives on nationalization of property in the final treaty. The U.S. wanted to protect creditors' interests to ensure that investors were compensated if nationalizations took place. The U.S. was outvoted and therefore refused to ratify the final treaty.

Without the ITO and its supporting treaty in place, the U.S. had to fall back onto another agreement. Prior to the Havana Conference, it had agreed with Britain to present a unified position in the talks. The two countries signed a compromise, the General Agreement on Tariffs and Trade (GATT). On the one hand, the U.S. wanted Britain to dismantle the Imperial Preference System, arguing that any new trade regime should be based on non-discrimination—tariffs on goods should be based on the nature of the good, not on the country of origin. Britain countered with the argument that the new regime should aim to liberalize trade; in other words, Britain wanted the Smoot-Hawley Tariff lowered. The GATT represented a compromise, since both nondiscrimination and liberalization became part of its basic goals.

Rationalist institutionalists point out two things about these negotiations. First, the U.S. could not completely force its own perspective on all other states. As powerful as it may have been at the time, it could not create the trade regime it originally intended but had to fall back on the GATT, which itself represented a compromise. Why would a hegemonic state have such failures? Why the need to compromise? Secondly, rationalist institutionalists argue that one of the chief lessons from the 1930s was the need to improve coordination and cooperation between states. No state could operate its economy in isolation; each country's policies had ramifications for others. If countries wanted to practise liberalism internationally, they would also need to coordinate their interventionism, or at least restrain themselves from the temptation to use "beggar thy neighbour" policies. Institutions facilitate that sort of cooperation or coordination. In short, the rationalist institutionalists argue that hegemonic leadership is not enough.

Consequences: An International Monetary Regime Based on "Embedded Liberalism"

The rules set down in 1944 were not supposed to be implemented until five years after the war ended, but in fact they did not officially come into operation until 1961. By then the monetary and economic situation had changed. Gold had already been displaced by the dollar as the primary reserve asset in the system. U.S. policies largely managed international liquidity, though this led to problems that grew to be major challenges in the late 1960s; by the early 1970s the rules set down with so much foresight in 1944 collapsed. Yet, the institutions created, the IMF and the World Bank, continue to operate to this day.

The U.S. maintains a strong say in the IMF. The quota it pays into the IMF, and therefore its voting power, was 19 per cent in 1991.[12] As long as the U.S. can vote with other Western financial powers, it can still have its interests largely protected. The IMF's original mandate, however, to assist in balance of payments adjustment under a fixed exchange rate regime, no longer holds. While it and the World Bank remain important and powerful legacies from the Bretton Woods regime, the time may have come for serious reforms.

Ruggie concluded his analysis of the establishment of Bretton Woods with the recognition that the balance struck in these regimes, what he labelled "embedded liberalism," has largely endured. Not only have the Bretton Woods institutions themselves lasted, but more importantly the reconciliation attempted between relatively free trade at the international level and domestic intervention in selected areas has also persisted.[13] The compromises have provided a stable foundation for a tremendous boom in international trade and international investment. While the specific aspects of the regime came unglued in the 1970s, as will be discussed in Chapter 20, the regime set down the broader practices of "embedded liberalism" with which we still live.

Notes

1. Perhaps the most important was the Atlantic Charter, signed in August 1941 by Roosevelt and Churchill. A reprint of the Atlantic Charter can be found in A.F.W. Plumptre, *Three Decades of Decision: Canada and the World Monetary System, 1944-75* (Toronto, ON: McClelland and Stewart, 1977) 32.

2. Plumptre, who participated as a representative of Canada in these talks, gives a great description of the role these other states could play. As he put it, Canadians' "major contributions to postwar economic plans probably lay in helping to find acceptable compromises between British and American positions which, in some respects were wide apart." See Plumptre 28-29.

3. This chapter will spend little time on the World Bank; for more information, see Robert Oliver, "Early Plans for a World Bank," *Princeton Studies in International Finance* 29 (1971).

4. As quoted in Joan E. Spero, *The Politics of International Economic Relations*, 4th ed. (New York, NY: St. Martin's Press, 1990) 22.

5. In Plumptre's assessment, "the new international institutions, largely fashioned in Washington, were designed to serve the international interests of the U.S." though he also notes how they were largely consistent with Canadian interests as well. See Plumptre 31.

6. J.G. Ruggie, "International Regimes, Transactions, and Change: Embedded Liberalism in the Postwar Economic Order," *International Organization* 36,2 (Spring 1982): 195-231.

7. Karl Polanyi, *The Great Transformation* (Boston, MA: Beacon Press, 1957).

8. Polanyi.

9. Ruggie.

10. Ruggie 197.

11. For more on this point, see Mark R. Brawley, "Political Leadership and Liberal Economic Subsystems: The Constraints of Structural Assumptions," *Canadian Journal of Political Science* 28,1 (March 1995): 85-103.

12. See Melissa H. Bird, "The IMF," *Dealing with Debt*, ed. Thomas J. Biersteker (Boulder, CO: Westview Press, 1993) 20. For more on the ways quotas have changed, and their impact, see Jacob S. Dreyer and Andrew Schotter, "Power Relationships in the IMF: The Consequences of Quota Changes," *Review of Economics and Statistics* 62,1 (February 1980): 97-106.

13. Ruggie.

Additional References

Dobson, Alan P. "Economic Diplomacy at the Atlantic Conference." *Review of International Studies* 10,2 (April 1984): 143-63.

Helleiner, Eric. "Chapter 2: Bretton Woods and the Endorsement of Capital Controls." *States and the Reemergence of Global Finance*. Ithaca, NY: Cornell University Press, 1994.

Ikenberry, John. "Creating Yesterday's New World Order: Keynesian 'New Thinking' and the Anglo-American Postwar Settlement." *Ideas and Foreign Policy: Beliefs, Institutions and Political Change*. Ed. Judith Goldstein and Robert O. Keohane. Ithaca, NY: Cornell University Press, 1993. 57-86.

Polanyi, Karl. *The Great Transformation*. Boston, MA: Beacon Press, 1957.

CHAPTER 19
South Korea Opts for Export-Oriented Industrialization

Little happened in the post-World War II trade regime during the 1950s. The institutional framework for reciprocal trade liberalization was in place, but countries remained reluctant to offer real concessions. The Kennedy Round negotiations, conducted between 1962-67, introduced new bargaining techniques. It marked the real beginning of a wave of tariff reductions by GATT members. The lower tariffs, plus the resulting expansion of trade, created the systemic environment in which countries had enormous opportunities to exploit trade.

It was in this setting that several economically less developed countries began to use trade as part of their economic strategy. The best known of these are South Korea, Taiwan, Hong Kong, and Singapore. This chapter focuses on the decision to pursue a development program based on trade made by South Korea in the early 1960s. South Korea's strategy is often touted as an economic success story. In evaluating economic development, most people refer to industrialization: the share of manufacturing in South Korea's gross domestic product (GDP) went from 14 per cent in 1960 to 30 per cent in 1983, and then still higher.[1]

Exports played an important role in the story. Between 1949 and 1960, South Korea's export earnings grew 3.9 per cent, about the same rate of growth as its GDP. While respectable, these figures are not very different from other industrializing countries, such as those in Latin America. But then, between 1963, after the decision was made to concentrate on exports and to let exporting sectors lead the country's growth, and 1990, South Korea's merchandise exports grew by an average of 23 per cent per year.[2] In terms of per capita gross national product (GNP), South Korea ranked eighty-fifth in 1962, but had risen to forty-fourth by 1986.[3] The final mark of successful industrial development came when South Korea was invited to join the Organization for Economic Cooperation and Development (OECD), which is generally considered the economically advanced countries' club.

South Korea's Initial Trade and Industrialization Strategy: Import-Substitution Industrialization (ISI)

In the immediate post-World War II years, South Korea pursued the trade and development program popular with most other economically developing countries: it blocked the import of industrial goods, so that domestic demand would stimulate domestic production. This strategy is referred to as import-substitution industrialization or ISI. In fact, South Korea is said to have pursued ISI in the years between 1950 and 1963 "with zeal."[4]

The typical liberal criticisms of ISI have been well documented.[5] By blocking foreign competition, ISI ensures that domestic manufacturers garner a profit, but this automatically means consumers are hurt by the lack of competition. ISI is a way of forcing a transfer of income from consumers to the industrial sector, which works through distorting prices in the market by eliminating cheaper priced competition. These price shifts can create distortions in the ability of other sectors to utilize inputs—distortions introduce greater inefficiencies throughout the economy. Take the example of local steel production, which was supported through ISI; any other producers using steel as an input had to pay more for it, and this made the price of their goods less competitive.

Along the same lines, though, there is no guarantee that greater profits accruing to the firm will be reinvested in the same industry. They might not be; instead, profits could be spent on many other things, including investment in unrelated sectors and conspicuous consumption (buying mansions and Rolls Royce limousines), or they might even be taken out of the country and invested somewhere else. The industry might get comfortable behind the protective tariffs and manage its captive market without improving productivity or levels of production but still receive a steady profit.

Sometimes ISI meant blocking imports that could not be fully replaced by domestic production in the short run. Say the import of steel was blocked to support higher prices for domestic steel producers. These steel producers would make more money, but also it would take some time for that profit to be reinvested into new steel plants. In the meantime, steel demand might not be met. Other producers who used steel as an input might have to slow down their production. So ISI could lead to bottlenecks.

In other areas, technology may be a barrier. ISI may not work very well if the country lacks the technical know-how or high-tech production facilities necessary for efficient production. For instance, many countries would like to make computers, but producing high quality chips and assembling the components in dust-free labs, etc., is expensive and difficult. Even the Soviet Union had tremendous problems in this area. While Third World countries might possibly achieve production in certain high-tech areas, they may be expending a tremendous amount of resources, which could be more effectively applied elsewhere.

In most cases, ISI was supposed to be a temporary policy, to be dropped after the local industry got on its feet. Unfortunately, that has rarely happened, because the local industry has no incentive to increase its competitiveness. This lack of competitiveness and distortions created in the domestic economy often lead to a slowdown in the pace of industrialization over time, even where ISI worked well in sparking or kicking off industrialization. It proved difficult to sustain industrial growth through ISI. The reasons for this should be fairly easy to understand. The domestic market in many economically developing countries is not very big (though there are some significant exceptions such as India, Brazil, and perhaps Argentina and a few others), nor do consumers have much purchasing power. The larger the market, the more likely ISI will last longer and perform better. Small countries may not have the domestic base of demand to support industrial factories because of economies of scale. In this instance, economies of scale refer to the optimal size of an efficient industrial plant. An efficient factory must maintain a high level of output per year to turn a profit. If a country bases its development strategy on ISI, but the level of domestic demand does not meet the production level of a modern efficient plant, it makes little sense to build the plant and then utilize it at less than full capacity.

All of these are the general liberal criticisms about protectionism addressed to the specifics of an ISI program. We can add to these the argument about social losses associated with rent-seeking. In other words, individuals and groups will expend resources in the pursuit of the right to participate in the ISI-protected sectors. Society as a whole loses, because the individuals seeking the special privileges accruing to the protected firms are burning up the country's resources without adding to the country's ability to produce anything extra. This kind of consumption of resources can become quite high in some settings and represent a serious drain on the economy.[6]

Problems did not arise with rent-seeking in South Korea at this time because of external political pressures on the country. The government couldn't plunder the capital which came its way because the country's political survival was at stake. The South was locked in a political and economic competition with the North. It had to develop stronger political loyalties among its citizens, and that meant improving the economy.[7] The government in South Korea certainly handed out privileges, and the entrepreneurs who benefited from ISI gave politicians kick-backs, yet the government was more self-restrained than it otherwise might have been.

Many of the problems associated with ISI identified by liberals and listed above did occur during South Korea's drive to industrialize in the 1950s.

Production of critical basic materials lagged behind schedule, and the production of many sectors remained well below standard. This had both economic and political consequences. On the one hand, the private business sector was not very well developed. Moreover, this community was not very powerful *vis-à-vis* the state. The business community could hardly argue that the state needed its support to survive—if anything, it was more the other way around. Economically, objective assessments recognized the need to modify policies. At the same time, in many ways the ISI period laid the economic foundation for South Korea's later success.[8] The country built up much of its basic industries, (though they were not internationally competitive yet), and identified some of its most pressing needs.

Export-Oriented Industrialization

The reverse of ISI is export-oriented industrialization (EOI). Instead of seeing international trade as a threat, EOI embraces it. With EOI, a country builds industrial plants for efficiency, then produces for international demand. It does not require large size; indeed, for small countries it may be the only way to support industrial development without introducing too many distortions into the domestic economy.[9] EOI promises to avoid many of the problems associated with ISI. Also, a developing country need not have a high level of per capita income, since production is supported by consumption in the rich markets of the economically advanced states.

Being tied into the international market entails certain risks, however. Countries utilizing EOI are basing their future on forces beyond their control. If the world economy grows, then EOI is more likely to work well; if it does not, and the economically less developed country has already invested in production, there is little it can do to stimulate international demand. Presumably domestic demand was weak to begin with, which is why international markets had to be sought out, so compensating for a fall in international demand can be difficult. This means the timing of introducing production for export trade (EOI) is critical.

EOI may be risky too in that it means entering a very competitive market system. If all states try to pursue the same markets at the same time, the chance of any of them being successful is lessened. In the steel sector, competition has been very high indeed. Since all countries wish to produce basic industrial products such as steel, many have entered this sector using an EOI strategy; but, as many countries try to produce steel for the European and U.S. markets, they saturate demand: prices fall and so do profits. So picking the right sectors to enter into, as well as doing so at the right time, is important for the success of EOI.

This is where strategic trade policy comes into play. Paul Krugman defines strategic trade policy as "government policy which can tilt the terms of oligopolistic competition to shift excess returns from foreign to domestic firms."[10] The state wishes to develop certain sectors that do not yet have the ability to compete. In essence, the state wishes to create a comparative advantage. That means government support for getting the necessary inputs, technical knowledge, or human capital (in terms of skill and experience). But, as Krugman also notes, strategic trade policy is far from perfect; there are problems with ISI, but a different range of dangers with EOI. What if international markets are suddenly cut off? After all, U.S. and European producers don't appreciate foreign competition, so they have responded to increased imports by asking for protection. The whole strategy of EOI assumes relatively free trade in the international economy. This is why many of the developing countries who relied on EOI led the battle to transform GATT into the World Trade Organization (WTO). These countries continue to emphasize the importance of clear rules enforcing trade liberalization in their foreign economic policies.

Also, ISI works with very little capital in place to begin with. As mentioned above, it is a way to transfer income from other sectors to industry in lieu of savings. ISI, then, is a way to raise capital. EOI is not a way to raise capital domestically, but can instead be a way to pay off foreign investments that have already been undertaken. But the capital has to be raised somewhere, either through forced savings domestically or borrowed internationally.

There is a potential problem for both strategies. Each may have difficulty in achieving diversification. ISI can lead to distortions and may direct resources out of the protected industries and into other sectors. This sort of thing can happen also with EOI, since it may increase wealth or capital savings in one sector, but not translate into wider changes. Broader economic transformations are perhaps more likely to occur with EOI, though, since it can improve industrial efficiency and build up certain sectors' competitiveness in such a way as to stimulate other local producers without introducing distortions into the domestic market. EOI is also a way of producing a surplus for investment in the longer run. Since a gain can be produced in trade, there may be more funds around after several years of EOI, while ISI is based on redistributing domestic wealth.

All of these factors came into play in South Korea's eventual economic success. It is an important point to remember that the decision to adopt an export orientation did not guarantee that success—EOI does not always work so well. For South Korea, the timing was right. The world's economy was booming in the 1960s, and the East Asian region in particular was growing. Strong economic expansion in Japan, plus heightened expenditures by the U.S. as that country prosecuted the war in Vietnam helped to stimulate growth. South

Korea's strategic importance to the U.S. also guaranteed that access to the U.S. market was always available. U.S. funds, both public and private, were available to finance EOI. As one of the first countries to use EOI, South Korea also entered several markets when international competition was fairly low. (Many of these same factors did not apply to countries attempting EOI in the 1990s.)[11] Another important point is that the EOI strategy that South Korea adopted was not a blanket liberalization. Some sectors were left protected; EOI was pursued only in certain areas, while ISI was left in others. The decisions made were tailored to the specifics of South Korea's situation. ISI and EOI policies were integrated so that they reinforced each other.

The remainder of this chapter looks at South Korea's decision to adopt EOI. It does not address the reasons such a policy proved successful. Instead, it examines several explanations offered for why South Korea chose to adopt a new development program employing EOI at a time when most other states were still pursuing ISI. To begin with, we shall take a closer look at just what the decision itself entailed.

The Shift to EOI

In practice, the shift to EOI introduced a new set of economic policies. In 1963-64, South Korea took a number of important steps, as well as several less obvious moves in support of the overall strategy.[12] First, exchange rate policy was changed. Until this time, South Korea had maintained a set of different exchange rates for different international economic transactions This practice was eliminated, and all the different exchange rates were unified into a single rate.

Second, the currency was devalued. This is close to what several liberal economists have referred to as "getting the exchange rate right." The currency was set at a value considered more realistic. (For judging how realistic an official exchange rate is, one can compare the official rate to that found on the black market.) By lowering the value of the currency, South Korean exports appeared cheaper to foreign consumers. Previously, a high exchange rate supported the protectionism inherent in ISI.

Third, the government enacted a set of domestic investment policies intended to aid the expansion of exports. It made a concerted effort to invest in education and infrastructure developments. Interest rates were raised, partially in hopes of increasing domestic savings, which had been very low prior to 1963, and partially in hopes of drawing in foreign investment. When this was combined with the government's ability to offer cheaper credits to exports, thanks to its control over the financial sector, the policies created a split financial market. For most Koreans, interest rates were high, and therefore they chose to consume less and save more; for exporters, interest rates were low, and therefore they expanded their operations. Overall, the country imported less and exported more.

Fourth, trade relations were liberalized—though not completely. Tariffs were reduced on certain items to make it easier to import inputs that exporters could not otherwise attain. This was especially important for the importation of capital goods necessary for manufacturing exports (i.e., machinery) and other critical inputs. In this way the exporters found it cheaper to produce goods than before; under ISI, they had had to pay higher prices for goods which were most often of inferior quality.

Fifth, a number of incentives were structured to entice businesses to engage in exporting. At one level this was by the most obvious route: some exports were subsidized. A special fund was created to help small firms enter the international market. But the state employed a wide range of techniques, including fostering the creation of exporter associations, so that different firms could share information and experiences; discounting energy prices for exporters; and modifying tax policies in many different ways, such as giving exporters breaks on their income tax. Credit necessary for foreign trade was especially subsidized by the government.

As an example, consider the treatment afforded South Korea's first auto assembly plant, which was set up in 1962. It received a variety of tax benefits. The government allowed components to be imported duty free and then placed stringent import controls on finished vehicles.[13] This allowed the firm to follow a pricing strategy similar to that used by Japanese firms: the home market became a reserved area, allowing the firm to charge high prices, offsetting any losses or small profit margins on products exported. This represents a mix of EOI and ISI.

Overall, these policies marked the swing to EOI, which in turn is related to South Korea's sustained industrialization. Economists such as Jagdish Bhagwati and Anne Krueger have argued that South Korea's economic success came from its willingness to stop discriminating against exports and instead promoting them.[14] Jung-en Woo credits the "back-and-forth dialectic between international and domestic realms" for the economic surge that followed.[15] What drove the government to undertake this set of policy changes?

The Regional and System-Level Forces Conducive to EOI

As mentioned above, one of the system-level factors that may have shaped the Korean decision was the expansion of opportunities to export. The regional economy was especially healthy. Japanese economists use the analogy of snow geese to illustrate the manner in which they believe regional factors helped pull South Korea into EOI. Geese fly long distances in a vee-formation; the first goose breaks air resistance, so that those at each trailing wing tip need less force to slice through the air. Economically, much the same can take place: Japanese firms pioneered electronics markets; as they moved their product lines into more differentiated, high-end goods, South Korean (and Taiwanese) firms started to export the basic models.[16]

This is somewhat against the understanding of North American political scientists. In fact, the decision to pursue ISI in the 1950s can be viewed in the opposite sense: South Korean policy-makers wanted to pursue ISI to get out from under the shadow of Japan's industrialization.[17] Korean leaders were afraid that they would remain stuck in the position of exporting raw materials to Japan and, in return, purchasing Japanese manufactured goods. This point does not shed much light on the choice between EOI and ISI, however.

Neither policy was all that risky, thanks to system-level factors. Korean leaders in the 1950s had the opportunity to pursue ISI with little or no risks because of their relationship with another major power: the U.S. South Korea was important for U.S. strategic interests in the Cold War. The massive inflows of U.S. aid (as a recipient, South Korea ranked only behind South Vietnam and Israel during the Cold War)[18] allowed the South Korean state to play a mediating role between international capital and the domestic economy. The funds were used to support both industrialization strategies.

It is worth noting that U.S. advisors were not in favour of ISI at the time. They were interested in seeing Japan develop economically and were ready to see South Korean interests and aspirations suppressed for the time being in order to achieve this broader goal. The South Koreans, however, ignored the advice.[19] Instead, they pursued the whole range of policies in the typical ISI package. They adopted numerous barriers to block international competition—namely, licencing and tariffs—but also put in place a multiple exchange rate system and a host of other devices designed to shield parts of the domestic economy.

Cutbacks in U.S. aid began in 1959, but the most severe cuts came in the early 1960s. Along with reduced aid during the Kennedy administration came new advice: push for greater democratization, economic growth (around expansion of light industries), and reduce military expenditures. The U.S. advice looked like a textbook application of Rostow's take-off model, one form of modernization theory.[20] While this at first glance may appear to be what happened, we need to look into the domestic politics of the situation to see what did, in fact, occur.

System-level factors provide insight into some of the constraints and opportunities South Korea faced, but they do not tell us about which way policy would move. Indeed, other countries in similar positions in the international political economy continued to pursue ISI. System-level factors may have been important for the success of EOI, as discussed above, but domestic forces seem more important in South Korea's decision to adopt new policies. In May 1961 there was a *coup d'état*, and a military government took over. While democratic institutions were restored in 1963, the military became firmly entrenched in society and government. Institutional arrangements were also altered in fundamental ways, thus changing how the government could interact with the economy.

Domestic-Level Theories: Strong State/Weak Society?

South Korea's adoption of EOI can best be explained perhaps by referring to the changes in the relationship between the South Korean state and other societal actors. The state became more powerful, as well as somewhat freer to resist the demands from other actors because of changing institutional arrangements and political economic practices, which allowed the state to intervene in the economy in more effective and selective ways.

The new institutional arrangements made in 1961 after the *coup d'état* play an important role in the 1963-64 policy reforms. A new, key economic planning institution was created, the Economic Planning Board (EPB). It was given authority over the setting of tariffs, administering direct subsidies to industries, and setting economic targets. It could carry out these functions without referring to the legislative branch. The EPB also had power over the government's budget.[21] In roughly the same period, KOTRA (the state's official trade promotion agency) and the Korean Development Institute were created. Many have argued that the EPB's actions worked hand-in-hand with market forces. The EPB and other government institutions were able to eliminate some of the risk and uncertainty of the market by generating and disseminating critical information. They were also able to convince businesses to invest, thus bringing about an expansionist environment—a sort of self-fulfilling prophecy.[22]

The state also stepped in and took over the banking sector at this time. According to Jung-en Woo, at the core of the state's strength *vis-à-vis* other actors is its ability to channel money into the economy. She characterizes the South Korean state as a prism, refracting international capital flows into different segments and sectors of the economy. In order to understand the strength of the South Korean state, one must therefore understand the working of the country's financial system.[23] Prior to 1961, the state had had funds at its disposal, thanks to U.S. aid. After 1961, U.S. aid declined, but the government began borrowing from private sources to make up the difference.

The state used the money in a variety of ways. Robert Wade is interested in the character of the state's intervention[24] and goes so far as to argue that the public/private distinction is often blurred in South Korea, thanks to government participation in ownership. The state also employed so-called "policy loans." These were special loans targeted for specific sectors of the economy the state decided to favour. The loans were at very favourable rates, and banks were forced to issue them—the banks were given no say in the application of the loans in either the rates or the level of participation.[25]

A false contrast is suggested in this approach, however. The emphasis tends to be on the characteristics of the state, but that is only one side of the equation. After all, the limited success of ISI meant that the business class was largely in favour of the shift to EOI. There were few powerful opponents to its use; in countries where ISI delivered more industrialization, it also created powerful, well-entrenched interests, which opposed state implementation of a similar policy shift. As it was, large firms were favoured by government policies encouraging exports, because large firms were in the best position to exploit the opportunities the policies created. The largest firms were able to gather and handle the information necessary for engaging in international trade. They were more capable of ensuring the consistent quality of their product, a very necessary ability for successful competition internationally. They also often had previous experience in international trade and therefore had connections and business relationships that could be built upon. Moreover, they had the collateral necessary for raising foreign loans.[26]

When looking at the state's relationship with business, the state's role in finance remains pivotal. South Korean firms became very reliant on funds from government sources or government-controlled sources. The typical debt-equity ratio for South Korean firms in the 1970s was between 300 and 400 per cent. (Just to compare, the average Brazilian or Mexican firms in the 1970s probably had a debt-equity ratio of 100 to 120 per cent.)[27] Thus, the firms were very sensitive to small changes in the interest rate. This gave the state additional leverage over them, since it was the state rather than the financial community who determined what interest rates would be.

Moreover, the state was relatively free from outside interference by other domestic forces. Not only was the business elite relatively weak compared to the state, but so was the agricultural elite. In many economically developing countries, traditional authority tends to rest with an elite based in the rural areas. Often the traditional elite has economic interests tied to the agricultural sector, which it seeks to protect. In South Korea, however, these landed interests had been broken years before. Land owned formerly by the Japanese had been redistributed by the U.S. Military Government before 1950; after the Korean War, the South Korean government itself engaged in reforms that reduced the power of the landed elite and helped equalize wealth within the country.[28]

Some people argue that another basis for the state's power *vis-à-vis* other societal actors comes from South Korea's corporatist political practices, which insulated the state and bureaucracy from particularist interests.[29] This insulation definitely promoted stability in policy. While this may not tell us much about why one policy was selected over another, it does tell us that the bureaucracies were likely to stick with their choices over the long term. Ministries themselves were very centralized, but then so were businesses, thanks to conglomerates, called *chaebol*s, and business associations.[30] South Korea's "hard state" had to deal with a centralized society, and the result was a situation where decisions could be made and implemented swiftly. Bruce Cumings developed a special term to refer to such strong states: "Bureaucratic-Authoritarian Industrializing Regimes" (or BAIRs). He describes them as "penetrating, comprehensive, highly articulated, and relatively autonomous of particular groups and classes."[31]

Bureaucratic Politics: The Power of the Ministry of Technology and the EPB

All this emphasis on the state's capabilities could still be undone by bureaucratic politics. What allowed for the successful turn to EOI? Did all bureaucracies share a common vision? For one thing, the bureaucracies were not equally strong. For instance, South Korea lacked an independent, autonomous central bank.[32] Instead, the central bank was subordinate to the Finance Ministry. One potential source of independent policy, then, was exempt from the picture. Monetary policy could easily be coordinated with other economic plans.

One of the most important ministries in the formulation of economic policy has been the Ministry of Trade and Industry. In some ways, this body was modelled after Japan's Ministry of International Trade and Industry as an agency with the specific duty of coordinating industrial activity, engaging in long-range planning, and developing technology. As part of these duties, the Ministry of Trade and Industry monitored exports and foreign markets.[33] It was the brains behind the development of a strategic trade policy. Because the central bank answered to the Ministry of Finance, and the Ministry of Finance had no clear authority over other ministries, these others could have a greater say in monetary policy. Thus, the Ministry of Trade and Industry wielded more influence than the central bank.[34]

Most important, however, was the Economic Planning Board (EPB). The new military government installed after 1961 had an immediate crisis to face: the reduction in U.S. economic aid. To respond to the impending fiscal crisis, the head of the government, Park Chung Hee, concentrated decision-making in a single agency. The EPB was formed by taking the old Ministry of Reconstruction and adding in agencies removed from two other ministries. The Bureau of the Budget was transferred from the Ministry of Finance, and the Bureau of Statistics was transferred from the Ministry of Home Affairs. The EPB took over the budgeting function and economic planning previously undertaken by other branches of the government.[35]

In short, policy-making powers were centralized in the EPB and the Ministry of Trade and Industry. Bureaucratic politics were circumvented by the concentration of power within these two agencies. The EPB produced the country's first development plan. While this first five-year plan (from 1962-66) wasn't based on an overt plan to use exports as the engine for economic growth, it was intended to improve South Korea's balance of payments. The policy changes undertaken to stimulate exports in 1963-64 became the basis of a more conscious attempt to use exports to stimulate economic development.

Individuals and Ideas?: The Role of Military Officers

While there were changes in the arrangement of political institutions, as well as between institutions and other elements of society, it is impossible to separate them from simultaneous changes in personnel at the top of the government. In May 1961, a military coup put Park Chung Hee in power. While Park's government carried through the institutional reorganization, it also placed new people in the top posts and drew on foreign experts to formulate policy.

The economic package that was instituted came mostly from the military government's U.S. advisers.[36] Similar advice also came from the IMF and other international organizations. Whether this advice was new or not, the relationship between the members of the military government and the U.S. advisers was presumably closer than had been the relationship between the civilian government and other U.S. counsellors.

It should also be remembered that the coup allowed the military not only to penetrate government bureaucracies but also the rest of society. Military officers were placed in key offices in the government, but, more importantly, they were also put in positions of authority within private firms.[37] This provided the organization and insulation necessary for the state to be stronger than other actors (as mentioned above), but the individuals entrusted to make decisions also could rely on their personal linkages and shared experiences.

Whatever its source, the evidence over the decades since 1963 makes it apparent that the South Korean elite has shared an ideological commitment to unity. Despite turnover in the individuals at the top, the elite has maintained its focus on its primary goals and has, therefore, given economic development priority while seeing it as the means to achieve enhanced defence, internal unity, ideological competition versus the North, and so on.

Consequences: South Korea's Trade-led Economic Success

South Korea's decisions translated into economic success. This has to be understood in terms of questions and answers other than this chapter has considered. For instance, system-level factors were critical for South Korea's ability to use EOI successfully. The U.S. market was largely open to Korean exporters, and the growth of the Japanese economy in the 1960s and 1970s also fuelled demand for Korean exports. Though U.S. aid was being slashed, the Vietnam War, which raged through the latter half of the 1960s and the early part of the 1970s, meant that regional demand for goods were being pushed up by U.S. military purchases. These included important new markets for South Korean exports, especially steel, chemical, and machinery goods, as well as construction and engineering contracts.[38] Without those external stimuli, the EOI strategy might not have succeeded.

In 1960, more than three-quarters of the population was still engaged in agricultural production. This changed rapidly as the manufacturing export sectors expanded. But with so many people in the agricultural sector creating very little surplus, there was little domestic saving and slow growth in domestic demand. Foreign markets were much more attractive.[39] Labour used in the production of exports more than trebled in the 1960s. Between 1960 and 1970, income from exports rose 7.4 times, while income from domestic output rose only 2.4 times. Exports became the engine for South Korea's industrialization. South Korea has its own multinational corporations: *chaebol*s such as Hyundai, Samsung, and Daewoo now rank among the largest firms in the world.[40] Government policies have clearly benefited these firms, thus concentrating economic power in a relatively small number of executive posts. This has been especially true since 1970.[41]

There has also been a downside, namely, that economic power remains in the hands of a select few. Labour has largely been excluded from decision-making, which naturally means that labour has not shared equally in all the benefits generated by industrialization. The greatest challenges for South Korea may still lie ahead. Can the country continue to diversify its production sufficiently that it no longer requires trade to maintain economic growth? Can wages be expanded in such a way that competitiveness is not hurt, but the domestic demand becomes the real engine of growth? Those are the ultimate goals of EOI, and South Korea has yet to reach them.

Notes

1. Robert Wade, *Governing the Market: Economic Theory and the Role of Government in East Asian Industrialization* (Princeton, NJ: Princeton University Press, 1990) 44.

2. Sebastian Edwards, *Crisis and Reform in Latin America: From Despair to Hope* (New York: Oxford University Press (World Bank), 1995) 49.

3. Wade 34.

4. Edwards 49-50.

5. See for instance, Bela Balassa, "The Process of Industrial Development and Alternative Development Strategies," *Princeton Essays in International Finance* 141 (December 1980); Wade 9.

6. This can best be seen in the development of certain African countries in those same years, such as Zaire.

7. Wade 33.

8. This argument is laid out by Wade 84-87; and see Bruce Cumings, "The Origins and Development of the Northeast Asian Political Economy: Industrial Sectors, Product Cycles, and Political Consequences," *The Political Economy of the New Asian Industrialism*, ed. Frederic Deyo (Ithaca, NY: Cornell University Press, 1987) 66-68.

9. In fact, the same sort of logic underpins the economic strategies of small industrialized states, such as Belgium, the Netherlands, etc.; see Peter Katzenstein, *Small States in World Markets* (Ithaca, NY: Cornell University Press, 1985).

10. See Paul R. Krugman, "Is Free Trade Passé?," *International Economics and International Economic Policy: A Reader*, ed. Philip King (New York, NY: McGraw Hill, 1990) 91-107.

11. Robin Broad and John Cavanaugh, "No More NICs," *Foreign Policy* 72 (Fall 1988): 81-103.

12. The following paragraphs build on descriptions from a number of sources. The most important have been: Edwards 49-50; Jung-en Woo, *Race to the Swift: State and Finance in Korean Industrialization* (New York, NY: Columbia University Press, 1991) 102-03; Youngil Lim, *Government Policy and Private Enterprise: Korean Experience in Industrialization*, Korea Research Monograph 6 (Berkeley, CA: Center for Korean Studies, Institute of East Asian Studies, 1981) 18-24, 31.

13. Wade 309.

14. See Jagdish N. Bhagwati and Anne O. Krueger, "Exchange Control, Liberalization and Economic Development," *American Economic Review* 63,2 (May 1973): 419-27.

15. Woo 116.

16. Wade 103.

17. Woo 53-54.

18. Woo 45.

19. Woo 53-60, 63-64.

20. Woo 71-72, 75-80.

21. Lim 2. The author's point in this monograph, however, is that the private sector always played the major role in the country's economic performance; for instance, the country usually exceeded EPB targets in the 1960s, thereby suggesting that planning could be overemphasized.

22. Lim 4.

23. Woo 2, 6-7.
24. Wade 157-158, 177-178, see especially fn. 19.
25. Woo 12.
26. Lim 39.
27. Woo 12.
28. Stephan Haggard, *Pathways from the Periphery* (Ithaca, NY: Cornell University Press, 1990) 51, 55.
29. Wade 298. Also see Stephan Haggard and Tun-jen Cheng, "State and Foreign Capital in the East Asian NICs," *The Political Economy of the New Asian Industrialism*, ed. Frederic Deyo (Ithaca, NY: Cornell University Press, 1987) 111.
30. Wade 322-24, 337-39.
31. Cumings 71.
32. Woo 51-52.
33. For a description of its activities see Lim 15.
34. Wade 323.
35. Cumings 72-73; Haggard and Cheng 111; and Chalmers Johnson, "Political Institutions and Economic Performance: The Government-Business Relationship in Japan, South Korea and Taiwan," *The Political Economy of the New Asian Industrialism*, ed. Frederic Deyo (Ithaca, NY: Cornell University Press, 1987) 154.
36. Cumings 70. Also see Haggard and Cheng 111.
37. Johnson 153-55.
38. Woo 85, 95-97.
39. Lim 81, 84, 86-87.
40. Woo 15.
41. Wade 309.

Additional References

Deyo, Frederic (ed.). *The Political Economy of the New Asian Industrialism*. Ithaca, NY: Cornell University Press, 1987.

Foster-Carter, Aidan. "Korea and Dependency Theory." *Monthly Review* 37,5 (October 1985): 27-34.

Haggard, Stephan. *Pathways from the Periphery*. Ithaca, NY: Cornell University Press, 1990.

Kreuger, Anne O. *Studies in the Modernization of the Republic of Korea, 1945-1975*. Cambridge, MA: Harvard University Press, 1979.

Wade, Robert. *Governing the Market: Economic Theory and the Role of Government in East Asian Industrialization*. Princeton, NJ: Princeton University Press, 1990.

Woo, Jung-en. *Race to the Swift: State and Finance in Korean Industrialization*. New York, NY: Columbia University Press, 1991.

CHAPTER 20

The Collapse of the Bretton Woods Monetary Regime

Bretton Woods in Operation

The goals of the Bretton Woods system, as it was designed under the guidance of officials from the U.S. Treasury, were to achieve an orderly balance of payments adjustment system, provide adequate liquidity for international trade, facilitate private international investment, and stabilize financial markets by limiting speculative flows, while maximizing the effectiveness of domestic monetary and fiscal policies.[1] The monetary system was intended to be subordinate to and supportive of the open international trading system, while governments would be allowed to intervene in the domestic economy.

The dollar assumed the chief functions of an international money under the Bretton Woods rules, even though this was perhaps not the intention. Supported by U.S. economic and political strength, the dollar became the primary medium of international payment, the primary reserve asset (serving along with gold and several other currencies), and the primary currency used by governments to intervene in exchange markets to stabilize the value of their own currency.[2] But since the U.S. dollar remained a national currency, U.S. monetary authorities were given two separate sets of goals: their own domestic goals versus the system's requirements.[3] During the early years of the Bretton Woods regime, these goals were not necessarily in conflict.

The U.S. allowed foreigners to increase their holdings of dollars not only because they wanted them to be able to pay for U.S. exports, but also because they did not necessarily want gold to flow out of the U.S. Since confidence in the dollar was so high, with the British pound being the only possible alternative, and with the U.S. market the largest open market in the world, demand for dollars soared. U.S. firms used dollars to purchase assets abroad. This situation also made it possible for the government to wield dollars as an international policy instrument in a number of fashions. Through these channels, U.S. policy provided enough international liquidity to support not only the resurrection of commerce but also the expansion of international trade and investment to new levels. The accumulation of dollar balances abroad accounted for approximately one half of the increase in world liquidity between 1949-58.[4]

The Emergence of the Dollar Overhang

The dollar shortage of the 1950s required the implementation of a conscious policy to get dollars into the world economy despite the underlying economic conditions driving the U.S. to a certain balance of payments surplus. This was done in three ways. First was foreign aid, the largest single chunk of which was the Marshall Plan, aimed at the reconstruction of postwar Europe. Second was increased military expenditures outside the U.S., which in Europe addressed strategic concerns over Soviet power. The outbreak of the Korean War stimulated U.S. expenditures in Asia further. Third was foreign direct investment—U.S. corporations took dollars abroad and spent them buying up foreign companies, foreign property, and so on. The end result was that the dollar became the principal reserve asset held by others, meaning that the U.S. federal reserve banks could control not only U.S. domestic monetary supply but the international supply as well.

The U.S. controlled exchange rate adjustment as well, but this was done through the auspices of the International Monetary Fund (IMF). Because the U.S. dominated voting within the IMF at this time, it ran things differently than the rules dictated. The convertibility of European currencies was suspended from 1947 to 1958. Non-IMF policies were linked to exchange rate adjustments—for instance, Marshall Plan money was linked to currency devaluations in 1949. The U.S. took several measures such as pushing for these devaluations in order to get other countries to discriminate against U.S. goods so that these other countries might gain more dollars through foreign exchange.

All these unilateral U.S. actions worked, slowly, so that by 1958, convertibility could be reinstituted among the economically advanced countries, and these countries could earn enough dollars through regular channels that the U.S. didn't have to run things by itself any more. The other countries were able to defend their parities on their own. So the IMF as originally designed finally came into force in 1958.

Unfortunately, there were some inherent instabilities built into the system; most importantly, some of the U.S. policies of running a balance of payments deficit continued (the U.S. learned to like them). The Cold War, U.S. military aid, and foreign expenditures continued, and so the dollar shortage of the early 1950s was by the early 1960s rapidly becoming a dollar glut. As the Vietnam War began to heat up, U.S. deficits and foreign expenditures increased even more.

One way of dealing with this monetary situation was to back out of the Cold War—which wasn't very likely. Another was to redress the U.S. balance of payments deficit and turn it into a surplus again. This is of course easier said than done, since it would have required deflating the U.S. economy; moreover, much of the European growth in the 1960s was being driven by U.S. demand, so a slowing down of the U.S. market would have slowed the growth of its largest export market too, meaning the balance would most likely have stayed in a deficit.

The third possibility for fixing the situation was devaluing the dollar—but this was problematic because so many countries held dollars as their primary reserve asset. By devaluing the dollar, all the other currencies' values would be affected automatically. And, as in Britain in the 1920s, there was fear that a devaluation would appear as a sign of weakness and would be bad psychologically for investors. These factors meant that the U.S. didn't do anything for several years, simply continuing to run deficits, thus making the problem worse. It became obvious that there were more dollars in circulation than could ever be converted into gold.

A related problem was the increasing amount of speculation in foreign exchange markets after the return of convertibility in 1958. This was tied to individual country's balance of payments problems. Think of the dollar glut as a market problem; there were more dollars out there than people wanted. People began to expect the dollar to be devalued in the later 1960s, and the IMF system of fixed exchange rates gave speculators a good deal. Remember how the IMF system committed governments to keep their currencies within 1 per cent of their pledged parities? If one expected the dollar to be devalued in the near future, one would ditch dollars and buy something else, say *deutschmarks* (DMs). If the dollar was in fact devalued, then the DMs could be sold for more dollars than what one started with. If nothing happened, and the dollar was not devalued, one sold the DMs for the same amount of dollars with which one began. That's why this type of speculation was known as a "one-way bet," as well as why speculation became such a problem—patient speculators never lost money!

The obvious problem was that, since everybody would have the same fears of a devaluation, everyone would try to sell the same currency. And who would buy? The governments committed to maintaining their parities. So if enough people feared a devaluation, and therefore bailed out of a currency, they could actually so drain government reserves that the government might actually be forced to devalue. This kind of large-scale market pressure first happened to the dollar in 1960; in 1961, when the British pound came under market pressure, the Bank of England's reserves were depleted, and the pound had to be devalued in just this fashion.

The designers of the IMF had not thought about what the situation would eventually become—billions of dollars floating across international lines transmitted electronically wherever the markets are highest. IMF reserves weren't large enough, so the U.S. had to begin several stop-gap measures to deal with the dollar glut and the speculation problem.

The first of these was the gold pool. The central banks agreed to pool their reserves of gold in order to centralize and coordinate interventions in the gold market to defend the dollar's value at \$35/ounce. This was an attempt to end speculation of the dollar being devalued versus gold. The second was the construction of the General Agreements to Borrow (GAB) in 1961 in response to the run on the pound and the realization that the IMF did not have reserves large enough to deal with immediate crises. The ten largest members of the IMF (G10—basically the U.S. and Western Europe) agreed to lend up to \$6 billion overnight whenever the whole group agreed to do so. The G10 also sought to augment IMF reserves. The third response was to establish swap agreements. Central banks agreed to make swaps of currencies (interest-free loans) on a quick basis so that each could intervene in markets without having to dip into their reserves. In other words, if there were a problem in the parity of the dollar versus the DM, because everyone expected the dollar to be devalued, the central bank in the U.S. would need DMs to sell in order to prop up the value of the dollar. The swaps are ways of sharing currencies in order to intervene in markets. The fourth was the establishment of Roosa Bonds, named after the U.S. Assistant Secretary of the Treasury who designed them. These bonds were denominated in foreign currencies which the U.S. government sold for dollars in order to draw some of the dollars back into the U.S.

But these were all just band-aid solutions, and their ultimate result was a failure to solve the problem. Ultimately, these temporary measures could not stem the market forces driving changes. The rules had to be changed, because countries, including the U.S. (despite the advantages it had obtained), were increasingly unhappy with the existing state of affairs. The U.S. wanted to improve its position, just when the other countries decided that it already had too many privileges. Additionally, other countries felt their own monetary policies were being adversely affected by U.S. policy; under the Bretton Woods rules, they were continually having to maintain exchange rate parities by buying up dollars. This forced their own money supplies up, with inflation as a consequence.[5] Negotiations stalled, and the result—at least in the late 1960s and the early 1970s—was for the U.S. to go its own way.

This period of tinkering with the rules—the beginning of the end of Bretton Woods—began in 1968. In that year, the U.S. acted to undercut market speculation between the dollar and gold. It had become clear to everyone that there were many more dollars floating around than there was gold in Fort Knox, and the official ratio of dollars to gold had to be changed. The gold pool deal still didn't provide central banks with the strength to dissuade speculation; if anything, their efforts simply fuelled it. So the U.S. unilaterally declared there would be two markets for gold—one for private citizens and the other for governments. The U.S. government would deal directly with other governments concerning the dollar's ratio to gold, but would no longer defend the ratio in private markets. In a sense, this broke the dollar's connection to gold, though the real break was yet to come.

The split of the gold market into two tiers signalled that the U.S. would no longer solve its balance of payments deficit problems. It had taken the first step towards adjusting the rules to fit the situation, rather than adjusting its policy to fit the rules. Next came the policy of "benign neglect." The U.S. stopped doing its share of intervening in exchange markets to defend the parity of the dollar. If other countries wanted to keep the parities fixed, let them use their own resources. This was an easy way for the U.S. to act unilaterally to force the costs of maintaining fixed exchange rates on the other countries. By the summer of 1971, the other countries could no longer sustain the system.

The Nixon Shocks

In the summer of 1971, the U.S. was experiencing both inflation from the Vietnam War build-up and the beginnings of high unemployment, as well as running a large trade deficit. But because of the practices followed in the previous two decades, there were lots of dollars out there internationally—there were perhaps as much as eight times as many foreign-held dollars as in the gold reserve. So any actions by the U.S. would affect the value of other countries' reserves. The Nixon administration wanted to devalue the dollar, without bearing any of the costs of adjustment. This was the only way to remove the immediate problem of speculation against the dollar. Because it didn't want to look weak (that is, didn't want to admit to a devaluation), the Nixon administration tried to pressure all the other major countries to revalue their currencies. The result would be exactly the same—the ratio would change—but the psychological impact would be smaller. In the words of Nixon's advisers, "devaluations are what small backward countries do, not the United States." The other countries would not agree to this, so in August 1971 the U.S. acted unilaterally in a series of moves known as the "Nixon shocks," which effectively ended the Bretton Woods system.

On August 15, 1971, the U.S. announced two actions that not only caught everyone off guard but fatally wounded Bretton Woods. First, it broke the convertibility of the dollar into gold. No longer could foreign governments expect to change their dollars into gold. Second, the U.S. imposed a 10 per cent surcharge (or tax) on all imports. This was not done to protect U.S. industry from competition but was, instead, punishment of other countries for not revaluing their currencies. It was an attempt to use the U.S. market as a lever in bargaining, because the U.S. made it clear that, if other countries would revalue, the surcharge would be dropped. These actions are important because they were done unilaterally. Other countries were neither warned nor consulted. The decision to undertake these "Nixon shocks" was made by members of the Nixon administration during a weekend at Camp David. They decided then that the U.S. position was unsustainable and foreign cooperation was missing.

The domestic economic situation and the dollar's role as a reserve asset were no longer compatible. By breaking the link between the dollar and gold, the U.S. severed more links between the domestic economy and the balance of payments situation. It could maintain a balance of payments deficit only as long as other countries were willing to accept dollars, which could be returned and exchanged only for U.S. goods and services, not for gold. The U.S. was now free to run a deficit without risking any loss of gold. The dollars in circulation internationally would have to be spent in the U.S. and so would stimulate business, further lessening the threat of inflation. In this way, the balance of payments deficit was no longer a problem for the U.S.

What this means is that the U.S. liked having the powers that belonged to a reserve asset currency, but didn't like the costs associated with that same role. U.S. decision-makers were trying to cut the best possible deal—they wanted to continue running a deficit, but didn't want to have to deal with the speculation that had accompanied those deficits in the Bretton Woods system. The Nixon shocks largely achieved those goals in the short run.

John Odell explored five possible explanations for this U.S. policy: the balance of payments situation, the international military-political situation, the domestic political situation, organization and internal bargaining, and the policy or ideological beliefs of key decision-makers. These five run the gamut of the levels of analysis, making Odell's work an important reference for our consideration.

System-Level Theory: The U.S. as a Declining Hegemonic Power

Two of Odell's five possible explanations work at the system level. One is purely economic: the balance of payments situation. The other is purely political: the consideration of the military and political environment. Let us take each of these in turn.

The balance of payments argument is essentially an argument about markets. That is, under the Bretton Woods arrangements, exchange markets were open for all buyers and sellers to come and purchase or sell their currencies. Governments had promised to "fix" the prices so that they would not be allowed to stray very far from announced parity rates. This meant that prices could not vary, as they should have, when demand and supply varied.

When governments are forced to intervene to fix the market price, they must expend resources. Getting the market price to match the pledged parity works only if the government buys up excess supply or meets excess demand. In the case of the U.S. dollar, there already was excess supply, thanks to the dollar overhang described above. But the overhang also identified the lack of resources in U.S. coffers. By definition, an overhang involves too much currency for reserves. If the holders of the currency doubt that they can get the nominal (or face) value for the currency, they are likely to offload that currency. Moreover, in a fixed exchange rate system, if one currency is grossly overvalued, some other currency or currencies are going to be undervalued. Thus, a wise currency trader would recognize that the dollar was no longer backed by much reserves; if the overhang was corrected, then each dollar would be worth less in terms of gold and, therefore, less in terms of other currencies. Other currencies would be worth the same amount of gold, but worth more dollars. (Remember the example of exchanging DMs for dollars above, page 321.)

The dollar overhang was not an overwhelming problem. Smart intervention by American authorities could move the currency market in one direction or another. But as more people became convinced of the need—or impending inevitability—of a devaluation, it became harder to convince them that minor intervention would work, since it would entail ever greater expenditure of resources by the government. Odell's point here was that, in such a situation, the market will eventually win. As long as authorities were willing to allow an open market in currencies, the market would reflect the underlying laws of supply and demand. No amount of marginal intervention would change that pattern. According to this argument, the U.S. would have to devalue the dollar at some point.

But we should remember what this argument is missing. The overhang had persisted for several years before the Nixon shocks. Why did the U.S. have to react to this problem in 1971 and not before? Several possible solutions existed as well; for instance, the U.S. could have devalued the dollar to an appropriate level (i.e., fixed the new value of the dollar to existing reserves). Yet it sought one solution. The balance of payments situation suggests that the U.S. could not hope to ignore this problem, but it also does not give us much insight into why one policy response was selected over another.

The international military-political setting was key to why some of the theoretically possible solutions were not attempted. In the monetary realm, the U.S. did not have any particular challengers.[6] At the same time, it was acutely aware of the fact that it was stretched in terms of commitments. The Vietnam War was not going well, and the U.S. was beginning to feel the pinch of economic competition from its allies.

The international setting must also be taken into account in the sense that the leading monetary challengers (namely, West Germany and Japan, but also Switzerland) were beholden to the U.S. in security terms. The West Germans were in the best position to challenge the U.S.'s predominant position in monetary affairs. Yet, they proved to be quite cooperative all things considered, largely because they did not want to antagonize their most important ally.

Domestic Level: The Changing U.S. Economy?

Instead of submitting domestic economic performance to the needs of the international monetary regime, the U.S. chose to destroy Bretton Woods with the "Nixon shocks" of August 1971. In her analysis in *Closing the Gold Window*, Joanne Gowa clearly stresses the Nixon administration's emphasis on the domestic economy and the need for autonomy in the domestic realm as the reasoning behind the shocks.[7] Instead of supporting the continuance of the international monetary regime it created, the U.S. destroyed the regime in order to throw off the constraints it placed on its own domestic policy.

The New Economic Policy Nixon announced in conjunction with the decision to take the dollar off gold also froze wages and prices in order to slow inflation, while seeking to stimulate employment by reducing taxes and spending.[8] Nixon presented these policy decisions as an effort to make the international economic competition a "fair game" for the U.S. Trade statistics issued in the summer of 1971 showed that the U.S. would have a yearly trade deficit for the first time in almost 80 years. As Nixon put it, "The time has come for exchange rates to be set straight and for the major nations to compete as equals. There is no longer any need for the United States to compete with one hand tied behind her back."[9]

Included in Gowa's assessment of these decisions is an examination of the sectoral explanation. She argues that the U.S. economy, because of its low reliance on international trade, lacked a powerful constituency that would support Bretton Woods at the expense of the domestic economy's performance. Saving Bretton Woods would require suppressing the U.S. economy to end the balance of payments deficit; as Gowa puts it, "The idea of increasing domestic unemployment in order to preserve the monetary regime commanded no political following either within or outside the executive branch... As a consequence, domestic economic policy was considered virtually sacrosanct, very largely immune from the conduct of U.S. balance-of-payments or international monetary policy."[10]

The primary actors which might be expected to support the hegemon-led international monetary regime, even at the cost of the domestic economy's performance, were those sectors which derived much of their income from international interactions. One obvious group were New York bankers, who had been so prominent in the creation of the Federal Reserve and the rise of the U.S. dollar as an international currency. Yet the internationally oriented banking community, multinational corporations, and other likely supporters of the Bretton Woods regime remained silent. It seems that they either had enough interests in the domestic economic performance of the U.S. to cancel out their international interests, or that they at least perceived rising protectionism to be a bigger threat than the loss of the Bretton Woods regime. Even they were unwilling to tradeoff the health of the domestic economy to save Bretton Woods.[11]

While no sector-based groups loudly defended the Bretton Woods regime, it is not apparent that any groups lobbied strongly for its downfall either. Gowa argues that the executive branch decision-makers saw electoral repercussions if the economy's performance sagged and were therefore indirectly constrained in evaluating policy trade-offs.[12] John Odell's analysis of these decisions challenges this interpretation, for he sees no such pressure building up; as he puts it, "an analyst monitoring only public opinion, electoral struggles, and group pressures would have had virtually no clue that a change in international monetary policy was imminent. Instead this analyst would have anticipated a shift in trade policy that did not occur." Thus, Odell puts little faith in the notion that domestic pressure was the source of the changes in monetary policy.[13]

Evidence confirms Odell's suggestion that instead of targeting international monetary policy, the domestic groups adversely affected by the dollar's overvaluation were interested in achieving more sector-specific traditional forms of protection. Some in the Nixon administration—advisers such as Gottfried Haberler and Hendrik S. Houthakker—saw the rising pressures for protectionism as a much more dangerous threat to the open international economy than any depreciation of the U.S. dollar. Since depreciation was the lesser evil, these advisers saw changes in monetary policy as a substitute for protectionism.[14]

Bureaucratic Politics:
The Volcker Group, the Treasury, and the Fed

Given the weakness in the sector-based interest groups argument, it is important to turn to any bureaucratic factors which might have come into play, especially if we think about how similar problems were resolved in Britain in the 1920s. In that case, the Treasury and the Bank of England experienced different pressures and expressed somewhat different policy goals. In the case of the U.S. response to its own currency overhang, Gowa claims the Treasury had the greatest say in international monetary affairs and that it opposed reform within Bretton Woods, preferring to abandon the monetary regime altogether. The Federal Reserve Board was less interested in international monetary policy—it consistently placed higher priority on domestic economic concerns. The exception to this pattern was the New York Federal Reserve Bank (the Fed), which was most concerned with international finance and which was also responsible for the execution of international monetary policy.[15]

The subtlety of this bureaucratic politics argument can best be appreciated when it is placed in comparison with the British case. During Britain's currency overhang in the 1920s, when there were too many pounds held abroad and there was also the threat of foreigners cashing them in for gold in order to transfer their holdings into a rival currency based on a rival financial centre, the Bank of England wanted to defend the pound with ever higher interest rates—even if that meant depressing national economic performance (an example of "*hegemonic afterglow*"). The Treasury increasingly resisted the Bank of England's position and in the early 1930s finally took the opportunity afforded by the creation of special financial accounts under its own control to influence international monetary policy and divorce it from domestic policy as much as possible. In the U.S. case, faced with a choice between supporting the role of the dollar at the cost of domestic economic performance or letting the international monetary regime crash, the U.S. quickly moved to the position we would expect to be supported by the Treasury but perhaps opposed by the Fed—protect the domestic economy. Yet the Fed accepted the decision to end the Bretton Woods regime, including eliminating the commitment linking gold to the dollar. Perhaps system-level factors still come into play, for the Fed could take this stand because there was no strong currency rivalling the dollar.

It would be wrong, however, to imply that international monetary policy was formulated by the Treasury alone. Instead, during the early years of the Nixon administration, international monetary policy flowed from an inter-agency team, known as the "Volcker Group," which consisted of members of the Council of Economic Advisors, the State Department, the Staff of the Assistant for National Security Affairs, the Treasury, and the Fed. Despite the broad composition of this group, all shared a common belief that national interest should be defined in terms of the domestic economy rather than preservation of the international monetary regime.[16] The conclusion this evidence suggests, which the work of other scholars supports, is that there was no disagreement along bureaucratic lines.

Other policy-making elements of the executive branch which discussed international monetary affairs were the Cabinet Committee on Economic Policy and the cabinet-level Council on International Economic Policy. Similar to the Volcker group, the Council on International Economic Policy included a broad representation of different agencies (in fact, it was even broader).[17] Perhaps none of this matters, as Odell claims, and Nixon selected policies on the advice of John Connally, the Secretary of the Treasury, and chose to ignore the others. But it is surprising to see how much consistency there was in the views of officials from different agencies; at first glance, this consensus suggests bureaucratic concerns did not factor into the decision.

It was the Fed, however, which put up the most significant opposition to Connally's decision to suspend the dollar's convertibility to gold. The Fed knew something had to change, but rather than see the Bretton Woods system undermined in one fell swoop, it argued for a more effective devaluation of the dollar. The Federal Reserve Chairman argued that devaluation was the most sensible policy because the dollar would still be difficult to defend on international markets at the existing rate.[18] Thus, the Fed may have valued the Bretton Woods system more than the Treasury, but it too wanted to see international monetary policy brought into line with domestic needs one way or another.

The end result of these discussions was a partial adjustment of the dollar's value which more accurately reflected the supply of the currency in circulation. The U.S. reduced the gap between resources and commitments by dropping commitments. This is precisely the response to a currency overhang we would expect if the central bank was not yet concerned about rival foreign currencies, whereas the Treasury was increasingly concerned with fiscal deficits.

Individual Level: Nixon, Kissinger, and Connally

In Odell's analysis, a shift in personnel was more significant than bureaucratic politics. Whenever a U.S. administration changes after a presidential election, a large number of top government officials are replaced. While the offices and positions remain largely the same, so bureaucratic interests do not change, the individuals filling those roles are different. Odell argues that when officials of the Nixon administration took office, the key players had very new ideas compared to members of the previous administration. In monetary affairs, we have already identified the key institutions: the Fed and the Treasury.

The Secretary of the Treasury under Johnson was Henry H. Fowler. Fowler was in that office from 1965 until 1969—so the entire time he was Secretary, there had been a currency overhang. He resisted any discussion of taking the dollar off gold. To him, a switch to floating exchange rates was a step towards the chaos of the 1930s. Reflecting on the problems of the interwar period, Fowler wanted to prevent any return to those sorts of policies. He saw a breakdown of the monetary regime as the first step to increased trade competition, the development of trading blocs, and perhaps even another war between major powers. Also, he had plenty of faith in the wisdom and capability of central bank intervention. He strongly believed that monetary authorities could move markets in such a way as to stabilize them and keep the fixed exchange rate system going.[19]

In late 1970 Fowler was replaced as Secretary of Treasury by the new president's appointee, John Connally. Connally, a former governor of Texas, was given a high profile post in hopes of bolstering the popularity of the Nixon administration in that large populous state. Connally's ideas on monetary policy were apparently not very fixed; he had little experience in this area and probably hadn't spent much time or invested much energy in formulating any ideas about it. The same could be said of Nixon himself; both Nixon and Connally were more interested in the administration's popularity at home, than in any particular ideological position.

The Undersecretary of the Treasury for Monetary Affairs was Paul Volcker. Volcker had much experience within both the Treasury and the Fed; he held beliefs like those of most others in those two bureaucracies, in line with Fowler's ideas. He was prepared to defend the Bretton Woods rules. By coincidence, a new Chairman of the Federal Reserve was named in 1970. Arthur Burns had experience as a banker and central banker, and thus was a strong believer in the fixed exchange rate system. The other important player on the scene, according to Odell, was George Shultz. As Director of the Office of Management and the Budget (OMB), Shultz was involved in planning and policy discussions, although he did not have the policy instruments at his disposal to shift policy in the directions he desired. Shultz's role is important, because he did not believe in government intervention in the marketplace; he did not fear the consequences of "closing the gold window." He argued for free market solutions and downplayed the dangers of economic repercussions or a repeat of the 1930s.[20]

According to this description, among the individuals making monetary policy in the early 1970s were several who lacked any fixed ideological positions on monetary issues. Nixon, Connally, and Kissinger were prepared to throw Bretton Woods and the fixed exchange rate system out the window for domestic political gains. Moreover, the frustrations in arriving at a multilateral solution to questions about the dollar's value had prompted Connally to turn his back on multilateral efforts. Connally and Nixon found the idea of striking out boldly and seeking diplomatic solutions later more attractive.

Would the same policies have been followed if different people had held these key positions? Why is it that some of those with entrenched beliefs, such as Burns or Volcker, were unable to prevent "the shocks"? Structural system-level factors shaped the problem, and may have largely outlined the only possible responses, providing us with insight into how to think about the different arguments coming together; individuals mattered, for they played a role in selecting and implementing the policies. The dollar-gold relationship was unsustainable; the only real question was how that relationship would be broken.

The Consequences of the End of Bretton Woods

Of course, the end of the regime did not terminate the dollar's role as the primary instrument for international payment because there were no readily available substitutes that could serve as an international media of exchange. Indeed, Nixon wanted to throw off the constraints of the Bretton Woods system, yet maintain the dollar's status as the main reserve currency for two reasons: prestige first, but also the leverage this brought the U.S. over other states.[21] The end of Bretton Woods meant the end of the promise to redeem foreign central banks' dollars into gold, but this merely underlined the lack of confidence in the dollar. When the dollar was devalued further in 1971, confidence waned further, and by the spring of 1973 the dollar could no longer be supported through interventions. The failure to reestablish any sort of binding international monetary regime in the 1970s can be traced back to the decision that the domestic economy's performance was of paramount importance. In discussions held in the fall of 1975 concerning the creation of a new international monetary regime, French and U.S. officials agreed that domestic economic stability was more important than exchange rate stability.[22] Yet large numbers of dollars continued to be held abroad, and the dollar's role as international medium of exchange remained largely unchallenged.

Other countries did not appreciate the U.S. actions. From August 1971 to 1976 the search was on for a new set of international rules to cover international monetary affairs. Before 1971 ended, the U.S., the West Europeans, and the Japanese had reached an agreement on meeting some of the U.S. desires. In this Smithsonian Agreement, as it was called, the U.S. did not get everything it wanted. The value of the dollar was changed by a little less than 10 per cent, and the West Germans, Japanese, and Swiss (all the countries which provided rival reserve assets) agreed to revalue their currencies by more than 10 per cent. Nixon was able to declare this a U.S. victory because the others moved their currency values more than the U.S. did, so he dropped the import surcharge.

At the same time, it was agreed that the Bretton Woods fixed exchange rate rules would be maintained, but the band of fluctuation would be increased to plus or minus 2.50 per cent. It was hoped that this would give the markets a little more room for manoeuvre and give the governments a respite from intervening in currency markets so often. So this wasn't a real reform of Bretton Woods, but a sort of crisis control (or, better yet, damage control) operation.

Speculators, of course, received a totally different message out of this. They felt that although the U.S. had withstood attacks on the dollar in exchange markets for more than a decade, the dollar should have been devalued way back in 1960. Now the dollar actually had been devalued, though not by very much. The likelihood of future devaluations suddenly seemed much greater. So after the Smithsonian Agreement, speculation increased.

By June of 1972, the British pound was under speculative pressure, and Britain decided it could no longer defend its parity even with the wider bands, so it became the first major country to float its currency (i.e., to let the market decide the currency's parity). Speculative pressures on the dollar continued, and in February 1973, the U.S. devalued it another 10 per cent—but again this was an insufficient amount to calm the speculation. Exchange markets had to be closed. When they were reopened, the pressures were so strong that on March 1, the Bundesbank was forced to buy up $2.6 billion in a single day.[23] At that point, central banks everywhere gave up on defending parities, and all currencies were allowed to float.[24]

Notes

1. Edward L. Morse, "Political Choice and Alternative Monetary Regimes," *Alternatives to Monetary Disorder*, ed. Michael Schwarz (New York, NY: McGraw-Hill, 1977) 81, 83.

2. John S. Odell, *U.S. International Monetary Policy, Markets, Power and Ideas as Sources of Change* (Princeton, NJ: Princeton University Press, 1982) 84.

3. Morse 85.

4. Barry Eichengreen, "Hegemonic Stability Theories of the International Monetary System," *Can Nations Agree? Issues in International Economic Cooperation*, ed. R.N. Cooper *et al.* (Washington, DC: Brookings Institution, 1989) 275.

5. For an examination of whether these charges that the U.S. exported inflation have merit, see Edgar Feige and James M. Johannes, "Was the U.S. Responsible for Worldwide Inflation under the Regime of Fixed Exchange Rates?," *Kyklos* 35,2 (1982): 263-77.

6. The one exception would be France, which under de Gaulle was mounting a systemic disruption to stress the need for independence from U.S. leadership. See the discussion in Jonathan Kirshner, *Currency and Coercion* (Princeton, NJ: Princeton University Press, 1995) 192-203.

7. Joanne Gowa, *Closing the Gold Window: Domestic Politics and the End of Bretton Woods* (Ithaca, NY: Cornell University Press, 1983) 14.

8. Odell, *U.S. International Monetary Policy* 165.

9. Odell, *U.S. International Monetary Policy* 166, 202.

10. Gowa 25.

11. Gowa 67; Odell, *U.S. International Monetary Policy* 238-39.

12. Gowa 151.

13. Odell, *U.S. International Monetary Policy* 233.

14. Odell, *U.S. International Monetary Policy* 192, 346-47.

15. Gowa 31, 107-08, 115.

16. Gowa 62.

17. Odell, *U.S. International Monetary Policy* 268-69.

18. Odell, *U.S. International Monetary Policy* 270.

19. John S. Odell, "The U.S. and the Emergence of Flexible Exchange Rates," *International Organization* 33,1 (Winter 1979) 65-66.

20. Odell, "The U.S. and the Emergence of Flexible Exchange Rates" 68.

21. Gowa 132.

22. Kenneth W. Dam, *The Rules of the Game* (Chicago, IL: University of Chicago Press, 1982) 256; Tom de Vries, "Jamaica, or the Non-Reform of the IMF," *Foreign Affairs* 54,3 (April 1976): 577-605.

23. The rapidity of the collapse certainly reflects another factor in modern international monetary relations: the advent of technology. It was possible even then, some 25 years ago, to undertake massive international transactions electronically.

24. There were possible advantages to flexible exchange rates—especially after the oil crisis hit, creating strains in international payments. See Otmar Emminger "International Financial Markets and the Recycling of Petrodollars," *The World Today* 31,3 (March 1975): 95-102.

Additional References

Block, Fred. *The Origins of International Economic Disorder: A Study of U.S. International Monetary Policy from World War II to the Present.* Berkeley, CA: University of California Press, 1977.

Krasner, Stephen. "U.S. Commercial and Monetary Policy; Unraveling the Paradox of External Strength and Internal Weakness." *Between Power and Plenty.* Ed. Peter Katzenstein. Madison, WI: University of Wisconsin Press, 1978. 51-87.

Gowa, Joanne. *Closing the Gold Window.* Ithaca, NY: Cornell University Press, 1983.

—. "State Power, State Policy: Explaining the Decision to Close the Gold Window." *Politics and Society* 13,1 (1984): 91-117.

Odell, John. "The U.S. and the Emergence of Flexible Exchange Rates: An Analysis of Foreign Policy Change." *International Organization* 33,1 (Winter 1979): 57-81.

—. *U.S. International Monetary Policy: Markets, Power and Ideas as Sources of Change.* Princeton, NJ: Princeton University Press, 1982.

CHAPTER 21

Brazil's Responses
to the Debt Crisis

The crisis began when Mexico announced in August 1982 it could no longer pay the interest on its international debts. Soon afterwards, the leading lenders to Brazil began to scale back their loans, anticipating similar problems with that country's finances. In October, Brazil declared that it would not need debt rescheduling, perhaps because it had already arranged a $1.2 billion loan from the U.S. Treasury. Nonetheless, by the middle of December 1982, Brazil was unable to meet its financial obligations, and by the end of the month it had stopped payment on the principal of its foreign debt.

Background: Sources of the Debt Crisis

According to Ethan Kapstein, there are three prominent theories explaining why debt crises occur.[1] The first emphasizes the role of external shocks, which upset the calculations of both borrower and lender. The second is overlending—banks err in loaning out more money than they should. The third looks at the borrowers, stressing how they fail to use their loans effectively.[2] Kapstein also points out the flaws with each of these explanations when applied to the debt crisis of the 1980s. For instance, the argument that an external shock hit the borrowers and lenders, and therefore made it impossible for borrowers to meet their obligations, can be only partially true. While there were shocks (discussed below), these hit all borrowers evenly, yet not all borrowers failed to meet their obligations. East Asian debtors, such as South Korea, were able to meet the increased interest payments because they had high enough export earnings.[3] Exports gained them U.S. dollars, so when the value of the dollar rose, their incomes rose as well. They were therefore in a much better position to make their payments on or near schedule.

It is perhaps also worth noting that the suddenness of the crisis caught the markets off guard. The interest rate spread (defined below) is the banks' measure of a borrower's riskiness. The spreads charged on Mexican and Brazilian bonds did not start moving up until the last few weeks before the crisis broke.[4] As for overlending, Kapstein points out that banks are supposedly prevented from overlending by regulations. The domestic authorities which are supposed to ensure that overlending does not occur were circumvented, at least partially, by the emergence of the Euromarket.[5] Nonetheless, this indicates that governments shared part of the responsibility if overlending is to blame.

Finally, Kapstein does not believe that the third explanation, which underscores the importance of how the borrowers used the funds, can fully account for the debt crisis. After all, debtors used their borrowings for a wide variety of uses. Some of these were guaranteed not to earn much of an economic profit—in certain cases, some of the money went to providing government services, rather than being invested in a directly profit-generating endeavour. Others appeared to be wise investments. Once again, the example of the East Asian countries illustrates that some of the transactions made perfect economic sense.

Most observers agree that the dynamics of the early 1980s upset the calculations of borrowers and lenders alike. The biggest movements came in interest rates. The interest charged on a loan is intended to earn the bank a profit; if the bank judges the loan to be a higher risk, it charges the borrower a higher price. This is reflected in the two parts of an interest charge: there is a base rate plus a "spread." The base rate is the rate the bank gives its best customers, called the prime rate in the U.S. (i.e., the rate given to the bank's prime customers). Internationally, the base is the rate at which banks loan money to each other in London, known as the London Inter-Bank Offer Rate (LIBOR). The spread is then added to the base, with the size of the spread reflecting the riskiness of the particular loan.

Interest rates in earlier days were almost always fixed at some nominal rate. That is, at the time the debt was undertaken, the interest rate for the entire term was established by taking the base and adding the spread. Inflation had made banks change their practices. Inflation rates had risen to such levels in the 1970s that fixed rate loans were losing money. Let's say a bank made a loan and charged the borrower 10 per cent per year. If inflation was rising at 10 per cent per year over that same period, the real value of the principal plus interest would only equal the real value of the original loan—the bank would earn no profit. When inflation was soaring in a period when most loans were at fixed rates, real interest rates were very, very low. It didn't take long for the banks to figure this out; they began to issue most loans on the basis of variable interest rates, so that the interest charge moved as the underlying base rate changed. Almost all of Brazil's borrowing after 1979 (something like 95 per cent between 1979-81) was at variable interest rates.[6] Any increases in LIBOR were passed along to Brazil as higher interest charges.

The base rate rose, but so too did the spread. Developing countries in the early 1970s may have been paying only about 1 per cent spreads; from 1975-

77 the spreads climbed slightly, but then fell off again, only to climb back up to 1.7 per cent by 1983 on average.[7] The riskier borrowers were paying even higher spreads. For Brazil, the spread charged by banks in 1980 was 1.5 per cent. It took an initial jump in late 1982 to an average of 2.25 per cent, but then stabilized after February 1983, when Brazil made its first deal with the International Monetary Fund (IMF), settling at 2.5 per cent.[8]

While the spreads paid by developing countries were higher than other borrowers might have faced, this had been true for some time. The major source of the rising interest charge came from movements in LIBOR and the U.S. prime rate. The U.S. Federal Reserve had decided to combat inflation by restricting the U.S. money supply. This goal was pursued through higher interest rates, which pulled LIBOR up as well. In 1978, LIBOR was 8.7 per cent; by 1981 it had risen to 17 per cent. This was a much higher interest rate than the borrowers had ever thought about paying. As part of debt servicing, interest payments went from 38 per cent in 1978 to 61 per cent in 1984.[9] (The real interest rate paid by Brazil on foreign debt went from an average of 4.236 per cent in 1979 to 9.232 per cent in 1981, and then 14.245 per cent in 1982.)[10]

These higher interest rates, plus the downturn in global markets, which were being slowed by the same pressures on credit, made Brazil's ability to service its debt nearly impossible: the debt service ratio (i.e., the ratio of debt payments to exports) for 1982 hit 98.5 per cent—and Brazil also had to pay for necessary imports, such as oil.[11] As Frieden illustrates in *Debt, Development, and Democracy*, the climbing interest rate after 1979 upset Brazil's domestic political and economic relations. In his words, "A political economy that had come to rely on foreign finance was driven into political and economic crisis by so major a reversal in its international financial position."[12]

The Role of Debt in Brazil's Development Strategy

Since the 1940s, Brazil had employed a development strategy based mostly on import-substitution industrialization (ISI). This was pursued even more aggressively after 1967, a few years after a military government took power and at a time when European and U.S. banks were expanding their international lending. The military government took advantage of these new opportunities for borrowing. As access to foreign loans increased, so did the government's role in the economy.[13] As an example of the increased foreign borrowing by the government, Frieden gives statistics on the distribution of private versus government components of the debt. In 1974, more than half of the country's medium- and long-term foreign debt was owed by the private sector; by 1979, the private sector owed only one-third of this type of debt.[14]

From the late 1960s until the debt crisis hit, the military ruled with the support of a political coalition oriented around ISI.[15] This coalition had four major components: (1) the modern industrial sector, (2) the domestic financial sector, (3) agricultural businesses (especially the largest farms, which produced commodities for both domestic and international markets), and (4) state-owned enterprises (SOEs). These four elements of the economy received the lion's share of the funds raised via international borrowing.

The government took some of its borrowing and, in good fashion with ISI strategy, invested it in SOEs producing basic inputs. By increasing domestic production of basic goods such as steel, electricity, etc., it was hoped the overall economy would be stimulated. As it turned out, SOEs were part of the problem. For instance, at the end of 1985, Siderbrás, the national holding company which ran the steel industry, held $15.6 billion in foreign debt. That amounted to roughly 14 per cent of the entire country's foreign debts. And while these debts had been incurred by the individual companies, it was possible for the SOEs to transfer these debts to the federal government.[16] The government invested elsewhere, too. Rudiger Dornbusch has used examples from Brazil to show just how deeply the government of an economically developing country can get involved in its economy, in ways that have little to do with industrialization; the Brazilian government owned such diverse businesses as motels and perfume stores![17]

Meanwhile, the government adapted to its own inflation by introducing indexation.[18] Just as the banks had adjusted to inflation by utilizing variable rate loans, other actors were building rising costs into their charges. In Brazil (and elsewhere) the government introduced policies to ensure that workers' wages would rise with inflation as well. Wages were indexed, so that they could be raised as inflation went up. Indexation kept workers from being hurt by inflation in the short run, but the practice made inflation a permanent fixture of the Brazilian economy.

None of these problems meant Brazil's strategy was necessarily headed towards failure. Its merchandise exports grew by an average of 9.4 per cent per year between 1965 and 1980. That outpaced Singapore over those same years, and was just behind Hong Kong's rate.[19] Yet the political economy created was vulnerable to rising interest charges; obstacles to adjustment were difficult to overcome.

Brazil's Situation Leading up to 1982

Brazil had already introduced austerity measures before Mexico announced its inability to meet its external debt obligations. As early as the year before, Brazil had struggled with its debt burden, which arose largely because of the expenses of importing oil after the second oil price shock.[20] In 1981, oil imports cost Brazil the equivalent of 43 per cent of the country's export earnings. Brazil was already borrowing from abroad simply to pay the interest on previous debts.[21]

The military government spent the initial period of the debt crisis trying to keep its domestic support satisfied—this meant maintaining future capital inflows. This in turn required Brazil to prove its creditworthiness. This was difficult, since the government was unable to increase taxes. The public sector would have to reduce its expenditures so that additional funds could be spent on interest charges. In order to ensure that local investors would not take their money to another country where interest rates were higher (such as the U.S.) in what is known as capital flight, and to perhaps entice foreign money to come in, Brazil had to have a high domestic interest rate. Finally, in order to raise (and to conserve) hard currency for debt repayment, it had to export more and spend less on imports. This policy could be enhanced by devaluing the currency.[22]

Debt service would be difficult, however. Thanks to the banks' higher interest rates, the debt-service ratio was profoundly affected. In 1977, debt service payments equalled 51 per cent of Brazil's merchandise exports. In 1982, they equaled 91 per cent.[23] Interestingly, the response by the military government was to pursue a set of policies much like those the IMF would advocate: the military government struggled to reduce its budget deficit and to limit growth of the domestic money supply. And this was in 1981 *before* Brazil had negotiated with the IMF! The result was a fall in gross output (by 1.6 per cent in 1980-81) while inflation climbed from 94 to 121 per cent.[24] This set the stage for the later problems Brazil would confront.

Inflation grew to 211 per cent by 1983, causing widespread problems. Domestic product fell 3.2 per cent that year, per capita income dropped 5.5 per cent, and real wages fell even further (16 per cent). The most modern industrialized sectors of the economy had to lay off workers. As a result, these sectors would no longer support the government. Meanwhile, the statistics on Brazil's international economic relations were not very encouraging. Gross foreign debt in 1983 grew by 17 per cent. The dollar total of that debt amounted to more than $81 billion. The only positive sign was that Brazil had earned a trade surplus in 1983 of $6.4 billion. The external accounts seemed headed in the proper directions. From 1982 to 1984, export earnings increased by 35 per cent, while imports fell by 30 per cent.[25] With an upsurge in this trade surplus, Brazil alone among the largest debtors in Latin America appeared to be able to finance its debt through trade.

The Initial International Responses to the Debt Crisis

At first glance, one might have expected the debtors to default on their loans; they were sovereign actors, after all, so how could the banks hope to collect? Both sides understood, however, that default would carry long-term repercussions. If borrowers defaulted, causing the collapse of several large banks, then other banks would not be willing to extend these countries new loans in the future. Also, default would open them up to possible retaliations by the creditor countries. The U.S. and Europe might put up barriers to trade against the debtors' exports. This would punish defaulting debtors and reward other countries still trying to meet their debt obligations.

The banks were similarly constrained in that they could not simply write off the loans as mistakes or losses, because they were simply too large. To have written off these debts in the early 1980s would have been tantamount to a default, since the result would have been the same—the banks going out of business. As it was the value of the banks' stock dropped precipitously once it was clear they would not meet projected earnings after 1982.

The other actors with so much at stake were the creditor governments. Since the major banks which were threatened by the debt crisis were U.S. and European, these governments might have to bail out some very large banks. This encouraged the U.S. in particular to take action. Likewise at the international level, the U.S. did not want to see any of its neighbours experience too much internal turmoil, nor did it wish to have to pay off any other country's debts. No one would benefit from a default; some would simply lose less than others. The response was for the U.S. to ask both sides to make every effort to ease repayment; it also made its own efforts to prevent the politicization of the debt crisis. U.S. goals were both short-term crisis management (i.e., preventing a collapse of the financial system) and long-term stabilization.[26]

The first stage of the debt crisis, then, was to pretend that it was manageable: with enough work the Third World borrowers would be able to repay their entire debts. The U.S. government and the banks also made efforts to keep the borrowers bargaining individually, rather than as a debtor cartel.[27] The banks organized on their own and picked lead banks to deal with each of the major borrowers, so that negotiations were simplified to one country dealing with one bank; all the other banks would go along with the agreement made. The Third World borrowers, on the other hand, did not use their collective power. And prior to 1985, the U.S. government eschewed any direct responsibility in the debt crisis, though it had already issued loans to several debtors.

From the U.S. perspective, the only possible long-term solution within the existing relationships (and maintaining existing economic principles) was for the debtors to expand their economies, earn more money through exports, and pay off the debts.[28] This left the debt crisis to be settled by individual debtor's policies. The most popular program initially used in Latin America was to refinance the debts, which meant getting new, cheaper loans to pay off the original debts. These new loans were available from the IMF and the U.S. government, as well as from renegotiating the terms on old commercial debts.

The IMF Finds a New Role

After the fall of the Bretton Woods monetary regime, the IMF's major responsibility disappeared. The IMF had been created in order to help deficit countries maintain their pledged parity on the fixed exchange rate system. Without a fixed exchange rate regime, its duty was less important. Now, if a country had a balance of payments deficit, it could simply allow its currency to float. Yet by 1992, the IMF had some sort of lending operation in effect with 56 countries.[29] The debt crisis had created a new opportunity for the IMF to employ its expertise and financial resources. The debtors needed cash to meet obligations, and they were unable to raise more funds from private sources. The IMF continued its policy of only making loans with conditions attached, but now private actors would look to it to help evaluate whether debtors were making the proper economic adjustments to earn the hard currencies needed to pay off debts.[30]

The orthodox IMF stabilization plan consisted of three elements, which actually reflect its earlier responsibilities under the fixed exchange rate regime. First, the IMF recommended devaluing the debtor country's currency. This was intended to affect the country's balance of payments, in order to help the debtor adjust its debt-service ratio. Second, the IMF advocated methods to control domestic inflation, including reducing domestic demand, which would also reduce demand for imports. Third, and for many of the same reasons, the IMF worked to reduce government spending, contracting the money supply and reducing wage demands. In application, the policies looked consistent from one country to the next: control the money supply, put in place controls on domestic credit, reduce real wages, and liberalize markets. Most importantly, the IMF began to stretch out the timeframe of its adjustment packages; prior to the 1980s, they had all been short term. It was only through the experience of the early 1980s that the IMF began to engineer medium-term packages.[31]

The IMF's typical package has been criticized on a number of counts. For one, such adjustment schemes tend to create large trade surpluses so that external debts can be paid, but which lead to higher rates of domestic inflation. They also cut back on domestic investment—suggesting that as long-term economic plans, they reduce growth and the ability to pay back debts.[32] Other economists have noted that these policy recommendations are based largely on models developed for analyzing industrialized countries; the assumptions behind such models may simply be inappropriate for less economically developed countries.[33] Along the same lines, many have argued that the IMF packages all looked alike. Notably, in the early years of the debt crisis, more than 80 per cent of IMF adjustment packages included devaluation. As one finance minister is said to have lamented, "The IMF uses devaluation like a man with a hammer who believes that everything is a nail."[34]

The orthodox structural adjustment loans (SALs) from the World Bank were conditional upon a similar set of policies. In effect, the longer term of the SALs gave the World Bank the opportunity to stress the need to institutionalize the practices emphasized by the IMF's conditions. In the words of John Loxley, the emphasis on "structural" adjustment "simply makes more explicit the fact that contemporary programs frequently imply substantial changes in the direction of the economy, in its sectoral priorities, and in its institutional make-up."[35] The term SAL was only used after September 1979. SALs were intended to give debtors a period of five to 10 years in which they could restructure their economies. IMF conditionality was a precondition to getting a SAL from the World Bank, but the SAL offered lower interest rates and longer terms than IMF loans.[36]

There were often four separate elements to a SAL. First was the elimination or reduction of macroeconomic imbalances, or what is usually referred to as "stabilization" (along the lines of the IMF policies). Second were policies aimed at shifting resources into the production of goods for the market, especially away from consumption and into the production of exports. This was also referred to as "switching." Third was improvement of economic efficiency through support for rationalization and deregulation. Finally came mobilization and coordination of the application of resources, especially those coming from outside the country. The SALs were conditional upon establishment of a longer term plan for making such changes. On an issue such as currency devaluation, instead of asking for a one-shot adjustment, the SAL would ask the country to adopt a longer term pattern of small adjustments. These changes were intended to have a deeper, more lasting impact: they included reforming taxes, tariffs, price controls or subsidization of parts of the economy, privatizing state-owned enterprises, and so on.[37]

The largest debtors had the most power to upset the international financial system. In due course, they received the most attention from both international organizations and the industrialized countries. These debtors (Brazil, but also Mexico and Argentina) were given lower interest rates, longer maturities on their debts, and longer grace periods in their debt reschedulings.[38] Brazil was the single largest Third World debtor at this time[39] and certainly received its share of breaks compared to smaller debtors.

Brazil's First Interactions with the IMF

Brazil initially negotiated with the IMF in December 1982, signing a letter of intent in early January 1983. Since Brazil was unable to uphold its end of the deal, the conditions were renegotiated over the next few months. Some economists have been critical of this initial plan, because they believe the IMF rushed into the agreement without taking Brazil's position into account; apparently, the IMF was more interested in showing that the crisis was solvable and that it could play a positive role in resolving the crisis.[40] In the deal struck in January 1983, the IMF made $5.9 billion available over 1983, 1984, and 1985, which Brazil could use in its negotiations with commercial lenders.[41] The commercial banks were to make fresh funds available and maintain Brazil's trade credits.

In 1983, some relief came as LIBOR fell back to 9.8 per cent.[42] Yet by May 1983 Brazil was no longer meeting the conditions as specified. Renegotiations were undertaken, but since Brazil was not heeding the earlier promises, the IMF would not release planned disbursements, and the commercial banks would not make new loans. Finally, a revised letter of intent was signed in September 1983, for which Brazil received new IMF funds. Unfortunately, this did not convince private creditors that Brazil was committed to reforms. Since no new private funds were forthcoming, yet another deal with the IMF was negotiated before the end of 1983.[43]

One of the reasons for the difficulties was a disagreement over how to measure particular facets of the economy and the government's macroeconomic policies. For instance, the IMF used the "credit-based" approach to measure Brazil's fiscal deficit. This tracked the deficit in terms of overall flows of revenues and expenditures. The Brazilian government preferred to use an "operational" measure, which took indexation as a given, and therefore increasing costs were built into the calculations. The two systems produced different numbers. But the biggest reason for problems was that the IMF's targets on defeating inflation were never hit.[44]

The conditions imposed by the IMF had a positive impact on Brazil's balance of trade. The policies Brazil adopted in 1983 resulted in a $12 billion trade surplus. At the same time, the country had difficulty meeting the terms of its agreements because it could not limit internal inflation. The IMF asked that any wage increases via indexation be limited to 80 per cent of any increase in the consumer price index—this at a time when inflation was roaring along at 200 per cent. Fresh loan disbursements from the IMF had to be put on hold while the government struggled with budget deficit reductions, as well. For these reasons, Brazil wound up signing four letters of intent with the IMF in 1983, then three more in 1984.[45] The latter stressed the IMF's desire to see Brazil pursue higher exports, continue the policy of small but regular devaluations of the currency, and liberalize trade. In the end, Brazil received a new "jumbo" loan of $6.5 billion and had another $5 billion in debts rescheduled.[46]

Brazil's exports did increase and hit levels well above the targets set by the IMF in the letters of intent. The 1984 surplus was $13.1 billion, the 1985 surplus $12.4 billion. That was the positive part of the story. Brazil was also able to reduce its needs for imports in dramatic fashion. Domestic production of aluminum and energy in several forms were all increased. Production for domestic markets was reoriented to exports with remarkable success.[47] Nonetheless, Brazil was once again unable to meet the austerity targets established by the IMF, so the IMF suspended credit in February 1985. Since the two sides were unable to reach an agreement that year, Brazil introduced its own adjustment package early in 1986.

On the downside, many of the domestic adjustments were difficult to implement. The IMF would have preferred an outright end to wage indexation.[48] Brazil had had indexation since 1964, which explains why the IMF would target it as a source of problems, but also tells us why it would be so difficult for the government to dismantle the policy. Indexation enforced expectations of wage and price increases. At the same time, it is intended to ensure that wages grow as fast as price increases; therefore, ending indexation would hurt wage-earners, at least in the short run. (In the long run Brazil's inflation was perhaps more detrimental to the poor than anything else.)[49] One of the conclusions reached by some economists was that the IMF approach had hit its limits. While Brazil's external accounts had been adjusted in the ways the IMF urged, and Brazil's export earnings increased, internal stabilization did not follow suit. Without the internal adjustment, the debt problem remained.[50] This illustrates how poorly equipped the IMF was to deal with these sorts of problems.

Brazil's Turn to Unorthodox Responses: From the Cruzado Plan to the Moratorium

Having first followed the recommendations from the IMF and others, Brazil then tried its own unorthodox responses to the debt crisis. President Jose Sarney announced the Cruzado Plan on February 28, 1986, which was to implement a sophisticated set of policies geared to achieve domestic adjustments without suffering the recessionary side-effects of traditional stabilization packages. The main goals were to eliminate inflation, but raise revenues for the government by stimulating domestic demand, making it similar to the Austral Plan introduced in Argentina at about the same time. The measures which kept inflation going were supposed to be torn down.[51]

The Cruzado Plan included several tough measures which had been avoided up to that point. First, indexation was finally to be ended, at least for short-term contracts. Second, there was an immediate and indefinite freeze on more than 80 per cent of goods and services. Third, the money was to be altered in hopes of changing the way people thought about the currency. In reality, this was only a redenomination of the currency, with a slight change in the name of the unit: 1,000 cruzeiros would now be worth one cruzado (hence, the name of the scheme: the Cruzado Plan). Fourth, wages were controlled. The minimum wage was increased by one-third, and other wage earners were given an 8 per cent bonus; future wage adjustments would be triggered only when the inflation rate hit 20 per cent (and then adjusted with every following 20 per cent increment in the inflation rate).[52] Another important aspect was the elimination of indexed government bonds, which were a popular method for holding savings. They were replaced by a non-indexed version, again with the aim of destroying the inertia propelling inflation.[53]

Each of these measures was intended to disrupt inflation. The greatest political difficulty was to implement the policies in a way that would be perceived as fair, as well as actually convincing everyone that inflation would in fact stop. Typical wage contracts in Brazil ran for six months. Rent contracts were sometimes for six months, but more often ran for a year. Since contracts were constantly turning over, if the government had merely picked a day and decided to enforce a freeze instantly, those individuals who had just renegotiated their wage contracts would be far ahead of those who were just days away from renegotiating theirs. In order to make the freeze fairer, the Cruzado Plan contained augmentations for some, plus rollbacks in some rent contracts with the amount of adjustment based on the rents' average real value during the previous year.[54]

The Cruzado Plan seemed at first to have stopped inflation "cold" according to one assessment.[55] The inflation rate remained low for about six months, but within a year it returned. From March 1986 until the end of the year, total consumption increased by 10.9 per cent in real terms, while GDP in real terms only rose only 7.6 per cent.[56] The inflation rate hit 20 per cent by January 1987, triggering the first wage adjustments. This brought on a whole number of other small policy changes. To counteract the impact of inflation on trade, small devaluations of the currency were reintroduced. Indexation of the economy was brought back. Soon inflation was running at an even higher rate than before.

These policies unleashed a splurge in consumer spending. The boom in consumption created shortages of many items, including foodstuffs. There had been a severe drought in late 1985, so the 1986 harvest was small. In order to meet increased demand, the import of food items was liberalized. The result was that Brazil's positive trade balance was reduced, and precious monetary reserves were spent. Brazil's trade surplus, which had averaged $12.8 billion in 1984-85, fell back to $8.4 billion in 1986. Even worse, the increasing demand and resultant shortages pushed inflation back into the economy. By the end of 1986, Brazilian interest rates hit 400 per cent; various elements of indexation were brought back. Even the savings bonds were indexed again. By February 1987 the price freezes were lifted, and the price of many goods immediately jumped 30-40 per cent. By the end of 1987, consumer prices in urban centres such as Rio de Janeiro hit an annual increase of 230 per cent or more.[57]

The Cruzado Plan failed to increase government revenues. The indirect taxes introduced as part of the overall plan were too small to generate large amounts of funds. What Brazil needed to do was something politically difficult in any country whenever the economy is in a downturn: reduce government expenditures while increasing taxes. Tax hikes were unpopular, further expenditure cuts were next to impossible, and now investments were being slashed.[58] Also, the Brazilian government had done little to prevent the expansion of domestic credit. This was intended to allow the government to raise funds to pay off debts, but had other consequences. Inflation was one, capital flight another.[59]

Rather than drop the Cruzado Plan, some minor adjustments were introduced. These came too late. Instead of enacting them when needed, the government postponed them until after congressional and gubernatorial elections in the fall of 1986.[60] The new policies were intended to raise new revenues. Compulsory deposits were required for the purchase of many consumer durables, such as automobiles. New taxes were put in place, aimed at the upper class. Also, sales taxes were put into effect.[61] Other adjustments included price increases on many goods, altering the inflation index, the announcement of a wage adjustment scheme, the implementation of a series of minor currency devaluations, and plans for some efforts to boost domestic savings. Naturally, the newly elected government's popularity dropped.[62]

The Moratorium

Brazil's inflation returned, and its monetary reserves were shrinking. Brazil now had $110.5 billion in long- and medium-term debt. This amounted to more than one-third of its gross domestic product (GDP). The country was completing a full 180-degree swing in policies; in the first years of the debt crisis, the military government had tried to retain Brazil's creditworthiness by increasing export earnings as the international organizations urged, but now, in 1987, Brazil was going to do what every one of the international monetary organizations had been arguing against. Brazil was no longer a well-behaved success, but instead a challenge to the debt regime.[63]

Brazil declared a moratorium on interest payments to commercial banks on February 20, 1987. The government expected this action to earn it greater popularity at home; perhaps, too, it thought that this would enable it to find other debtors willing to pursue a similar course. It was also hoped that the sheer size of Brazil's debt, backed now by a refusal to pay, would force the banks to make concessions.[64] The Brazilian government was disappointed. Domestic popularity was not boosted by the moratorium, nor did other debtors rally to Brazil's side.[65] Instead, other countries with heavy debt burdens rescheduled their repayments. Brazil stood alone.[66] Moreover, the banks were preparing themselves for losses—they were ready to call Brazil's bluff.[67]

In May 1987, Citicorp moved to bolster its loan loss reserves. This was an amazing turnaround. In 1983, Citicorp had earned a quarter of its gross profits from the interest paid by Brazil on its jumbo loan. Citicorp was the largest commercial bank in the U.S.; while it had engaged in foreign lending, it also had other streams of income, most notably the interest Americans paid on credit cards. It was able to set aside earnings from these other areas to cover losses on international loans. In short, Citicorp was positioning itself to say it could afford not to collect the debts. Its stock immediately rallied.[68] Other banks were pressured to take similar actions, though not all had the diversified income stream which Citicorp possessed.

As a result of Brazil's moratorium, the U.S. took punitive action. In order to force the Brazilians into some sort of repayment on interest charges, the U.S. imposed trade sanctions worth $100 million in November 1987. After further negotiations, Brazil resumed full interest payments in January 1988.[69] In September 1988 it was able to renegotiate its debts. A little more than $62 billion in debts were refinanced at lower interest rates, and the principal repayments were stretched out for several extra years. Brazil was also given $5.2 billion to meet future interest payments.[70]

Nonetheless, Brazil was able to increase its exports. The 1988 trade surplus ran at $19.1 billion, and in that year $10 billion in external debt was cut via debt-equity conversions. The country also easily met the IMF's goals for foreign exchange reserves. Yet GDP failed to grow, and the inflation rate neared 1,000 per cent.[71] Brazil's experiment with unorthodox policies had failed.

The System-Level Explanations for Brazil's Policies

The debt crisis erupted as a problem for many countries at once. The increases in LIBOR and the downturn of the global economy presented economic difficulties for many developing countries which had relied on international borrowing to finance development. The similarity of the crisis is perhaps especially true across Latin America.[72] Yet these countries, despite the similarity of their position in the international political economy, responded to these system-level stimuli with different policies. Brazil's moratorium, when the country stood alone, stands out most clearly.

Despite the fact that many of the same international organizations were involved in the development of responses to the debt crisis, and the obvious similarity in the problem each country faced in paying back debts, the responses debtors used were quite varied.[73] Such observations naturally turn us to domestic-level explanations. As Thomas Biersteker argues, any understanding of the responses adopted by the various debtor countries requires a two-level approach, bringing in both domestic- and system-level actors.[74]

Domestic Politics: The Military Government Falls

The military government in power when the crisis first broke was discredited by its handling of the issue. The developmental coalition which had been so solid for nearly 20 years came unglued. The debt crisis created a political opening for democratization which, in the words of Frieden, was "overtaken and accelerated" by the continuing evolution of the issue.[75] The military government relented to demands for greater participation by holding indirect elections in 1984, which it intended to swing to its own favour.

As noted above, the economic slow-down in 1982 and 1983 hit hard at some of the core groups in the military government's support. The modern industrial sectors, both businessmen and organized labour, now opposed the government. In July 1983, business leaders issued a policy paper urging the government to rethink its debt strategy. The paper argued that the government needed to renegotiate its deal with the IMF and that part of this renegotiation should include an end to austerity programs.[76] By 1985 the opposition groups—strengthened by defections from the military's support—were in position to have their own leader, Tancredo Neves, elected president. Neves, however, fell ill and died before taking office. Jose Sarney, who took his place, instituted the Cruzado Plan.

The Cruzado Plan, therefore, reflects the bases of Sarney's support. The unorthodox approach taken was an attempt to make the necessary adjustments to pay off the debt while maintaining the government's central role in the overall development strategy.[77] Organized labour did not support it.[78] Labour organizations are fragmented in Brazil; unions are divided along sectoral and regional lines, and there are also important urban-rural splits.[79] Thus labour did not voice a united opposition to any adjustment policies, though it had much at stake. Labour's opposition was important for creating the political standoff over how to distribute the costs associated with defeating inflation.[80]

The political standoff was worsened by the new constitution put in place when the military government ended. The new constitution gave the Congress and the President shared responsibility for approving the federal budget, prioritizing expenditures, and dealing with wage policies (such as indexation), privatizations, etc. Any redistribution of the costs of adjustment would require broad public support.[81] In 1984-90, the budget was gradually unified with the different elements being tied into a single package. But Congress and various governmental agencies worked to upset any attempts to control expenditures.[82] The adjustment policies were hamstrung by the need to ensure their popularity.

The Overlap Between Bureaucratic Politics and Domestic Politics

Kurt Weyland relies on a bureaucratic politics approach to explain, at least partially, the incoherence of Brazil's adjustment efforts.[83] Weyland makes the point that the Brazilian government is very fragmented, allowing for the typical factors in bureaucratic politics to come into play. But Weyland also tries to tie together the fragmentation of the state with pluralist models. He cites the arguments of Theodore Lowi, who argued that where the state was fragmented, policy-making gets driven towards distributive policies. In other words, each group can achieve access and capture a small part of the government, which it uses for its own purposes.

There is some support for this argument in the later policies implemented by the Brazilian government itself. President Fernando Collor's administration (1990-92) tried to combat this problem by introducing measures to centralize the federal agencies. The reorganizations of ministries may have lessened the problems, but certainly did not eliminate them. The next government, that of Itamar Franco, reversed many of these reforms.[84] The most important point to draw from this analysis is that bureaucratic politics probably mirrored the domestic politics discussed above.

Did Individuals Matter Most?

Weyland also notes that political parties fail to serve their traditional purpose in Brazil. Parties do not aggregate interests well. Instead, politics follows very personalistic and narrow interest lines.[85] This suggests that the personalities of individual leaders may hold key evidence for understanding policy decisions. Many observers have noted differences in the personalities of the various presidents who have led Brazil since the military government left power in 1985.[86] For instance, Jose Sarney took office as a result of Neves's death;

Sarney was not seen as a strong figure, able to stand above specific interest groups. Instead, he was seen to yield to sectoral pressures.

President Collor, on the other hand, ran on his own. His ability to hold off the pressures from narrow interest groups illustrates how an individual can make a difference. At the same time, we should recognize that the president shares powers with other institutions and therefore has little room to manoeuvre. While journalistic impressions make it appear that personalities matter, the evidence is much less clear.

Consequences: The Far-Ranging Impact of the Debt Crisis

The evidence suggests that while system-level pressures presented opportunities and constraints, the responses tried out in Brazil are best explained by considering the ways in which they were filtered through domestic politics. The pressures generated by the debt crisis hit groups within each country differently; each country had a particular domestic political economy which the pressures upset. Past practices created serious constraints on any adjustment policies, the most important in Brazil's case being indexation.

Brazil attempted to make its adjustments in ways which were not quite consistent with the recommendations of international financial organizations such as the IMF and World Bank. It hoped that a set of unorthodox policies would deliver it from the debt crisis with less pain and sacrifice than the orthodox strategies they recommended. These rival strategies never lived up to their promise, however. Their failure helped consolidate the dominance of orthodox economic policies, not just in the international organizations but also among the debtors themselves.[87] This may have been the most important consequence of Brazil's decisions.

For the borrowers, the 1980s were the lost decade in the sense that, for most, growth was problematic and investment difficult. This has not been purely the case, however; Brazil's real GDP grew by 16 per cent between 1984 and 1986 in the heart of the crisis. Overall, for Latin America, capital flowed out of the region. In 1982, the year the crisis started, the Latin American countries had $23 billion in new lending. By 1985, new lending to the region fell to $3.5 billion, while the interest being paid out amounted to $22 billion![88]

The commercial banks swallowed some of the losses and negotiated new loans with the debtors. Overtime, the U.S. and other creditor governments had to take more direct action in the crisis, however reluctantly. As a consequence, the creditor governments took steps to coordinate their regulatory efforts. They wished to force banks to be more prudent in their lending, as well as to lessen the competitive pressures associated with international lending. Their actions represent a remarkable example of international cooperation.[89]

Meanwhile, the IMF and World Bank found new roles for themselves. By 1988, the World Bank had issued more than 150 different loans as part of adjustment programs in 55 countries.[90] The two agencies were much more active than in the preceding years, though this brought them more criticism than ever before. Also, serious questions were raised about just what their mandates entailed and the appropriateness of the policy instruments and resources they used to deal with their evolving responsibilities.[91] These matters remain up for debate, as there are continued calls for reforming the international financial system. The failure of these institutions to provide successful assistance in the 1980s, and then again in the 1990s, fuels these calls for reform.

Notes

1. Also see Miles Kahler, "Politics and International Debt: Explaining the Crisis," *International Organization* 39,3 (Summer 1985): 357-82.

2. This and the next few paragraphs draw on Ethan B. Kapstein, *Governing the Global Economy* (Cambridge, MA: Harvard University Press, 1994) 84-85.

3. See Jeffrey Sachs, "External Debt and Macroeconomic Performance in Latin America and East Asia," *Brookings Papers on Economic Activity* 2 (1985): 523-64.

4. Sebastian Edwards, *Crisis and Reform in Latin America: From Despair to Hope* (New York, NY: Oxford University Press [World Bank], 1995) 19-21.

5. For more on the development of the Euromarket and its connections to the debt crisis, see John Loxley, *Debt and Disorder: External Financing for Development* (Boulder, CO: Westview, 1986) 65-71; James P. Hawley, "Protecting Capital From Itself: U.S. Attempts to Regulate the Eurocurrency System," *International Organization* 38,1 (Winter 1984): 131-65.

6. James Dinsmoor, *Brazil: Responses to the Debt Crisis* (Washington, DC: Inter-American Development Bank, Johns Hopkins University Press, 1990) 31.

7. Jeffry Frieden, *Debt, Development, and Democracy: Modern Political Economy and Latin America, 1965-1985* (Princeton, NJ: Princeton University Press, 1991) 61-64.

8. Edwards 21; Loxley 78; Dinsmoor 31.

9. Loxley 64.

10. These figures are from Table A.33 in Eliana Cardoso and Albert Fishlow, "The Macroeconomics of the Brazilian External Debt," *Developing Country Debt and Economic Performance*, Volume 2:, *Country Studies—Argentina, Bolivia, Brazil, Mexico*, ed. Jeffrey Sachs (Chicago, IL: University of Chicago Press, 1990) 385.

11. Dinsmoor 33.

12. Frieden 126.

13. Frieden 74-75; Cardoso and Fishlow 274.

14. Frieden 120.

15. This paragraph draws on Frieden's excellent analysis in Chapter 4 of *Debt, Development, and Democracy*.

16. Dinsmoor 65.

17. Rudiger Dornbusch, "From Adjustment with Recession to Adjustment with Growth," *Debt Disaster?: Banks, Governments, and Multilaterals Confront the Crisis*, ed. John F. Weeks (New York, NY: New York University Press, 1989) 209.

18. Cardoso and Fishlow 274.

19. Cardoso and Fishlow 335.

20. The first oil shock had been caused by OPEC's Arab members' embargo on oil sales after the Arab-Israeli conflict in 1973; the revolution in Iran in 1979 and the subsequent war between Iran and Iraq sparked the second oil price shock.

21. Cardoso and Fishlow 275; Dinsmoor 31.

22. Frieden 126-27.

23. Frieden 128.

24. Cardoso and Fishlow 295.

25. The statistics are drawn from Hugo Pregrave de A. Faria, "Brazil, 1985-1987: Pursuing Heterodoxy to a Moratorium," *Dealing with Debt*, ed. Thomas J. Biersteker (Boulder, CO: Westview Press, 1993) 176; Cardoso and Fishlow 275-76.

26. Kapstein, *Governing the Global Economy* 89.

27. For more on how the creditors were able to maintain a united front, and achieve cooperation to overcome the danger of free-riding, see Vinod K. Aggarwal, *International Debt Threat*, Policy Papers in International Affairs 29 (Berkeley, CA: Institute of International Studies, 1987); and Charles Lipson, "Bankers' Dilemma: Private Cooperation in Rescheduling Sovereign Debts," *World Politics* 38,1 (October 1985) 200-25.

28. Kapstein, *Governing the Global Economy* 96.

29. Thomas J. Biersteker, "Introduction," *Dealing with Debt* (Boulder, CO: Westview Press, 1993) 1. Interestingly, 28 of these countries were in Africa.

30. See Charles Lipson, "International Debt and International Institutions," *The Politics of International Debt*, ed. Miles Kahler (Ithaca, NY: Cornell University Press, 1986) 219-43.

31. See Robin A. King and Michael D. Robinson, "Assessing Structural Adjustment Programs: A Summary of Country Experience," *Debt Disaster?: Banks, Governments, and Multilaterals Confront the Crisis*, ed. John F. Weeks (New York, NY: New York University Press, 1989) 105-06.

32. Cardoso and Fishlow 302.

33. King and Robinson 106-08.

34. The quote is from Carl Greenidge, Finance Minister of Guyana in January 1988; Richard D. Fletcher, "Undervaluation, Adjustment and Growth," *Debt Disaster?: Banks, Governments, and Multilaterals Confront the Crisis*, ed. John F. Weeks (New York, NY: New York University Press, 1989) 125.

35. Loxley 26.

36. Loxley 125, 141.

37. Biersteker 5-6; see also Kapstein, *Governing the Global Economy* 96; Loxley 26; and Robert Liebenthal and Peter Nicholas, "World Bank-Supported Adjustment Programs," *Debt Disaster?: Banks, Governments, and Multilaterals Confront the Crisis*, ed. John F. Weeks (New York, NY: New York University Press, 1989) 94.

38. Biersteker 7.

39. Frieden, *Debt, Development, and Democracy*, 95.

40. See Cardoso and Fishlow 297-300.

41. Dinsmoor 35.

42. Dinsmoor 36.

43. Faria 176-77; Dinsmoor 36.

TWENTY-ONE | *Brazil's Responses to the Debt Crisis* [353]

44. Dinsmoor 75-78. These sorts of disagreements should sound familiar to any who have followed the budgetary debates within the U.S. government, where different accounting rules also exist.

45. Cardoso and Fishlow 300.

46. Dinsmoor 36-37.

47. Dinsmoor 36-37, 41-49.

48. Dinsmoor 83-85.

49. Kurt Weyland, *Democracy without Equity: Failures of Reform in Brazil* (Pittsburgh, PA: University of Pittsburgh Press, 1996) 25-26.

50. This point is stressed by Cardoso and Fishlow among others; see especially p. 301.

51. Cardoso and Fishlow 276.

52. Faria 186; Edwards 36-37; Dinsmoor. 96-97.

53. Dinsmoor 9.

54. Cardoso and Fishlow 311-13.

55. Cardoso and Fishlow 319; Edwards 37.

56. Dinsmoor 97.

57. Faria 189; Dinsmoor 9, 98-102.

58. Cardoso and Fishlow 353. See also Dornbusch 212-13.

59. Dornbusch 213. Also see Edwards 36-37.

60. Weyland 63.

61. Faria 187.

62. Faria, 189-90; Dinsmoor 99.

63. This characterization comes from Cardoso and Fishlow 277, 318.

64. Joan E. Spero, *The Politics of International Economic Relations*, 4th ed. (New York, NY: St. Martin's Press, 1990) 191.

65. Faria 192; and Kapstein, *Governing the Global Economy* 99.

66. Faria 193.

67. Bluff is Spero's term; see 191.

68. Kapstein, *Governing the Global Economy* 99; and Paul M. Sacks and Chris Canavan, "Safe Passage through Dire Straits: Managing an Orderly Exit from the Debt Crisis," *Debt Disaster?: Banks, Governments, and Multilaterals Confront the Crisis,* ed. John F. Weeks (New York, NY: New York University Press, 1989) 81; Aggarwal 16-17.

69. Faria, 194.

70. Dinsmoor 104.

71. Dinsmoor 105.

72. Dinsmoor 1.

73. Biersteker 4.

74. Biersteker 2.

75. Frieden 87.

76. Frieden 131-33.

77. Edwards 33.

78. Edwards 36-37, 40.

79. Weyland 55-56, 68.

80. Edwards 71.

81. Dinsmoor 112; Weyland 8.

82. Weyland 74.

83. Weyland 4-5, 184-85.
84. Weyland 75.
85. Weyland 78.
86. Weyland 187-89.
87. Edwards 42.
88. Kapstein, *Governing the Global Economy* 97; Dinsmoor 3.
89. Ethan B. Kapstein, "Resolving the Regulators' Dilemma: International Coordination of Banking Regulations," *International Organization* 43,2 (Spring 1989): 323-47 and "Between Power and Purpose: Central Bankers and the Politics of Regulatory Convergence," *International Organization* 46,1 (1992): 256-87.
90. Liebenthal and Nicholas 97.
91. See Richard E. Feinberg and Edward L. Bacha, "When Supply and Demand Don't Intersect: Latin America and the Bretton Woods Institutions in the 1980s," *Development and Change* 19,3 (July 1988): 371-99.

Additional References

Aggarwal, Vinod. *Debt Games: Strategic Interaction in International Debt Rescheduling.* New York, NY: Cambridge University Press, 1996.
Biersteker, Thomas J. (ed.). *Dealing with Debt.* Boulder, CO: Westview Press, 1993.
Cooper, Richard N. *Economic Stabilization and Debt in Developing Countries.* Cambridge, MA: MIT Press, 1992.
Frieden, Jeffry. *Debt, Development, and Democracy.* Princeton, NJ: Princeton University Press, 1991.
—. "Third World Indebted Industrialization: International Finance and State Capitalism in Mexico, Brazil, Algeria and South Korea." *International Organization* 35,3 (Summer 1981): 407-31.
Kahler, Miles. "Politics and International Debt: Explaining the Crisis." *International Organization* 39,3 (Summer 1985): 357-82.

CHAPTER 22

Canada and the Free Trade Agreement with the U.S.

Background: The Historical Parameters of the U.S.-Canada Relationship

Canada and the U.S. explored freer trade on several occasions after the failure of reciprocity in 1911. That episode was followed in the interwar period by the disastrous Smoot-Hawley Tariff, exacerbating the Great Depression. In the wake of this experience, Canada and the U.S. were able to strike several deals to liberalize their trade. Bilateral agreements in 1935 and 1938 were fuelled by the need to stimulate production and employment in any way possible. These were enhanced over time, most notably by the Auto Pact signed in 1965. Canada's high tariffs had attracted investment by U.S. producers who wanted to sell in the Canadian market. The pact introduced waivers on the duty for original equipment parts and automobiles, allowing U.S. firms to integrate their production in the two countries. In return, the U.S. manufacturers had to produce a certain percentage in Canada, with the amount relative to the level of their sales in that country. The target was to make sure that 60 per cent of the content of the vehicles sold in Canada was produced there. As Casper Garos points out, this is managed trade,[1] though it was liberalized compared to tariff barriers. Much of these agreements went against Canada's longer tradition of protectionism, especially those signed in the 1930s. As noted in Chapters 12 and 15, ever since Sir John A. Macdonald's National Policy (1879), higher tariffs had been seen as part of a policy package helping Canada to industrialize and supporting Canadian unity.

These same goals of national unity and industrialization had been put forth as the reasons to reject a U.S. offer to negotiate freer trade in 1911. Now, some 70 years later, it was the Canadians who initiated the talks to liberalize trade. The central question for this chapter, then, is why Canada chose to do so.[2] The impact of an economic downturn was perhaps, once again, one of the driving forces behind the decision to explore new economic relations. It was hoped that improvements in trade could be used as an engine to stimulate the economy.

By the mid-1980s, some of Canada's political leaders were also beginning to worry about ensuring access to the U.S. market. Industrial leaders and businessmen were increasingly concerned that if Canadian firms were to remain competitive, they would have to achieve higher economies of scale. That meant ensuring that a greater volume of goods produced could be sold—and the Canadian market itself wasn't large enough to support that. At Canada's initiative, negotiations with the U.S. on a free trade agreement were requested in late 1985.

Fears of the New Protectionism

Another issue, of course, was to provide insurance against several forms of potential problems in international trade. Of course, the General Agreement on Tariffs and Trade (GATT) had provided enormous benefits to countries such as Canada which rely heavily on trade. In the early 1980s, however, there were worries that GATT was in trouble. On the one hand, its principles and practices appeared to be under attack. As more and more countries entered international trade—including those such as South Korea which were using export orientation industrialization (EOI) as a development strategy—and the economically advanced countries were wracked with economic downturns coupled with rising interest rates, it was small wonder that protectionist pressures rose everywhere. These pressures were somewhat controlled by GATT rules; if a country actually raised tariffs, they allowed other states to retaliate with tariff hikes. The GATT rules, therefore, prevented tariffs from rising, but sparked an increase in non-tariff barriers (NTBs).

NTBs lie in the gray area of the GATT rules; they are clearly against its underlying principles, but they are difficult to control with explicit rules or codes of behaviour. NTBs are easily disguised as the exercise of a state's regulatory powers in the areas of the environment, safety, or health. If a state passes a law banning a particular form of fishing, or requiring products to include special features, this can effectively block imports from other countries. Yet, no international agreements would prevent a country from exercising its sovereignty or regulating its own internal affairs, though in GATT's Tokyo Round negotiations members had tried to do so. Their efforts were not entirely successful. A new form of protectionism was on the rise.

Canadians had a second fear concerning GATT. GATT's future hinged on the progress of multilateral negotiations, but the Uruguay Round was dragging on to ever greater lengths. Particular issues such as trade in services and trade in agricultural goods threatened to upset the talks. Without forward movement in these negotiations, many feared that GATT would no longer be a source of stability in economic relations, but would instead begin a steady erosion and decline.[3] As insurance against the possible decline of the GATT regime, in either a failure of the Uruguay Round talks or the rise of NTBs, Canadians sought a bilateral trade agreement with the U.S. The Free Trade Agreement was not intended to circumvent GATT, or replace it, but rather to supplement the existing regime.

Canada's Attitudes Toward the U.S.

Since 1972, Canada's official perspective on trade relations with the U.S. were dominated by views set out by Mitchell Sharp. His essay "Canada-U.S. Relations: Options for the Future" underlined Canada's vulnerability to threats from its powerful southern neighbour. Written just after the Nixon shocks, when Canada had been hurt by the import surcharge created, the essay stressed the need for Canada to pursue multilateral trade strategies. It was intended that Canada should lessen its economic dependence on the U.S. or at least find better safeguards for its trade via multilateral institutions.[4]

In step with this attitude, the Canadian government established several policies and agencies designed to carry out this distancing. In 1974, the Foreign Investment Review Agency (FIRA) was created to monitor and regulate foreign investments entering Canada. In 1980, the National Energy Program (NEP) was introduced to promote Canadian ownership of the energy sector. (This would automatically require reducing and limiting the percentage of U.S. ownership in that sector.) When, in 1982-83, the Canadian government reviewed its stand on trade policies, the Trudeau government chose to reemphasize a sector-based approach to trade policy matters.[5]

In the 1980s, the combination of monetary and fiscal policies in the U.S. increased capital flows into that country. Moreover, with the threat of rising U.S. protectionism, investors were beginning to calculate ways to avoid potential barriers. Even Canadian investors were looking to put their new investments in the U.S. rather than rely on continued access to that market.[6] Moreover, previous tariff reductions by Canada had increased trade levels, and this in turn had influenced decisions made by investors from other countries. Whenever Canada liberalized its trade relations, either bilaterally or multilaterally, foreign investors had responded by increasing their holdings in Canada. Thus, it was clear to Canadian decision-makers that investment levels were being, and could be, affected by trade policy.

Despite the Canadians' attempts to create some distance between the U.S. economy and their own, the two countries' economies remained—and remain to this day—quite intertwined, beyond having the largest trading relationship in the world. Canada supplies raw materials and energy to the U.S., is a very important market for U.S. manufactured goods, and receives large amounts of

U.S. investments. Not many people know it, but Canada is one of the top foreign investors in the U.S., so the relationship works in both directions.[7] While
the two countries have far-reaching economic connections, the relationship is
asymmetric—the U.S. clearly dominates.

Canada Initiates Talks

Canada's goals in initiating the talks included securing access to the U.S. market, opening up parts of the U.S. market previously blocked to Canadian exporters, and establishing special rules for some sectors (especially agriculture,
wine and spirits, energy, and autos). These talks were also seen as a way to
create precedents for other talks elsewhere—especially for introducing service
sector and investment issues, as well as establishing patterns which could be
replicated at the multilateral level.[8] Since any deal would supplement GATT,
these talks provided the opportunity to establish examples which could be referred to in multilateral trade negotiations.

Canada's first probing discussions in 1984 were aimed at replicating the Auto
Pact in other sectors. Unfortunately, the symmetry of such deals was missing,
which undermined the ability to reach an agreement. It was too difficult to
see where each side would win or lose; without knowing where the benefits
would accrue, it was impossible to create reciprocity. Rather than let this issue extinguish the talks, it was decided that any deal would have to be much
broader—and both sides seemed interested in this possibility.[9] Interestingly,
public support within Canada for some sort of free trade agreement with the
U.S. had existed for many years prior to the Canadian government taking any
action.[10] It appeared that there was an opportunity to make a far-reaching
economic arrangement.

U.S. Priorities

The U.S. saw Canada's offer to negotiate as an opportunity not only for immediate potential economic gains, but also as a way to establish important
precedents. For Canada, access to the U.S. market was an obvious priority,
since its trade and investments were concentrated there. For the U.S., Canada
was very important, but it had several other large trading partners as well.
The broader U.S. aims were to get issues such as the liberalization of trade in
services on the world's agenda, as well as to open up investment opportunities
and put in place controls on intellectual property.[11] The U.S., therefore, saw
these negotiations much more as a single facet in a much larger game.

This did not mean that the U.S. provided the most momentum in these talks.
Canada initiated the negotiations, not the U.S.—in fact, the U.S. wasn't well

prepared for the talks once they started. Instead, in 1985, thanks in large part to the rising value of the U.S. dollar, Congress was feeling all sorts of protectionist pressures. Among the strongest then being expressed came from the U.S. lumber industry and was specifically aimed at competition from Canadian firms.[12] Senator Robert Packwood from Oregon was chair of the Senate Finance Committee, and this gave him the vantage point to make the lumber industry's points a major issue in the passage of the Free Trade Agreement (FTA), since treaties have to be ratified in the Senate and the Committee is charged with reviewing treaties' impact.[13]

In short, the U.S. was interested in responding to Canada's offers, but it was unready to initiate the talks itself. It took some time for the Canadians to convince decision-makers in the U.S. that the issues at stake were significant. The talks remained low on the list of U.S. priorities for quite some time; therefore, the U.S. negotiators expended few resources in preparing their positions, and the talks seemed one-sided in their first few years. The onus for completing them rested heavily on the shoulders of the Canadian negotiating team. This poses another question for us—why did the Canadians place such importance on the FTA, given the somewhat indifferent attitude coming from the Americans?

Canada's System-Level Concerns: Insuring a Future with Free Trade

As suggested above, one of the possible factors shaping the position of Canadian decision-makers was the systemic environment. As the Uruguay Round negotiations dragged on, doubts emerged about the long-term viability of the GATT regime. As a nation dependent on exports, Canada needed some sort of insurance that it would have access to foreign markets in the future. The insurance aspect also helps us understand how the FTA relates to other multilateral agreements. The FTA was not meant to supplant GATT, but to reinforce and supplement the broader trade regime. Thus, this bilateral effort reflected Canada's fears about the collapse of the GATT.

Moreover, there were signs that the U.S. itself might start to practise more protectionism. It had already deployed some of its own NTBs, and more were possible. Tariffs were also possible, especially where the U.S. felt Canadian producers benefited from government support. Friction with Canada had occurred already, and the possibility that a new, tighter relationship could be constructed was apparent. One of the primary goals for Canada was to ensure that explicit rules governed more of the trade relationship. Within the set of goals about legal codes governing trade, there was naturally a set of issues concerning how disputes would be settled. This was very important for Canada, because in many disputes in the past the U.S. had taken unilateral action. Canada wanted a clear set of rules for the way in which disputes would be handled in the future. With clear adjudication, trade disputes could be settled with minimal risk of spiralling out of control as each side retaliated.

Canadian leaders stressed that since more than three-quarters of Canadian trade is undertaken with the U.S., Canada had to act.[14] There was too much at stake. If the GATT talks foundered, or if U.S. protectionism surged, Canada's economy would be seriously hurt. These broad calculations about the future systemic environment helped Canadian policy-makers decide to initiate the negotiations with the U.S.

Problems with System-Level Arguments

One of the problems with the system-level arguments just presented has to do with the timing of Canada's initiatives. After all, fears about the breakdown of the GATT regime had existed since the mid-1970s. The Tokyo Round negotiations were just as difficult as the Uruguay Round, though the number of states involved were fewer. The Tokyo Round was supposed to prevent the spread of NTBs, but it was quickly apparent that NTBs were going to be more numerous in the future. Nonetheless, the Mulroney government stressed system-level goals in its public explanations.

Mulroney and his Progressive Conservative Party (the Tories) also mentioned other reasons for pursuing the FTA. Prominent among these were the needs of Canadian businesses to improve their competitiveness. The economic arguments often centred on the need for new investment and investment in plants so that they could be as efficient as possible. Yet, the need for economies of scale had been present for a long time. The Tories still stressed the need for Canadian businesses to become more competitive, and that meant facing up to U.S. competition.[15] Perhaps the Tories were more sensitive to these needs than were previous governments.

Critics pointed out that Canadian firms had largely achieved whatever economies of scale were possible. The U.S. market was already largely open to manufacturers, according to Riel Miller. Certainly, in terms of tariffs, this point was true; in terms of other issues, there was dissatisfaction with the existing relationship. By giving up Canada's tariffs, Miller and other critics contended that Canada would be pushed to specialize along the lines of the country's comparative advantage in resource production, not manufacturing.[16] They predicted a decline in Canadian manufacturing if the FTA was signed.

Along similar lines, critics argued that the "New Protectionism" was no longer so new by the mid-1980s. Tariffs were already fairly low—as Duncan

Cameron wondered, what would their elimination bring? No more than a marginal impact on the final price of the goods.[17] However, there were other issues at stake. The Tories argued that Canadians needed to remove their trade disputes from U.S. courts; Canadian interests would be better served by the binational adjudication panels created by the FTA.[18]

All these points remained legitimate concerns, but they had been present for awhile. As far as the timing of Canada's initiative is concerned, therefore, the system-level arguments are too vague. They point out why such an effort may have seemed unnecessary prior to the early 1970s, but they cannot distinguish between time periods after that. Once again, we need to turn to domestic-level arguments to get a better understanding of just what was motivating the Canadian decision-makers.

Domestic Politics: The Electoral Strategy of the Tories

As Cameron, one of the more vocal academic critics of the agreement, argued, it was easier to identify those sectors likely to suffer losses in the agreement than it was to identify winners.[19] As with other free trade agreements, the big winners should be consumers—but consumers are notoriously difficult to mobilize as a political group. There is little evidence that consumers somehow pressured for this outcome. This begs the question: Why then did the Tories follow this policy? Shouldn't the opposition have been too costly?

One easily identifiable group likely to oppose the FTA, for instance, were the workers and owners of the large number of small U.S.-owned branch plants. These tended to be in Ontario; their operations often mirrored those of their parents, but were less efficient and had higher labour costs. They existed because U.S. firms wanted to leap behind Canada's tariff barriers. Once there was a free trade agreement, the U.S. firms could concentrate their production at the more efficient home plant—or so the Canadian employees feared.[20]

Thus, one of the domestic splits likely to emerge in Canada's domestic politics surrounding FTA had to do with differing provincial interests. On the one hand, the provincial governments themselves wanted a hand in the talks—which wasn't allowed, though there were regular consultations between the federal government and the provinces. Yet, as we might expect, in the end support for the talks fell largely along provincial lines. The west and Quebec were largely in favour of free trade, while opposition was centred in Ontario.[21] These splits set the stage for electoral political strategies by the federal parties.

As Michael Lusztig argues, the regional variation in support for free trade allowed the issue to become a pivotal question in federal elections.[22] According to his analysis, the Tories pursued free trade as a conscious campaign strategy to retain office. The Conservatives were strong traditionally in the western provinces; the pursuit of free trade with the U.S. would allow them to unite this established base of support with popularity in Quebec. Their main rivals, the Liberals, were divided over whether they should oppose the FTA.[23] Thus, the very strategy that boosted the Tories promised to split their opponents.

The Tories also had one thing going in their favour in 1988, when Canada embarked on this path: they had largely delivered on their economic policy promises from their last campaign. In 1984, they promised to deal with unemployment without spurring inflation—and this they had largely done, though the costs were a rising debt (which Canadians have had to live with ever since).[24] The electorate may have been persuaded by the Tories' campaign statements, since the Mulroney government could claim it had been successful in its overall economic policies. In the 1988 elections, where the FTA was the dominant issue, the Tories won 43 per cent of the vote, and 170 seats out of 295. The Liberals came second, with 32 per cent and 82 seats. The most vehement critics of the agreement, the NDP, won 20 per cent of the vote and 43 seats—this reflects the strong opposition to the agreement found in certain parts of the country.

Bureaucratic Politics: Canada's Trade Negotiator's Office

Besides domestic politics, there were bureaucratic divisions within the Canadian government concerning the wisdom of free trade with the U.S. For instance, the Department of Regional Industrial Expansion (DRIE) was one source of opposition to any free trade deal.[25] This department's job, after all, was to assist industrial sectors in trouble. Foreign competition was often the source of this trouble; certainly, DRIE was unlikely to welcome the elimination of tariffs. Within other departments opposition could also be found.

The Mulroney government perhaps circumvented much of the potential bureaucratic opposition by setting up a new agency to undertake these negotiations: the Trade Negotiator's Office (TNO). The TNO drew most of its staff from the Department of External Affairs. Since other agencies were wary of this new body, Simon Reisman, the head of the Canadian negotiating team, made a point of establishing a narrow agenda and laying out a limited scope of action.[26] His team also coalesced into a tight-knit group, whereas the U.S. team lacked a real mandate and suffered from weaker leadership.

The U.S. Trade Representative (USTR) office was not only understaffed, but the FTA talks were merely one job that it was concerned with, and that not even the most important one. Most of the USTR staff was concentrating their energy in the formulation of strategies and policies for the Uruguay Round. Moreover, the USTR was more tightly constrained in its mandate.

The U.S. team had to keep in touch with the other relevant agencies in the U.S.; most importantly, the executive branch agencies in general had to work with Congress if there was any hope of getting the agreement to final ratification. It could hardly have been more different on the Canadian side. Given the parliamentary and political party practices in Canadian government, decision-making has become centralized in the cabinet. When the cabinet moves forcefully in one direction, the Parliament and the bureaucracy follow.[27] The Canadian negotiating team was much more insulated from these other bureaucratic pressures because it had strong backing from the cabinet.

Political Leaders and the Ideas They Shared

Journalists have focused on another angle in explaining Canada's decision to pursue free trade with the U.S. This is hardly surprising, given that the political leaders of the two countries themselves have stressed how close their cooperation was. As conservative politicians, it is no surprise that Brian Mulroney and Ronald Reagan (and later George Bush) held similar ideological convictions. In the public's perceptions of the FTA, the ideological affinity of the two governments was paramount. The March 1985 Quebec City meeting, for instance, allowed Mulroney and Reagan to lay out their similar visions for free trade—and, as both are of Irish descent, they sang "When Irish Eyes are Smiling" from the stage at a public gala. The depth of their relationship was further illustrated when Ronald Reagan passed away in 2004. Mulroney was invited to serve as a pallbearer and to deliver a eulogy at Reagan's funeral.

No matter how close these two leaders were, we still may have doubts about the importance of their friendship to the trade agreement. As mentioned above, bureaucrats actually formulated and executed the negotiations. The top political leadership stepped in at only a few points along the way and then again at the end of the whole process. As Michael Hart described the talks' early months, the Canadians supplied the vision, the U.S. politicians enthusiastically endorsed it, but then U.S. bureaucrats put the brakes on.[28] The bureaucrats, as well as the politicians, were critical for reaching successful negotiations.

Even the ideological affinity of the two governments may not explain as much as one might think. The U.S. administration's support for the ideology of free trade did not necessarily mean it would take action to back up its verbal convictions. In fact, some have compared the Reagan administration's position on the FTA with its stand on budget deficits: "long on ideology and rhetoric but very short on policy and execution." What was more worrisome to Canadians was that the gap between rhetoric and reality seemed to expand the longer the administration was in office.[29]

In Canada, the Tories were ideologically behind liberalization, and they argued that they were simply following a longer trend in Canadian policy.[30] As for the negotiators themselves, on the Canadian side they were all "true believers" in the benefits of freer trade. That was part of the way the TNO team was assembled. As one, Michael Hart, explains the switch in Canadian policy, hitting the liberal arguments on efficiency, "...it had become clear that the resource base could no longer finance the maintenance of an inefficient manufacturing economy sheltered behind high tariff walls."[31] On the U.S. side, chief negotiator Peter Murphy was described as having "no vision and no compelling philosophy."[32] His experience had been in negotiations concerning the textile trade, the greatest area of managed trade in the postwar Western economy. Ideology may have been a motivating factor for the Canadians, but that point doesn't carry over to the U.S. negotiators.

Consequences: The Impact of the FTA

On January 2, 1988, Mulroney and Reagan signed the FTA. The preliminary agreement was reached just before midnight on October 3, 1987, after an erratic set of negotiations spanning 16 months. The FTA was intended to be a comprehensive and sweeping arrangement. All tariffs were to be eliminated over a span of 10 years. Goods were separated into three categories, with some having their tariffs eliminated right away, others in a period of five years, and the last group phased out in the ten-year period. The rules of origin (i.e., assessment of the content of a final product) referred to the value of the goods involved, with the limit being at least 50 per cent of the value of the good. This was one modification of the Auto Pact, since the rules of origin replaced the previous Canadian content rules. (And, of course, the duties on car components would be phased out along with other tariffs.) Investment and the service sector were also liberalized, though some areas were kept apart.[33] Also, Canada made the cultural industry (e.g., television, radio, newspapers, etc.) exempt, though there has since been pressure by the U.S. to alter practices in this area.

While the two countries signed a deal to coordinate technical standards (a common form of NTB) as part of the FTA, these rules are largely set by state/provincial governments, and therefore the agreement is not as binding as either federal government might have wished. Government procurement was also liberalized beyond the codes set in GATT. Agriculture was largely left in the hands of the GATT talks, though some Canadian special requests were maintained in the FTA. While there were promises made on the liberalization of trade in alcoholic beverages, these too remain largely in the hands of Canadian provincial governments, and little change has occurred so far.

Paul Wonnacott defends the agreement as the best possible deal Canada could expect.[34] The greatest success for Canada may well have been the institutionalization of new dispute settlement mechanisms. These have been expanded in the North American Free Trade Agreement (NAFTA), which adds Mexico to the mix. They serve to protect the free trade agreement from coercive uses of economic power, which obviously poses a greater threat to Canada than the U.S. The dispute settlement mechanisms also set up specific time limits for resolving cases, an improvement over GATT's rules and the mechanisms used in other free trade zones which allowed cases to drag on indefinitely.[35]

Within a few years, on August 12, 1992, the FTA was superseded by NAFTA.[36] NAFTA included several items the FTA did not, but in most ways it was built on the same base.[37] Moreover, the Uruguay Round was finally over, and it, too, borrowed certain features from the FTA. While Canada didn't need the FTA in the end, it was valuable as insurance and even provided a powerful precedent for other negotiations in other institutional settings.

In assessing the economic impact of the FTA on Canada (the initiator of the treaty), one must try to separate the impact of trade from the broader factors affecting the country's economy.[38] Critics claimed that Canadian manufacturing jobs would be lost in large numbers and that Canada would slip into the role of a resource exporter. In fact, the preferred jobs seem to have been retained, with adjustments in some sectors, and job losses best accounted for by other facets of economic policy. Canadian exports to the U.S. have grown at a faster rate than Canadian exports to other markets, suggesting that liberalization did have an impact.[39] On the other side of the border, the 1990s were a decade of unprecedented growth and sustained high employment, suggesting that the FTA and NAFTA were both good for the U.S.

A major question remains: Are regional arrangements such as the FTA or NAFTA a positive omen for the future of the trade regime? In this case, the regional trade agreement was intended to work alongside GATT. Fears that it would undermine GATT appear to be unfounded—though the same cannot be said about some of the other regional trade deals struck in recent years. Free trade blocs are not necessarily a problem for a broader regime based on similar principles, and there are those who argue that momentum for further liberalization might best come from regional agreements. Certainly, in this example, the FTA did not upset liberal trade relations elsewhere and may even have helped expand free trade by establishing a base for an agreement involving the U.S., Canada, and Mexico.

Notes

1. Casper Garos, *Canada-U.S. Free Trade* (Amsterdam: VU University Press, 1990) 8-9.

2. The fact that the U.S. was caught unprepared by the Canadian initiative is best captured by Michael Hart's title for the chapter covering the starting position of the U.S.: "No Anchor, No Rudder, No Compass." See Michael Hart (with Bill Dymond and Colin Robertson), *Decision at Midnight: Inside the Canada-U.S. Free-Trade Negotiations* (Vancouver, BC: University of British Columbia Press, 1994) Chapter 3.

3. Stephen D. Cohen, Joel R. Paul, and Robert A. Blecker, *Fundamentals of U.S. Foreign Trade Policy* (Boulder, CO: Westview, 1996) 239. Also see Murray G. Smith and Frank Stone (eds.), "Editor's Introduction," *Assessing the Canada-U.S. Free Trade Agreement*, ed. Murray G. Smith and Frank Stone (Halifax, NS: Institute for Research on Public Policy, 1987) 3-17, especially pp. 5-6.

4. Hart 14. For a very brief discussion of these ideas, see Garos 9-11.

5. Hart 17-22.

6. Hart 6.

7. Garos 4-6.

8. Simon Reisman, "The Nature of the Canada-U.S. Trade Agreement," *Assessing the Canada-U.S. Free Trade Agreement*, ed. Murray G. Smith and Frank Stone (Halifax, NS: Institute for Research on Public Policy, 1987) 42-48.

9. Hart 57-62.

10. Hart, especially 71-73, presents polling statistics in several places.

11. Hart 96.

12. Hart 114-19, 161-63.

13. Hart 142-52.

14. Duncan Cameron, "Introduction," *The Free Trade Deal*, ed. Duncan Cameron (Toronto: Lorimer, 1988) iv-vi; see also Richard G. Lipsey, Daniel Schwanen, and Ronald J. Wonnacott, *The NAFTA: What's In, What's Out, What's Next*, Policy Study 21 (Ottawa, ON: C.D. Howe Institute, 1994) 19-21.

15. Cameron iv-vi; also Lipsey *et al.* 19-21.

16. Riel Miller, "Assessing Economic Benefits," *The Free Trade Deal*, ed. Duncan Cameron (Toronto, ON: James Lorimer, 1988) 62-65.

17. Duncan Cameron, "Striking a Deal," *The Free Trade Deal*, ed. Duncan Cameron (Toronto, ON: James Lorimer, 1988) 19.

18. Cameron, "Introduction," iv-vi; see also Lipsey *et al.* 19-21.

19. Duncan Cameron and Hugh Mackenzie, "Manufacturing," *The Free Trade Deal*, ed. Duncan Cameron (Toronto, ON: James Lorimer, 1988) 118.

20. Hart 76-82.

21. Hart 128-29, 138-40.

22. Michael Lusztig, *Risking Free Trade* (Pittsburgh, PN: University of Pittsburgh Press, 1996).

23. Hart 122-24.

24. Cameron, "Introduction," iv-vi.

25. Hart 65.

26. Hart 124-25.

27. Hart 312-14.

28. Hart 68-71.

29. The quote is from Hart 313.

30. Cameron, "Introduction," iv-vi.

31. Hart 5.

32. Hart 239.

33. For a brief overview of the FTA, see Garos 42-47; for a more extensive assessment (and naturally a favourable one), see Hart, Chapter 17; also Smith and Stone 7-13.

34. Paul Wonnacott, "The Automotive Sector in the U.S.-Canada Free Trade Agreement," *Assessing the Canada-U.S. Free Trade Agreement*, ed. Murray G. Smith and Frank Stone (Halifax, NS: Institute for Research on Public Policy, 1987) 73-77.

35. Debra Steger, "Analysis of the Dispute Settlement Provisions: A Canadian Perspective," *Assessing the Canada-U.S. Free Trade Agreement*, ed. Murray G. Smith and Frank Stone (Halifax, NS: Institute for Research on Public Policy, 1987) 91-98.

36. Cohen *et al.* 240. For a comparison between the FTA and NAFTA, see Lipsey *et al.* 31-38.

37. For a description of the ways in which NAFTA builds off of FTA, and tries to improve on the latter, see Lipsey *et al.* 26-27.

38. For an overview of some of the literature on the subject, see Kenneth Woodside, "The Canada-U.S. FTA," *Canadian Journal of Political Science* 22,1 (March 1989): 155-70.

39. Lipsey *et al.* 149-53.

Additional References

Chase, Kerry. "Economic Interests and Regional Trading Arrangements: The Case of NAFTA." *International Organization* 57,1 (Winter 2003): 137-74.

Doern, Bruce, Les Pal and Brian Tomlin. *Border Crossings.* New York, NY: Oxford University Press, 1996.

Lipsey, Richard G. "Unsettled Issues in the Great Free Trade Debate." *Canadian Journal of Economics* 22,1 (February 1989): 1-21.

Lipsey, Richard G., Daniel Schwanen, and Ronald Wonnacott. *The NAFTA: What's In, What's Out, What's Next.* Toronto, ON: C.D. Howe, 1994.

Watson, William G. "Canada-U.S. Free Trade: Why Now?" *Canadian Public Policy* 13,3 (September 1987): 337-49.

CHAPTER 23

Japan, International Monetary Responsibilities, and Policy Coordination: The Louvre and Plaza Accords

U.S. Monetary Policy in the 1980s

Several prominent specialists in international political economy, including Susan Strange and David Calleo, describe U.S. monetary policy in the 1980s as the actions of a leader, but a leader behaving irresponsibly.[1] The U.S. moved to resolve its own problems with inflation, but these same policies had serious international repercussions. One we have already covered—the tight monetary policy pursued in the early 1980s drove up interest rates and sparked an international debt crisis. Since these same policies successfully raised the value of the dollar compared to other currencies in a very short amount of time, the financial and trade positions of the U.S. were affected. The U.S. soon was drawing in money from elsewhere as foreign investors sought high returns, shifting the country into the position of a net international debtor. The U.S. trade balance went into a large deficit, largely due to the dollar's overvaluation.[2]

Responding to Dollar Overliquidity Again

Due to the combination of policies pursued in the early 1980s, the gross national product (GNP) of the U.S. grew, as did total employment, while inflation and unemployment rates fell. Inflation was fought with high interest rates, while spending was maintained even though taxes were reduced. But a new problem emerged, as a large and consistent current account deficit appeared, and a massive foreign debt arose. Foreign financial centres were also on the rise, most notably in Japan. The positive U.S. economic performance, which was defeating stagflation, was financed by foreign capital. The combination of tight monetary policy and loose fiscal policy was arrived at more by accident than by plan.[3] In any case, the U.S. now faced a situation conducive to maladjustment with the central bank pushing for a higher exchange rate as it sought to reassert the dollar's international role, while the Treasury had to worry about a growing fiscal deficit.

During the first Reagan administration, official intervention in the exchange markets was avoided for ideological reasons. The Treasury's foreign activities instead focused on pressuring other countries to liberalize their capital markets. This was aimed at letting U.S. service-sector businesses enter foreign markets previously closed to them; particular attention was paid to Japan. The net effect of agreements such as the one reached with Japan in May 1984 was to encourage the flow of foreign funds to the U.S. The Treasury also began to woo foreign capital more directly that same year by altering tax laws on foreign holders of U.S. government and corporate bonds, and introducing new bond issues of its own aimed at the foreign market.

Several actors became concerned about the rising value of the dollar. Paul Volcker, now chairman of the Federal Reserve Bank of New York (the Fed), was still interested in defeating inflation, so he was unwilling to change domestic policy to reduce the dollar's international value. Instead, he spoke out against the consequences of the administration's lack of a coherent foreign exchange policy.[4] Not only were foreign governments increasingly asking the Treasury to intervene in currency markets, so too was the Fed.[5]

Who was in charge of international monetary policy? The Fed always guaranteed the Treasury that it would never intervene in exchange markets without Treasury approval, but at the same time the Fed never recognized the Treasury's right to veto any planned Fed actions. In the early 1970s, the Treasury blocked Fed interventions on several occasions.[6] The Treasury and the Fed coordinated foreign exchange intervention through regular consultation (the Fed Chairman and the Secretary of the Treasury have had the regular practice of meeting weekly for breakfast on Thursdays since the late 1930s), institutional bonding (through policies such as constant exchange of personnel), equal participation in operations (each agency contributing around half the funds for intervention and splitting the proceeds), and having all intervention for either agency handled by the New York Fed. But each bureaucracy was pulling monetary policy in its own direction: the Fed was tightening the domestic money supply, while the Treasury was running a loose fiscal policy. All the elements of maladjustment came together: other currencies were emerging as clear rivals to the dollar, other financial centres were developing to rival New York, and the Treasury had already begun borrowing heavily from abroad. The Treasury and the Fed shared responsibility for fiscal policy in the 1980s, with peripheral actors such as interest groups, Congress, and other executive branch agencies entering only after monetary issues became politicized by the mid-1980s. The fact that one of these other actors—Congress—posed a common threat helped drive the Fed and Treasury together, so that this example of maladjustment did not have the vitriolic public atmosphere one might expect.[7]

Although some sectors of the economy in manufacturing and agriculture were clearly hurt by the rising value of the dollar, the sectoral influence argument is not very persuasive, because these groups failed to take political action on monetary policy prior to 1985.[8] It was only after the split between the Fed and the Treasury became apparent that such groups focused attention on monetary policy. At that point, business leaders like Lee Iacocca of Chrysler and Lee Morgan of Caterpillar Tractor began to campaign for a lower dollar as the way to regain a competitive stance against Japanese firms.

Although some other actors benefited from the higher dollar, there is little evidence that they ever actually lobbied to support the dollar's rise in value. The most obvious candidates to engage in such lobbying activities in terms of both interests and access to the Treasury and the Fed were the large, money-centre banks, which had the most to gain internationally. These large banks had interests in the domestic economy, however, to counter their international interests; their portfolios were sufficiently mixed that they had no clear interest in supporting specific movements of the exchange rate. They had also learned how to turn exchange rate fluctuations into profits, so foreign exchange trading was increasingly important as a source of revenue. The rise and fall of the dollar in the 1980s did not elicit a strong reaction from the banking community until 1987, when the fall in the dollar's value made bankers concerned about a possible return of inflation.[9]

Despite these weak and varied signals from different economic sectors, a broad consensus among both political parties arose in Congress. Republicans and Democrats alike blamed the high dollar for the burgeoning trade imbalance.[10] In July 1985, Democrats in Congress, led by Lloyd Bentsen, Dan Rostenkowski, and Richard Gephardt, introduced a bill to impose a 25 per cent duty on imports from countries running large trade surpluses with the U.S. At the same time, other Democrats such as Bill Bradley, Daniel Patrick Moynihan, and M.S. Baucaus submitted bills in various banking committees to legislate specific foreign exchange market interventions when the U.S. was running large current account deficits. Similar pieces of legislation were later included as provisions of the 1988 Trade Act.[11] When Senator Byrd threatened to order the Fed to ease its policies via legislation on December 18, 1982, he reminded Volcker who was ultimately responsible by asking "To whom are you accountable?" Volcker responded by noting "the Congress created us and the Congress can uncreate us," although it would be hard to imagine that there would be popular approval for a radical change in the Fed's mandate.[12] Still, the threat of congressional action was made clear.

Within the executive branch, some Republican decision-makers whose offices were under pressure also fought to get a change in policy. Secretary of Commerce Malcolm Baldrige, Special Trade Representative William E. Brock, and Secretary of Agriculture John Block all argued in cabinet meetings in 1984 that the dollar's international value was too high. Secretary of State George Shultz identified the high value of the dollar as the main source of the trade imbalance, and thus international friction, with Japan. But each of these actors had no way to control monetary policy.[13]

In *Secrets of the Temple*, William Grieder titles his chapter summarizing the Fed's monetary policies of the late 1970s and early 1980s "The Triumph of Money," because the Fed achieved its objective of restoring confidence in the dollar. Inflation was reduced significantly, and the public's expectations of future inflation were altered. The Fed pursued its objective of strengthening the dollar regardless of the short-run economic repercussions on the dollar's international value, the trade balance, growth, or employment.[14]

Coordination to Bring the Dollar Down

The threat of congressional activity to mandate Treasury policy convinced the Treasury to respond to some of the problems related to the rising value of the dollar.[15] Once it decided to take action on the exchange rate, it had to abandon its earlier position of unilateral inaction in terms of the exchange markets and to seek to establish a policy based on multilateralism.[16] The multilateral approach was necessary in order to deal with the trade imbalance directly, while convincing other countries it could preempt the threat of protectionism.[17] In the second Reagan administration, Secretary of the Treasury James A. Baker led the efforts to coordinate the decline in the dollar's value.[18] During the 1985-86 negotiations the same split could be seen in almost all the major economic powers' negotiating teams. Finance ministers promoted currency coordination, while central bankers resisted. As a group, during these discussions the central bankers placed institutional independence ahead of other goals, including price stability and economic growth.[19]

For the Treasury and the Fed, the goals of policy were largely the same—ease monetary policy and get the value of the dollar down, without setting the dollar's market value into a downward spiral. At first glance bureaucratic politics do not seem to be a major factor, in the sense that each side agreed on the goals; there is still debate about the degree of coordination of their activities, however. The Treasury acted to push the dollar down, while occasionally Volcker used the Fed's policies to put the brakes on.[20] At the same time, use of the G5 (the group of France, Japan, Britain, the U.S., and West Germany, formed in 1985 to discuss international monetary policy) tended to reassert the

Treasury's control.[21] While the Fed and Treasury were interested in dealing with their own policy objectives, they seemed able to coordinate their actions in a satisfactory manner. As long as the two worked together, the domestic politicization of monetary policy subsided.[22]

This coordination of Fed and Treasury policies also required additional international coordination to be effective. In the Plaza Accords of September 1985, Baker found the other G5 countries willing to agree to help bring the dollar down in order to thwart the growth of protectionism in the U.S. Fears of inflation had also subsided by then.[23] In the Baker-Miyazawa Accord of late 1986, the Japanese agreed to lower their discount rate significantly, to proceed with tax reform, and to submit a supplemental budget to the Diet in order to increase government spending. The U.S., in return, agreed to take actions to stabilize the exchange rate between the dollar and the yen. In fact, by January 1987, the dollar was falling in value so rapidly that the Fed began to threaten to use interest rates to stabilize its value once again.[24]

The Plaza Accord: Japan's Rising Role in Monetary Affairs

As mentioned above, in September 1985 a secret meeting was held at the Plaza Hotel in New York. The U.S. agreed to take action, but only in coordination with Japan, Britain, West Germany, and France. While coordination in intervention in the exchange markets was agreed upon, countries pledged to make further commitments to ensure that monetary cooperation would work. The U.S. was asked to lower its budget deficit by reducing spending, while the other powers would increase their spending, thereby accepting a low rate of inflation. The aim was to bring the exchange rates of the dollar, yen, and deutschmark back into more reasonable patterns. The Plaza Accord ushered in a period of coordination among the major powers, at least in monetary affairs. Finance ministers began to meet regularly, coordinating not only their intervention in exchange markets, but also other aspects of economic policy.

What we are most interested in here is how the Plaza Accord denotes Japan's entry into a position of greater responsibility in managing the international monetary system. Japan clearly had reasons to take on a greater responsibility, due to its rise to the position of the foremost international financial creditor. The U.S. had been borrowing abroad, and in 1985 it became a net debtor for the first time since World War I. While it still invested a lot abroad, its borrowings now outweighed its lending. Japan, meanwhile, had used its large export earnings to build up its financial position, rising from $7 billion in external credits in 1976 to $241 billion in 1987. As Joan Spero points out, "Any efforts to stabilize the system and to coordinate economic policies would be meaningless without Japan."[25]

In May 1986, the major powers made an effort to institutionalize the spirit of the Plaza agreement via the G7 (the G5 plus Canada and Italy) economic summit in Tokyo. In particular, the leaders of the G7 countries stressed the need to coordinate their domestic economic policies in order to achieve their individual goals and stabilize the international monetary and trading systems.[26] They all wanted the same thing: steady growth with low inflation. The problem was how to attain this goal.

In accordance with these negotiations, the U.S. did take some steps to reduce its budget, while West Germany and Japan lowered their interest rates. The idea was to reverse the earlier trends set in motion. Now it was necessary to weaken the yen and deutschmark, while strengthening the dollar, so as to stop the dollar's descent in value versus rival currencies. But because each country was also worried about their own trade balances, each wound up not going as far as they could and then accusing the others of doing too little. This necessitated another meeting, in order to reaffirm the major powers' commitment to coordinated action.

The Louvre Accord

In the Louvre Accord of February 1987, the G5 (plus Canada) secretly agreed to stabilize the exchange values of the dollar, yen, and deutschmark (Italy also cooperated with these policies). By and large, these countries did not live up to their commitments.[27] The U.S. could not reach a domestic consensus on how much to reduce the budget deficit; since it took both Congress and the President to agree on the budget, the U.S. simply never got the reductions that the Reagan administration had committed to in the Louvre Accord. The other countries were reluctant to stimulate their economies as much as they had committed to as their part of the Accord. The one exception was Japan; it introduced a more expansionary fiscal policy in an effort to raise domestic demand and therefore to reduce its overall trade deficit with the U.S., among others.[28]

In lieu of macroeconomic coordination, foreign central banks were forced to intervene in currency markets. They aimed to keep their currencies from rising in value too fast as the dollar continued to fall in value. Soon the dollar not only stabilized on exchange markets, but began to appreciate. This result brought about the need to renegotiate the dollar-yen exchange rate. Also, the flow of private capital into the U.S. fell back to lower levels.[29]

On the U.S. side, domestic concerns continued to shape attitudes about foreign monetary policy, particularly the need to coordinate policies with other financial powers. The stock market collapse in late 1987 sparked renewed interest in monetary policy; there were many who were critical of the

Fed's policies. Scrutiny over monetary policy remained high in 1988. That year the Fed began to tighten monetary policy to restrain domestic demand in order to ensure that improvements in trade did not ignite domestic inflation.[30] The Fed was more concerned with domestic policy considerations than with the exchange rate, particularly given the upcoming elections and the apparent weakness of the U.S. economy. Monetary policy was aimed at stimulating the economy, while pressure was placed on other countries to change their policies and manage the dollar's international value for the Fed.[31]

Because the Treasury's actions had lessened the problems with exchange rates, domestic political activity aimed at monetary policy was reduced. Policy had deflated protectionist pressures, even as the legal aspects of earlier actions were coming into effect. The 1988 Trade Act gave Congress the power to review the Treasury's exchange rate policy every six months.[32] Under these arrangements, senior Fed officials come before congressional committees (or sub-committees) around 40 times per year, with the Chairman himself called upon to testify approximately 20 times a year.[33]

While the protectionist demands within the U.S. subsided, and the value of the dollar was eventually stabilized at a level satisfying U.S. policy-makers, we need to turn our attention to the other side in the negotiations. Most importantly, we wish to examine how Japan's policies were selected. Why did Japan choose to cooperate so fully in these accords?

System-Level Explanations: Japan as Rival Leader?

Traditionally in the postwar period, Japanese international monetary policy had been fairly passive, which meant that the undervalued yen remained undervalued. This helped make Japanese exports competitive. The Plaza Accord marked a change in Japanese policy. Japan became more active and also began to support the appreciation of the yen relative to other currencies.[34]

In the early 1980s, Japan had done nothing to alter its previous policies in monetary affairs. Between 1980 and 1985, Japanese interventions never included any significant purchases of the dollar. The U.S. was running its policy of "benign neglect," and Japan was also pursuing a form of unilateralism. The yen remained weak compared to the U.S. dollar. But by 1983, the governor of the Bank of Japan, Haruo Maekawa, was calling for some sort of "international concerted action." He added that the floating exchange rate regime "hasn't come up to our expectations." The main thrust of his position was that the yen needed to increase in value.[35]

The U.S. was hardly ready to encourage the rise of the yen to the same international status as the dollar. The distribution of power within financial relations had shifted, but the dollar remained the most popular currency to use in international transactions, especially since the defeat of inflation had helped to maintain its attractiveness. Now the U.S. wanted to counteract some of the side-effects associated with the higher dollar—it probably would have resisted attempts to see the yen replace the dollar internationally anyway regardless of the popularity of that move in Japan. In short, there were a few people in Japan who felt that the country's changing financial status required new policies, but most Japanese were interested in continuing to support those international economic policies which had built up the country's financial reserves—and that meant expanding exports. Exports would be helped by a lower value yen, not a highly valued yen. Such disagreements naturally make us turn to the domestic level.

The Domestic Sources of International Monetary Cooperation

The traditional undervaluation of the yen, plus the rising value of the U.S. dollar in the early 1980s, combined to create the demands for policy actions from the sphere of domestic politics. The currency trends accentuated the trade imbalance between the U.S. and Japan. The higher interest rates in the U.S. pushed the value of the dollar up, but also brought on a serious recession. Japan was able to expand exports, and while its growth rate slowed down from previous years, it was the only G7 country not to drop into a recession.[36]

As noted earlier, protectionist threats were on the rise in the U.S., where businesses which were losing ground to Japanese imports, including such important manufacturing sectors as machinery and automobiles, called for some sort of action. Sector-specific trade protection was one possibility raised, as these firms lobbied Congress. Changes in monetary policy were another. In order to head off demands for tariff barriers, the Reagan administration sought to use monetary cooperation to resolve the trade imbalance with Japan.

The first measures of coordination between the U.S. and Japan, the Yen-Dollar Agreement struck between Secretary of the Treasury Regan and Finance Minister Takeshita, occurred in April 1984. The central effort was to liberalize Japan's domestic financial markets. This was meant as a counter to any pressures for protectionism beginning in the U.S whose service-sector businesses would presumably have new opportunities in Japan and so would support the administration in countering any demands for protectionist policies against Japan. The end result of the international agreement, however, was not to change the relative values of the two currencies. Instead, as Japan continued to run a loose monetary policy, even more capital flowed from Japan to the U.S. [37]

The protectionist threat in the U.S. hit a new high the following year. Japanese businesses became more concerned in 1985, as U.S. businessmen began testifying before Congress about the need to take legislative action in trade policy. As Japanese businesses started to worry, so did Japanese bureaucrats and policy-makers. Domestic politics in one country soon influenced domestic politics in the other. At the same time, members of the Reagan administration also decided that changes needed to be made. Secret negotiations were carried out in the summer of 1985 by Finance Minister Takeshita's team and the U.S. Treasury, now headed by James Baker.[38]

If the Japanese had hoped to defuse the protectionist threat in the U.S., as many analysts think, they probably underestimated how much the yen would have to move to affect trade flows. Henning argues that the Japanese misjudged the amount of correction needed by a wide margin. The relevant Japanese decision-makers made a private assessment at the beginning of the process in 1985 that the value of the yen would probably have to rise to 210¥ to the dollar. (Readers should remember that when a currency rises in value compared to another, it takes less of the currency to buy the same amount of the other.) This target was further adjusted to 200¥ to the dollar.[39] At the Plaza meeting (September 22, 1985), when the yen stood at 242 to the dollar, Japan agreed to intervene to alter the value of the dollar and the yen. Over the next month and a half, Japan spent $3 billion in interventions.

Japan also agreed to other policy changes. It committed itself to further liberalization of the domestic financial markets and to a reduction of the government's budget deficit. There were also promises to allow greater use of the yen internationally; the U.S. extracted similar promises from the Germans, though most observers agree that the Japanese respected their commitments in these areas more than the Germans did.[40]

When the yen had risen to 200¥ to the dollar and then continued to rise in February-March 1986, Japanese businesses became concerned about the currency's value. They now wanted the rise to stop. The policy-makers shared the business community's concerns, though there was some disagreement between the Bank of Japan and the Finance Ministry (see below) over where the levelling off of the currency's value should be. From April to August, the business sector's concerns about the yen's value solidified and broadened, thus bringing greater pressure to bear on the politicians and bureaucrats. In response, the Bank of Japan wound up taking unilateral action to strengthen the dollar versus the yen by purchasing $12.4 billion.[41] What was necessary was some sort of concerted action with the U.S., and the necessary agreement was elusive. In February 1987, both countries were finally ready for a new agreement, the Louvre Accord.

Bureaucratic Politics: The Cabinet's
Relations with the Bank of Japan

In this particular instance, we once again have the ingredients for a bureaucratic struggle between a central bank and a finance ministry. The relationship
between the Bank of Japan and the Japanese government is a little different
from the same sort of institutional arrangements we have considered in other
countries. One might be mislead by impressions formed by journalistic cover-
age, too. The governor of the Bank of Japan holds the spotlight in relations
with the press. The governor announces policy on exchange rates and other
areas, though in fact, the governor is not entirely responsible for making such
policy. Unlike the Fed in the U.S., the central bank is under the supervision
and authority of the Ministry of Finance. Any decisions about intervention
in exchange markets, or international agreements, are made by the minister
of finance (though the prime minister can become more involved as well, of
course) rather than the central bank's governor.[42]

In 1983, when the Bank of Japan's top official was encouraging some sort of
coordination to increase the value of the yen, the Ministry of Finance seemed
to be on a different policy direction altogether. The prime minister and the
cabinet simply did not want a tighter monetary policy.[43] Because the Bank of
Japan is responsible to the Finance Ministry, the cabinet has the final say in
policy. Though the institutional arrangement is straightforward, there is still
room for disagreements to surface, as they did soon after the Plaza Accord
was reached.

The Bank of Japan was quite willing to increase the value of the yen as
required under the agreement. In fact, the bank's targets were perhaps even
above those of the cabinet. The Ministry of Finance and the cabinet anticipated less of an increase in the yen's value. The bank's governor, Sumita, and
the finance minister, Takeshita, publicly differed over the goals of Japan's
international monetary policies in February 1986. The value of the yen went
past the initial targets of 200 ¥; as the value rose higher however, even the
Bank of Japan thought it had risen as far as it should. Bureaucratic splits
subsided. From March 1986 the Japanese again presented a united front, this
time to stop the further appreciation of the yen. The U.S. on the other hand,
continued to urge the Japanese to push the yen higher, though the U.S. agreed
the pace of the increase should be slowed.[44] The yen continued to rise in value,
however. In about a year (i.e., by February 1987) even the U.S. policy-makers
agreed that the yen had risen enough, thus providing the basis for the Louvre
Accord.

How Miyazawa's Background Played a Role

In late 1986 and early 1987, Japanese officials sought to slow down the rise of the yen, but they needed cooperation from the U.S. to achieve this goal. Many people argue that joint action as taken in the Louvre Accord was possible only because of a change in personnel. Kiichi Miyazawa took over the post of finance minister; Miyazawa was a former official in the Ministry of Finance, who had developed extensive relationships with his U.S. counterparts over the years. He spoke English well, which also enhanced his ability to reach out to U.S. negotiators. Moreover, his personal beliefs about Japan's proper policies were reflected in his approaches to the Americans.

In September 1986, Miyazawa met with Treasury Secretary Baker, and they reached rough agreement on several subjects. Miyazawa's belief in the importance of a more expansive role for the Ministry of Finance (and therefore of Japan internationally) meant that he was willing to strike an agreement with Baker on the need for Japan to have a more expansive fiscal policy.[45] In return, Baker agreed that the U.S. would help stabilize the yen-dollar rate at 153-163¥.

These ranges were adjusted slightly in the Louvre Accord, which included similar negotiations with Germany; the yen's rate was now set at 153.5¥ +/- 5%. These ranges were secret. They were too high for Miyazawa, however. Psychologically, the rate of 150¥ to the dollar was an important barrier. He did not want the rate to go up to that barrier, let alone go beyond it. Unfortunately, he had already staked out some of his positions before coming to the meeting; when the agreements forced him to make greater concessions, he was left dissatisfied.[46] Even with the agreement, and the massive interventions that were carried out as part of the Accord, the yen continued to rise in value. The targets soon had to be adjusted, so that the yen stabilized at 146¥ to the dollar—still too high for Miyazawa, but he had to accept the rate if he was to get foreign assistance in achieving those targets.

By April 1987 the yen was at 137¥ to the dollar, and it would go even higher by the end of the year. All told, Japan carried out massive interventions in 1987. If looking at the combined amounts which the Bank of Japan and the Ministry of Finance spent over the course of the year in interventions in the exchange markets, it comes to the staggering total of $35 billion, greater than 1 per cent of Japan's GNP that year.[47]

Summary and Consequences: Currencies and Trade

The potential problem of dollar overliquidity remains, though it is a manageable issue, at least until a rival currency emerges (the euro may come to play that role). Japan has long accepted the higher value of the yen, as well as the need for further international coordination in international monetary affairs.[48] Japan is prepared to accept a greater, more active role in international monetary affairs. While it plays this greater role, it has not sought to displace the U.S.—the framework for successful cooperation is in place.

In the early 1980s, Japan and the U.S. pursued almost opposite policies. The U.S. had a loose fiscal policy while tightening monetary policy; Japan had a loose monetary policy with a tight fiscal policy. In Japan this caused a surge in asset prices.[49] Real estate became massively overvalued, for instance. The resulting bubble burst at the end of the decade, when the value of real estate came crashing down. This became a serious problem for Japanese financial actors when international capitalization accords were struck. In most other countries, banks are not allowed to count real estate as an asset in their portfolios; in Japan, the banks' portfolios had been massively inflated by their valuation of property holdings. International agreements on how to value real estate would use an Anglo-American standard, forcing the Japanese banks to lower the value of their assets considerably. While Japan can still boast of some of the world's most powerful financial actors, their relative strengths have receded.

The trade imbalance between the U.S. and Japan, and the tensions and struggle between the two countries over how to resolve this issue, continue. The relationship between the dollar and the yen will remain a point of concern for businesses, policy-makers, and politicians in both countries for some years to come. Fortunately, the agreements of the 1980s have provided the basis for some sort of bilateral management of their relationship, averting what could easily have been a major trade war. Instead, monetary cooperation has helped build cooperation on trade and strengthened the economic ties between the two powers.

Notes

1. Susan Strange, *Casino Capitalism* (London: Basil Blackwell, 1986) and David P. Calleo, *Beyond American Hegemony* (New York, NY: Basic Books, 1987).

2. See Jeffrey Frankel, "Six Possible Meanings of 'Overvaluation': The 1981-85 Dollar," *Princeton Essays in International Finance* 159 (December 1985).

3. I.M. Destler and C. Randall Henning, *Dollar Politics: Exchange Rate Policymaking in the United States* (Washington, DC: Institute for International Economics, 1989) 2, 28.

4. Destler and Henning, *Dollar Politics* 31.

5. Yoichi Funabashi, *Managing the Dollar: From the Plaza to the Louvre* (Washington, DC: Institute for International Economics, 1988) 68; Destler and Henning, *Dollar Politics* 2-3, 29.

6. Destler and Henning, *Dollar Politics* 88.

7. Destler and Henning, *Dollar Politics* 12, 89; David M. Jones, *The Politics of Money: The Fed Under Alan Greenspan* (New York, NY: New York Institute of Finance, 1991) 119.

8. Funabashi 69-74.

9. Destler and Henning, *Dollar Politics* 132-33.

10. I.M. Destler and C. Randall Henning, "From Neglect to Activism: American Politics and the 1985 Plaza Accord," *Journal of Public Policy* 8, 3/4 (June 1988): 323.

11. Destler and Henning, *Dollar Politics* 39.

12. William Grieder, *Secrets of the Temple* (New York, NY: Simon and Schuster, 1987) 473-74.

13. Destler and Henning, *Dollar Politics* 40.

14. Grieder.

15. Destler and Henning, *Dollar Politics* 43-44.

16. Destler and Henning, "From Neglect to Activism" 317.

17. Destler and Henning, "From Neglect to Activism" 326-27.

18. Destler and Henning, *Dollar Politics* 2-3.

19. Funabashi 46.

20. Destler and Henning, *Dollar Politics* 53.

21. Destler and Henning, "From Neglect to Activism" 326-27.

22. In short, I am arguing that domestic interests are reluctant to try to alter monetary policy unless there is an overt bureaucratic split between the agencies responsible for monetary policy which they could possibly exploit. Otherwise, it makes more sense for such groups to focus their efforts on changing trade policy, which is more easily broken down into discrete elements.

23. Destler and Henning, *Dollar Politics* 43-44.

24. Destler and Henning, *Dollar Politics* 58-59.

25. Joan E. Spero, *The Politics of International Economic Relations*, 4th ed. (New York, NY: St. Martin's Press, 1990) 60-61.

26. Spero 61.

27. Spero 62.

28. Spero 62.

29. Destler and Henning, *Dollar Politics* 60-61.

30. Destler and Henning, *Dollar Politics* 67-68.

31. Funabashi 57.

32. Destler and Henning, *Dollar Politics* 74-75.

33. Jones 113.

34. C. Randall Henning, *Currencies and Politics in the United States, Germany, and Japan* (Washington, DC: Institute for International Economics, 1994) 134.

35. Henning 137-39.

36. Henning 135.

37. Henning 140-41.

38. Henning 144-45.

39. Henning 145.

40. Henning 145-46.

41. Henning 147-48.

42. Henning 80.

43. Henning 137-39.

44. Henning 146-47.

45. Henning 149-50.

46. Henning 152.

47. Henning 154.

48. Hirohisa Kohoma and Shujiro Urata, "The Impact of the Recent Yen Appreciation on the Japanese Economy," *The Developing Economies* 26,4 (December 1988): 323-40.

49. Henning 158.

Additional References

Funabashi, Yoichi. *Managing the Dollar: From the Plaza to the Louvre.* Washington, DC: Institute for International Economics, 1988.

Ito, Takatoshi. "The Yen and the International Monetary System." *Pacific Dynamism and the International Economic System.* Ed. C. Fred Bergsten and Marcus Noland. Washington, DC: Institute for International Economics, 1993.

Naoki, Tanaka. "The Dollar's *Fin de Siècle*, the Yen's Debut." *Japan Quarterly* (April-June 1989): 120-26.

Rosenbluth, Frances McCall. *Financial Politics in Contemporary Japan.* Ithaca, NY: Cornell University Press, 1989.

Miyazaki, Yoshikazu. "Debtor America and Creditor Japan: Will There Be a Hegemony Change?" *Japanese Economic Studies* 15,3 (Spring 1987): 58-96.

Sachs, Jeffrey. "The Uneasy Case for Greater Exchange Rate Coordination." *American Economic Review* 76,2 (May 1986): 336-41.

CHAPTER 24

Germany's Role in European Monetary Union

With the potential for economic and financial disruptions associated with floating exchange rates, some countries have sought to recreate stability through regional arrangements. This has been most apparent in Western Europe where the members of the European Common Market had strong incentives to ensure that exchange rate movements did not undercut their efforts to construct a free trade zone after the fixed exchange rates of the Bretton Woods era collapsed. Detailed plans for European monetary unification were first developed as part of a broader scheme for political economic cooperation in the Werner Report in 1969. The report was developed in the context of the Bretton Woods system; the collapse of that regime made its specific recommendations inapplicable. However, the six original members of the European Common Market (Belgium, France, West Germany, Italy, Luxembourg, and the Netherlands) decided to retain some sort of stable exchange rates, maintaining their currencies within a band of plus or minus 2.25 per cent. This system was referred to as the "Snake."[1] As other states joined the European Community in 1973 (Denmark, Britain, and Ireland), they too joined the Snake. However, they found it difficult to maintain their commitments, given their very different economic circumstances.[2]

By 1976, the Snake consisted only of Germany and those countries able to match its tight monetary policies: the Netherlands, Belgium, Luxembourg, and Denmark. Yet, talks with the other European Community members about the desirability of closer monetary links continued. These led to the establishment of the European Monetary System (EMS), constructed out of the Snake. In March 1979 the EMS was enacted with its Exchange Rate Mechanism (ERM). (Britain declined to join at this time.) Under the ERM, states again pledged to maintain their currencies in a plus or minus 2.25 per cent band, but this time the currencies were anchored to a basket composed of the participating currencies. In other words, each currency had to fix its value against a single "basket" of currencies, rather than against each other individually; at the same time, each currency involved accounted for part of the basket itself. The lira was given special treatment with a 6 per cent band.[3] The EMS was designed to avoid some of the problems of earlier fixed exchange rate systems by having more frequent realignments of currency values. There were also special arrangements made to assist those countries needing assistance to uphold their commitments in the face of balance of payments shocks.

The Performance of the EMS

In the first few years of the EMS (1979-83), there were seven currency realignments. In the next few (1983-87), the number of realignments fell to four; then in the years 1987-92 there were no major realignments at all. The arrangement became more rigid than intended. Between 1979 and 1983, the deutschmark (DM) was revalued while the French franc and the lira were devalued. The higher rates of inflation in France and Italy continually drove down the value of the latter two currencies. The result of the realignments in those first four years of the EMS were downward shifts for those two currencies of 27 per cent and 25 per cent respectively.[4]

Despite some of these movements, or perhaps because of them, the European countries were pleased with the performance of the EMS in the 1980s. The system seemed to offer the stability of exchange rates they wanted, without locking them in permanently. It allowed countries with traditionally disparate domestic monetary practices to create some sort of exchange rate stability. Adjustments were made when necessary, but in normal times, exchange rates were firm.[5]

The next step was to create a single currency—one representing in practice the basket to which each of the individual currencies was fixed. The creation of the "ecu" was supposed to help make the impact of monetary factors become more equal across the board. However, because the ecu was never issued as an actual currency, it never had its intended impact.[6] Moreover, as a basket currency, it was comprised of parts of each of the member's currencies; thus, asymmetries within the system persisted. Since the single largest component of the ecu was the deutschmark (DM), many observers concluded that the EMS was little more than a deutschmark-zone.[7] Wherever the DM moved, the basket had to follow—it was impossible for the DM to be out of alignment with the ecu. In other words, Germany's central bank, the Bundesbank, was free to set an independent policy, while the central banks of the other EMS members could not. They had to follow the basket's trends, and hence the Bundesbank's lead. At the same time, the realignments of exchange rates and the existence of capital controls allowed countries such as France, Italy, and later Spain some room for independent policy manoeuvres.[8]

The EMS seemed to satisfy the needs of the European Community members for exchange rate stability, yet conceded them enough freedom to pursue their own macroeconomic policy goals. Why, then, would these countries give up that room for manoeuvre? Why would Germany, in particular, push to modify this regional regime?

Deciding on the Next Step: Monetary Union

In 1989, the Delors Committee recommended making the exchange rate rules the basis for even tighter monetary coordination—monetary union was the long-term goal.[9] Its report recommended that the European Union (EU), as the European Community was now called, should have a single currency. Unification of currencies was the next step forward; it would be an improvement on stable exchange rates, for all the risk in currency instability would be eliminated, and transaction costs associated with economic activity among the member states would be reduced. The committee recommended that the move be made in three phases.

First, the committee suggested a period in which the last national capital controls were removed. This would allow for the complete integration of financial markets. EU member countries would all join the EMS and hold to the ERM at this stage. Second, the members would coordinate their macro-economic policies. Monetary policies would be synchronized by having each member's central bank become a member of the European System of Central Banks. Third, an EU-wide central bank (the ECB) would be created, a new common currency introduced, and coordinated fiscal policies followed.[10] As with many other phased integration plans developed in Western Europe, the easiest steps were to be taken first, with each progressive stage being increasingly more difficult.

Since the EMS appeared to be working smoothly in 1989, these recommendations were accepted, providing the basis for negotiations over the following two years. By December 1991, the members of the EU signed the Maastricht Treaty,[11] which spelled out the obligations of the members in the various steps to monetary union, as well as establishing a timetable for the entire project.

The Goals of Monetary Union

There were two strands of economic arguments in support of monetary unification, both of them extensions of those made concerning the benefits of a monetary regime based on liberal principles, such as stable exchange rates and open capital flows. The first strand emphasizes that monetary unification eliminates the costs of currency conversion. To illustrate how high these costs could be, proponents of monetary union gave the example of a tourist travelling among the EU members, converting his or her currency after crossing a border. Since commissions must be paid with each exchange, the cost of converting currency added up. Moreover, there were risks associated with the changing value of the currencies, given that some were still not fixed.

Some analysts, such as Barry Eichengreen and Jeff Frieden, argued that the overall benefits of unification for eliminating the costs of currency conversion would probably be small. Though the example of a tourist paying fees to convert funds as he or she moved from one country to the next might resonate with many individuals' experiences, it was not typical of larger international economic transactions. Large firms and banks had already developed several techniques to accommodate the instabilities of floating or flexible exchange rates. Because the currency markets worked fairly efficiently, and with great speed, large businesses could hedge their interests; that is, they could cover their assets so that exchange rate changes did little damage to them.[12]

The second strand of economic arguments accepted German leadership of the new monetary union as a given. They emphasized the benefits other states would receive by joining a monetary system where Germany served as the anchor. Since it would be very difficult to opt out of monetary union once it went into effect, individual countries would, in effect, be forced to follow the group's monetary and macroeconomic policies. Germany had to work very hard to ensure that the ECB would be independent of political pressure. Historically, independence has been a good indicator of a central bank's stand against inflation. If Germans wanted to ensure that future monetary policy would be directed towards their long-standing preferences, ECB independence was critical. At the time, many assumed that the ECB would be a mere reconstruction of the Bundesbank and that Germany would indeed be the anchor—or rather, that the system would necessarily emulate German practices. As Eichengreen and Frieden pointed out at the time, there were good reasons to doubt such thinking.[13]

There were, of course, important political goals behind monetary unification. Many Europeans believed that economic integration required steady progress. If forward movement was halted, the entire process would be put in jeopardy. Many also believed that the EMS had been too costly to maintain precisely because it reflected a compromise between fixed and floating exchange rates. Rather than go to a system of floating exchange rates and the problems therein, they pushed the whole arrangement to the ultimate fixed exchange rate system: union. Paramount among the political concerns driving European integration has always been the desire of the member states to control German ambitions, or at least to lessen friction between the major European powers. Monetary union can be seen as an important element in the process of economically binding the European states together in order to achieve these broader aims.

Germany's Bargaining Position and the Process of EMU

Perhaps the single most problematic point in negotiations concerning EMU was the process to be employed. Some states saw the act of union as a way to force monetary policy convergence; others saw policy convergence as a necessary ingredient in the process leading up to monetary union. The two views distributed the costs of policy convergence differently and also created different projections as to what the policies of the ECB would be like. Germany had very hard and clear positions on these issues, which it wanted included in the Maastricht Treaty.

Germany wanted to force policy convergence before union. In other words, it wanted states to prove their ability and willingness to adhere to the union's stated goals before they would be allowed in.[14] Since the monetary policy aims associated with monetary union were largely those which Germany had long held—and successfully attained for some time—Germany did not want to jeopardize its own policy success by participating in monetary union. German policy-makers held that countries must make the commitment to the policy goals of low inflation and tight monetary supplies first; if they could not or would not make such commitments on their own, the new institutional arrangements would not be able to force them to do so. German policy-makers wanted to prevent having to pay for costly efforts to maintain monetary union once it was attained, so they felt that states needed to make the difficult adjustments up-front.

A second sticking point centred on questions about how new members would be admitted to the monetary union. Two formulas were proposed. One required the existing members to vote unanimously in favour of admission; the other required that a qualified majority of the existing members approve admission. Germany supported unanimity voting on membership, because it wanted to ensure that it held a veto over new entrants to the monetary union.

A third point of debate concerned the methods for disciplining members of the union. Germany wanted automatic fines to be built into the system; that is, any countries violating the union's performance criteria would be penalized automatically. This would force countries whose policies were disrupting the union's policies to bear additional costs so long as they continued to be a source of disturbance. Moreover, such punishments would serve as a deterrent to poor behaviour on the part of other members.

The poorer states in the EU asked for compensation as part of their fee for their entrance. As Lisa Martin has pointed out, their demands for compensation were made very explicitly.[15] As one of the richest members, and the one with the most to lose if monetary union went in a different direction than it intended, Germany would be expected to pay for these compensations. This followed the longer tradition of bargaining in European monetary affairs, for Germany had often made side-payments to persuade other states to participate in monetary arrangements.

Germany's preferences, revealed in its bargaining in these years, made it clear that foremost among its aims were to balance the achievement of monetary unification with the desire to keep maintenance costs down. Germany wanted to exercise some sort of leadership in this issue-area in Europe, yet keep the price of leadership to a minimum.

Also high among Germany's priorities were monetary relations with non-European states. Germany undoubtedly wanted to see the impact of third-party relations softened. There were always problems with the DM's relationship to the dollar, as there had been under the Bretton Woods monetary regime.[16] Whenever confidence in the dollar was shaken, people would transfer out of their dollar holdings and into DMs. As soon as confidence in the dollar was restored, DM holdings might be lowered. These were the risks of having a strong currency which foreigners wished to possess—a side-effect of having a currency with low inflation. A strong currency was attractive internationally, but international use left the DM vulnerable to international shocks, causing difficulties for monetary authorities. By having the rest of Europe behind the DM, it was hoped that the increases in the money supply caused by international flows would be spread out among the other members of the union, as well.[17]

System-Level Changes:
The Impact of the Long Decline of the Dollar

After the fall of Bretton Woods, experts predicted the downfall of the dollar out of the "top" or "key" currency role. Yet, the dollar continued to hold on, remaining, for the most part, the preferred currency for international transactions. However, asset-holders began to move away from the dollar and switch to other currencies. This had a different impact on various European countries, because some currencies were more attractive than others. Due to the relative independence of the Bundesbank, and that institution's historically embedded commitment to resist inflation, the DM was a good bet to retain its value over the long term[18] and so was a good substitute for the dollar in many ways.[19] Moreover, Germany was quite open to capital flows and had the largest domestic financial base in Europe, though London was still Europe's most important international financial centre.[20]

Germany preferred to spread the pressures created by the dollar's decline. Instead of letting the dollar's decline lead to increased usage of the DM internationally, the Germans, and the Bundesbank in particular, wanted to have people switch dollars for other currencies besides DMs. This meant finding a way to make these other currencies just as attractive as the DM. That had been the strategy behind the Snake and the EMS. In return, the other European countries hoped to have Germany's credibility in monetary affairs transferred to them, but without all the policy repercussions which go with earning that credibility. Germany had an attractive currency because it had kept a tight lid on monetary policy, which may have cost it jobs at times. For others to maintain that same credibility, even under monetary union, they would have to accept similar costs.[21]

The chief obstacle in getting others to follow German-style policies in the first post-Bretton Woods arrangements typically came down to the resources required for stabilizing currencies. If the others were to use DMs in their stabilization efforts, the Germans would fail to achieve their goal through other means. Handing over loans of DMs for intervention purposes to buy up French francs or Italian lire simply put more DMs in circulation anyway. So the main challenges for the Germans were to devise a way to create a zone of monetary stability in Europe and to diffuse pressures created by the decline of the dollar, but still maintain independence in their own domestic monetary affairs (i.e., not to let foreign holdings of DMs increase substantially).[22] While they refined these efforts in the EMS, its shortcomings left them in favour of monetary union. Thus, they exhibited leadership in moving to EMU, but they also made their preferences about the end-product clear to all.

The Domestic Pressures For and Against EMU

By most accounts, the strongest supporters of EMU were large corporations and financial institutions, which had holdings among the many different members of the EU and did business across borders. They stood to gain from the elimination of costs associated with converting currencies with each cross-border transaction.[23] At the same time, these very same firms were in the best position to deal with the costs of converting currencies. In fact, the banks were the ones making profits from handling currency conversion!

Of course, banks had another interest in seeing monetary union: the anti-inflationary results expected if the system adopted fell along German lines. Bankers always oppose inflation, because inflation makes money—the banks' primary asset and source of income—worth less and less over time. Thus, financial firms pushed for monetary union, perhaps as a second-best outcome.

The domestic opposition to monetary union came largely from those economic actors who did their business almost entirely within their national borders. Actors who earned their incomes largely from domestic business, and who also benefited from inflationary policies, could find little to gain but much to lose with EMU. Moreover, the real appreciation of their national currencies in the wind-up to monetary union invited imports, meaning greater competition for their output within their own market. The best examples of such actors were workers in sectors such as steel or auto manufacturing in France or Italy in the early 1980s.[24]

There were also two other sorts of opposition to monetary union, which in fact highlight the way the Maastricht Treaty covered much more than monetary relations.[25] There were those who opposed any sort of political union, since they saw it as a loss of national sovereignty. This sentiment remains strong in Britain, where it has ensured Britain has not participated in EMU. Similar sentiments played a role in the Danish public's initial rejection of the Maastricht Treaty. The same feeling arose in Germany, where the DM had become a sign of Germany's success in the postwar period. Giving up the DM for a new currency required the sacrifice of one of Germany's most potent national symbols.

There were also those who opposed the transfer of so much decision-making power to European-wide institutions which did not seem to have to answer to any particular electorate. Journalists referred to this situation as the "democratic deficit." Those who disliked the concentration of decision-making in EU institutions were hardly likely to favour the creation of a new, independent, supra-national central bank. Indeed, with the ECB's board playing a critical role in policy-making, naming directors became an immediate point of conflict between EU members. Given the distance between policy-making and accountability, these concerns may grow over time, rather than recede.

As for the policies this ECB was expected to pursue, greater support existed within Germany than perhaps anywhere else. Germans have long expressed a consensus around support for domestic price stability. Pursuit of this goal assured that the DM stayed strong. At the same time, Germany relied extensively on trade, which meant that the country was very interested in seeing a lower value of the DM, so as to enhance the competitiveness of its exports. This goal was clearly subordinated to the domestic goal of price stability, however.[26] Perhaps this is because many of Germany's exports are sold on the basis of quality, not price; Germany has long been a major exporter of machinery and other products where reliability is more important than price. Since Germany was likely to dominate the ECB, Germans expected to be satisfied with the ECB's policies. But, of course, the reverse was true for people in other countries. France and Italy had been known for having lax monetary policies aimed at ensuring employment levels, rather than currency values. To the extent that Germans were satisfied with negotiations leading up to EMU, other member publics were unhappy.

These points having been made, it is no surprise that negotiations led to compromise. Although the German government got the treaty it was after, Bundesbank officials were not altogether pleased with the results of the Maastricht negotiations.[27] The federal government carried the day in this dispute, since it was responsible for international negotiations, yet it had to rely on the Bundesbank to execute policy decisions.[28] Hence, we need to examine bureaucratic politics next.

Bureaucratic Politics: Bundesbank Independence

In a comparison of the array of institutions in charge of monetary policy in the U.S., Germany, and Japan, C. Randall Henning concluded that Germany has the most independent central bank.[29] This is consistent with most assessments of central banks. At the same time, Henning argued that policy outcomes can best be understood by analyzing both the structure of domestic institutions and their connections to groups within the private sector.[30]

Technically, the Bundesbank's autonomy derives from its statutory basis, the Bundesbank Act of 1957. This legislation not only established the bank's independence from direct political authority, it also identified the institution's policy goal: stability. However, as Henning pointed out, its real power stemmed from the broad political consensus in Germany that supported its independence, and the goal of stability. It was this broad political support for independence that prevented the federal government from "packing" the Bundesbank's upper ranks with appointees sharing a particular slant.[31]

The Bundesbank's independence sets the stage for bureaucratic politics, for its bureaucratic turf overlaps that of other agencies. Frictions between the two chief institutions in Germany in charge of monetary policy—the Bundesbank and the Foreign Ministry—occurred because they had different goals and experienced different political pressures. The Bundesbank was in charge of domestic policy and relied primarily on interest rates as the tool for executing policy. The Foreign Ministry, on the other hand, was in charge of exchange rate policy and of negotiating the commitments of concern here. It also handled decisions about foreign exchange intervention, though the execution of policy remained in the Bundesbank's jurisdiction.

In EMU, the Bundesbank was always distrustful of what the Foreign Ministry was doing. The Bundesbank's power came from its independence; since it would essentially be giving up its position in EMU, one would expect it to resist the changes. As Henning remarked, the Bundesbank's views on EMU were "publicly cool and privately hostile."[32] But as discussions on EMU proceeded, this position evolved; since it could hardly veto such a step, it decided to go along with the process. It used its participation to stress the need for strict conditions to be met before a country could participate in the EMU. This was perhaps meant to dissuade others from joining the project; if that was the plan, it didn't work. Bundesbank officials were probably surprised by the other European countries which gladly signed on to the severe conditions they laid out.[33]

The Bundesbank then had to fight to have the criteria for membership established as a condition to be met *before* membership.[34] Thus, its positioning, which was influenced by domestic bureaucratic conflicts, had a dramatic impact on the way the entire negotiations unfolded. Bureaucratic politics generated Germany's policy stance, which in turn shaped the results of the international agreement.

Consequences: Bumps along the Way, But Monetary Union Achieved

A variety of changes in the international system threw these plans askew. Most importantly, the end of the Cold War gave Germany the opportunity to push for national unification. By bringing together East and West Germany, the West German government took an extremely popular and long dreamed-of step—but also a step which proved to be quite costly. The economic adjustments and investments necessary to modify the East resulted in a hefty bill. As a result, Germany's central government budget deficit went from .5 per cent of GDP in 1989 to 5 per cent in 1991.[35]

Some countries had trouble meeting the criteria for convergence in the first place, without any extraordinary circumstances. Already, Britain and Italy were not meeting the performance criteria. Then came the real shocker: Danish voters, asked in a referendum to support Maastricht, rejected the treaty in June 1992. The EMS was thrown into turmoil.[36] Speculators did not believe that the countries could maintain their exchange rate commitments, so they began heavy trading on currency markets.

The Germans were forced to carry out extensive and heavy interventions in 1992. In September alone, the Bundesbank spent 92.7 billion DM buying up the British pound and the Italian lira. September 16 was the single largest intervention, when 36 billion DM were spent on propping up those two currencies before they fell out of the ERM. While the purchases of currency were sterilized (i.e., kept separate from the domestic money supply), a tight monetary policy had to be initiated, which brought on an economic recession. This in turn led to negotiations between various levels of government and the financial sector; a widespread solidarity pact on public-sector borrowing was eventually reached.[37]

In some ways, these crises within the ERM represented a victory for the Bundesbank over its opponents within and outside Germany. First, as noted above, realignments in the EMS had been fewer and fewer. The Bundesbank argued that other states needed to alter their exchange rate commitments to fit more closely with their domestic policies. The Bundesbank was pleased to see realignments used again, though this was a costly way to reach this conclusion. Second, the failure of several countries to stay within the EMS effectively meant that the preferred process for EMU would move ahead in the way the Germans wished; only those already seriously committed to the target policies remained. Policy convergence would have to come before union. Third, the explicit timetable laid out in the Maastricht Treaty was placed in serious doubt.[38]

As a result of these speculative attacks and the ensuing crises on the currency markets, the EMS band had to be widened to 15 per cent in August 1993. This gave the members relief from speculative attacks by making their commitments extremely loose. Critics wondered aloud whether a band so wide was really a band at all.[39] One economist, Paul Krugman, noted the irony of discussions about the politics of monetary policy coordination in the 1990s. In his view, such debates came full circle. In the early 1970s, fixed exchange rates were dropped because countries needed their independence. Then it proved that the independence gained was much less than expected. By the late 1980s, countries realized a need to coordinate their monetary policies, and thus monetary union was proposed as a mechanism for coordination.[40]

Despite these problems in the early 1990s, monetary union remained a central goal for the EU. The timetable had to be adjusted, and political leaders had to step forward to convince skeptical publics of the worthiness of the project. Their determination and will to pursue monetary union carried the day in most countries. In January 1999, 11 members of the EU fixed their currencies against each other so tightly as to make them completely interchangeable. This was one of the most significant preliminary steps to the final stage of monetary union. Despite the obstacles and technical problems of replacing circulating monies with a brand new currency, the final stage of EMU—the introduction of the euro into circulation—was achieved in 2002.

Notes

1. John B. Goodman, *Monetary Sovereignty* (Ithaca, NY: Cornell University Press, 1992) 186-87.

2. Barry Eichengreen and Jeffry Frieden, "The Political Economy of European Monetary Unification: An Analytical Introduction," *The Political Economy of European Monetary Unification*, ed. Barry Eichengreen and Jeffry Frieden (Boulder, CO: Westview, 1994) 2-3.

3. Goodman 191-93.

4. Eichengreen and Frieden 2-3; and also Jeffry Frieden, "Making Commitments: France and Italy in the EMS, 1979-1985," *The Political Economy of European Monetary Unification*, ed. Barry Eichengreen and Jeffry Frieden (Boulder, CO: Westview, 1994) 33.

5. Jose Vinals, "The EMS, Spain and Macroeconomic Policy," *The EMS in the 1990s*, ed. Paul de Grauwe and Lucas Papademos (New York, NY: Longman, 1990) 202; and Niels Thygesen, "Institutional Developments in the Evolution from EMS towards EMU," *The EMS in the 1990s*, ed. Paul de Grauwe and Lucas Papademos (New York, NY: Longman, 1990) 19.

6. Rainer Stefano Masera, "An Increasing Role for the ECU: A Character in Search of a Script," *Princeton Essays in International Finance* 167 (June 1987).

7. Patrick Honohan and Paul McNelis, "Is the EMS a DM Zone?—Evidence from the Realignments?," *The Economic and Social Review* 20,2 (January 1989): 97-110.

8. Paul de Grauwe and Lucas Papademos, "Introduction," *The EMS in the 1990s*, ed. Paul de Grauwe and Lucas Papademos (New York, NY: Longman, 1990) xiii.

9. Niels Thygesen, "The Delors Report and European Economic and Monetary Union," *International Affairs* 65,4 (Autumn 1989): 637-52.

10. Eichengreen and Frieden 4.

11. Eichengreen and Frieden 4.

12. Eichengreen and Frieden 4-8.

13. Eichengreen and Frieden 5-8. Also see the contribution by Geoffrey Garrett, "The Politics of Maastricht," *The Political Economy of European Monetary Unification*, ed. Barry Eichengreen and Jeffry Frieden (Boulder, CO: Westview, 1994), especially pp. 47-50.

14. This and the next sections build off of Garrett, especially p. 55.

15. Lisa Martin, "International and Domestic Institutions in the EMU Process," *The Political Economy of European Monetary Unification*, ed. Barry Eichengreen and Jeffry Frieden (Boulder, CO: Westview, 1994) 90.

16. Elke Thiel, "Die D-Mark zwischen dem Dollar und dem EWS," *Aussenpolitik* 33,1 (1982): 37-46.

17. Garrett 54.

18. For more on the Bundesbank's independence, and the connection between this and the DM's performance, see Ellen Kennedy, *The Bundesbank: Germany's Central Bank in the International Monetary System* (London: Pinter, 1991), and Goodman, Chapter 3.

19. See C. Randall Henning, *Currencies and Politics in the United States, Germany and Japan* (Washington, DC: Institute for International Economics, 1994) 317, Table 7.2, for international use of DM. Also see George Tavlas, "On the International Use of Currencies: The Case of the Deutsche Mark," *Princeton Essays in International Finance* 181 (1991).

20. Thygesen 17.

21. Paul Krugman, "Policy Problems of a Monetary Union," *The EMS in the 1990s*, ed. Paul de Grauwe and Lucas Papademos (New York, NY: Longman, 1990) 57.

22. Henning 185-86.

23. Eichengreen and Frieden 13.

24. Eichengreen and Frieden 13.

25. The following paragraphs draw on Wolfgang Rieke, "Alternative Views on the EMS in the 1990s," *The EMS in the 1990s,* ed. Paul de Grauwe and Lucas Papademos (New York, NY: Longman, 1990) 31.

26. Henning 178.

27. Garrett 64.

28. Henning 178.

29. Henning 84-85.

30. Henning 177.

31. This is similar to the sort of obstacles formed by public opinion in the U.S. which restrained Roosevelt from changing the number of justices on the Supreme Court. For the points on the Bundesbank's independence, see Henning 90-93.

32. Henning 230.

33. Henning 230-31.

34. Henning 231-32.

35. Garrett 58.

36. Eichengreen and Frieden 4.

37. Henning 241.

38. Henning 243-44.

39. Eichengreen and Frieden 5.

40. Krugman 56.

Additional References

Cobham, David. "Strategies for Monetary Integration Revisited." *Journal of Common Market Studies* 27,3 (March 1989): 203-18.

Eichengreen, Barry, and Jeffry Frieden (eds.). *The Political Economy of European Monetary Unification.* Boulder, Co: Westview, 1994.

Fratianni, Michele, Jürgen von Hagen, and Christopher Waller. "The Maastricht Way to EMU." *Princeton Essays in International Finance* 187 (June 1992).

Gros, Daniel. "Paradigms for the Monetary Union of Europe." *Journal of Common Market Studies* 27,3 (March 1989): 219-30.

Minford, Patrick. "The Path to Monetary Union in Europe." *The World Economy* 16,1 (January 1993): 17-28.

CHAPTER 25
Mahathir, Financial Crisis, and Malaysia's Capital Controls

In the early 1990s, many countries opened their national financial markets to international investors. In the second half of the decade, several crises struck the international financial system, drawing in many of these countries. Investors shifted assets to avoid risks, and the rapid movement of capital upset exchange rates, undid development plans, and wreaked havoc on local economies, particularly among the newly industrializing countries of Asia. Some pointed their fingers at the countries themselves, accusing them of lax internal regulation that left them vulnerable. Others blamed the policy advice from the IMF and World Bank. These two institutions held incredible ideological power, especially in the years after the collapse of the Soviet Union. They had encouraged the liberalization of financial markets across the globe. Now, less than a decade later, the countries that had followed their advice were swept up in enormous international financial crises.

Debates linger over the relative importance of different factors as the source of the East Asian financial crisis. Unsurprisingly, evidence suggests that both internal and external factors conjoined to make it particularly severe. Liberalization had been urged without adequate attention to internal regulatory practices, making both the international financial institutions (IFIs) and the national governments responsible for the situation. In the wake of the crisis, the IMF and World Bank have seriously reconsidered the sort of advice they had been giving. Some of the sharpest criticisms have come from those within the organizations.[1] Numerous countries have also rethought their acceptance of policy recommendations from the IFIs, though market liberalization remains the general trend.

In this chapter, we consider one country that bucked the trend—Malaysia. As countries struggled to respond to the mess in financial markets, Malaysia did the one thing almost all economists had argued against: it reversed course from market liberalization, instituting capital controls instead. Capital controls are legal restrictions on the movement of invested capital into or out of a country. The vast majority of economists had strenuously argued against capital controls for several reasons. The most obvious was that in a world where so many countries had opened up their economies to international investments, any state that chose to put restrictions on capital inflows would likely drive investors to put their money elsewhere. Capital controls can also distort investors' decisions by forcing them to calculate risks based on non-market factors.

Of course, those in favour of capital controls emphasize this last point in their own arguments. Markets are not always stable, and in the post-Cold War era, international investments have grown to tremendous size. Moreover, these investments are mostly short-term flows—they reflect money moving over borders rapidly, capturing profits by exploiting shifting exchange rates. Such short-term flows dwarf not only the volume of trade in goods, but also in long-term investments. Those who argued that capital controls could be beneficial typically emphasized the difference between long- and short-term flows. The market effects of short-term flows were often too disruptive, with few benefits for economically developing countries, and they often introduced great risk. These countries needed foreign capital, but in the form of long-term investments. When short-term flows fled, they typically destroyed the investment climate for long-term investors and hurt domestic financial actors as well. Thus, there was a good logic for using capital controls to limit short-term flows while still encouraging more lasting investments.

Malaysia Turns Its Back on the IFIs

In the early 1990s, Malaysia had been one of the favourite destinations for international capital. Unlike other Asian countries, it had fairly strong domestic regulations in place for its financial actors. Foreign investment focused on the local stock market, but to prevent certain risks, the government did not allow banks to borrow heavily from abroad, although it did so itself. It then redirected the capital to those sectors or firms it targeted in its development plans. Because the country had struggled with a steady current account deficit in the 1990s, it could only afford to run this deficit by continued inflows of foreign capital. Thus, when a worldwide financial crisis occurred in the spring of 1997, Malaysia soon became involved. Investors withdrew their funds from abroad, either to cover losses elsewhere or simply as a cautionary step. When investors fled the Malaysian stock market and refused to extend new credit to the government, Malaysia's economic strategy was no longer tenable. Little had changed within the Malaysian economy to spark these moves, other than the loss of Malaysian exports to its neighbours who were already in the throes of the crisis.

The situation was starkly reminiscent of the debt crisis of the early 1980s. As the IMF and World Bank hastened to put together fresh packages of capital for the countries caught up in the crisis, they also tried to develop coherent policy recommendations aimed at fixing the economic situation and retrieving investors' confidence in these developing countries. Knowing investors would be shy for some time to come, the IFIs were considering the longer-time horizon. They therefore argued against capital controls, suggesting that such regulations would only dissuade investors from returning. Instead, they urged the same sort of policies for all countries: decrease government spending, reduce imports while increasing exports, amass foreign exchange, and improve standing in the eyes of creditors.

In September 1998, Malaysia rejected this advice and introduced capital controls, becoming the first country to reverse course. These regulations had two separate goals.[2] One was to prevent further speculation against Malaysia's currency, the ringgit. The laws enacted limited the ability of foreigners to hold the currency and also forced the repatriation of ringgit held abroad. The second goal was to prevent further capital flight, so portfolio investments held by foreigners were blocked from exiting the country for one year, and the ability of Malaysian citizens to move investments out of the country was severely restricted. Long-term investments were largely unaffected by the new laws. In coordination with these capital controls, the government also pegged the exchange rate. By locking international capital in place and preventing speculation against the ringgit, the government then instituted policies aimed at stimulating the domestic economy. This was its solution to the trade-offs captured in the Mundell-Fleming model (described in Chapter 8): by fixing the exchange rate and controlling capital flows. It had regained autonomy over domestic monetary policy, allowing the government to lower interest rates and increase fiscal expenditures in an effort to stimulate the economy, quite the opposite of the IFIs' advice.

To many observers, the capital controls may have garnered more attention than they deserve. Such regulations might have been effective in limiting incoming short-term capital flows, thereby decreasing the country's vulnerability to a shock, if they had been instituted prior to the crisis occurring. Some say that by September 1998, there were no short-term capital flows to be concerned about. If anything, the problem had become encouraging short-term capital back into the country. Long-term capital investments had already reacted to the crisis. Though foreign direct investments were still in place, much of the international portfolio investments had already been withdrawn.[3]

The question addressed in this chapter, however, is how we can understand Malaysia's decision. It appeared to be the lone exception to the pattern, the one country thumbing its nose at the IMF and World Bank. Indeed, Malaysia's leader, Dr. Mahathir Mohamad, was one of the most vociferous critics of the IFIs and of international investors. As described below, his criticisms were often overblown, and some were certainly misguided. Some observers therefore emphasize his role in the decision. Competing explanations exist, including those that stress the discrediting of liberal market practices. In a crisis so severe, policy-makers were interested in exploring alternative ideas. Certainly Malaysia's actions reignited a debate among economists over the efficacy of capital controls. One thing should be clear, however: the system-level pressures seemed to have pushed most other countries away from capital controls.

The Pressure for Conforming to Orthodoxy

As the financial crisis broke in the spring of 1997, the IMF and World Bank reacted as they had in previous international emergencies. They urged a set of policies designed to rectify balance of payments deficits. These policies promote exports and make importing more expensive; they also assist governments in amassing capital. If governments institute these policies in an effort to place themselves in a better position for the longer term, the IFIs extend short-term credit. Typically, loans from the IFIs signal an endorsement of the borrower's efforts, thereby triggering increased flows of private credit.

These policies can be very helpful for countries facing monetary policy problems sparked by trade adjustment. Yet, the countries caught up in the 1997 financial crisis were facing a variety of problems. Though we still debate the reasons for the crisis, there is a general consensus that these countries were vulnerable. As financial markets tightened, the countries of East Asia could not afford the withdrawal of capital. While it is true that in most of these countries prices of certain assets had been pushed to unsustainable heights by rapid economic growth, other sources of vulnerability varied. South Korea faced a liquidity crisis. As its debts were called in and capital withdrawn, South Korean banks or firms could not liquidate assets quickly enough to make up the difference. Once short-term financing was made available by the U.S. and the IFIs, the crisis eased. In Indonesia, the problem was much more severe, because the financial system was much weaker. Indonesia's banks had been loosely regulated, with many ties between the financial actors, politicians, the state, and favoured private firms. In systems where cronyism has taken hold, risks are calculated according to political rather than economic factors. The crisis forced a return to economic calculations, exposing how foolish (in economic terms) much of the lending had been. As the economic situation deteriorated, so did the political position of the governing elite. The two collapsed together.

Malaysia had been doing well in trade up to the beginning of the crisis, and its economy was healthy according to most assessments. Why then was it caught up in the crisis? The one soft spot was its current account deficit, but this had not been a problem in the previous several years, so it could hardly be considered the source of the difficulty now. Some economists, including Jeffrey Sachs, argued that Malaysia and others were simply caught up in market panic. As investors lost money in Indonesia and elsewhere, they pulled out of international investment altogether. These pull-outs affected the markets negatively, signalling weaknesses to other investors. Once the financial markets turned against a country, the withdrawal of funds grew from a trickle to a flood. Investors therefore generated a self-fulfilling prophecy.

Sachs and others offered this description because they were critical of the IFIs' policy recommendations. The IFIs viewed the problem through a particular lens, though they also saw the cronyism in Indonesia as another problem to be dealt with. The IFIs had encouraged financial market liberalization earlier in the 1990s, but now realized that liberalization without prudential domestic regulation had been a recipe for disaster. They therefore recommended their traditional policies of balance of payments adjustment along with calls for new rules for overseeing domestic financial systems. Yet, as noted above, the sources of vulnerability differed greatly from one country to another—the policy recommendations looked similar across cases. And when considering Malaysia's situation, the solutions did not look terribly attractive.

Still system-level theories hold that Malaysia would have to comply with the IFIs' policies. There were no other clear sources of capital in the short-term, other than the IFIs, the governments that provide the IFIs their funding, or private capital markets that rely on the IFIs' expertise when calculating where to place investments. Ignoring the IFIs' advice involved the great possibility of losing access to all three of these sources of capital. It was quite rare to see countries reject the IFIs' policies so dramatically. As discussed in Chapter 21, Brazil tried to develop policies out of step with the IMF's recommendations in the 1980s debt crisis. It stood alone in these efforts and gained little before returning to orthodoxy. Malaysia's actions in the 1990s were more successful, if only because so many were now critical of the IMF and World Bank.

Mahathir, Anwar, and the Struggle for Leadership

In deciding to reject the IFIs' recommendations, Malaysia's policy-makers were surely focusing on the domestic scene. The IFIs' policies would naturally create economic hardships, which Malaysia's leaders wanted to avoid. Just as importantly, the crisis had already exposed splits within the ruling party, the United Malays National Organization (UMNO). Deciding how to respond to the crisis exacerbated these splits, since any policy would affect powerful domestic interests. It should be no surprise, then, to find a link between the fight over policy and an internal struggle for leadership of the UMNO.

Since Malaysia's independence from Britain in 1957, the UMNO has been the country's most powerful party. In the 1970s, Dr. Mahathir Mohamad became one of its leaders, eventually becoming prime minister in 1981. Thus, he had been in office for 16 years by the time the East Asian financial crisis struck. While he could take much of the credit for guiding Malaysia's successful economic development in the 1980s, he had faced several leadership challenges in those years as well. On the one hand, Mahathir's political success was due to his close links with indigenous big business, since the UMNO championed ethnic Malay entrepreneurs, or *bumiputera*, favouring them over ethnic Chinese businessmen. On the other hand, Mahathir showed he was willing to use heavy-handed tactics against his critics. In 1987, his election as leader of the UMNO was challenged. He responded by closing down some newspapers, jailing opponents, and exercising pressures on the judicial system. These two elements—his close connections with the *bumiputera* and his choice of tactics in dealing with opposition—resurfaced in the East Asian financial crisis.

As investment dropped off steeply in the early stages of the crisis, those large businesses that had succeeded because of connections to the UMNO government, preferential treatment, and/or cheap credit from banks with close government ties, were under threat. This translated into divisions within the UMNO. Deputy Prime Minister Anwar Ibrahim signalled that he would pursue orthodox economic policies. Anwar had risen to his powerful post because he was Mahathir's heir-apparent. He warned the *bumiputera* that the country could not afford to protect them from losses. He would not bail them out, suggesting instead that the firms weather the storm, with the healthiest surviving but the weakest failing. Mahathir saw this as a threat to his power base. Others also saw this as Anwar's attempt to speed up a transition from Mahathir's leadership to his own. As the crisis continued, Anwar's supporters suggested that Mahathir had corrupt links to some of the businesses demanding government help.

Anwar favoured steps paralleling those imposed in IMF-sanctioned programs, indicating to investors that Malaysia would implement conservative policies to their liking. In December 1997 he authorized a reduction in government spending by 18 per cent, and other stiff measures were announced. This was meant to reassure international investors, since Mahathir continually voiced complaints that were bound to be scaring them off. As long as Anwar had control over economic policy, he kept it along orthodox lines and maintained investors' confidence. However, Mahathir would not allow his supporters to continue to be hurt by government policy.

Mahathir had to know that removing his deputy would spark panic among foreign investors. A similar situation had already unfolded in neighbouring

Indonesia, where the political upheaval surrounding the fall of Soeharto had triggered a crash of the stock market. Given that investors were already jittery by the summer of 1998, Mahathir would not be able to remove Anwar without worsening the economic situation. He must have thought capital controls could cushion Malaysia from these economic and political blows and was determined to remove his rival.[4] Capital controls can thus be seen as a measure lowering the costs of removing Anwar.

Capital controls also afforded Mahathir's government the opportunity to take other steps that would have driven international investors to withdraw their funds. Most obvious, the capital controls gave the government a solution to the Mundell-Fleming conditions: it now had domestic monetary policy autonomy. After the controls were announced, the government introduced a stimulus package ($12 billion in new spending) and reduced domestic interest rates. It also forced banks to increase their lending significantly. Such policies helped the economy recover and would never have been possible if the government had been following the recommendations of the IFIs.

Of course, this also allowed Mahathir to rescue the economic fortunes of his supporters. One major benefactor of this policy was Renong, an investment firm tied to the ruling party. The government also forced the consolidation of the private financial sector by ordering the 58 existing firms to reorganize into six large groups.[5] The danger of having such large groups, formed under government direction and of sizable fiscal expenditures, is that the state leaders can use these measures for their own political advantage. Additional spending often targets political allies, not enemies. The same can be said when politicians reconfigure business sectors, as in this case: their friends come out on top.

Mahathir now moved swiftly. Capital controls were announced on September 1, 1998. Anwar was sacked from his office as deputy prime minister the next day. The top officials of Malaysia's central bank were also ousted for opposing the new regulations. By September 18, Mahathir had Anwar jailed for corruption and homosexuality. (Since the majority of Malaysians are Muslim, not only is homosexuality a crime, but something the majority finds extremely unpopular.) In line with earlier leadership struggles, Mahathir used the UMNO's power over the press and his control of the judiciary to attack Anwar and his supporters. Anwar's backers reacted by rioting in the streets.

In June 1998 Mahathir had already positioned Anwar's replacement to take over economic policy. He appointed Daim Zainuddin Minister Responsible for Economic Development. Daim, a millionaire businessman, had served as finance minister before, but was closely linked to several large Malay firms. Mahathir and Daim introduced the capital controls, stimulated the economy, and directed funds to aid their supporters within the UMNO. Their blunt actions—especially the trumped-up charges against Anwar—drew international criticism and helped enliven Malaysia's Islamist movement. But for Mahathir, it was all a political success. He not only rode out the financial crisis, he remained in office until deciding to retire in November 2003, when he handed over power to Abdullah Ahmad Badawi.

Mahathir's Views: Conspiracies and the Crisis

In almost all accounts, Mahathir plays a central role in the story. As prime minister, the central authority in Malaysia's government, he had a say in any policy of this importance. His take on the sources of the East Asian financial crisis gives us cause to consider his personality or at least his beliefs, for his ideas lean towards the bizarre. For more than a year before introducing capital controls, he had voiced troubling statements to the media and the public. He blamed the financial crisis on conspiracies of "Jewish speculators" and even singled out international financier George Soros as a culprit.[6] He went on to describe the IFIs' policy recommendations as a concerted effort by the West to re-colonize Asia. His declaration of such ridiculous theories suggests he made decisions irrationally.

It is possible, therefore, that he held a strange set of beliefs about the way international markets work or about the economics behind IMF and World Bank policy. If, indeed, he viewed the world in terms of racial and religious competition, he might well see capital controls as a useful tool for defending "his people" against "others." As noted earlier, the UMNO is based on ethnic political divisions within Malaysia, and Mahathir's political career was built around exercising favouritism in economic policies by egging on competition between ethnic groups. It is quite possible, then, that he truly saw the world in terms we find morally repugnant.

On the other hand, Mahathir may simply have been saying things he believed would prove popular with his constituents as cover for his oppressive actions. The existence of the power struggle within the UMNO suggests that while his comments may have had political appeal within Malaysia, not everyone agreed with him. Indeed, Anwar continued to criticize Mahathir from jail, spawning the "reformasi" movement. Anwar's calls for reform focused on corrupt practices by highlighting how Mahathir had used power and government finances to benefit his cronies. Preferences based on ethnicity were used as an excuse for such policies, so we may never know whether we were hearing Mahathir's actual beliefs or simply watching a politician perform an act to cover his corrupt policies. One significant clue, of course, is that capital controls were enacted only during the internal power struggle. As economists have emphasized, capital controls are best suited as tools to prevent being swept up in an international financial crisis, but here we had the legislation enacted much too late for that purpose.

Ideas: The Debate over Capital Controls

By almost all accounts, conventional economic theory prior to the 1997 crisis had little good to say about capital controls. As barriers between countries, economists considered them the source of distortions to economic decisions. They blocked the inflow of the capital necessary for economically developing countries to invest in growth. As with most barriers at borders, they encouraged the expansion of black market activity and corruption. And just as important, they also gave domestic political actors leeway to follow more autonomous policies—including policies that were not economically viable. Many economists suggested that the international capital markets constrain states, since states dependent on outside capital must behave responsibly lest they lose their backing.

One prominent voice advocating capital controls prior to the East Asian financial crisis was Paul Krugman of MIT. A well-known international economist, Krugman argued in several places that capital controls might make sense for developing countries. These were limited controls, however, to make economically developing countries less vulnerable to short-term currency fluctuations. Capital controls of this type could encourage investors to be prudent, while still keeping countries open to long-term investment. His stance echoed the position of some others, such as James Tobin, who had earlier tried to develop a tax that would decrease the amount of very short-term investments crossing borders, while leaving long-run investment capital freedom to move internationally.

Yet Krugman made strong efforts to distance himself from Malaysia's decision.[7] This was not least because Mahathir continued to point an accusatory finger at a concocted conspiracy of Western investors as the source of the crisis. As Krugman put it, "Sometimes bad men make good policies, and vice versa."[8] Krugman also noted that the point of capital controls is to prevent an international shock from devastating the domestic economy. Malaysia's capital controls came too late for that. Instead, the capital controls could be considered an important tool in fostering economic recovery, but even this Krugman was reluctant to endorse. Other Asian countries affected by the crisis recovered at a pace similar to Malaysia's without implementing similar measures. Even when considering the ingredients specific to Malaysia's post-crisis performance, it isn't clear that capital controls were so critical, though they did afford the government a freer hand in setting domestic monetary policies.[9]

Conclusions: Malaysia's Recovery and the Return of an Old Idea

Malaysia's regulations came after the East Asian financial crisis had peaked. In that sense they did not prevent the damage from being done. Comparisons between Malaysia's economic recovery and that of others affected by the crisis that refused to introduce capital controls, such as South Korea, suggest that the controls may not have made that much difference. That conclusion means that capital controls did not hurt Malaysia's chances either. Statistics show that Malaysia surely was not hurt by the policies in the short run. Foreign exchange reserves rose from $20 billion in August 1998 to $27 billion in April 1999. Short-term interest rates dropped from an average of slightly over 7 per cent in 1997 to slightly over 3 per cent by the summer of 1999.[10]

By 1999, Malaysia was also already easing some of the restrictions. This may have given international investors some renewed confidence in the country. It isn't clear that investors have shunned Malaysia, but they haven't favoured it either. Malaysia recovered well, but so did others, such as South Korea, that followed orthodox policies laid out by the IFIs. The capital controls, therefore, are viewed by some as a success, but by others as largely irrelevant. However, simply pointing out that they did no damage has encouraged other states to consider them more carefully. If they can do the most good before a crisis hits, and do not cause the harm economists often claim, might they be a good idea?

Notes

1. Joseph Stiglitz is perhaps the best known of these critics. See "Must Financial Crises be This Frequent and This Painful?," *Policy Options* 20,5 (June 1999): 23-32.

2. The set of regulations introduced are nicely summarized in Ethan Kaplan and Dani Rodrik, "Did the Malaysian Capital Controls Work?," NBER Working Papers #8142, February 2001.

3. See the statistics in K.S. Jomo (ed.). *Malaysian Eclipse: Economic Crisis and Recovery* (New York, NY: Zed Books, 2001).

4. Dwight Perkins and Wing Thye Woo, "Malaysia: Adjusting to Deep Integration with the World Economy," *The Asian Financial Crisis: Lessons for a Resilient Asia*, ed. Wing Thye Woo, Jeffrey Sachs and Klaus Schwab (Cambridge, MA: MIT, 2000) 227-56.

5. "Malaysia's Dubious Recovery," *The Asian Wall Street Journal* 2 September 1999.

6. Perhaps surprisingly, such language was largely tolerated by Western governments at the time. Such toleration eroded when Anwar was arrested and largely ended after September 11, 2001.

7. "Capital Control Freaks: How Malaysia got away with economic heresy," <http://slate.msn.com>, originally posted 27 September 1999.

8. "Capital Control Freaks."

9. "Malaysia's Dubious Recovery."

10. Hali J. Edison and Carmen M. Reinhart, "Capital Controls During Financial Crises: The Case of Malaysia and Thailand," *Board of Governors of the Federal Reserve System International Finance Discussion Papers* 662 (March 2000): 11.

Additional References

Edwards, Sebastian. "How Effective are Capital Controls?" *Journal of Economic Perspectives* 13,4 (Fall 1999): 65-84.

Chang, Ha-Joon (ed.). *The Rebel Within: Joseph Stiglitz and the World Bank*. London: Wimbledon, 2001.

Helleiner, Eric. "Post-Globalization: Is the Financial Liberalization Trend Likely to be Reversed?," *States Against Markets*. Ed. Robert Boyer and Daniel Drache (London: Routledge, 1996). 193-94.

—. "States and the Future of Global Finance." *Review of International Studies* 18 (1992): 31-49.

Williamson, John, and Molly Mahar. "A Survey of Financial Liberalization." *Princeton Essays in International Finance* 211 (November 1998).

CONCLUSION

Theories, Evidence, and the Evolution of the International Political Economy

Having now read about theories that seek to explain international outcomes, examined particular descriptions of issues and problems within the different areas of international political economic relations and, finally, reviewed a number of cases illustrating how critical foreign economic policy decisions were made, it is time to pull this material together. What do the cases, taken together, tell us about the evolution of the international political economy? How can they help us understand the application of theories, so that we may refine them or at least apply them more effectively in the future?

The Evolution of Regimes Governing the International Political Economy

Let us begin by thinking about what the historical examples have illustrated in terms of the ways in which the international regimes in the issue-areas of trade, investment, and monetary affairs changed over time. The story of the evolution of the trade regime began with Britain's Repeal of the Corn Laws in the 1840s. This signals Britain's desire to lead the liberalization of the international economy, although this unilateral action had only a limited impact on the behaviour of other states. Direct negotiations with another country, France, resulted in the Cobden-Chevalier Treaty in 1860. This treaty sparked a chain reaction among European states, thereby creating a relatively open trading system. This regime was built in an ad hoc fashion out of numerous bilateral relations. It lasted for only a brief time, for already by the late 1870s several countries were again raising barriers to trade; Canada's National Policy illustrates the beginning of this trend. Just as the regime had been created in an ad hoc fashion, it fell apart in the same way. Notable among the defectors was Germany, where the proponents of free trade were unable to install and maintain their preferred policy. Britain considered retaliations against such defectors but, as we saw, declined to raise its own tariffs before 1914.

World War I disrupted trade relations. After the war, the victorious powers attempted to rebuild a trade regime around liberal economic principles, but this attempt soon fell victim to protectionist pressures. The U.S. Smoot-Hawley Tariff led the closure. After World War II, an open international system was established around the General Agreement on Tariffs and Trade (the GATT); in contrast to the earlier trade regimes, the GATT is much more explicit and institutionalized. These characteristics may make it less susceptible to erosion, though the rise of non-tariff barriers (NTBs) has presented a serious challenge to GATT's principles. Nevertheless, this open trading system has remained intact, although there are some signs of the emergence of threat of closure. Regional trading blocs have been added to the picture in recent years, as has the further institutionalization of GATT (as it evolves into the World Trade Organization, or WTO); whether the WTO and regional trading blocs can function alongside one another remains to be seen.

In the issue-area of international investment, the story is a bit simpler. In the nineteenth century, there were increased levels of international investments, which primarily took the form of portfolio investment. The gold standard facilitated such flows. Britain was at the centre, though other European countries also invested capital internationally. These interests in international investment shaped Britain's attitudes about trade and monetary relations, as was evident in its attitude towards German protectionism prior to World War I and the need to resume the gold standard in the 1920s. After World Wars I and II, the U.S. emerged as the primary source of international investments, and U.S. investments were dominated by foreign direct investments by multinational corporations (MNCs). In the 1970s, the expansion of eurodollar holdings laid the basis for a massive growth in international lending. When U.S. monetary policy was tightened in the early 1980s, these international loans created an enormous debt crisis and a clash between private international actors, international agencies, and the creditor states, as well as the debtor states. As a result, new patterns and rules governing international banking and international investment have been developed.

In international monetary relations, a much more diverse pattern can be observed. There have been periods with very strict rules, as well as times when the regime exerted little constraint on monetary policies. When trade was finally opened in the mid-nineteenth century, the gold standard was adopted in order to regulate international monetary affairs and to facilitate the free trade and investment regimes. The gold standard operated on a strict model—though practice often diverged from theory. The outbreak of World War I effectively destroyed it; it was not successfully rebuilt in the interwar period, despite the tremendous efforts Britain made. After World War II, a new monetary regime was created around the U.S. dollar, and the institutions of the International Monetary Fund and the World Bank. This Bretton Woods regime, however, had difficulty balancing liquidity with confidence in the dollar. The system collapsed under these pressures in the early 1970s and has not been replaced by a new set of real regulations. Instead, rules have been written to allow countries to do whatever they wish. This has required greater cooperation among the major financial powers and ignited desires among the Europeans to tie their currencies more strongly together.

Explaining Regime Change: The Development of Theoretical Paradigms

By taking a broader perspective on the evolution of international regimes, we may appreciate the reasons for the popularity of particular paradigms in international political economy (IPE). A more comprehensive consideration of the ways in which we explain regime change may also shed light on the directions in which more recent research in IPE has been headed. The popularity of realism springs from its ability to provide insight into numerous cases across issue-areas and over time. Structural realists have centred their explanations on the role of hegemonic leaders in the international system. Realists base their arguments on states and power and the pursuit of power. They associate periods of stable economic relations with stable political power; regimes reflect the distribution of power. Realists face several tough questions, though. Why do hegemonic states follow these policies of maintaining an open trading system, with high levels of international investment and so on? In the cases we've closely studied, the trade and investment regimes supported first by Britain and then by the U.S. have ultimately led to the relative decline of the hegemonic country. Given that the U.S. remains a dominant military power, although the future of its relative economic position has been questioned, how should we expect international regimes to develop in the future? Realists must look at issues such as the creation of regional trading blocs as signs of the future demise of the trade regime; examples of coordinated adjustment, as in monetary affairs in the 1980s, raise questions as to how well realist theories can explain current outcomes.

These questions also provide insight into some of the reasons for the rise of variations in realism. Neo-realism, in particular, has attempted to compensate for some of the apparent weaknesses in realist explanations by opening up assumptions about the goals of states. If states are doing other things besides maximizing power, such as maximizing wealth, then some of these questions disappear—though we are left with new questions, about the ways in which we as theorists should make assumptions about states' goals.

In contrast, classical liberals relate changes in the international political economy to the ways in which individuals pursue their—usually material—interests. For classical liberals and their modern descendants, the swings of the IPE from more open relations to closure and back again are evidence of too much politicization of international political economic relations. What liberals tend to ignore is the need for political order to underwrite or support these relations. Politics are always a force in the international political economy, but all political orders do not support markets. Classical liberals now tend to spend time thinking about how to get politics out of international economic relations. By examining the role of individuals and firms, they provide insight into the connections between domestic politics and foreign economic policy. As a paradigm, liberalism has failed to present a coherent set of arguments for the explanation of foreign economic policy, even though liberal assumptions are the starting point for many—if not most—analyses from the domestic level (as will be examined below).[1] As a paradigm for explaining regime change, Liberalism's apparent weakness has led its proponents to create two new paradigms: institutionalism and constructivism.

Institutionalists have observed the realists' difficulties in explaining why regimes persist after hegemonic powers decline. Where does continued cooperation come from? Institutionalists have focused their efforts on explaining these anomalies and then used these theories to illuminate how cooperation can be created without relying on the expression of international power. They offer a much more optimistic picture of the future, when compared to the realists. Cooperative management of existing regimes is not only possible, it is likely.

Constructivists have picked up on a different set of anomalies in the realists' analyses. Realists have been unable to explain much of the content of the regimes hegemonic states played a role in creating; constructivists use the formation of identities as a stepping-off point to develop a better understanding of how all states, including hegemonic powers, have formulated their interests. Since constructivists see outcomes flowing from the formation of interests as well as the exertion of power, they offer more optimistic projections of the future of IPE. As long as states understand that their interests lie in cooperation within existing regimes, they will not only adhere to those regimes' rules, but will even be prepared to enhance these international arrangements. One of the challenges confronting the proponents of constructivism is to go back and illustrate in several cases how their analyses provide a better understanding of past events. Ruggie's analysis of the creation of the Bretton Woods regimes is an excellent example of the manner in which this can be done, but more such interpretations need to be created. Moreover, we need more serious tests of this young paradigm, so that we can refine its explanations, come to grips with its advantages and disadvantages, and grasp its policy implications more fully.

Other, older paradigms have provided contrasting analyses of past events, as we saw in some of the chapters in Part III. Marxists see politics at the heart of IPE, but relate changes in the international political economy to changing economic bases, which are filtered through politics. They see the rise of capitalism and markets as an economic activity resulting in political manifestations of exploitation by capitalists, such as imperialism. These analyses in turn spawned newer paradigms, such as the modern world-system approach, which shares both strengths and weaknesses with some of the realist models.

If there is one thing we have learned from the examination of the cases presented in this textbook, it is that these paradigms are simple ways of approaching some rather complex phenomena. No single paradigm provides correct interpretations of each and every event; none works well for all the questions we have posed about IPE. The exercise of academic inquiry is to engage in debates, appreciate what is right and what is wrong with each approach, and use those lessons to learn how to improve existing theories. Only by appreciating a paradigm's deficiencies, and knowing the strengths of alternatives, can we hope to refine and adapt our theories in ways that overcome their current weaknesses.

State Behaviour and The Levels of Analysis

These same points hold for the theories when we group them together by levels of analysis. By seeing what realism or other system-level theories can do—and what they cannot do—we can appreciate the value of other approaches. Reflect on the value of domestic-level theories, the ones using models of domestic politics to explain how state policies were developed. For traditional questions in IPE, such as tariff changes or agreements to fix exchange rates at particular levels, economic models provide excellent material for constructing theories about the domestic political basis of foreign economic policies.

We also reflected on the impact of specific decision-makers. Decision-makers may get locked into roles, with the roles determining how they formulate and execute foreign economic policy. In such cases, we can understand policy as a result of bureaucratic politics and/or organizational process. Policy may be formulated to achieve bureaucratic goals as much as, or more often than, for national interest. Policy may not make sense as a comprehensive package, because different bureaucracies formulate different policies, putting their own institutional twist on the interpretation of foreign policy, so that overall policy may not appear to be rational. Below the level of bureaucratic politics, we examined individuals and their idiosyncratic characteristics to try to come to grips with state behaviour. How do individuals differ, and how do their differences show up in foreign economic policy? How would policy have differed if different individuals were in power?

At the outset of this book, I stressed that one of the key tasks we face as theorists in international relations is the simplification of reality. We know that the world is a complicated place and that coming up with persuasive explanations for past events is difficult; accurate prediction is even harder. Yet, if we want to get some sort of control over the future—to prevent wars, ensure smoother handling of international crises, conduct more satisfactory economic negotiations, or whatever—we have to have some ideas about the consequences of our own actions in order to form expectations about how others are likely to react to our deeds. Which of these various theoretical approaches should we rely on? First, let us reflect on the strengths and weaknesses of each of the levels of analysis in turn, remembering not only that each level of analysis represents a whole array of theories sharing a few common assumptions, but also that such theories do not necessarily say the same things.

System-level theories explain state behaviour by looking at characteristics of the system. For Waltz (and most other realists), a key characteristic of the system is its anarchic nature that forces all states to become concerned with preserving their own interests and allows states to choose to use force to resolve disputes. Realists wind up focusing on the role of power in international relations. But what can we say about arguments made about the causal weight of systemic characteristics? Well, first, they are generalizable; that is, they can be used to talk about the foreign policy or behaviour of many different states, in different issue-areas, and across long spans of time.

System-level theories also tend to be parsimonious. Whether or not the theory is accurate depends on the specific theory examined out of this grouping, and indeed we can picture two different system-level arguments making opposite predictions (such as balancing and bandwagoning). Both may operate with similar assumptions about actors and actors' goals and thus exhibit similar strengths and weaknesses. On the whole these theories are generalizable and parsimonious, so if they are accurate as well, they may be doing well across the board—hence the popularity of system-level theories.

By focusing on specific factors that characterize nation-states, national or state-level theories are naturally limiting their generalizability. By saying that some states are not like others, and therefore are likely to behave differently, these theories say that the same logic cannot be applied to predict the actions of all states. We know specific theories drawn from this group are not as generalizable as system-level theories. They may be just as parsimonious, since they may need only small amounts of information, but they can also become much more complicated and require greater detail. To counterbalance the lack of generalizability, however, we often see that these theories are more accurate in the sense that they integrate more details into their analysis. They are also often more descriptive.

When we come to the next kind of argument, bureaucratic politics, the picture becomes even more complicated. To make such theories work we need information about the decision-making structure, the bureaucracy. That should tell us two things. These theories are likely to be less parsimonious, since the information required is more detailed, and they are certainly going to be specific to particular countries. So they are not likely to be very generalizable across cases, or for that matter across time, for bureaucracies change over time, too. Though widespread applicability is sacrificed, as is parsimony, supporters of this approach argue that accuracy is gained.

When we drop down to the lowest level theory, the individual level with its emphasis on idiosyncratic features, we need even more specific, detailed information. We need to know who is making decisions, the background information on the personal level. So, again, we see a trade-off between generalizability, parsimony, and accuracy: if you want generalizability, we often have to give up some detail.

These trade-offs matter when we remember the tasks of theories—describing, explaining, and predicting foreign policy. The more detail-oriented theories are great for describing and might be very useful when all the evidence needed for supporting the theory has been gathered. They may be weaker when used to formulate predictions. The more generalizable and parsimonious theories are better at prediction, for they allow for faster theorizing and reaching conclusions with less information. If we were to think about predicting Russian foreign economic policy five years from now, what kind of information would we need to employ theories from each level of analysis? A prediction based on the individual level would have to begin by predicting who would be in charge of foreign economic policy in five years. Will Putin's government still be in power? Who will be in charge of particular ministerial portfolios? If we turn to the next level of analysis, and consider domestic politics, we have to wonder what the Russian government would look like. Will there be constitutional changes? How will different interest groups compete? What will the role of political parties be in the future? Will the country keep its democratic institutions, or will these be modified? This brief example illustrates how these issues of parsimony, generalizability, and accuracy interact to influence the qualities of theories.

Combining Theories for a More Complex and Comprehensive Understanding of Events

With a few exceptions, the analyses in the cases have primarily presented these theories as rivals. That is not the only way they are used; increasingly, we create theories by drawing causal variables from different levels of analysis. We use these variables in combination to make a better theory than we could by limiting ourselves to factors from a single level of analysis. This eclecticism may make it harder for students new to the subject to understand why the theories look the way they do, but, by creating stronger theories, such eclecticism may be the mark of the advances we've made.[2] Addressing more complicated theories may be a subject for more advanced courses in international relations, but it should already be evident that, by creating a complex mix of variables, we can construct a bigger picture than we could otherwise. Moreover, combining analyses from different levels may be the most effective way to extract the best from each. The challenge is to understand when to use particular theories, to figure out which types of theories are best for what sort of questions, and to determine how they may be used together to derive theories that are better in all characteristics: more accurate, more generalizable, and more parsimonious.

Having finished this book, the reader should not only appreciate how particular decisions shaped the evolution of the international political economy, but also have a better understanding of the ways IPE theories (and political science theories more generally) are formed. Knowing that is the first step towards testing theories, which leads to the next step: refining and improving theories. These are the challenges for the next generation of theorists.

Notes

1. See Andrew Moravscik "Taking Preferences Seriously: A Liberal Theory of International Relations," *International Organization* 51,4 (1997): 513-54.

2. A good example of how this can be done can be found in the concluding chapter of Deborah Larson's *The Origins of Containment* (Princeton, NJ: Princeton University Press, 1985).

Glossary

Please note that this glossary does not refer to the general definition of these terms, nor even to their general usage in political science, but rather refers merely to their common usage within the subfield of international political economy. Some frequently used political economic terms are also provided.

absolute advantage: An actor has an absolute advantage in the production of a good or service if it can produce that good or service with fewer resources than other actors.

accuracy: One of the qualities we can use in evaluating and comparing theories, referring to the probability that the theory will provide the correct answer.

ad valorem tariff: A tariff where the duty charged is a proportion of the value of the good (e.g., 5 per cent of the good's declared value).

adjustable peg: A type of exchange rate regime where rates are fixed, but countries retain the right to change rates whenever they see fit. See *exchange rate.*

assumption: The basic starting point for a causal theory. Something assumed to be true; a simplification, used to bring clarity to a complex situation or relationship.

autarky: A situation where there are no international economic transactions taking place.

balance of payments: Tracks a nation's international economic transactions; a nation's accounting records.

balance of payments adjustment: This refers to the way in which states settle their bills.

balance of power: A term with many meanings, it usually refers to either any distribution of power (it doesn't matter if power is evenly distributed or not), or a perfectly even distribution of power.

beggar-thy-neighbour policy: A policy intended to transfer unemployment problems from one country to another via protectionism.

behaviouralists: Those who believe that the proper way to construct and to test theories involves making many observations of variables, aggregating the information, and applying methods of data analysis (statistics) to interpret the evidence. This view is contrasted with that of the *traditionalists.*

belief-systems: A set of beliefs about how the world works and/or how it ought to work. See *ideology.*

bipolar: One of several different possible distributions of power; in this case, a distribution where two states or alliances have power concentrated in their control.

bolstering: Bolstering occurs when a decision-maker stops engaging in the broad search for information and, instead of exploring the full range of policy options, merely searches for information that supports the choice he or she has already made.

bureaucratic politics: One of the commonly used levels of analysis; theories in this group concentrate their explanations for state policy on divisions within the state itself, which pit one bureaucracy against another.

capital account: A subset of the balance of payments, which records the borrowing, selling, or purchasing of assets.

classical liberalism: The earliest form of liberalism, which promised that national wealth would be increased if individuals were free to compete against each other (pursuing their own narrow self-interest), as opposed to having the state interfere with the market.

classical Marxism: The earliest form of Marxism, which emphasized that social classes are the most important actors in domestic or international politics. See *Marxism.*

classical realism: The earliest version of realism, which, in order to counter the arguments of Idealists, assumed human nature to be selfish and driven by a desire for power.

Coase Theorem: An argument describing possible situations where problems with externalities can be overcome, even in the absence of government. The Coase Theorem states that if (1) there is a legal framework to establish liabilities, (2) there is perfect information (and also everyone understands their own preferences), and (3) there are zero negotiating costs, actors can resolve problems arising from externalities through deal-making.

commercial liberalism: An early version of liberalism, which argued that free trade was not only beneficial to individuals in an economic sense, and therefore economically beneficial to states (since states are merely agglomerations of individuals), but would also provide the basis for a harmony of interests in the international system. See *liberalism.*

comparative advantage: If two actors have different opportunity costs for producing a good or service, the one with the lower opportunity cost has a comparative advantage in that good or service.

competitive devaluation: A reduction in the value of a currency in order to gain a competitive advantage in trade.

complex interdependence: An approach developed by Keohane and Nye in the 1970s to open up the realms of theorizing away from the narrow assumptions of Realism.

Concert of the Great Powers: The management of the European state system after the defeat of Napoleon in 1815 through a conscious coordinated effort by the most powerful states.

confidence: A characteristic of a currency, referring to the faith people place in it as a store of value.

constructivism: A commonly used paradigm in international relations. It poses questions that come prior to the analysis undertaken in most paradigms. Key concepts are that interests have no meaning without establishing actors' identities and that actors and interests should be placed in social context.

convertibility: The ability to switch from a currency to another currency or asset.

crawling peg: A type of exchange rate regime where rates are fixed only for the very short run, with many frequent small changes in rates. The intention is to prevent any large changes. See *exchange rate.*

crisis: Most definitions of an international crisis include (1) a high threat to something valued very highly, (2) surprise, and (3) the need for a quick response.

culture: A set of characteristics shared by a group of individuals or a nation; this has been used as a causal factor for explaining international outcomes.

current account: A subset of the balance of payments, denoting net changes in a country's claims on foreigners.

deductive theorizing: One method of reasoning, which involves first postulating a logical relationship between cause and effect, then making repeated observations to evaluate and refine the relationship. See *inductive theorizing.*

defensive procrastination: Occurs when someone refuses to deal with a problem in the hopes that the problem will resolve itself.

deflation: A decline in the average level of prices.

dependent variable: The variations of the dependent variable depend upon the variations of the independent variables.

description: One of the basic tasks of a causal theory; the act of forming a representation.

dirty float: On a floating exchange rate, a situation where a state has intervened in the market to set its exchange rate at a level it desires. See *exchange rate.*

division of labour: The breaking up of the stages of production into different tasks. See *specialization.*

domestic level: One of the commonly used levels of analysis; theories in this group concentrate their explanations for state policy on domestic characteristics of countries or on the politics that takes place within their borders. See *societal level.*

dumping: Selling a good in foreign markets at a price lower than the price charged in the home market.

epistemic communities: A group of experts whose consensus on what constitutes knowledge creates a shared view of an issue.

eurodollars: U.S. dollars held by banks outside the U.S. government's jurisdiction.

exchange rate: The price of one national currency in terms of another. Systems of exchange rates are either fixed (i.e., the prices are set and not allowed to vary very much) or floating (i.e., the prices fluctuate as in most other markets).

export-oriented industrialization (EOI): A strategy for developing a country's industrial sector by selling its output abroad, rather than relying on domestic demand. See *import-substitution industrialization (ISI).*

externality: Situations where the market fails to cover the entire set of costs and benefits associated with a particular transaction.

externalization: Occurs when a society is becoming unstable, and in order to reconsolidate their control, elite policy-makers instigate an international incident, crisis, or conflict to divert the population from domestic problems or domestic differences.

extraterritoriality: The extension of national jurisdiction beyond a nation's own borders.

factor mobility: The ease with which a factor of production can be moved from one application to another.

factors of production: The inputs necessary for producing a good or service. In the simplest models, the factors are capital and labour.

falsifiability: One of the qualities we can use in evaluating and comparing theories. It refers to our ability to test a theory; if a theory is falsifiable, there are explicit terms under which it could be said to fail.

foreign direct investment (FDI): International investment involving the direct ownership and operation of the venture. See *portfolio investment.*

generalizability: One of the qualities we can use in evaluating and comparing theories, referring to how widely the theory can be applied.

Gresham's Law: The observation that bad money will drive good money out of circulation.

Heartland: A geopolitical notion developed by Mackinder to describe the centre of the Eurasian landmass, which he considered to be the most important strategic terrain in the world. See *Rimland.*

Heckscher-Ohlin (H-O) model: A model intended to explain the content and direction of trade flows. It expects each country to export goods that intensively use the locally most abundant factor(s) and to import goods whose production requires intensive use of locally scarce factor(s) of production.

hegemonic: See *unipolar.*

hegemonic stability theory: A realist explanation for the creation and main-tenance of international regimes; according to this view, regimes are an outcome of the exercise of power. Therefore, regimes are only strong and stable when international power is concentrated in the hands of one state (a hegemonic power), which supports the international regime in question.

horizontal integration: One strategy for expansion of a firm; it entails monopolization of one step in the production process.

idea: A thought or belief; recently being used as a causal factor in theories in international relations.

idealism: A commonly used paradigm in international relations. It was the first dominant paradigm to emerge after World War I. Idealism stresses the possibility of perfecting the behaviour of man (usually through the creation of institutions or laws) and thus perfecting the actions of states, thereby reaching international peace and harmony.

ideology: A set of beliefs about how the world works, and/or how it ought to work. See *belief-system.*

import-substitution industrialization (ISI): A strategy for developing a country's industrial sector by blocking imports of industrial goods, forcing domestic demand to support national industries. See *export-oriented industrialization (EOI).*

independent variable: The causal factor in a theory.

indifference curve: A diagram showing the possible mix of two goods, which then depicts on a curve all the points between which an actor is indifferent.

individual level: One of the commonly used levels of analysis; theories in this group concentrate their explanations for state policy on idiosyncratic characteristics of individuals.

inductive theorizing: One method of reasoning, which involves first making repeated observations, then inferring the logical relationship between cause and effect. See *deductive theorizing.*

inflation: A rise in the average level of prices.

institutionalism: A recently developed paradigm, developed originally to explain the persistence of regimes outside of hegemonic stability theory. Institutionalists argue that if regimes deliver benefits to the participants, the participants would have reasons to maintain or even create international regimes. (Also referred to as *rationalist institutionalism.*)

instrumental Marxism: A version of Marxism, made popular by Lenin, which focuses on explaining the actions of states, but views states as instruments of the interests of each country's capitalists. See *Marxism.*

interdependence: Interdependence can be defined as a situation where changes or events in any single part produce some reaction or have a significant consequence in other parts of the system or, more simply, as the mutual contingency of policies.

international political economy: The analysis of the interaction of power and the processes of wealth creation at the international level.

international regime: An international regime is a set of implicit and explicit norms, rules and principles guiding actors' behaviour.

international relations: The study of politics involving an international dimension; relations between states and external actors (states and non-state actors), as well as between non-state actors and other external actors (states and non-state actors), or involving the formulation of a policy that has repercussions for actors outside the country.

key currency: A national currency that plays the role of international money.

Keynsianism: A view of macroeconomics that prescribes an active, positive role of government in managing the economy through manipulation of fiscal and monetary policy.

law: Laws are connections between variables of which we have repeated observations of such strength and number that we can safely expect the relations to continue into the future.

Leontief Paradox: The paradoxical results produced in empirical analysis of the imports and exports of the U.S., which seem to disconfirm the *Heckscher-Ohlin model.*

levels of analysis: A method for grouping theories together, based on the types of assumptions made about the most important actors.

leverage: One of the qualities we can use in evaluating and comparing theories. The ability to explain as much as possible with as little as possible.

liberalism: A commonly used paradigm in international relations, which bases its arguments on the actions of rational utility-maximizing individuals.

liquidity: A characteristic of a currency, referring to its availability, which in turn determines how well it can serve as a medium of exchange.

Marxism: A commonly used paradigm in international relations, which bases its explanations of politics on the relationships between social classes.

mercantilism: A practice in foreign economic policies of the seventeenth and eighteenth centuries that entailed a set of policies designed to maintain an inward flow of money, but these policies were barriers to trade and international investment.

modern world systems: A set of works which blend history, sociology, and political science to develop a deeper understanding of the historical development of the international political economy. It is rooted within Marxist traditions and looks at actors at several levels of analysis.

monopoly: A market in which there is only one seller.

most-favoured-nation (MFN) clause: A clause in a trade treaty which commits a country to impose no greater barriers to imports of the signatory than it imposes on imports from any other country.

multinational corporation (MNC): A corporation which carries on business operations in several countries.

multipolar: One of several different possible distributions of power; in this case, a distribution where more than three states or alliances have power concentrated in their control.

Mundell-Fleming conditions: When choosing policies in the three dimensions of monetary policy (domestic autonomy, exchange rate, and open or closed capital markets), policy makers only have freedom to select two—they have no freedom on the third policy dimension, as it must be consistent with the other two.

national level: One of the commonly used levels of analysis; theories in this group concentrate their explanations for state policy on characteristics of the country or on internal political economic activities. See *societal level.*

neo-realism: A recent version of realism, which recognizes the importance of other goals which states might have by modifying the assumption that states seek to maximize power.

non-tariff barrier (NTB): A broad concept, used to denote impediments to trade (excepting tariffs).

normative goal: One of the basic tasks of a causal theory; a vision of the way things ought to be.

oligopoly: A market in which there are only a few sellers.

opportunity cost: The amount that an input could earn in its next best possible application; the alternative foregone when something is produced.

organizational processes: The argument that bureaucratic organizations are entirely flexible and thus may affect the implementation of policy; policy may be rationally formulated, but then bureaucracies and organizations may not be able to carry them out as originally intended, making policy appear irrational.

paradigm: An example which others copy and employ as well, or a set of core assumptions (often established in a single example on which theorists draw) shared by many similar theories. The set of core assumptions define a grouping of theories and separates one paradigm from another.

parsimony: One of the qualities we can use in evaluating and comparing theories. It refers to the degree of simplicity; it reflects the ability to explain much of the variation in the dependent variable with as little information or theory as possible.

Phillips curve: A diagram used to portray the relationship between inflation and unemployment.

policy paradigm: A concept developed by P. Hall, which he defines as an overarching set of ideas that specify how the problems actors face are to be perceived, which goals might be attained through policy, and what sorts of techniques can be used to reach those goals.

portfolio investment: An indirect investment, one where ownership or investment does not entail direct management of the economic activity resulting from their investment.

power: In political science, usually defined as control over actors, especially their actions (i.e., the ability to get an actor to do something which he/she otherwise would not do).

power transition: A term originated by Organski to identify a period when internally driven changes rapidly alter a country's strength, thereby altering the systemic distribution of power.

prediction: One of the basic tasks of a causal theory, referring to the act of foretelling an event.

prescription: One of the basic tasks of a causal theory, referring to the act of providing advice or direction.

prisoners' dilemma: An example from game theory, which illustrates a situation where two egoistic actors interact yet fail to attain their harmony of interests.

product cycle: An argument developed by Vernon to explain when *foreign direct investment (FDI)* takes place; it is based on the notion that products go through a characteristic life-cycle, reflecting the varying ability of firms to produce the good over time.

production possibility frontier: A curve illustrating the limits of output which can be produced with various combinations of inputs.

public good: A good characterized by both non-excludibility and non-rival consumption.

quota: A typical barrier to trade, which limits the volume of goods coming into a country.

rally-round-the-flag effect: A concept used to identify the tendency for domestic differences to be set aside in a foreign policy crisis.

rate of transformation: The rate at which production can be shifted from one product to another.

rationality: A common assumption made about actors in our theories, which states that actors will try to attain their highest preferences at the least cost. The assumption of rationality contains three conditions: first, the actor is assumed to have perfect information—it is assumed the actor knows all its options and knows all the costs and benefits (the ramifications) associated with each option; second, the actor must understand the causal effect of each possible choice; third, the actor must be able to rank its choices, which requires that it be able to relate what it values into some sort of schedule of preferences.

rationalist institutionalism: See *institutionalism.*

realism: A commonly used paradigm in international relations, realism emerged as the dominant paradigm in the 1940s and remained so until recent years. It has stressed the importance of power in international relations and the continuity in states' behaviour. It also emphasizes the anarchic nature of the international system, which allows states to use power to resolve differences.

reflectivist institutionalism: A very recent version of *institutionalism*, which argues that existing institutions and norms shape the ways in which actors' preferences are defined. The institutionalists using a reflectivist approach stress that international regimes are rarely the product of purely rational design, but instead are shaped by existing norms and institutions.

republican liberalism: A version of liberalism, emphasizing the political aspects of liberalism by arguing that republics behave differently; where individuals have a say in the formulation of national policy, national policy will be peaceful and pursue the creation of wealth. See *liberalism.*

reserves: Commodities or assets held as backing for a currency.

Rimland: A geopolitical notion developed by Spykman to describe the outer edge of the Eurasian landmass, which he considered to be the most important strategic terrain in the world, due to the concentration of economic and industrial power in these regions. See *Heartland.*

role level: See *bureaucratic politics.*

sector specificity: An assumption made in some trade models concerning the ability of an input to be deployed into different industries. If there is high sector specificity for a factor of production, it means that factor is best suited for use in that industry. This shapes its preferences on trade policy—by tying its interests to that sector. See the competing ideas of the *Stolper-Samuelson theorem.*

security dilemma: A concept used to describe relations between sovereign states in the context of international anarchy, where each state treats its neighbours as the potential source of threats; as each increases its power, it makes the other insecure. The overall result is competition for power and insecurity.

specialization: The act of concentrating production on one type of good, or even one stage in the production of a good, to exploit *comparative advantage.*

societal level: One of the commonly used levels of analysis; theories in this group concentrate their explanations for state policy on characteristics of the country's society or on internal political economic activities. See *national level*.

sovereignty: Sovereignty refers to the ability to exercise the ultimate legitimate political authority.

stagflation: A situation where an economy suffers both high inflation and high unemployment.

standard operating procedures: In order to function smoothly, large organizations such as government bureaucracies must practise routine operations; the range of manoeuvres a bureaucracy can perform may constrain policy choice or affect the way policy is actually implemented. See *organizational processes*.

state level: One of the commonly used levels of analysis; theories in this group concentrate their explanations for state policy on characteristics of the country overall, such as the type of governing institutions it has.

status inconsistency: A concept borrowed from sociology, which denotes differences in the status an actor is accorded in the various facets of interactions with other actors. Inconsistency in the levels of status may be the root of frustrations and aggressive behaviour.

Stolper-Samuelson theorem: A theorem developed to understand the distribution of gains and losses from international trade. The relatively scarce factor of production will lose real earnings when trade levels rise, while the relatively abundant factor of production will gain real earnings.

strategic trade policy: A policy intended to change the benefits from trade, either by altering the position of particular firms or by changing the position of their economies in the international division of labour.

structural Marxism: A version of Marxism which explains the actions of states by arguing that states act politically to maintain the overall political economic structure of capitalism.

structural realism: A version of realism laid out by Waltz in *Theory of International Politics* (1979). It stresses the characteristics of the structure of the international system in its explanations of state behaviour.

structure: A way of depicting the relations of the units or the composition of a system.

system level: One of the commonly used levels of analysis; theories in this group concentrate their explanations for state policy on characteristics of the international system.

tariff: A typical barrier to trade; a tax on goods as they cross a border.

theory: A speculative process for explaining observed relationships between variables.

traditionalists: Those who believe that the best way to construct theories is to make detailed observations of a few cases, relying more on historical analysis and seeing the uniqueness of each event. This view is contrasted with that of the *behaviouralists.*

tripolar: One of several different possible distributions of power; in this case, a distribution where three states or alliances have power concentrated in their control.

unipolar: One of several different possible distributions of power; in this case, a distribution where one state or alliance has power concentrated in its control. Also possibly described as *hegemonic.*

utopianism: See *idealism.*

value-complexity: A term created by George to describe situations where policies may entail trade-offs in values a decision-maker would rather not face.

variable: A term used in our construction of theories, which can refer to the forces or factors of both cause and effect.

vertical integration: One strategy for forming a large firm; it entails capturing the various stages of production within one firm.

wealth: A central concept in economics, referring to affluence and/or abundance.

Bibliography

Achen, Christopher, and Duncan Snidal. "Rational Deterrence Theory and Comparative Case Studies." *World Politics* 41 (January 1989): 143-69.

Aggarwal, Vinod K. *International Debt Threat*. Policy Papers in International Affairs 29. Berkeley, CA: Institute of International Studies, 1987.

Allison, Graham. "Conceptual Models and the Cuban Missile Crisis." *American Political Science Review* 63 (September 1969): 689-718.

—. *The Essence of Decision*. Boston, MA: Little, Brown, 1971.

Andriole, S.J. "The Levels of Analysis Problems and the Study of Foreign, International and Global Affairs: A Review Critique, and Another Final Solution." *International Interactions* 5, 2/3 (1978): 113-33.

Angell, Norman. *The Great Illusion*. New York, NY: Putnam's, 1910.

Art, Robert. "Bureaucratic Politics and American Foreign Policy—A Critique." *Policy Sciences* 4 (1973): 467-90.

Axelrod, Robert. *The Evolution of Cooperation*. New York, NY: Basic Books, 1984.

Baker, Ray S., ed. *Woodrow Wilson and World Settlement*. Garden City, NJ: Doubleday, Page and Co., 1922.

Balassa, Bela. "The Process of Industrial Development and Alternative Development Strategies." *Princeton Essays in International Finance* 141, December 1980.

Baldwin, David A. "Security Studies and the End of the Cold War." *World Politics* 48,1 (October 1995): 117-41.

Beaulieu, Eugene, and J.C.H. Emery. "Pork Packers, Reciprocity and Laurier's Defeat in the 1911 General Election." *Journal of Economic History* 62,4 (December 2001): 1083-1101.

Bergsten, C. Fred. *The Dilemmas of the Dollar*. New York, NY: New York University Press, 1975.

Bhagwati, Jagdish N., and Anne O. Krueger. "Exchange Control, Liberalization and Economic Development." *American Economic Review* 63,2 (May 1973): 419-27.

Biersteker, Thomas J. "Introduction." *Dealing with Debt*. Ed. Thomas J. Biersteker. Boulder, CO: Westview Press, 1993. 1-15.

Bird, Melissa H. "The IMF." *Dealing with Debt*. Ed. Thomas J. Biersteker. Boulder, CO: Westview Press, 1993. 19-36.

Blewett, Neal. "Free Fooders, Balfourites, Whole Hoggers. Factionalism within the Unionist Party, 1906-1910." *The Historical Journal* 11,1 (1968): 95-124.

—. *The Peers, the Parties and the People, The General Elections of 1910*. London: Macmillan, 1972.

Boulding, Kenneth. *Conflict and Defense*. New York, NY: Harper and Row, 1963.

Braudel, Fernand. *The Perspective of the World: Civilization and Capitalism, 15th-18th Century*. Volume III. New York, NY: Harper and Row, 1984.

—. *The Structures of Everyday Life: Civilization and Capitalism, 15th-18th Century*. Volume I. New York, NY: Harper and Row, 1979.

—. *The Wheels of Commerce: Civilization and Capitalism, 15th-18th Century*. Volume II. New York, NY: Harper and Row, 1982.

Brawley, Mark R. *Afterglow or Adjustment?* New York, NY: Columbia University Press, 1999.

—. "Factoral or Sectoral Conflict? Partially Mobile Factors and the Politics of Trade in Imperial Germany." *International Studies Quarterly* 41,4 (December 1997): 633-53.

—. *Liberal Leadership: Great Powers and Their Challengers in Peace and War*. Ithaca, NY: Cornell University Press, 1993.

—. "Political Leadership and Liberal Economic Sub-Systems: The Constraints of Structural Assumptions." *Canadian Journal of Political Science* 28,1 (March 1995): 85-103.

Brecher, Michael. "State Behavior in International Crisis." *Journal of Conflict Resolution* 23,3 (September 1979): 446-80.

Brenner, Robert. "The Origins of Capitalist Development: A Critique of Neo-Smithian Marxism." *New Left Review* 104 (1977): 25-92.

Broad, Robin, and John Cavanaugh. "No More NICs." *Foreign Policy* 72 (Fall 1988): 81-103.

Brown, Michael. *After Imperialism*. London: Heinemann, 1973.

Brown, Robert, and Ramsay Cook. *Canada 1896-1921: A Nation Transformed*. Toronto, ON: McClelland and Stewart, 1974.

Bull, Hedley. *The Anarchical Society*. London: Macmillan, 1977.

Bullock, Alan. *Hitler: A Study in Tyranny*. New York, NY: Harper and Row, 1964.

Byman, Daniel L. "Al-Qaeda as an Adversary: Do We Understand Our Enemy?" *World Politics* 56 (October 2003): 139-63.

Cain, Peter. "Capitalism, War and Internationalism in the Thought of Richard Cobden." *British Journal of International Studies* 5,3 (October 1979): 229-47.

Cairncross, Alec, and Barry Eichengreen. *Sterling in Decline*. Oxford: Basil Blackwell, 1983.

Calleo, David P. *Beyond American Hegemony*. New York, NY: Basic Books, 1987.

—. *The German Problem Reconsidered*. New York, NY: Cambridge University Press, 1978.

Cameron, Duncan. "Introduction." *The Free Trade Deal*. Ed. Duncan Cameron. Toronto, ON: James Lorimer and Co., 1988. i-xviii.

—. "Striking a Deal." *The Free Trade Deal*. Ed. Duncan Cameron. Toronto, ON: James Lorimer and Co., 1988. 16-25.

Cameron, Duncan, and Hugh Mackenzie. "Manufacturing." *The Free Trade Deal*. Ed. Duncan Cameron. Toronto, ON: James Lorimer and Co., 1988. 117-24.

Cardoso, Eliana, and Albert Fishlow. "The Macroeconomics of the Brazilian External Debt." *Developing Country Debt and Economic Performance*. Volume 2: *Country Studies—Argentina, Bolivia, Brazil, Mexico*. Ed. Jeffrey Sachs. Chicago, IL: University of Chicago Press, 1990. 269-391.

Carr, E.H. *The Twenty Years' Crisis, 1919-1939*. 1939. New York, NY: Harper, 1964.

Caves, Richard. *Multinational Enterprise and Economic Growth*. New York, NY: Cambridge University Press, 1982.

de Cecco, Marcello. *Money and Empire*. Totowa, NJ: Rowman and Littlefield, 1975.

Chan, Steve. "In Search of the Democratic Peace: Problems and Promise." *Mershon International Studies Review* 41,1 (May 1997): 59-91.

—. "Mirror, Mirror on the Wall ... Are the Freer Countries More Pacific?" *Journal of Conflict Resolution* 28,4 (1984): 617-48.

Chandler, Lester V. *Benjamin Strong, Central Banker*. Washington, DC: Brookings Institution, 1958.

Chase, Kerry. "Economic Interests and Regional Trading Arrangements: The Case of NAFTA." *International Organization* 57,1 (Winter 2003): 137-74.

Chase-Dunn, Christopher. "Comparative Research on World-System Characteristics." *International Studies Quarterly* 23,4 (December 1979): 601-23.

—. "Interstate System and Capitalist World-Economy: One Logic or Two?" *International Studies Quarterly* 25 (March 1981): 19-42.

Clarke, Stephen V.O. *Central Bank Cooperation 1924-1931*. New York, NY: Federal Reserve Bank of New York, 1967.

—. "The Reconstruction of the International Monetary System: The Attempts of 1922 and 1933." *Princeton Studies in International Finance* 33 (November 1973).

Cline, Ray. *World Power Assessment*. Boulder, CO: Westview, 1977.

Coats, A.W. "Political Economy and the Tariff Reform Campaign of 1903." *Journal of Law and Economics* 11 (April 1968): 181-229.

Cohen, Benjamin J. *In Whose Interest?* New Haven, CT: Yale University Press, 1986.

Cohen, Stephen D., Joel R. Paul, and Robert A. Blecker. *Fundamentals of U.S. Foreign Trade Policy*. Boulder, CO: Westview, 1996.

Cooper, Richard N. "Prolegomena to the Choice of an International Monetary System." *International Organization* 29,1 (1975): 63-97.

Cumings, Bruce. "The Origins and Development of the Northeast Asian Political Economy: Industrial Sectors, Product Cycles, and Political Consequences." *The Political Economy of the New Asian Industrialism*. Ed. Frederic Deyo. Ithaca. NY: Cornell University Press, 1987. 44-83.

Creighton, Donald. *A History of Canada*. Cambridge, MA: Houghton-Mifflin, 1958.

Dafoe, John W. *Clifford Sifton in Relation to His Times*. Toronto, ON: Macmillan, 1931.

Dahl, Robert. "The Concept of Power." *Behavioral Science* 2,3 (July 1957): 201-15.

Dam, Kenneth W. *The Rules of the Game*. Chicago, IL: University of Chicago Press, 1982.

Denemark, Robert A., and Kenneth P. Thomas. "The Brenner-Wallerstein Debate." *International Studies Quarterly* 32,1 (March 1988): 47-65.

Dessler, David. "What's at Stake in the Agent-Structure Debate?" *International Organization* 43,3 (Summer 1989): 441-73.

Destler, I.M. *Making Foreign Economic Policy*. Washington, DC: Brookings Institution, 1980.

Destler, I.M., and C. Randall Henning. *Dollar Politics: Exchange Rate Policymaking in the United States*. Washington, DC: Institute for International Economics, 1989.

—. "From Neglect to Activism: American Politics and the 1985 Plaza Accord." *Journal of Public Policy* 8,3/4 (June 1988): 317-33.

Dinsmoor, James. *Brazil: Responses to the Debt Crisis*. Washington, DC: Inter-American Development Bank, Johns Hopkins University Press, 1990.

Doran, Charles. *The Politics of Assimilation: Hegemony and Its Aftermath*. Baltimore, MD: Johns Hopkins University Press, 1971.

Dornbusch, Rudiger. "From Adjustment with Recession to Adjustment with Growth." *Debt Disaster?: Banks, Governments, and Multilaterals Confront the Crisis*. Ed. John F. Weeks. New York, NY: New York University Press, 1989. 207-21.

Dos Santos, Theotonio. "The Structure of Dependence." *American Economic Review* 60,2 (May 1970): 231-36.

Doyle, Michael. "Liberalism and World Politics." *American Political Science Review* 80,4 (1986): 1151-61.

—. "Thucydidean Realism." *Review of International Studies* 16 (July 1990): 223-37.

Dreyer, Jacob S., and Andrew Schotter. "Power Relationships in the IMF: The Consequences of Quota Changes." *Review of Economics and Statistics* 62,1 (February 1980): 97-106.

Dunham, Arthur Lewis. *The Anglo-French Treaty of Commerce of 1860*. Ann Arbor, MI: University of Michigan Press, 1930.

Dunn, Robert M., Jr. "The Many Disappointments of Flexible Exchange Rates." *Princeton Essays in International Finance* 154 (December 1983).

Eaton, Diane, and Garfield Newman. *Canada A Nation Unfolding*. Toronto, ON: McGraw-Hill Ryerson, 1994.

Edelstein, Michael. "Rigidity and Bias in the British Capital Market, 1870-1913." *Essays on a Mature Economy: Britain after 1840*. Ed. Donald N. McCloskey. Princeton, NJ: Princeton University Press, 1971. 83-105.

Edison, Hali J., and Carmen M. Reinhart. "Capital Controls During Financial Crises: The Case of Malaysia and Thailand." *Board of Governors of the Federal Reserve System International Finance Discussion Papers* 662 (March 2000): 11.

Edwards, Sebastian. *Crisis and Reform in Latin America: From Despair to Hope*. New York: Oxford University Press (World Bank), 1995.

—. "How Effective Are Capital Controls?" *Journal of Economic Perspectives* 13,4 (Fall 1999): 65-84.

Eichengreen, Barry. "Hegemonic Stability Theories of the International Monetary System," *Can Nations Agree? Issues in International Economic Cooperation*. Ed. R.N. Cooper *et al.* Washington, DC: Brookings Institution, 1989. 255-98.

Eichengreen, Barry. "The Political Economy of the Smoot-Hawley Tariff." *Research in Economic History* 12 (1989): 1-43.

Eichengreen, Barry, and Jeffry Frieden. "The Political Economy of European Monetary Unification: An Analytical Introduction." *The Political Economy of European Monetary Unification*. Ed. Barry Eichengreen and Jeffry Frieden. Boulder, CO: Westview, 1994. 1-23.

Eichengreen, Barry, and Jeffrey Sachs. "Exchange Rates and Economic Recovery in the 1930s." *Journal of Economic History* 45,4 (December 1985): 925-46.

Elbaum, Bernard, and William Lazonick. "The Decline of the British Economy: An Institutional Perspective." *Journal of Economic History* 44,2 (June 1984): 567-83.

Ellis, L. Ethan. *Reciprocity 1911: A Study in Canadian-American Relations*. New Haven, CT: Yale University Press, 1939.

Emminger, Otmar. "International Financial Markets and the Recycling of Petrodollars." *The World Today* 31,3 (March 1975): 95-102.

Emy, H.V. *Liberals, Radicals, and Social Politics 1892-1914*. Cambridge: Cambridge University Press, 1973.

Evangelista, Matthew. *Innovation and Arms Races: How the United States and the Soviet Union Develop New Military Technologies*. Ithaca, NY: Cornell University Press, 1988.

Falkus, M.E. "U.S. Economic Policy and the 'Dollar Gap' of the 1920s." *Economic History Review* (Second Series) 24,4 (November 1971): 599-623.

Feierabend, Ivo K. "Expansionist and Isolationist Tendencies of Totalitarian Political Systems: A Theoretical Note." *Journal of Politics* 24 (November 1962): 733-42.

Feige, Edgar, and James M. Johannes. "Was the U.S. Responsible for Worldwide Inflation under the Regime of Fixed Exchange Rates?" *Kyklos* 35,2 (1982): 263-77.

Feinberg, Richard E., and Edward L. Bacha. "When Supply and Demand Don't Intersect: Latin America and the Bretton Woods Institutions in the 1980s." *Development and Change* 19,3 (July 1988): 371-99.

Ferns, Henry, and Bernard Ostry. *The Age of Mackenzie King.* Toronto, ON: James Lorimer and Co., 1976.

Finlayson, Jock A., and Mark W. Zacher. "The GATT and the Regulation of Trade Barriers: Regime Dynamics and Functions." *International Organization* 35,4 (Autumn 1981): 561-602.

Fishlow, Albert. "Lessons from the Past: Capital Markets during the Nineteenth Century and the Interwar Period." *International Organization* 39,3 (Summer 1985): 37-93.

Flanders, M. June. *International Monetary Economics, Between the Classical and the New Classical.* New York, NY: Cambridge University Press, 1989.

Fletcher, Richard D. "Undervaluation, Adjustment and Growth." *Debt Disaster?: Banks, Governments, and Multilaterals Confront the Crisis.* Ed. John F. Weeks. New York, NY: New York University Press, 1989. 125-30.

Frank, André Gunder. *World Accumulation, 1492-1789.* New York, NY: Monthly Review Press, 1978.

Frankel, Jeffrey. "Six Possible Meanings of 'Overvaluation': The 1981-85 Dollar." *Princeton Essays in International Finance* 159 (December 1985).

Frieden, Jeffry. "Capital Politics: Creditors and the International Political Economy." *Journal of Public Policy* 8,3/4 (July-December 1988): 265-86.

—. *Debt, Development, and Democracy: Modern Political Economy and Latin America, 1965-1985.* Princeton, NJ: Princeton University Press, 1991.

—. "The Economics of Intervention: American Overseas Investments and Relations with Underdeveloped Areas, 1890-1950." *Comparative Studies in Society and History* 31,1 (1989): 55-80.

—. "Invested Interests: The Politics of National Economic Policies in a World of Global Finance." *International Organization* 45,4 (Autumn 1991): 425-51.

—. "Making Commitments: France and Italy in the EMS, 1979-1985." *The Political Economy of European Monetary Unification.* Ed. Barry Eichengreen and Jeffry Frieden. Boulder, CO: Westview, 1994. 25-46.

—. "Sectoral Conflict and U.S. Foreign Economic Policy, 1914-1940." *The State and American Foreign Economic Policy.* Ed. John Ikenberry, David A. Lake, and Michael Mastanduno. Ithaca, NY: Cornell University Press, 1988. 59-90.

Fukuyama, Francis. "The End of History?" *National Interest* (Summer 1989): 3-18.

Funabashi, Yoichi. *Managing the Dollar: From the Plaza to the Louvre.* Washington, DC: Institute for International Economics, 1988.

Garos, Casper. *Canada-U.S. Free Trade.* Amsterdam: VU University Press, 1990.

Garrett, Geoffrey. "The Politics of Maastricht." *The Political Economy of European Monetary Unification.* Ed. Barry Eichengreen and Jeffry Frieden. Boulder, CO: Westview, 1994. 47-65.

Garrett, Geoffrey, and Peter Lange. "Internationalization, Institutions and Political Change." *International Organization* 49,4 (Autumn 1995): 627-55.

Garrett, Geoffrey, and Barry Weingast. "Ideas, Interests, and Institutions: Constructing the European Community's Internal Market." *Ideas and Foreign Policy*. Ed. Judith Goldstein and Robert Keohane. Ithaca, NY: Cornell University Press, 1993. 173-206.

George, Alexander, "The Causal Nexus between Cognitive Beliefs and Decision-Making Behavior: The 'Operational Code' Belief System." *Psychological Models in International Politics*. Ed. Lawrence S. Falkowski. Boulder, CO: Westview Press, 1979. 95-124.

—. "The 'Operational Code': A Neglected Approach to the Study of Political Leaders and Decision-Making." *International Studies Quarterly* 13 (June 1969): 190-222.

George, Alexander, and Juliette L. George. *Woodrow Wilson and Colonel House*. New York, NY: John Day, 1956.

—. "Woodrow Wilson and Colonel House: A Reply to Weinstein, Anderson, and Link." *Political Science Quarterly* 96 (Winter 1981-82): 641-65.

Gilpin, Robert. *The Political Economy of International Relations*. Princeton, NJ: Princeton University Press, 1987.

—. *U.S. Power and the Multinational Corporation*. New York, NY: Basic Books, 1975.

—. *War and Change in World Politics*. Cambridge: Cambridge University Press, 1981.

Goldstein, Judith. *Ideas, Interests and American Trade Policy*. Ithaca, NY: Cornell University Press, 1993.

Goldstein, Judith, and Robert Keohane. "Ideas and Foreign Policy: An Analytical Framework." *Ideas and Foreign Policy*. Ed. Judith Goldstein and Robert Keohane. Ithaca, NY: Cornell University Press, 1993. 3-30.

—, eds. *Ideas and Foreign Policy*. Ithaca, NY: Cornell University Press, 1993.

Goodman, John B. *Monetary Sovereignty*. Ithaca, NY: Cornell University Press, 1992.

Gourevitch, Peter. "International Trade, Domestic Coalitions, and Liberty: Comparative Responses to the Crisis of 1873-1896." *Journal of Interdisciplinary History* 7 (1977): 281-313.

Gowa, Joanne. *Allies, Adversaries, and International Trade*. Princeton, NJ: Princeton University Press, 1994.

—. *Closing the Gold Window: Domestic Politics and the End of Bretton Woods*. Ithaca, NY: Cornell University Press, 1983.

de Grauwe, Paul. *International Money: Postwar Trends and Theories*. Oxford: Clarendon Press, 1989.

de Grauwe, Paul, and Lucas Papademos. "Introduction" *The EMS in the 1990s*. Ed. Paul de Grauwe and Lucas Papademos. New York, NY: Longman, 1990. xi-xvi.

Grieder, William. *Secrets of the Temple*. New York, NY: Simon and Schuster, 1987.

Grieco, Joseph. *Cooperation Among Nations*. Ithaca, NY: Cornell University Press, 1990.

Griffiths, Martin. *Realism, Idealism, and International Politics: A Reinterpretation*. New York, NY: Routledge, 1992.

Guiseppi, John. *The Bank of England*. Chicago, IL: Henry Regnery Co., 1966.

Haas, Peter M. "Epistemic Communities and International Policy Coordination." *International Organization* 46,1 (1992): 1-36.

Haggard, Stephan. *Pathways from the Periphery*. Ithaca, NY: Cornell University Press, 1990.

Haggard, Stephan, and Tun-jen Cheng. "State and Foreign Capital in the East Asian NICs." *The Political Economy of the New Asian Industrialism*. Ed. Frederic Deyo. Ithaca, NY: Cornell University Press, 1987. 84-135.

Ha-Joon Chang, ed. *The Rebel Within: Joseph Stiglitz and the World Bank*. London: Wimbledon, 2001.

Hall, David J. *Clifford Sifton*, Volume 2. Vancouver, BC: University of British Columbia Press, 1985.

Hall, John A. "Ideas and the Social Sciences." *Ideas and Foreign Policy*. Ed. Judith Goldstein and Robert Keohane. Ithaca, NY: Cornell University Press, 1993. 31-54.

Hall, John A., and T.V. Paul, eds. *International Order in the Twenty-First Century*. New York, NY: Cambridge University Press, 2001.

Hall, Peter. "The Movement from Keynesianism to Monetarism: Institutional Analysis and British Economic Policy in the 1970s." *Structuring Politics*. Ed. Sven Steinmo, Kathleen Thelen, and Frank Longstreth. New York, NY: Cambridge University Press, 1992. 90-113.

Halperin, Morton H. "The Decision to Deploy the ABM: Bureaucratic and Domestic Politics in the Johnson Administration." *World Politics* 25,1 (October 1975): 62-95.

Halperin, Morton H., and Arnold Kanter. *Readings in Foreign Policy: A Bureaucratic Perspective*. Boston, MA: Little Brown, 1973.

Harris, Richard G. "The New Protectionism Revisited." *Canadian Journal of Economics* 22,4 (November 1989): 751-78.

—. "Why Voluntary Export Restraints are 'Voluntary.'" *Canadian Journal of Economics* 18,4 (November 1985): 799-809.

Hart, Jeffrey. "Three Approaches to the Measurement of Power in International Relations." *International Organization* 30,2 (Spring 1976): 289-305.

Hart, Michael, with Bill Dymond and Colin Robertson. *Decision at Midnight: Inside the Canada-U.S. Free-Trade Negotiations*. Vancouver, BC: University of British Columbia Press, 1994.

Hawley, James P. "Protecting Capital From Itself: U.S. Attempts to Regulate the Eurocurrency System." *International Organization* 38,1 (Winter 1984): 131-65.

Heckscher, Eli. *Mercantilism*. Volumes 1, 2. London: George Allen and Unwin, 1934.

Helleiner, Eric. "Post-Globalization: Is the Financial Liberalization Trend Likely to be Reversed?" *States Against Markets*. Ed. Robert Boyer and Daniel Drache. London: Routledge, 1996. 193-94.

—. "States and the Future of Global Finance." *Review of International Studies* 18 (1992): 31-49.

Henning, C. Randall. *Currencies and Politics in the United States, Germany, and Japan*. Washington, DC: Institute for International Economics, 1994.

Henning, Friedrich-Wilhelm. "Vom Agrarliberalismus zum Agrarprotektionismus." *Die Auswirkungen von Zöllen und anderen Handelshemmnissen auf Wirtschaft und Gesellschaft von Mittelalter bis zur Gegenwart*. Ed. Hans Pohl. Stuttgart: Franz Steiner Verlag, 1987. (Vierteljahrschrift für Sozial- und Wirtschaftsgeschichte, Beiheft 80). 252-74.

Hiscox, Michael. *International Trade and Political Conflict: Commerce, Coalitions and Mobility*. Princeton, NJ: Princeton University Press, 2002.

Hobson, J.A. "Imperialism: A Study, 1902." *The Theory of Capitalist Imperialism*. Ed. D.K. Fieldhouse. London: Longmans, 1967. 65-72.

—. "The Theory of Underconsumption, 1894." *The Theory of Capitalist Imperialism*. Ed. D.K. Fieldhouse. London: Longmans, 1967. 54-59.

Holborn, Hajo. *A History of Modern Germany 1840-1945*. Princeton, NJ: Princeton University Press, 1982.

Honohan, Patrick, and Paul McNelis. "Is the EMS a DM Zone?—Evidence from the Realignments?" *The Economic and Social Review* 20,2 (January 1989): 97-110.

Howson, Susan. *Domestic Monetary Management in Britain 1919-1938*. New York, NY: Cambridge University Press, 1975.

Huntington, Samuel. *The Clash of Civilizations and the Remaking of World Order*. New York, NY: Simon and Schuster, 1998.

—. "Transnational Organizations in World Politics." *World Politics* 25 (April 1973): 333-68.

Irwin, Douglas. "The Political Economy of Free Trade: Voting in the British General Election of 1906." *Journal of Law and Economics* 37 (1994): 75-108.

Jaeger, Hans. *Unternehmer in der deutschen Politik (1890-1918)*. Bonn: Ludwig Röhrscheid Verlag, 1967.

James, Scott, and David Lake. "The Second Face of Hegemony: Britain's Repeal of the Corn Laws and the American Walker Tariff of 1846." *International Organization* 43,1 (Winter 1989): 1-29.

Jervis, Robert. "Cooperation under the Security Dilemma." *World Politics* 30,2 (January 1978): 167-214.

Johnson, Chalmers. "Political Institutions and Economic Performance: The Government-Business Relationship in Japan, South Korea and Taiwan." *The Political Economy of the New Asian Industrialism*. Ed. Frederic Deyo. Ithaca, NY: Cornell University Press, 1987. 136-64.

Johnston, Richard, and Michael Percy. "Reciprocity, Imperial Sentiment, and Party Politics in the 1911 Election." *Canadian Journal of Political Science* 13,4 (1980): 710-29.

Jomo, K.S., ed. *Malaysian Eclipse: Economic Crisis and Recovery*. New York, NY: Zed Books, 2001.

Jones, David M. *The Politics of Money: The Fed Under Alan Greenspan*. New York, NY: New York Institute of Finance, 1991.

Jones, Kent. "The Political Economy of VER Agreements." *Kyklos* 37,1 (1984): 82-101.

Kahler, Miles. "Politics and International Debt: Explaining the Crisis." *International Organization* 39,3 (Summer 1985): 357-82.

Kant, Immanuel. *Perpetual Peace*. New York, NY: Columbia University Press, 1939.

Kaplan, Ethan, and Dani Rodrik. "Did the Malaysian Capital Controls Work?" NBER Working Paper #8142, February 2001.

Kaplan, Morton A. "The New Great Debate: Traditionalism versus Science in International Relations." *World Politics* 19,1 (1966): 1-20.

—. *System and Process in International Politics*. 1957. Huntington, NY: Robert Krieger, 1975.

Kapstein, Ethan B. "Between Power and Purpose: Central Bankers and the Politics of Regulatory Convergence." *International Organization* 46,1 (1992): 256-87.

—. *Governing the Global Economy*. Cambridge, MA: Harvard University Press, 1994.

—. "Resolving the Regulators' Dilemma: International Coordination of Banking Regulations." *International Organization* 43,2 (Spring 1989): 323-47.

Katzenstein, Peter. "The Role of Theory in Comparative Politics: A Symposium." *World Politics* 48,1 (October 1995): 1-49.

—. *Small States in World Markets*. Ithaca, NY: Cornell University Press, 1985.

—, ed. *Between Power and Plenty*. Madison, WI: University of Wisconsin Press, 1978.

Kehr, Eckhart. *Economic Interest, Militarism and Foreign Policy*. Ed. Gordon Craig. Los Angeles, CA: University of California Press, 1977.

Kennedy, Ellen. *The Bundesbank: Germany's Central Bank in the International Monetary System*. London: Pinter, 1991.

Kennedy, Paul. *Strategy and Diplomacy, 1870-1945*. Aylesbury: Fontana Paperbacks, 1983.

Keohane, Robert. *After Hegemony*. Princeton, NJ: Princeton University Press, 1984.

—. "The Demand for International Regimes." *International Organization* 36,2 (Spring 1982): 141-71.

—. "International Institutions: Two Approaches." *International Studies Quarterly* 32 (December 1988): 379-96.

—. "The Theory of Hegemonic Stability and Changes in International Economic Regimes, 1967-1977." *Changes in the International System*. Ed. Ole R. Holsti, R.M. Siverson, and Alexander L. George. Boulder, CO: Westview Press, 1980. 131-62.

—, ed. *Neorealism and Its Critics*. New York, NY: Columbia University Press, 1986.

Keohane, Robert, Gary King, and Sidney Verba. *Designing Social Inquiry*. Princeton, NJ: Princeton University Press, 1994.

Keohane, Robert, and Joseph Nye. *Power and Interdependence*. Boston, MA: Little Brown, 1977.

—. "The Role of Transnational Forces." *International Organization* 25 (Summer 1971): 721-48.

Kettl, Donald F. *Leadership at the Fed*. New Haven, CT: Yale University Press, 1986.

Kindleberger, Charles P. "Dominance and Leadership in the International Economy." *International Studies Quarterly* 25,2 (June 1981): 242-54.

—. "The Functioning of Financial Centers: Britain in the Nineteenth Century, the United States since 1945." *Princeton Essays in International Finance* 157 (September 1985): 7-18.

—. "International Public Goods without International Government." *American Economic Review* 76,1 (March 1986): 1-13.

—. "The Rise of Free Trade in Western Europe." *Journal of Economic History* 35,1 (March 1975): 20-55.

—. *The World in Depression, 1929-1939*. Berkeley, CA: University of California Press, 1973.

King, Robin A., and Michael D. Robinson, "Assessing Structural Adjustment Programs: A Summary of Country Experience." *Debt Disaster?: Banks, Governments, and Multilaterals Confront the Crisis*. Ed. John F. Weeks. New York, NY: New York University Press, 1989. 103-23.

Kirshner, Jonathan. *Currency and Coercion*. Princeton, NJ: Princeton University Press, 1995.

Kissinger, Henry. *American Foreign Policy*. New York, NY: W.W. Norton, 1969.

Kohoma, Hirohisa, and Shujiro Urata. "The Impact of the Recent Yen Appreciation on the Japanese Economy." *The Developing Economies* 26,4 (December 1988): 323-40.

Krasner, Stephen, *Defending the National Interest*. Princeton, NJ: Princeton University Press, 1978.

—. "State Power and the Structure of International Trade." *World Politics* 28,3 (April 1976): 317-47.

—. *Structural Conflict: The Third World Against Global Liberalism*. Berkeley, CA: University of California Press, 1985.

—. "Westphalia and All That." *Ideas and Foreign Policy*. Ed. Judith Goldstein and Robert Keohane. Ithaca, NY: Cornell University Press, 1993. 235-64.

—, ed. *International Regimes*. Ithaca, NY: Cornell University Press, 1983.

Krugman, Paul R. "Capital Control Freaks: How Malaysia Got Away with Economic Heresy." Available at <http://slate.msn.com>, 27 September 1999.

—. "Is Free Trade Passé?" *International Economics and International Economic Policy: A Reader*. Ed. P. King. New York: McGraw Hill, 1990. 91-107.

—. "Policy Problems of a Monetary Union." *The EMS in the 1990s*. Ed. Paul de Grauwe and Lucas Papademos. New York, NY: Longman, 1990. 48-64.

—, ed. *Strategic Trade Policy and the New International Economics*. Cambridge, MA: MIT Press, 1986.

Kuhn, Thomas. "Reflections on my Critics." *Criticism and the Growth of Knowledge*. Ed. Imre Lakatos and Alan Musgrave. New York, NY: Cambridge University Press, 1970. 231-78.

—. *The Structure of Scientific Revolutions*. Chicago, IL: University of Chicago Press, 1962.

Lakatos, Imre. "Falsification and the Methodology of Scientific Research Programmes." *Criticism and the Growth of Knowledge*. Ed. Imre Lakatos and Alan Musgrave. New York, NY: Cambridge University Press, 1970. 91-196.

Lake, David. "International Economic Structures and American Foreign Economic Policy, 1887-1934." *World Politics* 35,4 (July 1983): 517-43.

—. "International Relations and Internal Conflict: Insights from the Interstices." *International Studies Review* 5,4 (December 2003): 81-90.

Lairson, Thomas D., and David Skidmore. *International Political Economy: The Struggle for Power and Wealth*. New York, NY: Harcourt Brace, 1993.

Lambi, Ivo. *Free Trade and Protection in Germany 1868-1879*. Weisbaden: Franz Steiner Verlag, 1963.

Larson, Deborah. *The Origins of Containment*. Princeton, NJ: Princeton University Press, 1985.

Lebow, Richard Ned. *Between Peace and War*. Baltimore, MD: Johns Hopkins, 1981.

—. "Generational Learning and Conflict Management." *International Journal* 40,4 (Autumn 1985): 555-85

Lenin, V.I. "The Mature Marxist Theory, 1916." *The Theory of Capitalist Imperialism*. Ed. D.K. Fieldhouse. London: Longmans, 1967. 99-109.

Levitt, Joseph. *Henri Bourassa and the Golden Calf*. Ottawa, ON: Les Éditions de l'Université d'Ottawa, 1972.

Liebenthal, Robert, and Peter Nicholas. "World Bank-Supported Adjustment Programs." *Debt Disaster?: Banks, Governments, and Multilaterals Confront the Crisis*. Ed. John F. Weeks. New York, NY: New York University Press, 1989. 91-102.

Lim, Youngil. *Government Policy and Private Enterprise: Korean Experience in Industrialization*. Korea Research Monograph 6. Berkeley, CA: Center for Korean Studies, Institute of East Asian Studies, 1981.

Lindert, Peter. "Key Currencies and Gold, 1900-1913." *Princeton Studies in International Finance* 24 (August 1969).

Lipsey, Richard G., Daniel Schwanen, and Ronald J. Wonnacott. *The NAFTA: What's In, What's Out, What's Next*. Policy Study 21. Ottawa, ON: C.D. Howe Institute, 1994.

Lipson, Charles. "Bankers' Dilemma: Private Cooperation in Rescheduling Sovereign Debts." *World Politics* 38,1 (October 1985): 200-25.

—. "International Debt and International Institutions." *The Politics of International Debt*. Ed. Miles Kahler. Ithaca, NY: Cornell University Press, 1986. 219-43.

List, Friedrich. *The National System of Political Economy*. 1841-44. New York, NY: Augustus M. Kelley, 1966.

Lowi, Theodore. "Making Democracy Safe for the World: National Politics and Foreign Policy." *Domestic Sources of Foreign Policy*. Ed. James N. Rosenau. New York, NY: Free Press, 1967. 295-331.

Loxley, John. *Debt and Disorder: External Financing for Development*. Boulder, CO: Westview, 1986.

Lusztig, Michael. *Risking Free Trade*. Pittsburgh, PA: University of Pittsburgh Press, 1996.

—. "Solving Peel's Puzzle: Repeal of the Corn Laws and Institutional Preservation." *Comparative Politics* 27,4 (July 1995): 393-408.

Mackinder, Halford. *Democratic Ideals and Reality*. New York, NY: Norton, 1962.

—. "The Geographical Pivot of History." *Geographical Journal* 23 (April 1904): 421-44.

Magee, Stephen. "The Political Economy of Protectionism: Comment." *Import Competition and Response*. Ed. J.N. Bhagwati. Chicago, IL: University of Chicago Press, 1982.

—. "Three Simple Tests of the Stolper-Samuelson Theorem." *Issues in International Economics*. Ed. P. Oppenheimer. London: Oriel Press, 1978. 138-53.

Mahan, Alfred T. *The Influence of Seapower on History, 1660-1783*. Boston, MA: Little, Brown, 1897.

Mallet, B. *British Budgets 1887-88 to 1912-13*. London: Macmillan, 1913.

Mansfield, Edward D. *Power, Trade and War*. Princeton, NJ: Princeton University Press, 1994.

Marr, William, and Donald Paterson. *Canada: An Economic History*. Toronto, ON: Macmillan, 1980.

Marrison, A.J. "Businessmen, Industries and Tariff Reform in Great Britain, 1903-30." *Business History* 25 (July 1983): 148-78.

Martin, Lisa. "An Institutionalist View: International Institutions and State Strategies." *International Order in the Twenty-First Century*. Ed. John A. Hall and T.V. Paul. New York, NY: Cambridge University Press, 2001.

—. "International and Domestic Institutions in the EMU Process." *The Political Economy of European Monetary Unification*. Ed. Barry Eichengreen and Jeffry Frieden. Boulder, CO: Westview, 1994. 87-106.

Masera, Rainer Stefano. "An Increasing Role for the ECU: A Character in Search of a Script." *Princeton Essays in International Finance* 167 (June 1987).

May, Trevor. *An Economic and Social History of Britain, 1760-1970.* New York, NY: Longman, 1987.

Mayer, Arno. "Internal Causes and Purposes of War in Europe, 1870-1956." *Journal of Modern History* 41 (September 1969): 291-303.

McCloskey, Donald N., and Richard J. Zecher. "How the Gold Standard Worked, 1880-1913." *The Monetary Approach to the Balance of Payments.* Ed. Jacob A. Frenkel and Harry G. Johnson. London: Allen and Unwin, 1976. 184-208.

McDiarmid, O.J. *Commercial Policy in the Canadian Economy.* Cambridge, MA: Harvard University Press, 1946.

McKeown, Timothy. "Hegemonic Stability Theory and Nineteenth-Century Tariff Levels in Europe." *International Organization* 37,1 (Winter 1983): 73-92.

Mearsheimer, John. "Back to the Future: Instability in Europe after the Cold War." *International Security* 15 (1990): 5-56.

Mielke, Siegfried. *Der Hansa-Bund für Gewerbe, Handel und Industrie 1909-1914, Der gescheiterterte Versuch einer antifeudalen Sammlungspolitik.* Kritische Studien zur Geschichtswissenschaft (Band 17). Göttingen: Vandenhoek and Ruprecht, 1976.

Miller, Riel. "Assessing Economic Benefits." *The Free Trade Deal.* Ed. Duncan Cameron. Toronto, ON: James Lorimer and Co., 1988. 59-70.

Milner, Helen. "A Critique of Anarchy." *International Politics: Enduring Concepts and Contemporary Issues.* Ed. Robert Art and Robert Jervis. New York, NY: HarperCollins, 1996. 70-80.

Modelski, George. *Long Cycles in World Politics.* Seattle, WA: University of Washington Press, 1987.

Moggridge, D. E. *British Monetary Policy 1924-1931.* New York, NY: Cambridge University Press, 1972.

—. *The Return to Gold, 1925: The Formulation of Economic Policy and its Critics.* London: Cambridge University Press, 1969.

Moir, John S., and D.M.L. Farr. *The Canadian Experience.* Toronto, ON: McGraw Hill Ryerson, 1969.

Moravscik, Andrew. "Taking Preferences Seriously: A Liberal Theory of International Relations," *International Organization* 51,4 (1997): 513-54.

Morgenthau, Hans. *Scientific Man vs. Power Politics.* Chicago, IL: University of Chicago Press, 1946.

Morse, Edward L. "Political Choice and Alternative Monetary Regimes." *Alternatives to Monetary Disorder.* Ed. Michael Schwarz. New York, NY: McGraw-Hill, 1977. 65-139.

Morton, W.L. *The Kingdom of Canada.* 2nd ed. Toronto, ON: McClelland and Stewart, 1969.

Neill, Robin. *A History of Canadian Economic Thought.* New York, NY: Routledge, 1991.

Nipperdey, Thomas. *Deutsche Geschichte 1866-1918, Zweiter Band, Machtstaat vor der Demokratie.* München: Verlag C.H. Beck, 1992.

—. "Interessenverbände und Parteien in Deutschland vor dem Ersten Weltkrieg." *Moderne deutsche Sozialgeschichte.* Ed. H.-U. Wehler. Berlin: Kiepenheuer and Witsch 1966.

Norrie, Kenneth, and Douglas Owram. *A History of the Canadian Economy.* Toronto, ON: Harcourt Brace, 1996.

North, Robert C. "Towards a Framework for the Analysis of Scarcity and Conflict." *International Studies Quarterly* 21 (December 1977): 569-91.

Nye, John Vincent. "The Myth of Free-Trade Britain and Fortress France: Tariffs and Trade in the Nineteenth Century." *Journal of Economic History* 51,1 (March 1991): 23-46.

O'Brien, Patrick K., and Geoffrey Pigman. "Free Trade, British Hegemony, and the International Economic Order in the Nineteenth Century." *Review of International Studies* 18 (April 1992): 89-113.

Odell, John. "From London to Bretton Woods: Sources of Change in Bargaining Strategies And Outcomes." *Journal of Public Policy* 8,3/4 (1988): 287-315.

—. "The U.S. and the Emergence of Flexible Exchange Rates." *International Organization* 33,1 (Winter 1979): 57-81.

—. *U.S. International Monetary Policy*. Princeton, NJ: Princeton University Press, 1982.

Oliver, Robert. "Early Plans for a World Bank." *Princeton Studies in International Finance* 29 (1971).

Organski, A.F.K. "The Power Transition." *World Politics*. New York, NY: Knopf, 1958.

Pastor, Robert. *Congress and the Politics of U.S. Foreign Economic Policy, 1929-1976*. Berkeley, CA: University of California Press, 1980.

Percy, Michael, Ken Norrie, and Richard Johnston. "Reciprocity and the General Election of 1911." *Explorations in Economic History* 19 (1982): 409-34.

Perkins, Dwight, and Wing Thye Woo. "Malaysia: Adjusting to Deep Integration with the World Economy." *The Asian Financial Crisis: Lessons for a Resilient Asia*. Ed. Wing Thye Woo, Jeffrey Sachs, and Klaus Schwab. Cambridge, MA: MIT, 2000. 227-56.

Plumptre, A.F.W. *Three Decades of Decision: Canada and the World Monetary System, 1944-75*. Toronto, ON: McClelland and Stewart, 1977.

Polanyi, Karl. *The Great Transformation*. Boston, MA: Beacon Press, 1957.

Popper, Karl. *The Logic of Scientific Discovery*. New York, NY: Basic Books, 1959.

Pregrave de A. Faria, Hugo. "Brazil, 1985-1987: Pursuing Heterodoxy to a Moratorium." *Dealing with Debt*. Ed. Thomas J. Biersteker. Boulder, CO: Westview Press, 1993. 175-97.

Pruessen, Ronald W. *John Foster Dulles: The Road to Power*. New York, NY: Free Press, 1982.

Puhle, Hans-Jürgen. "Parlament, Parteien und Interessenverbaende 1890-1914." *Das kaiserliche Deutschland, Politik und Gesellschaft 1870-1918*. Ed. Michael Stürmer. Düsseldorf: Droste Verlag, 1970. 340-77.

Pzerworski, Adam, and Henry Teune. *The Logic of Comparative Social Inquiry*. New York, NY: Wiley, 1970.

Quester, George. *Offense and Defense in the International System*. New York, NY: John Wiley and Sons, 1977.

Rees, J.F. *A Short Fiscal and Financial History of England*. London: Methuen, 1921.

Reisman, Simon. "The Nature of the Canada-U.S. Trade Agreement." *Assessing the Canada-U.S. Free Trade Agreement*. Ed. Murray G. Smith and Frank Stone. Halifax, NS: Institute for Research on Public Policy, 1987. 41-50.

Ricardo, David. *Principles of Political Economy and Taxation*. 1817. London: Dent, 1965.

Rich, G. *The Cross of Gold*. Ottawa, ON: Carleton University Press, 1988.

Richardson, J. David. "The Political Economy of Strategic Trade Policy." *International Organization* 44,1 (Winter 1990): 107-35.

Rieke, Wolfgang. "Alternative Views on the EMS in the 1990s." *The EMS in the 1990s.* Ed. Paul de Grauwe and Lucas Papademos. New York, NY: Longman, 1990. 29-39.

Riendeau, Roger. *A Brief History of Canada.* Markham, ON: Fitzhenry and Whiteside, 2000.

Rogowski, Ronald. *Commerce and Coalitions.* Princeton, NJ: Princeton University Press, 1989.

Röhl, John C.G. "Beamtenpolitik im Wilhelminischen Deutschland." *Das kaiserliche Deutschland, Politik und Gesellschaft 1870-1918.* Ed. Michael Stürmer. Düsseldorf: Droste Verlag, 1970. 287-311.

Rosecrance, Richard. *Action and Reaction in World Politics.* Boston, MA: Little, Brown, 1963.

—. *The Rise of the Trading State.* New York, NY: Basic Books, 1986.

Rosenau, James R., and Mary Durfee. *Thinking Theory Thoroughly.* Boulder, CO: Westview, 1995.

Roskin, Michael. "From Pearl Harbor to Vietnam: Shifting Generational Paradigms." *Political Science Quarterly* 89,3 (Fall 1974): 563-88.

Ruggie, J.G. "International Regimes, Transactions, and Change: Embedded Liberalism in the Postwar Economic Order." *International Organization* 36,2 (Spring 1982): 195-231.

Russett, Bruce. *Grasping the Democratic Peace.* Princeton, NJ: Princeton University Press, 1993.

Russett, Bruce, and Harvey Starr. *World Politics: The Menu for Choice.* 4th ed. New York, NY: Freeman, 1992.

Sachs, Jeffrey. "External Debt and Macroeconomic Performance in Latin America and East Asia." *Brookings Papers on Economic Activity* 2 (1985): 523-64.

Sacks, Paul M., and Chris Canavan. "Safe Passage Through Dire Straits: Managing an Orderly Exit from the Debt Crisis." *Debt Disaster?: Banks, Governments, and Multilaterals Confront the Crisis.* Ed. John F. Weeks. New York, NY: New York University Press, 1989. 75-87.

Saywell, John T. "The 1890s." *The Canadians 1867-1967, Part I.* Ed. J.M.S. Careless and Roger Craig Brown. Toronto, ON: Macmillan, 1968. 108-36.

Scammell, W.M. *The Stability of the International Monetary System.* Totowa, N.J.: Rowman and Littlefield, 1987.

Schattschneider, E.E. *Politics, Pressures and the Tariff.* New York, NY: Prentice Hall, 1935.

Schneider, Jürgen. "Die Auswirkungen von Zöllen und Handelsvertrgen sowie Handelshemmnissen auf Staat, Wirtschaft und Gesellschaft zwischen 1890 und 1914." *Die Auswirkungen von Zöllen und anderen Handelshemmnissen auf Wirtschaft und Gesellschaft von Mittelalter bis zur Gegenwart.* Ed. Hans Pohl. Stuttgart: Franz Steiner Verlag, 1987 (Vierteljahrschrift für Sozial- und Wirtschaftsgeschichte, Beiheft 80). 293-327.

Schonhardt-Bailey, Cheryl. "Specific Factors, Capital Markets, Portfolio Diversification and Free Trade: Domestic Determinants of the Repeal of the Corn Laws." *World Politics* 43 (1991): 345-69.

Schull, Joseph. *Laurier: The First Canadian.* Toronto, ON: Macmillan, 1965.

Simmons, Beth. *Who Adjusts?* Princeton, NJ: Princeton University Press, 1994.

Singer, John David. "The Level-of-Analysis Problem in International Relations." *The International System: Theoretical Essays.* Ed. Klaus Knorr and Sidney Verba. Princeton, NJ: Princeton University Press, 1961. 77-92.

Skelton, Oscar. *The Canadian Dominion*. New Haven, CT: Yale University Press, 1919.

Smith, Adam. *The Wealth of Nations*. 1776. Oxford: Clarendon Press, 1976.

Smith, Murray, and Frank Stone. "Editor's Introduction." *Assessing the Canada-U.S. Free Trade Agreement*. Ed. Murray G. Smith and Frank Stone. Halifax, NS: Institute for Research on Public Policy, 1987. 3-17.

Snyder, Glenn H. "'Prisoner's Dilemma' and 'Chicken' Models in International Politics." *International Studies Quarterly* 15 (March 1971): 66-103.

Snyder, Glenn, and Paul Diesing. *Conflict Among Nations*. Princeton, NJ: Princeton University Press, 1977.

Snyder, Jack. *Myths of Empire*. Ithaca, NY: Cornell University Press, 1991.

Spero, Joan E. *The Politics of International Economic Relations*. 4th ed. New York, NY: St. Martin's Press, 1990.

Spykman, Nicholas. *America's Strategy in World Politics*. New York, NY: Harcourt Brace Jovanovich, 1942.

——. "Geography and Foreign Policy, I." *American Political Science Review* 32 (February 1938): 213-36.

Steger, Debra. "Analysis of the Dispute Settlement Provisions: A Canadian Perspective." *Assessing the Canada-U.S. Free Trade Agreement*. Ed. Murray G. Smith and Frank Stone. Halifax, NS: Institute for Research on Public Policy, 1987. 91-98.

Stein, Arthur A. "The Hegemon's Dilemma: Great Britain, the United States, and Economic Order." *International Organization* 38,2 (Spring 1984): 355-86.

——. *Why Nations Cooperate*. Ithaca, NY: Cornell University Press, 1990.

Steinberg, Blema. *Shame and Humiliation*. Montreal, QC: McGill-Queens University Press, 1996.

Stiglitz, Joseph. "Must Financial Crises be This Frequent and This Painful?" *Policy Options* 20,5 (June 1999): 23-32.

Stoessinger, John. *Crusaders and Pragmatists*. New York, NY: W.W. Norton, 1979.

Strange, Susan. *Casino Capitalism*. London: Basil Blackwell, 1986.

——. "The Politics of International Currencies." *World Politics* 23,2 (January 1971): 215-31.

——. *Sterling and British Policy: A Political Study of an International Currency in Decline*. New York, NY: Oxford University Press, 1971.

Tavlas, George. "On the International Use of Currencies: The Case of the Deutsche Mark." *Princeton Essays in International Finance* 181 (1991).

Thiel, Elke. "Die D-Mark zwischen dem Dollar und dem EWS." *Aussenpolitik* 33,1 (1982): 37-46.

Thygesen, Niels. "The Delors Report and European Economic and Monetary Union." *International Affairs* 65,4 (Autumn 1989): 637-52.

——. "Institutional Developments in the Evolution from EMS towards EMU." *The EMS in the 1990s*. Ed. Paul de Grauwe and Lucas Papademos. New York, NY: Longman, 1990. 3-26.

Ullmann, Hans-Peter. *Der Bund der Industriellen*. Göttingen: Vandenhoek and Ruprecht, 1976 (Kritische Studien zur Geschichtswissenschaft, Band 21).

Vasquez, John A. *The Power of Power Politics: A Critique*. New Brunswick, NJ: Rutgers University Press, 1983.

Vernon, Raymond. "International Investment and International Trade in the Product Cycle." *Quarterly Journal of Economics* 80,2 (1966): 190-207.

Vinals, Jose. "The EMS, Spain and Macroeconomic Policy." *The EMS in the 1990s*. Ed. Paul de Grauwe and Lucas Papademos. New York, NY: Longman, 1990. 201-26.

Viner, Jacob. "Power versus Plenty as Objectives of Foreign Policy in the Seventeenth and Eighteenth Centuries." *World Politics* 1,1 (October 1948): 1-29.

de Vries, Tom. "Jamaica, or the Non-Reform of the IMF." *Foreign Affairs* 54,3 (April 1976): 577-605.

Wade, Robert. *Governing the Market: Economic Theory and the Role of Government in East Asian Industrialization*. Princeton, NJ: Princeton University Press, 1990.

Wallerstein, Immanuel. *The Modern World-System*. Volume I. New York, NY: Academic Press, 1974.

—. *The Modern World-System*. Volume II. New York, NY: Academic Press, 1980.

—. *The Modern World-System*. Volume III. New York, NY: Academic Press, 1989.

Walt, Stephen M. *The Origins of Alliances*. Ithaca, NY: Cornell University Press, 1987.

Walter, Andrew. *World Power and World Money*. Hertfordshire: Harvester Wheatsheaf, 1991.

Waltz, Kenneth. *Man, the State and War*. New York, NY: Columbia University Press, 1954.

—. "The Stability of a Bipolar World." *Daedalus* 93 (Summer 1964): 881-909.

—. *Theory of International Politics*. Reading, MA: Addison-Wesley, 1979.

Weede, Erich. "Democracy and War Involvement." *Journal of Conflict Resolution* 28,4 (1984): 649-64.

Wehler, Hans-Ulrich. *The German Empire 1871-1918*. Dover, NH: Berg, 1985.

Weinstein, Edwin A., James William Anderson, and Arthur S. Link. "Woodrow Wilson's Political Personality: A Reappraisal." *Political Science Quarterly* 93 (Winter 1978): 585-98.

Weitowitz, Rolf. *Deutsche Politik und Handelspolitik unter Reichskanzler Leo von Caprivi 1890-1894*. Düsseldorf: Droste Verlag, 1978.

Wendt, Alexander. "Anarchy is What States Make of It." *International Organization* 46,2 (Spring 1992): 391-425.

Weyland, Kurt. *Democracy without Equity: Failures of Reform in Brazil*. Pittsburgh, PA: University of Pittsburgh Press, 1996.

Wicker, Elmus. *Federal Reserve Monetary Policy 1917-1933*. New York, NY: Random House, 1966.

Williamson, John, and Molly Mahar. "A Survey of Financial Liberalization." *Princeton Essays in International Finance* 211 (November 1998).

Wolfers, Arnold. "National Interest as an Ambiguous Symbol." *Discord and Collaboration*. Baltimore, MD: Johns Hopkins University Press, 1962. 147-65.

Wonnacott, Paul. "The Automotive Sector in the U.S.-Canada Free Trade Agreement." *Assessing the Canada-U.S. Free Trade Agreement*. Ed. Murray G. Smith and Frank Stone. Halifax, NS: Institute for Research on Public Policy, 1987. 73-77.

Woo, Jung-en. *Race to the Swift: State and Finance in Korean Industrialization*. New York, NY: Columbia University Press, 1991.

Woo, Wing Thye, Jeffrey D. Sachs, and Klaus Schwab, eds. *The Asian Financial Crisis: Lessons for a Resilient Asia*. Cambridge, MA: MIT Press, 2000.

Woodside, Kenneth. "The Canada-U.S. FTA." *Canadian Journal of Political Science* 22,1 (March 1989): 155-70.

Yee, Albert S. "The Causal Effects of Ideas on Policies." *International Organization* 50,1 (Winter 1996): 69-108.

Index